SOCIAL SKILLS TRAINING
FOR PSYCHIATRIC NURSES

SOCIAL SKILLS TRAINING FOR PSYCHIATRIC NURSES

Brian Pope

Director of Nursing Services (Psychiatry)
Wigan Health Authority

Harper & Row, Publishers
London

Cambridge
Singapore
Philadelphia
New York

San Francisco
Mexico City
São Paulo
Sydney

First published 1986

Harper & Row Ltd
28 Tavistock Street
London WC2E 7PN

British Library Cataloguing in Publication Data

Pope, B.
  Social skills training for psychiatric nurses.
  1. Mentally ill — Rehabilitation 2. Social
  skills — Study and teaching
  I. Title
  362.2'1   RC489.S63

  ISBN 0-06-318338-2

Typeset by Burns & Smith, Derby
Printed and bound by Butler & Tanner Ltd, Frome and London

To Rosi, Jan, George and Mildy

CONTENTS

Appendices

PREFACE

This book has been written at a time of considerable change in psychiatry. The old institutions that have provided care for so long are being run down and the services that will replace them are not yet clearly established. In addition, psychiatric nursing is changing, partly because of the decline of the institutions and partly because of pressures from within the profession. Over the past few years there has been a considerable debate about the nature of psychiatric nursing and the role of the psychiatric nurse. This self-scrutiny has been of considerable benefit and has led to a questioning attitude which has had many positive effects.

There has been a gradual emergence of individual accountability for interactions with clients in all areas of psychiatric nursing, fostered by such tools as the nursing process, primary nursing and key worker systems. These developments have encouraged individual nurses, nurse managers and nurse educationalists to look closely at the organisation of the skills necessary for this new role. They have also culminated in the new 1982 syllabus for Registered Mental Nurse training in which the emphasis focused much more on what an individual psychiatric nurse is able to offer a client in a clinical situation.

This book was written in the belief that the acquisition of clinical skills is the right road for psychiatric nursing to go down. This does not denigrate in any way the caring role of the psychiatric nurse but, in a time of increasing scrutiny of performance, psychiatric nursing — in common with all other professions in the health service — needs to be able to describe what it is able to achieve. This provides a base on which to build a profession for the future.

One of the strengths of psychiatric nursing has always been an ability to interact with people on an everyday level. One of the dangers of developing formal clinical skills is a tendancy to intellectualise problems, leading to a remoteness from people who need help. This should be strongly resisted by nurses at all times.

Social skills training is an ideal clinical skill for psychiatric nurses to develop. It is directly applicable to the problems people have with living skills, and can be conducted in everyday language. It is not a universal panacea for psychiatric illness and does not cure, but it does offer a realistic method for helping people to acquire the skills necessary for successful living. It can be applied to anybody coming into contact with the psychiatric profession, however it has a particular application to people experiencing "long-term" psychiatric illness.

Chapter 3 addresses these issues in detail but it now seems clear that, to date, the methods applied to this group of clients have been woefully inadequate. To assume that people who have been in hospital for 20 or 30 years would respond to a six to eight week social skills training course now appears highly optimistic. A much more comprehensive programme has to be devised for an effective retraining programme. It is probable that a thorough assessment will identify a number of such problem areas. However, it should be emphasised that social skills training programmes for this group of clients should be individual, comprehensive and relevant to the client's needs.

In the author's experience, time periods of one to two years should be considered as appropriate for training with this group. This should include a gradual transition from the institution to the client's new residence. The method of training clients in hospital settings and then leaving them to fend for themselves in the community has proved to be both inadequate and, in some ways, cruel.

This book has been written to help nurses acquire the necessary skills for this type of therapy. There is no substitute for practical experience, and the practising nurse is strongly advised to work as a co-therapist with someone experienced in social skills training before beginning unsupervised therapy. One of the difficulties the author has found is that although psychiatric nurses are enthusiastic about developing clinical skills such as social skills training, and many have attended workshops and training courses, the transition from initial training to acquiring the confidence to undertake clinical practice is not always easy. This book has been written to help the nurse acquire this confidence.

To this end, it is essentially a practical book describing problems and methods of dealing with them. None of the techniques require any special expertise other than an ability to be able to interact with people in a considerate manner, and with understanding. Some experience of working with groups of people is beneficial, especially of how to deal with the possible difficulties of interaction. All of these aspects can be learnt by working with an efficient therapist for a period of time. For those interested people who have no access to an experienced therapist, Appendix II contains a list of therapists who have agreed to act as contacts.

To achieve its aims, the book is divided into three parts:

Part 1

Theory: This is the "dry" part of the book, providing the basic background information necessary for practice. Social skills training is a rapidly evolving field with techniques continually being refined and developed. The intention is to give the reader an entrance into the literature on social skills training, which can be pursued according to interest.

Part 2

Practice: This comprises the bulk of the book. It describes various techniques which have developed and are currently in use in social skills training. The author has taken a broad view of social skills training and has included cognitive techniques in the belief that this area has been sadly neglected. In addition, there is a chapter on video techniques, an important component of many social skills training programmes.

Part 3

Specific applications: This final part looks in more detail at three specific applications of social skills training which are commonly encountered. These are: social anxiety, cognitive therapy and assertion training.

All three parts can stand in isolation and the reader is encouraged to use the book as he feels appropriate.

It is the author's hope that this book will stimulate interest in this field and will encourage psychiatric nurses to practice these skills for which they are ideally equipped.

Brian Pope
Wigan 1986

ACKNOWLEDGEMENTS

I would like to take this opportunity to thank all the people who have helped me in the preparation of this book. In particular, Frank German, Director of Nursing Services (Psychiatry), Exeter Health Authority, for encouraging me when I was struggling to develop both clinically and educationally. In addition, his help and support as a friend have been invaluable. I would also like to thank all those who have participated in the social skills courses in which I have been involved; both clients and professionals who have helped to evolve my ideas. Particular mention should be made of my long-suffering colleagues, Tim Matthews and Judy Mallett.

Principally, I would like to thank my wife Rosi, who contributed so much to this book by reading proofs, criticising ideas, typing drafts and generally supporting me when I became unbearable. Finally, I would like to thank Linda Churchward for her patience, tolerance and help. Without these people this book would not have been written.

PART 1

THEORY

CHAPTER 1

SOCIAL SKILLS

The purpose of this chapter is to provide a basic introduction to the complex field of social behaviour and social learning on which the practice of social skills training is based. To achieve this, the chapter has been divided into three parts:

1. Learning;
2. Social behaviour;
3. Social skills.

Learning

Learning can be defined as an adaptive change in behaviour resulting from past experience. Learnt behaviour is therefore acquired during the lifetime of an individual as a result of constant experience. Learning is characterised by flexibility — what is learnt may vary from one individual to another — and the resulting behaviour can be modified if the environment changes. Clearly, a learnt behaviour pattern cannot be inherited, although the ability to learn is almost certainly inherited.

Categories of learning

Learning has been classified by biologists into five categories:

1. Habituation;
2. Associative learning;
3. Imprinting;
4. Exploratory learning;
5. Insight learning.

Habituation   If an animal is subjected to repeated stimulation, it may gradually cease to respond. If the stimuli are not harmful the animal tends to learn not to react to them. The purpose of this type of learning is to prevent an animal performing an escape response so frequently that it has no opportunity to do anything else.

Associative learning   In this process, an animal learns to associate a particular response with a reward or punishment. The animal remembers its past experience and modifies its behaviour accordingly. This is not necessarily a conscious response. This type of learning will be considered in more detail later.

Imprinting   Lorenz (1952) described how geese followed the first thing they could see after they were born. Although this was usually their mother, Lorenz found that they would follow any moving object. The story illustrates the basic principle of imprinting, or that young animals tend to follow their parents. This is obviously advantageous during the early stages of an animal's life, when parental protection is important for survival. There is an increasing body of evidence that imprinting also plays a profound role in determining the individual's behaviour in later life.

Exploratory learning   A hungry rat placed in a maze will master it after about 12 trials. This assumes that it is rewarded at the end of each trial and that it has never been in the maze before. However, if a rat that is not hungry or thirsty is allowed to spend some time in the maze without any reward before the trials begin, it is found that it subsequently requires fewer trials to gain complete mastery of the maze. Exploratory behaviour is extremely important in the lives of many animals for it enables them to find their way about their environment. They learn all its characteristics and remember its landmarks.

Insight learning   This is the highest form of learning and, in many ways, the most difficult to interpret. It has been defined as the "immediate comprehension and response to a new situation without trial and error". As such it would appear to involve some kind of mental reasoning or intelligence. It is difficult to decide to what extent an apparent insight is based on past experience, trial and error, imprinting and so on.

Theories of learning

Theories of learning form the basis of the behaviour modification approaches. These are usually considered under four processes:

1. Classical conditioning;
2. Operant conditioning;
3. Vicarious learning;
4. Cognitive learning.

Classical conditioning   One of the most important areas of learning was discovered by the Russian physiologist Pavlov at the turn of the century while conducting research into the reflex processes associated with digestion. While observing the behaviour of the dogs with which he was working, he noticed that the flow of saliva occurred not only when food was placed in the dog's mouth, but also at the sight of food, that is, *before* it was in the dogs' mouths.

Pavlov considered the dogs' salivary response to food in the mouth to be an innate automatic reflex, but that the response before presentation of the food was a learnt (conditioned) response. Pavlov found that the conditioned response (salivation) could be initiated not only by the sight of food but by other stimuli (conditioned stimuli) such as ringing a bell. The equation shown in Figure 1.1 has been proposed to account for this associative learning.

Figure 1.1   Classical Conditioning

1. *FOOD* (unconditioned stimulus ⟶ *SALIVATION* (unconditioned
   — UCS)   response — UCR)

2. *BELL* (conditioned stimulus ⟶ *NO RESPONSE*
   — CS)

3. *FOOD* (UCS) + *BELL* (CS) ⟶ *SALIVATION* (UCR)

4. *BELL* (CS) ⟶ *SALIVATION (CR)*

Concept of generalisation When the conditioned response has been established it has been found that similar responses can be obtained from stimuli that are similar in nature to the original stimuli. This type of associative learning has great biological survival value as it allows the organism to learn by association the functional relationship between objects and events in its environment.

Concept of extinction If the bell in Pavlov's experiment is rung repeatedly, but without any food appearing, the classically conditioned response eventually disappears. This is clearly advantageous biologically as there is no survival value in responding indiscriminately to unreliable associations. This mechanism is called extinction.

Operant conditioning This refers to the way an organism affects its environment, which in turn increases the likelihood of certain behaviours being performed again. This can happen either accidentally or because the environment is designed to encourage some types of behaviour and discourage others.

An operant is a sequence of behaviour that produces an environmental consequence. Much of the work in developing the operant conditioning model is attributed to Skinner (1938), who investigated with great precision the variables that affect this type of learning. His experiments were conducted largely on animals using the "Skinner box", a glass-sided box equipped with a food dispenser which, when discovered by the animal, could be operated either by the animal or the operator.

Concept of reinforcement Reinforce simply means to strengthen. A reinforcer is a stimulus which, when paired with a response, increases the frequency of that response. There are two main types:

1. Positive. A reinforcer is said to be positive when it strengthens the behaviour that follows it;
2. Negative. A reinforcer is said to be negative if its removal increases the probability that a response will occur.

Discriminative stimuli are stimuli which, as a result of learning, signal that reinforcement is available in the environment. They are especially important in complex social settings and much of the process of human socialisation is taken up with establishing finely tuned responses in relation to discriminative stimuli. In therapy, these stimuli are important because if the therapist can learn the signals that preceed certain behaviours, it is possible to intervene at this early stage, for example, if a particular style of conversation procedes aggressive behaviour.

So far this chapter has considered the way that different stimuli affect behaviour. Therapeutically, reinforcement can be controlled to achieve certain effects, and the way in which reinforcement schedules are controlled is of considerable clinical importance. Three factors are particularly important in the establishment of reinforcement schedules: the number and ratio of responses; whether regular or irregular patterns of reinforcement are used; and the interval that occurs between reinforcements.

1. Fixed ratio schedules: Reinforcement is given at a fixed rate. For example, every three times the behaviour occurs reinforcement is given. Clinically fixed ratio schedules are used when a high regular rate of easily definable responses is required. Their effects are relatively easily extinguished.

2. Continuous reinforcement: Reinforcement is given every time a target behaviour occurs. This method of reinforcement is often used initially in therapeutic programmes to establish a response. It is again easily extinguished if reinforcement stops. One commonly used therapeutic approach is to establish behaviours using continuous reinforcement then to maintain them on a variable ratio schedule.

3. Variable ratio schedules: Reinforcement occurs for an average number of responses, however the precise ratio of reinforcement to responses is variable over a given period. The individual is unable to predict easily when the next reinforcement will occur. If this type of reinforcement is withdrawn, the rate of responding stays the same for a long period and is therefore highly resistant to extinction. Many interactions with the environment are maintained on variable ratio schedules, and so many maladaptive behaviours can be just as resistant to extinction. Variable ratio schedules are an important clinical method of providing therapeutic reinforcement.

Concept of shaping By selectively reinforcing features of a behavioural programme, it is possible to gradually alter the nature of a response. This technique has been widely used in dealing with psychological disorders (see, for example, Isaacs, Tomas and Goldiamond 1966), and for altering undesired behaviours. Over time, the reinforcement given to the person emitting the behaviour is also gradually altered so that longer sequences of desired behaviour are performed for each reinforcer.

Concept of fading This is the process whereby control of a sequence of behaviour is gradually shifted from one set of reinforcers to another. It is an essential component of socialisation, for example, when regular positive reinforcement for performing a desired behaviour, such as toilet training, is gradually withdrawn to be replaced by other methods of reinforcement such as social approval. This is an important procedure in many behavioural programmes, especially in ensuring that generalisation of the learnt response occurs.

Vicarious learning This method of learning is also often called observational learning, modelling or imitation. Vicarious means something which is established at a distance. Vicarious learning is the method by which new responses are acquired, reinforced, or extinguished at a distance (vicariously), through observation of the behaviour of others. A large proportion of the behavioural repertoire of everyone is developed in this way, not through direct personal experience, but through watching what others do in particular circumstances and how they fare as a consequence. It is essentially the mechanism by which people learn how to speak, and is a major influence in human socialisation. Through vicarious learning, people select, observe and learn to imitate in approximate form elements of the behavioural patterns of other people. This mechanism of learning is especially apparent when animals are in strange environments, when they search for models about how to behave. In adolescent humans, in particular, models are actively sought and copied as the young person experiments with different styles of behaviour. As with all forms of learning, an individual can acquire either useful or maladaptive responses.

Concept of modelling People learn through modelling by observing and imitating, in approximate form, other people's behaviour. Therapeutically, these techniques have been extensively used to re-establish behaviours which were in an individual's repertoire but which have been extinguished, and to teach behaviours which have never been learnt.

Cognitive learning Over the past few years there has been a considerable increase in a type of learning which is argued to be largely independent of the types of learning so far described. This type of learning stresses the importance, especially in complex learning tasks, of understanding, imagination, prior knowledge, memory and creative intelligence. The importance of these cognitive components has been increasingly realised, and the implications for therapy have been enormous. This is a complex subject involving factors such as an individual's style of thinking, an individual's problem-solving ability and the roles of language and memory in behaviour. In addition, much of human behaviour is controlled by a set of complex social rules. It is now argued that cognitive events are not disconnected, nonphysical phenomena which have little to do with behaviour, but that they are inextricably entwined with the behaviour that a person emits, and as such need to be assessed, evaluated and involved as part of any treatment programme.

Social learning theory

Social learning theories focus on the ways in which people learn life skills through their behavioural and cognitive interactions with the external environment. Effective human functioning is seen as resulting from a satisfactory compromise between people and the environment that facilitates this learning process. The focus is on the person in the environment rather than only on characteristics of people's inner conflicts or strivings.

Rotter: Expectancies as guides for living Social learning theory proposes that people handle life's challenges by developing expectancies. Expectancies are subjective predictions about the consequences of different courses of actions. Two types of expectancies are viewed as crucial. The probable outcomes of an action are the consequences that the person has learned to expect from each of the potential responses to a situation. The subjective value of each outcome is the person's evaluation of the importance of each potential outcome. Rotter (1966) also hypothesised that people are guided by generalised expectancies. These are rules for understanding and dealing with the world that are seen as developing as a result of many consistent learning experiences. He proposed a central, generalised expectancy, the "locus of control", which involves the belief that one is either controlled by external forces such as luck or other powerful factors (an external locus of control), or that one is the master of one's own destiny (an internal locus of control). Effective living requires expectancies which guide the person toward rewards and away from punishment.

Bandura: Reciprocal social learning   Bandura (1977) views effective personal functioning as the product of continuous reciprocal interactions involving: learning experiences provided by the social environment; the cognitive processes through which the person understands these experiences and plans reactions to them; and the behaviours that the person uses to cope with and also to alter the environment.

All three of these components need to be considered for a complete analysis of any individual's functioning. Bandura highlighted the importance of vicarious learning in addition to the direct rewards and punishments that had been emphasised in earlier learning theories. Although direct learning was viewed as more powerful, observational learning is a safer and more versatile means of acquiring cognitive behavioural skills.

Bandura (1977) also furthered Rotter's analysis of expectancies, distinguishing between outcome expectancies — the estimate by a person that a given behaviour will lead to certain outcomes (that is, "This is what will happen if I take that action") — and efficacy expectancies — the belief that a person can successfully execute the behaviour required to produce a specific outcome ("I am/am not a skilful (capable) person").

A person may thus believe that the future holds the promise of many rewards but yet feel depressed because these rewards are seen as coming due to luck and despite a lack of personal skill. These expectancies mediate between the person's environment and his or her behaviour, sometimes leading to responses that appear incongruous in the light of the objective situation.

Mischel: Cognitive and behavioural skills   Mischel (1968, 1973), proposed a cognitive and behavioural model of skill that he believed underlay effective human functioning. According to Mischel, each new situation requires new tactics for action, but certain behavioural skills and cognitive strategies are always necessary to enable the person to select the most appropriate course of action.

Competencies are the specific skills that are required by different situations, while self-regulatory systems and plans are the underlying skills that enable the person to set goals, select specific behaviours, and regulate these plans and actions. For example, skill in evaluating one's past actions, and either rewarding oneself for success or developing new tactics for the future, are essential to personal happiness and effective interaction with other persons. Thus, Mischel emphasises an analysis of people's skills for handling the challenges of their environment, rather than a focus on internal conflicts or strivings for self-improvement.

Social behaviour

Social behaviour refers to the interactions humans undertake with others. Human beings engage in social behaviour to achieve certain goals. These goals have been described by Argyle (1983) as:

1. Biological needs — eating, drinking and bodily comfort;
2. Dependency — help, support, protection and guidance, at first from parents, later from people in positions of power or authority;
3. Affiliation — warm and friendly responses from, and social acceptance by, peers, shown by physical proximity, smiles and gaze;
4. Dominance — acceptance by others, and groups of others, as the task leader, being allowed to talk most of the time, taking the decisions, and being deferred to by the group;
5. Sex — physical proximity, bodily contact, and so on, eye contact, warmth, friendly and intimate social interaction, usually with attractive peers of the opposite sex;
6. Aggression — harming other people physically, verbally or in other ways;
7. Self-esteem and ego-identity — for other people to make approving responses and to accept the self-image as valid;
8. Other motivations which affect social behaviour — the need for achievement, money, interests and values.

These goals are likely to be satisfied in different social situations. In any culture there are established rules about how social interaction should proceed in different situations and how they affect different people. These rules cover the kinds of behaviour which are suitable in the situation, and the structure or sequence of events which must be followed.

These rules and structures have developed during the evolution of the particular culture as acceptable ways of conducting different kinds of social encounter. One reason for cultures needing to develop this kind of organised social behaviour is the basic human need for predictability. Because of the vast and complex repertoire of behaviours that are available to human beings, each individual would live in a state of continual anarchy if there were no social rules to control behavioural interaction. As much of social interaction is predictable, the individual does therefore not need to pay so much attention to his behaviour, thus freeing his mental resources for tasks which are unpredictable in their outcome or exceptionally complex.

Goffman (1971) described social interaction as the class of events which occurs during co-presence and by virtue of co-presence. He later went on to distinguish between two levels of interaction, co-presence and focused interaction.

1. Co-presence is, in fact, the basic level of interaction. By this term Goffman meant that individuals are co-present when they signal through bodily and facial signals, their personal space, their awareness of the other person's presence, and their availability for social interaction. An example of co-presence can be seen in social situations such as doctors' waiting rooms, when individuals signal their co-presence by slightly adjusting their seating positions with each new arrival, by non-verbal behaviour such as nods and smiling. However, the interaction remains minimal because there is no co-operative action to sustain a joint focus of attention. Co-presence is characterised by two features: individuals are *monitoring and controlling their own behaviour* as they always do in public but not in private; and each individual is *monitoring the behaviour of others* and adjusting their own behaviour accordingly.
2. Focused interaction occurs when people gather together and co-operate to sustain a single focus of attention, as occurs in much of social interaction. This type of interaction occurs in conversations, games and many other social situations.

Goffman has pointed out that people frequently participate in co-presence and focused interaction simultaneously. Social interaction at any level displays an orderly and patterned quality which suggests the presence of implicit as well as explicit rules. This order appears in the fulfilment of a number of social functions: maintaining normal appearances; controlling access to oneself; indicating the social structure of social occasions; and the maintenance of positive relationships. The impression may have been given of social interaction being an active dynamic process, with individuals using the social rules for their own particular purposes. However, much of social interaction is not undertaken in this controlled way: it is more a continuous series of interactions occurring against the backdrop of the social rules. Many social situations are already in existence and individuals can interact with them as they feel able and willing.

Elements of social behaviour

All social behaviour is composed of two main elements, the individual and the social situation in which he finds himself. There has been considerable debate in the social psychology literature about the relative importance of each of these factors, which will here be considered separately.

The person   One of the major purposes of social interaction is for people to communicate. Communication is an everyday word in contemporary British society, yet it encompasses a variety of complex behaviours, which are often difficult to categorise. People tend to assume that they have developed fairly good communication skills. However, if someone fails to understand a message that is sent, it is usually assumed that the receiver of the message is at fault. The study of communication involves the study of people relating to one another, to their groups, their organisations and to their societies. To understand the process of communicating, people need to understand how they relate to each other. Until recently the following criteria were described as being necessary for good communication:

1. It has a specific purpose;
2. It is directed towards a specific audience;
3. It is appropriate to the situation;
4. It is clear and precise.

It could be argued that this type of definition applies only to verbal communication as it ignores the spontaneous, unplanned responses that use non-verbal systems of delivery. Most of these definitions imply that communication has a definite beginning and a definite end, and that both these points are relatively identifiable and definable. However, it is now thought that communication has evolved as a much more ongoing, dynamic, everchanging and continuous process. Communication has become labelled as a process. It is not static but is constantly moving. The ingredients within a process continually interact, each affecting the other.

Components of the communication process   A model for communication usually includes the following components:

1. The message;
2. The source of origin of the stimulus (encoder);
3. The channel, signal, code or medium that carries the stimulus;
4. The responder or recipient (decoder);
5. The context;
6. The feedback.

This model is not to be viewed as a turn-taking process. Responses under most situations are multiple and continuous, since while the first encoder is transmitting the first message, the second person is simultaneously decoding the first message, while encoding his own messages. Each person is both sending and receiving messages simultanously. Feedback is an important concept as it provides information to the encoder about the message and how it has been received. The word feedback also helps to describe the nature of the process of communication and underscores the overlapping and continuous role of the participants as both encoders and decoders of messages.

Elements of communication Communication between people is commonly considered to consist of two major components: verbal communication and non-verbal communication.

Verbal communication Human beings have the capacity for conveying messages to one another by language. Linguists have analysed language into a number of components, which can be combined and recombined according to rules of grammar or syntax. Thus language consists of a finite set of elements and a finite set of rules for combining these elements. This characteristic gives the system of language two important qualities:

1. Redundancy. There exists more information than is actually needed for sending the message. In the message "Please sit down, dixxer is sexxxd", a number of letters have been removed as if the message was being received in a noisy environment. Most native speakers of English would be able to supply the defaced items from their implicit knowledge concerning English syntax. From both the existing letters and the preceding words, and from the non-linguistic context too, the listener has sufficient information to understand the message. Those items are therefore redundant. The redundancy of language allows it to remain an effective system where listening conditions are far from perfect.
2. Generative power. The language system allows for the creation of new elements and therefore new messages. New words come into a language virtually every day which are quickly understood by listeners who have never heard these particular words before. As culture, technology and society evolve, language evolves too.

It is beyond the scope of this chapter to consider the linguistic elements which make up language, but there are many elements of language such as conversation which appear to be structured in a predictable fashion. Conversations themselves, for example, tend to be bounded by the following rules: each participant has a chance to talk; only one person speaks at a time; the gaps between utterances are brief; the order of speaking is not fixed in advance; the person who initiates the conversation provides the first topic; the elements of conversation consist, to a considerable extent, in adjacency pairs, as in: request-grant, question-answer, and offer-acceptance/rejection. The purpose of these rules is that conversation will be severely disrupted if one person does not follow the rules.

Non-verbal communication   Non-verbal behaviour plays an important role in people's communication and relationships with others. In communicating, the spoken word tends to be emphasised. However, much of the meaning of the message, up to 65 per cent or more, is conveyed by non-verbal behaviour (Birdwhistell 1970). Non-verbal behaviour has been defined as being all human communication events other than spoken or written words. Wiener *et al.* (1972) argued that to use the term non-verbal communication, there should be non-verbal behaviours with shared meanings that constitute a code through which messages are conveyed by an encoder, and responded to systematically and appropriately by a decoder. To date, there have been numerous methods of conceptualising non-verbal behaviour which have indicated that a vast range of channels are open for conveying non-verbal communication.

A distinction has been made between verbal and non-verbal and between vocal and non-vocal communication. Vocal behaviour has been defined as all actions involved in the production of speech, whereas non-vocal behaviour refers to communicative activities other than speech and, therefore, include such features as facial and bodily movements. The verbal elements in conversation are taken to mean the actual words used (as distinct from vocal considerations of how they might be pronounced), while non-verbal behaviour refers to all vocal and non-vocal behaviour which is not verbal in the sense defined above. The term non-verbal then is a definition by exclusion.

If the verbal elements in conversation are taken to mean only the actual words used, then the term non-verbal can refer to non-verbal vocal features, such as tone of voice, stress and intonation. It can also refer to facial movement, gaze, pupil size, body movement and inter-personal distance. In addition, it can refer to communication through touch, smell and various kind of artifacts such as masks, clothes or formalised communication systems such as semaphore; in fact, the number of features which can be included are virtually limitless. Four distinctive approaches to the study of non-verbal communication have been distinguished:

1. Ethological approach. Ethology developed initially as a branch of zoology but in recent years the techniques of ethology have been applied to human behaviour. There are a number of distinctive features which characterise the ethological approach. Special emphasis is laid on observational, natural history techniques as a starting point. Ethologists have also worked on the assumption that human behaviours depend on inherited adaptive predispositions and they therefore try to interpret behaviour in this framework. Consequently, they seek to study behaviour in its natural environment, and the typical research methods employed are naturalistic observations. They have developed a number of techniques for concealed filming in order not to upset the natural flow of behaviour.

2. Structural approach. This is best exemplified by the work of Birdwhistell (1970). According to this approach, many aspects of social interaction are programmed; that is, they occur in specific sequences and those sequences can be ordered hierarchically. Such behaviours do have meanings, but their meanings can be best understood only in the context in which the behaviour occurs. This approach criticises those psychological studies which rely simply on frequency counts of isolated units of behaviour. According to Scheflen and Scheflen (1972), non-verbal cues are linked together through a system of rules. The task of the researcher is to describe those rules not through the isolation of single variables but through a structural analysis where the significance of particular aspects of behaviour can be understood in their total context.

3. Sociological approach. Closely related to the structural approach is the sociological approach, the most well-known exponent of which is Goffman (1971). He proposed an analysis of social interaction in terms of theatre, according to which people set out to project certain impressions of themselves through appropriate performance. According to Goffman, to present a performance is to sustain the relevant standards of behaviour, often without awareness or intention to be dishonest; in presenting such a performance, non-verbal cues may be of considerable significance. How others perceive the performance will depend on the framework in which they structure events. Thus exactly the same behaviours can be re-interpreted in different ways according to the frame in which they are

perceived. Goffman's approach is very similar to that of the structuralists, but where as the structuralists maintain that the significance of behaviour cannot be understood without reference to its sequential and hierarchical ordering, Goffman argues that its significance cannot be appreciated without an understanding of the roles and relationships of the performers.

4.   Psychological approach. Essential to this approach is the use of laboratory experimentation and statistical analysis. This approach divides non-verbal behaviour into encoding and decoding, which are analysed in a laboratory setting to try to understand its component parts.

Three dimensions of non-verbal behaviour with significant effects on communication are kinesics, paralinguistics and proxemics.

Kinesic behaviour, includes gestures, body movements, facial expressions, eye behaviour and posture. Associated with the work of Birdwhistell, kinesics also involves physical characteristics that remain relatively unchanged during a conversation, such as bodily characteristics (Figure 1.2).

Figure 1.2   Kinesics

Component	Function	Possible effects
Eyes	Eye contact can indicate expressions of feeling or willingness for inter-personal communications.	1. Lack of eye contact or looking away can indicate withdrawal, embarrassment or discomfort.
		2. Eye contact can indicate a desire to pause in the conversation, or to say something.
		3. Reduced eye movement may indicate rigidity, or preoccupation of thought.
		4. Direct eye contact should be interpreted differently across cultures. For example, in Japan avoiding eye contact can be seen as a mark of respect.

(continued)

Figure 1.2   (continued)

Component	Function	Possible effects
Facial expression	A major communicator of emotional expression.	1. Different facial areas tend to express different emotions: — mouth, jaw and eyes tend to convey happiness and surprise — eyes tend to convey sadness. 2. It is difficult to understand someone's emotions by facial cues alone, but these cues tend to be supported by other non-verbal messages. 3. Head nods and smiles are an important reinforcer in interpersonal communication.
Shoulders	May give an indication of a person's attitudes to interpersonal exchanges.	1. Shoulders leaning forward may indicate eagerness, attentiveness and receptiveness. 2. Slouched, stooped shoulders may mean that a person is unreceptive to interpersonal exchanges. 3. Shrugging shoulders may indicate uncertainty or frustrations.
Arms and hands	The arms and hands are the principal method by which gestures are generated. They are an important communicator of cultural and emotional messages.	1. Arms folded across the chest may signal avoidance of interpersonal exchanges. 2. Trembling or fidgety hands or clenched fists can indicate tension, anxiety or anger.

(continued)

Figure 1.2   (continued)

Component	Function	Possible effects
		3. Relaxed, unfolded arms and hands gesturing during conversation can signal openness to interpersonal involvement.
Legs and feet	An important indicator of a person's emotional state. Some researchers argue they are a more accurate general indicator than a person's face or arms as they are less likely to be under conscious control.	1. Shuffling feet or a tapping foot may indicate that a person is experiencing anxiety, frustration or wants to make a point. 2. Repeatedly crossing and uncrossing the legs may indicate anxiety, depression or impatience. 3. A person who appears to be very "controlled" or to have "stiff legs" may be anxious or unwilling to be involved in interpersonal exchanges.
Total body	Body movements and body postures, in total, can be indicative of a person's emotional state.	1. Rocking back and forward in a chair or sitting rigidly can indicate tension or worry. 2. Body orientation at an angle or slouching can indicate an unwillingness to engage in interpersonal communication. 3. Leaning forward in a relaxed manner and facing the other person squarely can indicate openness and an eagerness to seek interpersonal involvement.

Note: It is important to view the above components in context with all the other factors involved in social interaction when making assumptions about their role.

Paralanguage or paralinguistics can provide a wealth of information about a person's emotional state and attitudes. Paralanguage refers to how the message is delivered. Some of these elements include vocal cues such as voice level, pitch and fluency of speech (Figure 1.3).

Proxemics refers to the concept of environmental and personal space. It also includes the concept of territorality (Figure 1.4).

Congruence   One important part of the assessment procedure of a person's social behaviour is to establish whether the verbal and non-verbal elements of the messages are congruent (in agreement). An example of incongruent behaviour is a person who says something like, "I'm really happy with the way things are going", while at the same time avoiding eye contact, sitting crunched up in a ball in the corner. An example of congruent behaviour is a person who expresses confusion about a situation accompanied by squinting of the eyes or furrowing of the brow.

An important concept when assessing non-verbal behaviour is the *concept of leakage*. Leakage is the communication of messages that are valid yet are not sent intentionally. It has been suggested that non-verbal leakage can convey more accurate messages than verbal communication. This is usually on the assumption that non-verbal behaviours are generated more spontaneously than verbal behaviours.

The purpose of non-verbal messages is generally to support verbal messages. There are six principle ways that this can be achieved:

1. *Repetition*: the verbal message is "go to your room"; the finger pointing to the room is a non-verbal repeater.
2. *Contradiction*: the verbal message is "I like you", communicated with a frown and an angry tone of voice. Some evidence suggests that when a contradictory verbal and non-verbal message is received, the decoder tends to believe the non-verbal one.
3. *Substitution*: a non-verbal message is often used in place of a verbal one. For example, if someone is asked, "How are you?" and the receiver smiles, the smile substitutes for, "Very well, thank you".
4. *Complimentation*: a non-verbal message can compliment a verbal message by modifying or elaborating the message. For example, if someone is talking about feeling uncomfortable and they begin talking faster with more speech errors, those non-verbal messages add to the verbal one of discomfort.

Figure 1.3   Paralinguistics

Component	Function	Possible effects
Voice level and pitch	Voice level refers to the volume of speech, whereas pitch refers to intonation. A person who speaks in whispers or at an almost inaudible level may have difficulty in communication.	1. Irregular changes in pitch may mean that sensitive issues are being discussed. 2. Voice level may vary among cultures. Lower voice volume should not necessarily be assumed as indicating weakness or shyness.
Fluency in speech	Refers to hesitations, stuttering and speech errors.	1. Hesitation and speech errors may indicate a person's sensitivity about topics in conversation. 2. Shifts in topic or content also can result in changes in the rate or rhythm of speech.

Figure 1.4   Proxemics

Component	Function	Possible effects
Distance	A person can communicate anxious feelings, an increased level of arousal or infringement of personal space by certain reactions to the physical environment.	1. A person who moves back or does not move closer may be indicating a need for more space. 2. There is probably some cultural differences as Latin Americans, Africans and Indonesians have been found to feel more comfortable conversing at less distance.
Position in room	Refers to the concept of environmental and personal space, and includes the concept of territory.	The size of a room has been found to influence client verbal behaviour and possibly the level of arousal.

5. *Accent*: non-verbal messages can emphasise verbal ones and often heighten the impact of a verbal message. For example, if verbal concern is being communicated the message may come through more strongly with non-verbal cues such as furrowing of the brows, frowning or crying. The kind of emotion one conveys is detected best by facial expressions, the body conveying a better description of the intensity of the emotion.

6. *Regulation*: non-verbal communication helps to regulate the flow of conversation. This can be clearly demonstrated as a factor in regulating the flow of conversation. If the decoder continues to nod his head after he has finished speaking, the encoder tends to keep talking. But if the decoder looks away and shifts his body position, the encoder tends to stop talking, at least momentarily. Whether or not it is realised, certain non-verbal cues are relied upon as feedback for starting or stopping conversations and for indicating whether the other person is listening.

Social situations   Like social roles and identities, social situations can be regarded as being created by individuals during their interactions with others. On the other hand, they can also be regarded as existing independently of any participant or set of participants. Like social roles, social situations can be viewed as scenarios awaiting actors to bring them to life. Social situations tend to determine certain features of social interaction, and these situations tend to be common to particular groups in society. In particular, the physical environment can facilitate or impede many features of social interaction, from its basic frequency to its emotional quality. The research into social situations is still at an early stage, and although it is clear that social situations have an important effect on social behaviour, their particular impact is at present unclear. This is likely to be an area of considerably growing research over the next few years. The important concept when considering social behaviour is that the person and the social situation interact in a reciprocal manner. It is impossible to consider the person functioning in social behaviour without being in a social situation, and *vice versa*.

Social skills

Concept of social competence

Social competence means the ability, the possession of the necessary skills, to produce the desired effects on other people in social situations. There is no evidence of social competence as a general factor: a person may be better at one aspect of social skill than another, such as interviewing rather than lecturing, or in one situation than another. Social competency is a general evaluative term referring to the quality or adequacy of a person's overall performance in social interaction. It can also be applied to a person's overall functioning at a particular task.

Concept of social skill

Social skills are the specific abilities required to perform competently a task. They are the skills that are necessary for people to be involved in everyday conversations, encounters and relationships. It is the ability to give and obtain information and to express and exchange attitudes, opinions and feelings. It is fairly obvious that some individuals are better social interactors than others. This has lead to a considerable interest in the field of social interaction, principly at three levels:

1. A theoretical analysis of how and why people behave as they do has resulted in various conceptualisations of socially skilled behaviour;
2. Research has been conducted into the identification and effects of different types of social behaviour;
3. A number of different approaches to training in social skills have been introduced in order to ascertain whether it is possible to improve the social performance of the individual.

The above explanations of social skills are in some ways unhelpful as they are global definitions implying what social skills are used for rather than what they are.

Definition of social skills   Van Hasselt *et al.* (1979) attempted to evaluate recent attempts to define social skills. He concluded that there were two main elements which were central to the concept:

1. Social skills are situation-specific. Few, if any, inter-personal behaviours have the same significance across situations and cultures;

2. Inter-personal effectiveness is determined by the acquisition of verbal and non-verbal response components, which constitute the social repertoire of the individual. They argue that social behaviour is learnt and that failure to learn social skills can therefore result in social inadequacy.

These two elements encompass the main aspects of social skill. A socially skilled individual will possess an ability to behave in an appropriate manner in any given situation. Thus, social skills refer to behaviours displayed by an individual.

Hargie *et al.* (1981) concluded that there were five main features of social skills:

1. Socially skilled behaviours are goal-directed. The behaviours the individual employs are used in order to achieve a desired outcome;
2. Socially skilled behaviours are inter-related, in that they are synchronised behaviours which are employed to achieve a common goal. Thus the individual may employ two or more behaviours at the same time;
3. Social skills are defined in terms of identifiable units of behaviour that the individual displays. Socially skilled responses are hierarchically organised in such a way that large elements are comprised of smaller behavioural units, such as looking;
4. Social skills are comprised of behaviours which can be learnt;
5. Social skills are considered to be under the control of the individual.

The modern concept of social skill arose in the early 1960s from the application of the concepts of skill then current in studies of man—machine interactions. The concept of human beings using motor skills can be traced back to Bessel in 1820, an astronomer, and included studies of human beings interacting with various machines (Bryan 1899, learning morse code; Book 1908, using typewriters).

The modern concept of skill evolved in the 1940s with the development of the information—processing approach to human performance. The concept of social skill appears to have come into focus with the study of automation by Crossman in the 1960s. Crossman was an expert in human information processing and he teamed with Michael Argyle, a social psychologist, to explore analogies between man—machine and man—man interactions.

At the same time, other people were exploring similar areas. In 1953,

Farrer-Brown, director of the Nuffield Foundation, was urging the ergonomics research society to apply the principles of ergonomics to social problems. This society began to hold seminars to explore the concepts of skill applied to social relationships to industry. In 1964 an international conference was held to apply operational analysis to social interaction. However, these developments were concerned more with social performance than with social skill.

Argyle's social skills model

In 1969, Argyle defined skill as "an organised, co-ordinated activity in relation to an object or situation which involves the whole chain of sensory and motor mechanisms". He considered that the sequence of individual behaviour which occurs during social interaction could usefully be looked at as a kind of motor skill.

His model (Figure 1.5) was based on the following premises: that interactors seek goals, consisting of desired responses on the part of others, that one social act leads to another, and that social behaviour consists of a certain range of verbal and non-verbal signals.

Argyle argued that a motor skill operator had definite immediate goals, for example, to screw a nut on a bolt. He also had further goals under which the immediate ones were subsumed, for example, to make a bridge. These goals, in turn, are linked to basic motivators, for example, he may be paid for each unit of work completed. He considered that a "social skill" operator could have similar goals.

Argyle considered that the pattern of motor responses has a hierarchical structure where the larger, high-level units consist of integrated sequences or groupings of lower level units. The sequences making up smaller units tend to become habitual and automatic, for example, independent of external feedback. This concept has become well established in the social interactional literature, with the higher level units of behaviour being known as molar sequences which are composed of molecular subunits.

Elements of Argyle's model   Argyle's original model implied that social difficulties could arise for several reasons:

1. An individual's goals may be internally inconsistent, inappropriate or even unattainable in a given situation;

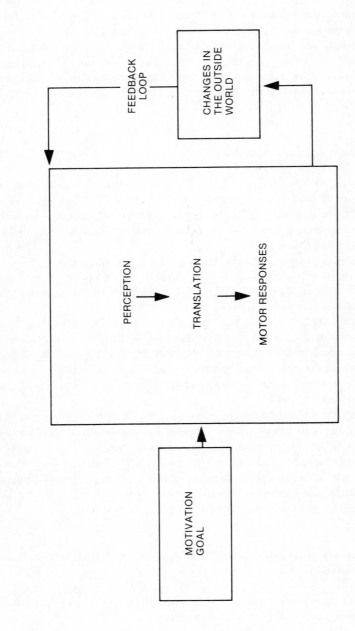

Figure 1.5 Argyle's Social Skills Model (Adapted from figure 8, Argyle 1983 and reprinted by permission of Penguin Books Ltd)

2. There may be failures of perception, such as selection, bias or inattention so that changes in the outside world are not seen at all;

3. Changes in the outside world can be misinterpreted;

4. The person may not be able to generate an appropriate motor response because that response is either inappropriate, inadequate, or has never been acquired by the person.

Argyle's model has had considerable impact in the field of social behaviour, mainly in the following areas:

1. It has formed a theoretical framework for extensive research, notably on the minutiae of social behaviour such as gaze, proxemics, gestures and so on;

2. It has formed the theoretical basis for a considerable amount of clinical work, for example, as outlined by Trower *et al.* (1978) in Social Skills and Mental Health.

3. This model has been used by many people working in professional fields to improve the competence of the professional workers.

Problems with Argyle's model Although it has had considerable influence, there are some difficulties with this model:

1. It contains no cognitive component;
2. It contains no clear affective component;
3. It combines several different types of perception;
4. It is not an interactive model.

McFall's model of social skills

McFall (1982) reviewed the concept of social skills and some of its common uses, which he concluded fitted within two general conceptual models — a trait model and a molecular-behavioural model.

The trait model assumed that social skill was a general underlying personality characteristic or response predisposition. It is not, therefore, directly observable. The more adequately a person performs in a social situation, the higher that individual's inferred level of social skill is assumed to be. It also assumes that the level of a person's social skill is reasonably stable over time and relatively consistent across situations. This is actually a commonly occurring assumption when people talk about social skills. An example of the trait model approach can be found in assessment techniques such as self-report inventories: the intention here is to obtain a representative sample of a subject's responses to a wide variety of items, which are often summarised as one score and then equated to the person's level of social skill. This can also be seen in some role play assessments, which are scored by judges in terms of the amount of social skilfulness displayed by each subject. Scores on individual items are usually summed to give an overall score.

McFall (1982) considered the concept to be an abstraction designed to integrate observed performance across various measures, and indicators of the trait. However, he concluded that psychological research has shown little to support the concept of social skill as a trait (see, for example, Bellack and Hersen 1979; Curran and Monti 1977).

In many ways the molecular model is the polar opposite of the trait model. Social skills are construed in terms of very specific observable units of behaviour, the building blocks of an individual's overall performance in each inter-personal situation. In this model the person does not have a certain amount of social skills, rather the person behaves more or less skilfully in a particular situation at a particular time. Social skills are viewed as learned behaviours in specific situations. This model's definition of social skill is complicated by its emphasis on situational specificity — no particular behaviour can be considered intrinsically skilful, independent of its context. The judgement of whether a response is effective in a particular situation will depend on the objectives, values and perspectives of the person making the judgement. This type of technique does not generally use assessment measures such as self-report measures, global self-ratings, and so on, but tends to use role-play techniques or naturalistic observation.

In McFall's opinion, this model attempts to avoid the ambiguities and problems of the trait approach by defining social skills operationally in terms of specific responses to specific situations. However, he considers that the model does not yet show how to divide the complex unbroken stream of events into meaningful units of behaviour.

McFall then goes on to define the concept of social skill as *the specific abilities that enable a person to perform competently at particular social tasks*. These abilities are not simply the molecular behaviours comprising the total performance, but include the following:

Figure 1.6 McFall's Two-Tiered Model of Social Competence and Social Skills (Source: McFall 1982, reprinted by permission of Pergammon Press)

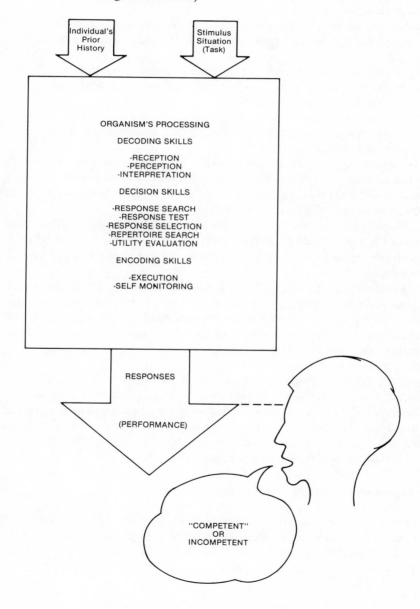

1. There will be no competent performance if all the prerequisite skills are not present;
2. The notion that social skills are specific abilities implies that they should be fairly stable;
3. It should be possible to predict the competence of a person's task performance on the assessment of a finite and manageable number of requisite skills;
4. If a person's incompetent performance on a task is due to a deficit in the required skill, then the person should perform competently once all the necessary skills have been acquired.

The assessment procedure using McFall's definition is aimed at identifying specific skill deficits.

Intervention programmes are aimed at helping subjects to acquire the specific skills they needed. It has to be assumed that some people will never acquire the skills required to perform certain tasks competently, regardless of the amount or kind of skilled training they received.

McFall then went on to develop his own three systems approach to social skill. He considered that performance can be analysed in terms of three relatively distinct systems: physiological (emotional); cognitive; overt motor behaviour.

These systems interact but can be analysed separately. Using this model, social skills are depicted as sequential, organismic steps through incoming stimuli, or as situational tasks that are transformed into the responses or task performances, which are then judged as competent/incompetent social performance (Figure 1.6).

Using McFall's model, the assessment of social skills is concerned with identifying specific areas of skill deficits rather than with measuring a person's social skill level. However, a comprehensive assessment would be far too difficult to carry out, and so social skills assessment should be problem-focused. The whole system should be considered as consisting of sub-systems which can be worked through to identify target behaviours.

Trower — "organism" versus "agency" approach

In a radical reappraisal of the social skills training literature, Trower (1984) evaluated the progress of social skills training to date and questioned the premises on which it was based. In particular, he noted that the following problems were being experienced:

1. There was no agreed definition of social skills, making it difficult to carry out research, assessment and training in a systematic way;
2. There was no standard by which to define a skill deficit, and so many clinicians were having difficulty in deciding what to measure;
3. There was no standard objective source for guiding the selection of any skills, making it difficult to select clear training targets;
4. Assessment instruments and procedures were of doubtful validity, particularly role-play tests, which were often considered to be too artificial for either assessment or training, and global measures, which were widely regarded as being unreliable and subjective;
5. Trained behaviours were considered not to maintain well in time;
6. Trained behaviours did not transfer well to situations outside the training setting;
7. Attempts were rarely made to measure or change the patient's negative cognitions which may successfully block social skills training.

Trower considered that most of the social skills training techniques devised so far came under the heading of the "organism" approach. The main tenet of this approach was that behaviour is under the control of external and/or internal forces — with behaviouralists holding the former and psychiatrists the latter view of the location of control. Behaviour is usually taken to include what other people would call voluntary actions and even thoughts, both of which are construed as overt and covert responses, respectively, to emphasise their control by other variables. Therefore, it is concluded from this approach that people cannot control their thoughts, let alone their social actions.

Another feature of the organism approach (behavioural) is to analyse the behaviour of the organism into basic elementary parts in the belief that the complex whole is the sum of its simple constituent parts, each of which can be separated, identified, measured and modified if found to be deficient.

The trainer is recommended to view the patient "objectively" (that is, externally), as the behaviourally deficient organism (problem) who needs to be modified (treatment goal). The trainer proceeds to examine the patient for these deficiencies (behavioural assessment), and applies a treatment (behavioural social skills training) designed to instigate the missing or deficient response components skills. The now modified and good-as-new patient should "work". To date, social skills training has invariably stopped at this point.

Trower went on to propose a new model for social skills training — the "agency" approach — which allocated a central role to cognitions, and did not separate mental and physical actions, as occurs in the "organism" approach. It adopts the following position:

1. A model of man as an agent who can initiate and direct his actions towards a goal and who can also monitor this activity so that he can evaluate, plan and comment on it as well as actually perform it;
2. A causal theory in which actions are related to their productive cognitions, and *vice versa*.

Trower's approach is cited as an example of the position that social skills training now finds itself in. Initially, it took off in a wave of euphoria that a ready-made answer had been found for many social difficulties. After several years of rapid growth, social skills training is now going through a period of self-evaluation. Social skills training has proved to be an effective form of therapy for many problems, but it needs to be further refined and developed.

Social skills training is a form of therapy that has a relatively short history. In recent years, however, interest in the field has greatly increased, especially within those professions that "deal with people". This has included careers officers, teachers, social workers, health visitors, youth leaders, doctors, clergymen and officers in the armed forces. Each of these professions has its own particular communication skills or social skills.

Social skills training has expanded rapidly over the past five years. It is now used as an important training procedure in a wide variety of settings and with many different types of client, including psychiatric patients, the mentally and physically handicapped, young offenders, long-term prisoners, and school and college students. There are many different approaches to the design of social skills training programmes. There are those that are designed to give a general training in a wide range of social behaviours and situations, whereas other programmes are concerned with training specific behaviours such as assertiveness skills.

While the precise relationship of psychiatric illness to social skills deficits is unclear, it is recognised that many psychotic and non-psychotic people have problems with social relationships that can play a major part in their adjustment. The need to have some form of social skills training in the treatment and rehabilitation of psychiatric clients was well expressed in "Better Services for the Mentally Ill" (DHSS 1975):

> Mental illness often fundamentally affects social adjustment even after the primary symptoms of the illness have been treated. If the patient is to resume his place in a busy competitive society, he will need help in regaining social skills which in the ordinary person are taken for granted.

Social skills training is now an accepted form of therapy in its own right, widely practised in schools, prisons, psychiatric hospitals and management training schools. The meteoric rise in research and training in social skills over the past decade has not always been tempered by scholarly appraisal of social skills theory and therapy outcomes. However, as with the development of most new therapeutic techniques, a period of rapid expansion and euphoric expectations has been replaced by a period of critical evaluation. There are many criticisms of social skills training. In particular, the definition of models developed have not yet been convincing, and many different types of therapy have flourished under the same name. However, there are certain specific advantages of social skills training which make it a particularly efficient form of therapy. For example, social skills trainers do not require years of psychological or analytical training before they can lead a group, although a certain amount of theory must be learnt. Trainers must also have had experience of leading groups and a knowledge of behaviour therapy in general. There are many useful manuals available for this purpose.

Another advantage is that social skills training can be adapted easily for the precise needs of specific groups who have special problems resulting from psychological or physical handicap. It can also be conducted beneficially in small groups or in one-to-one situations. Further, results can be obtained relatively quickly with some client groups.

In addition, social skills training is a positive educational behavioural approach to personal problems and adjustment as it asserts that social competence is learnt rather than biologically inherited or the result of mysterious intra-psychic forces. Thus it is a tenet of social skills theory that skills can be learnt for the first time if absent previously, or they can be relearnt or improved if the skill is inadequate. Finally, there is an increasing body of evidence in many fields that social skills training is an effective form of therapy.

References

Argyle M (1969) Social Interaction, Methuen

Argyle M (1983) The Psychology of Interpersonal Behaviour, Penguin

Bandura A (1977) Social Learning Theory, Prentice Hall

Bellack A S and Hersen, M (Editors) (1979) Research and Practice in Social Skills Training, Plenum Press

Birdwhistell R (1970) Kinesics and Content, University of Pennyslvania Press

Curran J P and Monti, P M (Editors) (1982) Social Skills Training: A Practical Handbook for Assessment and Training, Guildford Press

DHSS (1975) Better Services for the Mentally Ill, HMSO

Goffman E (1971) Relations in Public, Allen Lane

Hargie O et al. (1981) Social Skills In Interpersonal Communication, Croom Helm

Isaacs W, Tomas J and Goldiamond I (1966) Application of operant conditioning to reinstate verbal behaviour in psychotics, in R Ulrich, T Stachnic, and J Mabry (Editors), Control of Human Behaviour, volume 1, Scott Foresman

Lorentz K (1952) King Solomon's Ring, Methuen

McFall R M (1982) A review and reformulation of the concept of social skills, Behavioural Assessment, 4:1–33

Mischel W (1968) Personality and Assessment, Wiley

Mischel W (1973) Toward a cognitive social learning reconceptualisation of personality, Psychological Review, 80:252–283

Pendleton D A (1979) Assessing Communication Difficulties in General Practice (Editors, D J Osbourne, M M Gruneberg, J R Eiser) Academic Press

Rotter J B (1966) Generalized expectancies for internal V external control of reinforcement, Psychological Monographs Supplement, 80:609

Scheflen A E and Scheflen A (1972) Body Language and the Social Order, Prentice-Hall

Skinner B F (1938) The Behaviour of Organisms, Appleton-Century-Crofts

Trower P et al. (1978) Social Skills and Mental Health, Methuen

Trower P (Editor) (1984) Radical Approaches to Social Skills Training, Croom Helm

Van Hasselt V B et al. (1979) Social skills training for children: an evaluation review, Behaviour Research and Therapy, 17:413–437

Weiner M et al. (1972) Non-verbal behaviour and non-verbal communication, Psychological Review, 79:185–214

CHAPTER 2

SOCIAL SKILLS AND PSYCHOLOGICAL DISORDER

The concept of social skills has been applied to many different areas, including professional skills training. A considerable amount of time and effort has been expended on developing skill acquisition techniques in fields such as management and teacher training. In addition, this approach has been applied to the training of workers in the "helping" professions, particularly social workers. At times, this has reached a fairly sophisticated level in projects such as the development of courses by Argie *et al.* in Ulster.

This chapter attempts to relate the concept of social skills to the field of psychological disorder. It is a vast field and has led, therefore, to a selection of material. The author's sole intention is to direct interested readers into this fascinating and complex field. Thus the chapter is divided into two parts exploring:

1. The concepts of social competence and social inadequacy, with particular reference to various models of social inadequacy and some related factors;
2. Some of the research concerning non-verbal behaviour and psychological disorders, and a more detailed consideration of the effects of social skills defects in people experiencing depression.

Hill (1974), in a discussion of the role of non-verbal behaviour in mental illness, commented that psychiatrists of a previous generation had commonly believed that they could diagnose the likely mental state of their patients simply by observing their behaviour. Hence, for example, a tense obsessional person might display rigid body postures and use very precise movements, while a retarded depressive might use slow movement and display an immobile facial expression. He considered that this practice had essentially died out over the preceding 30 years. However, since Hill's paper in 1974, there have been a number of systematic studies investigating the relationship between social behaviour and psychological disorder.

In 1976, Bryant, Trower, Yardley *et al.* provided detailed evidence of what is meant by lack of social skill in a psychiatric setting. Their study concentrated on a group of outpatients who had been diagnosed as suffering from neurosis or personality disorders. The survey was carried out at a small psychiatric unit attached to a general hospital, chosen because it provided a representative sample of the referrals from that area.

Essentially, the study was composed of a comparison between a group of patients considered to be socially adequate, and a group who were judged to be lacking in social skills. Each person took part in an eight-minute structured social situation test, involving conversation with a stranger. Their behaviour was then rated by two psychologists on 24 categories of behaviour. In most of these categories there were significant differences between the two groups. Primarily, these differences were judged to occur because the socially unskilled group tended to show "too little of most forms of behaviour". In particular, they showed little variation in facial expression, adopted closed or inflexible postures, and they looked very little at their partner, tending to speak softly, indistinctly, slowly and in a flat, monotonous tone of voice. In addition, their speech tended to lack continuity, being punctuated with many silences, and they failed to hand over or take up the conversation thus leaving the other person to make all the conversational moves. They also tended to choose stereotyped and dull topics of conversation, showing little interest in the other person. The only behaviour in which the "socially unskilled" group exceeded the "socially skilled" group was in talking about themselves. The assessors also rated the clients in broad descriptive terms. In general, the socially unskilled group were rated as significantly more cold, non-assertive, socially anxious, sad, unrewarding and uncontrolling.

Bryant *et al*'s paper was essentially an attempt to provide a practical definition of social inadequacy, which they considered to be an "ill-defined and ambiguous term". Their approach was to view social inadequacy from a behavioural perspective, primarily concerned with verbal and non-verbal signals in communication, and their social consequences. They contrasted this approach with the traditional psychiatric approach, which mainly confined interest to social inadequacies of personality type that emphasised enduring traits such as weakness, timidity, anxiety and passive attitudes.

Their reason for adopting this approach was two-fold: there has been a very poor level of agreement between psychiatric professionals when attempting to assign individuals to personality types and there currently was no clear account of personality that fitted the picture of the inadequate person who specifically lacked social skills.

Social competence and social inadequacy

In the field of social psychology there has been a considerable debate over the concepts of social competence and social inadequacy. Many people view them as useful constructs: the majority of people display social competence or effectiveness in their social interactions, while a minority are unable to conduct their social interactions successfully. Other approaches argue that the two terms are value-laden and virtually meaningless as they are so broad, and that they do not significantly identify effective or ineffective social behaviour. They are, however, commonly used terms that are frequently encountered both clinically and among the lay population.

Concepts of social competence crop up in many branches of psychiatry, especially in relation to the field of rehabilitation, where the assessment of an individual's fitness to return to society has resulted in several different measures of social competence.

The concept of social inadequacy is a notoriously difficult one, and it has come to mean different things to different people in psychiatry. It is largely derived from social norms and consequently suffers from the inevitable difficulties of subjectivity and imprecise definition. Nowadays, social inadequacy is often used to refer to the inability to cope with a limited range of social situations essential to day-to-day life, such as shopping, going on buses and regular time-keeping at work. Confusingly, the term is also used to describe the gross social withdrawal exhibited by institutionalised psychotic patients.

Social inadequacy and psychological disorder have been connected in a number of ways.

1. The "medical model" suggests that psychiatric disorders are basically a biologically determined abnormality that has adverse effects on a wide range of functions and behaviour, including social behaviour. Disturbances in social behaviour are a common feature of many psychiatric conditions. The medical model assumes that the disturbance

in social functioning is a consequence of this basic biological disorder. Other approaches to psychiatry use a similar mechanism based on the belief that social behavioural disturbances are the consequence of innate causes, for example, psychoanalysis.

2. The "inadequate learning model" suggests that social inadequacy occurs because the person has not learnt the appropriate social skills, and it predisposes that person to the development of psychological disorder. The person has failed to learn the appropriate skills for effective social interaction in childhood, which leads to social rejection and failure to cope with the demands of everyday living. This, in turn, can lead to psychological disorder.

3. The "handicap model". Wing (1978) proposed a model which did not have a direct cause-effect relationship between psychological disorder and social inadequacy. He regarded both as areas of handicap that required separate assessment and treatment, if the client was to be satisfactorily treated. He proposed three levels of handicap: primary handicaps that are the symptoms of the biological disease process (for example, delusions, hallucinations); secondary handicaps that develop as a response to the illness or other factors such as institutionalisation (for example, social withdrawal, negative attitudes); and tertiary handicaps, that are the result of additional factors unassociated with the illness (for example, poor social circumstances, poor family support).

   Zigler and Phillips (1961) have undertaken research which indicates that a person's social adjustment before admission to hospital is an important indicator of how that person will function after discharge — a better prognosis is given for those people with more effective social functioning before admission.

Whatever the primary cause of social skills deficits, the elements involved interact in such a way as to maintain and exacerbate each other. This can easily become a vicious circle of maladaptive behaviour. For example, a state of high arousal, such as an anxiety state, might lead to reduced social functioning. The person becomes isolated and withdrawn if this state is maintained, there is less social contact and the person does not have the opportunity to develop his social skills. He is less able to cope with social situations and suffers an exacerbation of his anxiety when in contact with other people, which perpetrates the vicious circle.

In these circumstances, it is important to identify the current problems that the person is experiencing rather than search for causes which may be buried in the past. This problem-solving approach is then used to target individual problems. Treatment of these problem areas frequently involves several techniques, for example, medication to control delusions and, when these are under control, social skills training to improve the client's social functioning.

Social competence

Social competence or social skill means the ability to engage effectively in social behaviour. It is often easier to notice a lack of social skill than it is to notice social competence, which is a difficult concept to define.

Two factors have been identified which correlate highly with social competence:

1. *Rewardingness* — one goal of social behaviour is to maintain social interaction that is rewarding for all participants. This tends to come across in behaviours indicating warmth, friendliness and sensitivity.
2. *Controlling* — this aspect of social skill directs and controls the social interaction. It is comprised of elements which contribute to the impression of dominance, strength and assertiveness.

Social inadequacy

The concepts of social competence and social inadequacy can be applied either in a wide-ranging global fashion or to populations of people suffering from psychological disorders. Without doubt, many people in society exhibit varying degrees of social inadequacy in their everyday social functioning. These difficulties range from an inability to express oneself clearly to an inability to make friends. However, these people may be otherwise well adjusted and never be considered as having a psychological disorder.

Other people's difficulties with social interaction are much more severe and are often related to psychological disorders. Several investigators have tried to analyse the components of these skills. Eisler (1973) attempted to define assertiveness in terms of voice, volume, length and spontaneity of speech. Unassertiveness was defined as a lack of initiative in conversation, lack of spontaneous speech and soft volume. He defined coldness as silence, failure to hand over the conversation, dull expression and a fixed posture.

In psychiatric populations, people with social skills deficits tend to show a particular style of behaviour. They will probably appear to be cold, unassertive, unrewarding to others, to have inexpressive facial expressions, look infrequently at other people, and make little effort to produce a spontaneous and interesting flow of conversation.

Inadequate clients tend to report more difficulty across a wide range of situations than people who function adequately. The situations most likely to be experienced as difficult are contact with relative strangers, particularly of the opposite sex, approaching others and making the first move in starting up a friendship, going out with someone of the opposite sex, and going to social functions such as parties.

Additionally, socially inadequate people have considerable difficulty with what to socially competent people are relatively undemanding situations, such as using public transport, going to the shops and walking down the street.

Factors affecting social inadequacy   An examination of the factors related to social inadequacy have indicated the type of person who is most likely to be inadequate. However, there is currently very little direct evidence and considerable further research needs to be undertaken in this field.

1. Sex. It is generally agreed that boys and girls show different behaviour patterns at an early age. However, how this comes about is not yet clear. A common stereotype of the male/female is to categorise the male as independent and assertive, and the female as warm and empathic. The behaviour of socially inadequate patients seems to depart from both these stereotypes. However, there have been some differences noted between the sexes. Hall (1978) reviewed 75 studies in which the decoding accuracy of men and women were compared. These studies showed a pronounced advantage for women, with 24 studies showing a significant sex difference. These differences indicated that women looked more than men at other people, showed a preference for closer inter-personal distances with each other, smiled more and could encode more clearly than men. Hall then tried to relate these studies to other work. In particular, he noted that a number of studies have shown that women are more empathic than men. Of special interest was a comparison between the levels of assertion of men and women. There appears to be a concensus of opinion that assertion is an inter-personal behaviour that is socially defined and whose form varies as a function of its situational context. Some reports now suggest that when confronted with identical

rights infringement situations, the behaviour of women is objectively as assertive as that of men. Much of this research also suggests that the differences between men and women are in the antecedents and consequences of the actual behaviour, and that the behaviour of women when asserting their rights is more likely to be either disregarded or negatively sanctioned. This is a complex subject that can be used to indicate some of the variables that exist when attempting to assess social skills deficit.

In Trower *et al.*'s study (1978) the conclusions were interesting. Although the raters felt that the women performed inappropriately, they still did not rate them as inadequate. Again, although the women showed the same behavioural deficits as men, in that they had the same longstanding difficulties in mixing and reported as much difficulty in social situations, they were not reported as being socially inadequate as were the men. In practical terms, the implications of this study are enormous. Social norms change and many of the values and underlying attitudes to women in society are currently being questioned. An important issue raised from this is that it is very easy for therapists to impose their own standards on people during therapy. Each therapist should therefore confront the social and moral implications of what they are doing.

2. Marital state. Marriage is considered a natural and highly desirable state in society, and great pressures are put on individuals to conform to this expectation. Successful courtship and the establishment of a stable marital relationship require considerable inter-personal skills. As previously discussed, inadequate men tend to be single, but not women. A possible explanations is that the male skills needed for courtship are just those that socially inadequate men lack, in particular the skills of assertiveness and control. The explanation is probably less straight-forward in the case of women. Women are required to take less initiative in courtship, and so inadequate women would be less likely to encounter difficulty than inadequate men.

Within marriage it has long been assumed that communication deficits were a major source of marital conflict. However, the supporting evidence for this has been largely anecdotal. The marital interaction coding system developed by Weiss *et al.* was an interesting development in this field (Weiss and Engel 1971). Interactional behaviours were first given one of 30 behavioural codes and then summarised into one of six primary codes:

(a) Positive verbal behaviour;
(b) Positive non-verbal behaviour;
(c) Negative verbal behaviour;
(d) Negative non-verbal behaviour;
(e) Problem-solving behaviour;
(f) Neutral problem description.

This study demonstrated that distressed couples engaged in significantly greater frequencies of negative behaviour than did non-distressed couples, on both the conflict resolution task and in casual conversation. Positive behaviours were significantly more common in the repertoires of non-distressed couples during the conflict resolution, but there were no differences between distressed and non-distressed couples during casual conversation. These differences did not reflect general communication deficiencies since they were not apparent in interactions with opposite-sex strangers. Thus the observed differences were relationship-specific.

Goffman (1959, 1972) has reported a number of studies that both replicate and extend these findings. Interestingly, he concluded that verbal behaviour was a much less powerful force than non-verbal behaviour. He used a verbal code based on speech content and a non-verbal code based on affect, which was inferred from vocal, facial and kinetic cues. Most of the striking discrepancies occurred in the non-verbal dimension. Goffman also concluded that distressed couples exhibited negative reciprocity; that is, the probability of one spouse responding with a negative affect following a partner's negative affect is significantly greater. Basically, this means that distressed couples tended to produce chains of negative behaviours, with one negative tending to initiate another. Non-distressed couples, on the other hand, tended to disperse their negative behaviour in a way that made such a change less likely.

3. Social class. Links between social skill and social class have received little direct attention, although the effects of social class on intellectual attainment, patterns of childrearing and patterns of language use have received considerably more attention.

It has been claimed that middle-class parents provide more opportunity for learning in problem-solving strategies that can generalise to future problem-solving situations than do lower-class parents. If this could be validated, it would be an important variable for therapists, leading them to place more emphasis on goal-directiveness. This would obviously have considerable impact on some of the cognitive aspects of social skills training. It is also well known that middle-class language patterns are much more flexible and less context-bound, resulting in a greater scope for operating within a wider range of alternatives.

Goal-directiveness and problem-solving skills are essential to the social skills model, and Spivack and Shure (1976) found that a high level of problem-solving skills are related to better social adjustment at all socio-economic levels. From this argument it could be concluded that one component of assessment in any social skills assessment procedure should be to look at a person's socio-economic status, as this could lead one to assume that more cognitive skills would need to be taught to people from lower socio-economic backgrounds. However, this is obviously contentious.

Particular patterns of use of non-verbal and verbal signals are culturally determined, and it is fairly obvious — although in a subjective way — that they vary between social classes in as far as people largely meet with people from the same social level as themselves. Difficulties might be encountered in situations of upward or downward mobility, as are frequently encountered in psychiatric situations. This may be a complicating factor when assessing the social context of social skills, as an unfamiliar social environment may make people's customary behaviour inappropriate.

4. Clinical considerations. There is usually little to distinguish the inadequate from the competent patient, although a diagnosis of depression in men can indicate a greater likelihood of inadequacy. If "pre-morbid" personality is included, the inadequate patient is likely to have a history of poor mixing with others and to report considerable difficulty in a wide range of social situations, particularly those involving strangers and members of the opposite sex.

On psychometric tests, inadequate patients tend to score rather higher than other patients on measures of introversion and social imcompetence, but not on neuroticism.

Social skills model and psychological disorder

The social skills model assumes that the individual has goals which he seeks in order to obtain rewards. Goal achievement is dependent on skilled behaviour, which involves a continuous cycle of monitoring and modifying performance in the light of feedback. Failure in skill is defined as a breakdown or impairment at some point in the cycle, which results in a failure to achieve targets, leading to negative outcomes and abnormal behaviour. If social inadequacy occurs it can conceivably be due to difficulties at many points in the social skills model.

Perception

An individual needs accurate, relevant information for skilled social behaviour in order to respond appropriately. The perception of this information is subject to a considerable amount of distortion in the "normal population", but this distortion can reach serious levels among psychiatric populations. One assumption of effective social skill is that there is a need for adequate perception: many studies support this view and its corollary that perception is impaired in some psychiatric illnesses. Forgus and de Wolfe (1969, 1974) have shown that disturbed patients can suffer impairment in selective attention, and Silberschatz (1978) has shown that an improvement in clinical state is marked by improved attention across a wide range of disorders.

Interestingly, some research has indicated the reverse: Cunningham (1977) found that "neurotics" were more accurate than a normal group at perceiving emotions displayed by other people, and La Russo (1978) suggested that paranoid people were better than a normal group at detecting negative emotional expression.

Performance

Social skills are often considered as consisting of two elements, namely, molecular or single elements of behaviour which, when combined, form molar sequences. Both elements can be effected in social inadequacy.

Molecular behaviour   Social skill deficits in individual components of behaviour have been reported across a wide range of psychiatric disorders. Rutter (1976) found that schizophrenics look less in situations where personal facts are being discussed. Other research has found that schizophrenics tend to choose less face-to-face orientation when seated and prefer a larger inter-personal distance. Ekman and Friesen (1974) found that people suffering from depression used fewer "illustrators" (gestures to "illustrate" what is being said verbally). In addition, they look less in some situations and tend to have a characteristic "lowered" posture.

Molar behaviour The elements of social skill do not usually occur in isolation, but as part of larger units which usually include verbal and non-verbal elements. Once these molar components of social functioning are established they are usually resistent to change. Molar sequences of social skill consist of two main influences, person variables and situation variables.

Person variables usually refer to stable patterns of behaviour that the individual "takes" with him to different situations. They include attitudes, social class and so on. Goffman (1959) proposed the idea of "self-presentation" in which an individual attempts to present himself in a positive manner by using factors such as clothes. The impression the person was attempting to convey was "competence" in the various "roles" the individual had to fulfil. Social failure was a faulty performance. Various components of "self-presentation" can be affected, such as personality, inter-personal attitudes and emotion.

Some aspects of social behaviour appear to correlate with the concept of personality. For example, Hendrick and Brown (1971) have shown that extroverts are more popular than introverts, and Crozier (1979) reviewed a number of studies that found that "shyness" was a personality factor characterised by phenomena such as self-consciousness, fear of meeting new people, fear of being criticised and looking foolish, and, in some cases, social anxiety.

Two important dimensions of inter-personal attitudes have been considered: dominance (assertiveness, superiority) versus submissiveness (inferiority); and friendly (warmth) versus hostile (cold).

Research has shown that both styles are conveyed largely by non-verbal behaviour. Both dimensions are a major component of social skills problems among patients, as both submissive and hostile behaviour tends to create inter-personal difficulties. These styles are commonly associated with psychological disorders.

Libet and Lewinsohn (1973) found that depressed people tended to appear unfriendly or cold to other people which, in turn, generated unfriendly responses. Mehrabian (1972) found that anxious people tended to convey negative and submissive feelings during social interaction.

Some research into person variables in social skill interaction has implicated emotional expression. Studies have shown that submissive, unskilled patients tend to have a "flat" tone, have a blank expression and generally are emotionally inhibited. Buck (1979) has suggested a relationship between high physiological arousal and low facial expression.

The other main influence in molar sequences of social skill is situation variables, that is, the situation in which the behaviour occurs. These "social rules" can have a considerable impact on a person's social functioning if they are not followed. For example, in the rules of conversation, research has shown that conversation is controlled by a complex system of signals that accompanies the verbal components of speech. At a basic level of analysis, this system consists of "turn-taking": social difficulties can occur if these rules are broken, for example, if people talk simultaneously or if there are long silences. Fischetti, Curran and Wessberg (1977) showed that socially incompetent people were poor at timing their responses and did so in a more random fashion than did a more socially skilled group.

Pilkonis (1977) found that, compared to "shy" (subjects)', his "not shy" group allowed fewer silences to develop and broke a larger percentage of any silences that did occur.

With social routines, Goffman (1972) has described a number of social situations which require a more formal use of social skill. These routines tend to be ritualistic and serve to initiate, terminate, confirm, restore and change social relationships, for example, greetings, apologies. Serious social consequences tend to follow if the correct social routine is not followed, for example, the failure to return a greeting. Many socially unskilled people either lack the knowledge of or fail to use the correct social routine. Argyle (1981) has listed a number of components of social situations such as these.

Rosenthal et al. (1979) has carried out an extensive series of studies on individual differences in decoding non-verbal cues using his profile of non-verbal sensitivity (pons). This test comprises a 45-minute film in which a number of short scenes are portrayed. The information to the decoder includes both bodily cues and speech especially processed to disguise the actual words spoken. Rosenthal has applied this test to study various aspects of decoding non-verbal cues:

1. Age. There has been considerable argument as to whether the decoding of emotional expression is innate. Rosenthal et al. found that the accuracy of decoding skills gradually improved between the ages of eight to 25 years. This has confirmed the findings of earlier studies.

2. Culture. Rosenthal administered the pons test to nationals from 20 different countries. His findings were consistent with the interactionist

approach to non-verbal communication, where certain facial expressions of emotion are regarded as innate, while display rules, emblems, illustrators and regulators were seen as variable across cultures.

3. Personality. He next compared the performance of a number of groups on the pons test with their responses to a number of personality tests. These studies provided some evidence that people who are more skilled at decoding non-verbal cues are more confident, more socially mature and less dogmatic, but there was no clear relationship between pons scores and extroversion.

4. Psychopathology. He next investigated the performance of psychiatric patients by comparing the performance of psychiatric patients in Northern Ireland, America and Australia. There were no significant differences on any measure. He then compared the performance with high school students and found that, in general, the psychiatric patient's performance was significantly lower. Interestingly, he also found that the psychiatric patients did not benefit from practice from the first half of the test to the second, whereas other people did.

There is considerable support for his findings that psychiatric patients are inferior to normal groups in the decoding of non-verbal cues.

Non-verbal communication

It has been shown that the relationship between people in terms of age, acquaintanceship and sex can be determined on the basis of non-verbal communication, even by quite young children. Hence, in addition to communicating information about emotion, language and individual differences, non-verbal communication can also communicate information about interpersonal relationships to observers of the relationship. The role that non-verbal communication plays for the participants within a particular relationship has been assessed as conveying information in areas such as affiliation and dominance.

Studies of mother/infant interactions suggest that non-verbal communication between mother and infant increasingly comes to resemble adult conversation in form, for example, clusters of expression are produced by each partner in turn. Studies of marital relationships show that poor marital relationships are indicated by poor verbal communication and also that poor marital adjustment is associated with insensitivity to non-verbal communication. Non-verbal communication can also be examined within the context of a particular situation. In particular, research has been conducted into the following situations:

1. Therapeutic relationships. Research has shown that the perception of the therapist by the client is strongly influenced by non-verbal communication. In particular, Teppar and Hasse (1978) have assessed the factors relating to empathy in therapeutic relationships. Their results showed that non-verbal factors were important, with facial expression being the most influential factor. When the principal factors alone were considered, non-verbal cues accounted for twice as much of the variance in judged empathy as speech content, five times as much of the variance for respect, and 23 times as much of the variance for genuineness.
2. Teaching. Research in education suggests that although a pupil's perception of the teacher is affected by non-verbal cues, they are more affected by the actual verbal content. It has been argued that non-verbal communication is of considerable significance in education, and that it is important in facilitating and inhibiting communication, too many teachers being unaware of their non-verbal behaviour which may inadvertently inhibit a pupil's behaviour. This obviously has applications to social skills training, and any therapist should be aware of the therapeutic impact of his own non-verbal behaviour. An experiment was conducted in which children were given an intelligence test, 20 per cent of them being randomly assigned to an experimental group in which the teachers were told that they would show unusually good academic development. At the end of the year, the children completed another intelligence test and the results showed a considerable improvement for the experimental group. Although contentious, this experiment has been replicated on a number of occasions and, to some extent, can be explained by the concept of a self-fulfilling prophecy.
3. Interviewing. Research into interviewing shows that although interviewers are affected by non-verbal communication in their assessment of an interviewee, they are more affected by the content of what the interviewee says. A number of studies of interviews have been carried out with reference both to the way in which the behaviour of the interviewee affects the judgement and decisions of the interviewer, and to the way the interviewer may affect the interviewee through his own behaviour. Wexley, Fugita and Malone (1975) examined the affects of

bodily cues on the judgement of American male and female students assessing a candidate's suitability for a loan. The results showed that there were significant effects on the students' judgement of the candidates' suitability, from both the responses to the questionnaire and from the degree of non-verbal enthusiasm.

Keenan and Wedderburn (1975) have investigated the ways in which interviewee behaviour has been influenced by interviewer behaviour. They were particularly interested to test the hypothesis that the approval or disapproval of the interviewer might lead to significant differences in the amount the interviewee was prepared to say in the interview. A simulated interview was used consisting of two conditions, approval and disapproval.

In the approving condition, candidate utterances were acknowledged with smiles, positive head nods and eye contact. In the disapproving condition, the interviewer used frowns, head shakes and avoided eye contact. Candidates were perceived as significantly more comfortable and at ease in the approval interview, and were also judged to have created a significantly better impression. At the same time, their perceived competence was not significantly affected.

These studies of simulated interviews suggest that non-verbal behaviour can influence the way the interviewee is perceived and that the behaviour of the interviewer, in turn, can influence interviewee behaviour. Forbes and Jackson (1980) attempted to assess the role of non-verbal communication in non-simulated interviews on British school leavers who were being interviewed by a four-man panel for places on an engineering apprenticeship scheme. A decision was made after each interview to either accept or reject the candidate. Their observations showed a number of significant relationships between interview outcome and the non-verbal behaviour used by the interviewee. Interviewees made significantly greater use of eye contact in acceptance interviews, and significantly greater use of gaze avoidance in rejection interviews. Interviewers smiled significantly more in acceptance interviews and showed a neutral face significantly more in rejection interviews. Finally, interviewees showed significantly more head-shaking and head-nodding in acceptance interviews. Forbes and Jackson's work clearly shows that non-verbal behaviour is in some ways related to the outcome of interviews.

4. Deception. It appears possible that deception can be detected on the basis of non-verbal behaviour, but the relative importance of different bodily

cues in leaking information about deception has yet to be firmly established. If a person is attempting to conceal the fact that he is experiencing a particular emotion, he might not succeed in suppressing all the expressive movements associated with that particular emotion, or he may respond by omitting certain important features or by mismanaging the timing. These types of assumptions are implicit in Ekman and Friesen's (1969) concept of "non-verbal leakage". They argued that the sending capacity of a particular part of the body can be measured in terms of three indices: average transmission time; the number of discriminable patterns which can be produced; and visibility.

According to these criteria, the face is the best sender of information, the legs and feet the worst. The facial muscle changes are rapid, allow for a wide variety of expressions and are usually clearly visible. The feet and legs move much less quickly, are capable of only a limited number of movements and are often screened from view by furniture. Ekman and Friesen went on to hypothesise that because of the greater sending capacity of the face, people are more careful to control their facial expressions; hence attempts at deception may more often be "leaked" through movements of the legs and feet. They also found that observers trained in using the facial action coding system they developed were able to detect deception at a level significantly above chance from seeing just the face during interview.

Ekman, Friesen and Scherer (1976) also found that, during deceptive interviews, the interviewee displayed significantly fewer hand illustrators than during a non-deceptive interview. Ekman and Friesen (1975) also identified a number of facial styles which were seen as examples of non-verbal deficits. These included: *ever-ready expressors* — people who invariably show one emotional expression as a characteristic response to any event; and *substitute expressors* — people who substitute one expression of emotion for another without being aware of it.

In conclusion, it is still open to question to what extent it is appropriate to search for specific cues indicative of deception. One difficulty is that the relevant cues may vary as a function of the situation and the information that the encoder is attempting to conceal. However, what does seem clear is that deception can be detected from non-verbal communication alone, even if the cues themselves may vary according to particular situations and particular individuals.

Social skills deficits and depression

Depressed people are often assumed to want to avoid others. They can often also show similar behaviour to socially inadequate people, but return to normal patterns of behaviour on alleviation of the symptoms, and therefore it is important to be able to differentiate some of the non-verbal aspects of depression from those of social inadequacy. Waxer (1977) showed silent films of depressed and non-depressed patients. He found that the judges were able to identify the depressed patients from bodily cues alone. The particular cues he identified as characteristic of depression were: *lack of eye contact; downward angling of the head; a drooping mouth;* and *lack of hand movement.*

Waxer showed that observers can identify depressed patients on the basis of non-verbal behaviour alone, thus suggesting that depression can be communicated by bodily cues. Ekman and Friesen (1974) described a study in which the hand movements of American female inpatients were observed on hospital admission and on discharge. All hand movements were classified as either "illustrators" or "self-adaptors". It was hypothesised that the number of "illustrators" would increase with enthusiasm or involvement. Observations were taken of people suffering from psychotic depression, neurotic depression and schizophrenia. It was found that people suffering from psychotic depression showed the fewest number of illustrators on admission, and that there was a significant increase in their use of illustrators at discharge.

Gaze and depression   Rutter and Stephenson (1972) gave a standardised interview to 20 men and women suffering from depression who had just been admitted to hospital which were then, compared to a control group. The people with depression spent significantly less time looking at the interviewer than did the control group, regardless of whether they were speaking or listening. This study has been replicated. Rutter and Stephenson argue that since reduced gaze is not associated with all psychiatric patients, an interpretation in terms of, say, stigma is ruled out. This kind of social behaviour associated with depression can be interpreted as a way of communicating a desire to reduce social contact that is not necessarily going to be alleviated by just modifying those particular behaviours.

Libet and Lewinsohn (1973) have produced evidence to suggest that depressive people develop deficiencies in their social skills during their illness. In particular, they found that depressed individuals do indeed have a lower activity level, a narrower inter-personal range, a lower rate of emitted positive reactions and a longer action latency than control subjects. They also discovered that depressed people are more sensitive to adversive inter-personal stimulation and have especially long action latencies following a negative social interaction. Moreover, when participating in groups, depressed individuals tended to emit fewer actions, following the group members' behaviour who were the least depressed. Lewinsohn also investigated social skills deficits in the depressed individual's natural environment. Here the depressed individual was seen to have little ability to elicit positive re-enforcement from other family members. This suggests that therapeutic interventions that increase the levels of emitted assertive behaviour may prove useful in the treatment of depression (Libet and Lewinsohn 1973).

Cognitive aspects of depression   Beck *et al.* (1967) developed the hypothesis that a depressive's thought processes involve a number of maladaptive strategies which produce and maintain the depressive condition. He specified four major strategies:

1. *Arbitrary inference.* Conclusions are drawn from limited evidence or no evidence at all: "He is talking to that other woman. Therefore, I am unattractive to him."
2. *Selective abstraction.* Conclusions are drawn from selected aspects of a situation, other aspects being neglected: "Although he is holding my hand, he cannot love me since he has looked once or twice at someone else."
3. *Over-generalisation.* "Since she avoids my company, I am obviously repugnant to most people."
4. *Magnification and minimisation.* Large errors in evaluating performance: "Although she has praised me repeatedly, she obviously does not care for me since she told me off for forgetting her birthday."

A wealth of clinical material has been collected to demonstrate that these strategies do characterise depressive individuals and that attempts to modify these attitudes using cognitive therapies can have positive effects on the outcome of depressive illnesses.

Effective clinical psychiatric practice and social inadequacy

The current diagnostic practices in Great Britain are not a very useful way of identifying people who lack social skills. There is not much relationship, if any, between social inadequacy and diagnosis, symptoms or length of illness. Symptoms of depression and anxiety tend to be as prevalent in the socially competent as they are in the socially incompetent, though, as previously discussed, there is some possible relationship between social inadequacy in men and depression.

An important clinical issue in assessing social skills deficits is the pre-morbid personality. Social skills training is not designed to deal with temporary disturbances of skill caused by psychiatric disorder, but with enduring difficulties. Therefore, a careful assessment has to be made of social skills deficits caused by the onset of a current psychiatric illness, and those enduring from learning difficulties in the past. A positive road for social skills training to take would be for it to be used in a preventative way during adolescence to prevent later social isolation and perhaps psychiatric breakdown.

Argyle (1972) has argued that breakdown within the social skills model leads to socially inadequate behaviour. He argues that all psychiatric patients exhibit some breakdown in social behaviour and that some of these breakdowns might be termed primarily inadequate.

There is considerable practical evidence showing that most forms of recognised psychiatric illnesses include measurable behavioural changes in specific interactional features, such as eye gaze and posture, with depressives being characterised as emitting fewer rewarding behaviours, and schizophrenics as showing strange patterns of eye gaze. However, it is essential not to dismiss all such deviant behaviours as being merely unskilful. Taking one isolated inappropriate unit of social behaviour, such as the too-brief eye gaze, is not necessarily a breakdown of a unit within the hierarchical organisation of emotive skill, but more probably an act of communicational intent. For instance, if A is talking to B and B refuses to make the appropriate amount of eye contact, B is not merely failing to achieve an integrated emotive skill, but is communicating something about his attitude to the interaction in allowing, consciously or not, the attitude to be observed.

References

Argyle M (1972) The Psychology of Interpersonal Behaviour, Penguin

Beck A T (1967) Depression: Clinical, Experimental and Theoretical Aspects, Hoeber

Buck R (1979) in Rosenthal R see below

Bryant B, Trower P, Yardley K, et al. (1976) A survey of social inadequacy among psychiatric outpatients, Psychological Medicine 6:101–112

Crozier W R (1979) The interaction of value and subjective probability in risk decision making, British Journal of Psychology, 70(4):489–495

Cunningham J L (1977) A comparison of the didactic interactions of mothers and fathers with their pre-school children, Dissertation Abstracts International, 34(6B) 2757–2758

Eisler R M, Miller P M and Hersen M (1973) Components of Assertive Behaviour, Journal of Clinical Psychology, 29:295–299

Ekman P and Friesen W V (1969) Non-verbal leakage and clues to deception, Psychiatry, 32:88–106

Ekman P and Friesen W V (1974) Non-verbal behaviour and psychopathology, in R J Freidman and M M Katz (Editors), The Psychology of Depression: (Contemporary Theory and Research), 203–232, Wiley

Ekman P and Friesen W V (1975) Unmasking the Face: A Guide to Recognising Emotions From Facial Clues, Prentice Hall

Ekman P, Friesen W V and Scherer K R (1976) Body movement and voice pitch in deceptive interaction, Semotica, 16:23–27

Fischetti M, Curran J P and Wessberg H W (1977) Sense of timing: A skill deficit in heterosexual-socially anxious males, Behaviour Modification 1:179–194

Forbes R J and Jackson P R (1980) Non-verbal behaviour and the outcome of selection interviewers on candidates' impressions, Journal of Occupational Psychology, 53:65–72

Forgus R H and de Wolfe A S (1969) Perpetual selectivity in hallucinatory schizophrenics, Journal of Abnormal Psychology, 74:288–292

Forgus R H and de Wolfe A S (1974) Coding of cognitive input in delusional patients, Journal of Abnormal Psychology, 83:278–284

Goffman E (1959) The Presentations of Self In Everyday Life, Doubleday-Anchor

Goffman E (1972) Relations in Public, Harper Colophon Books

Hall J A (1978) Gender effects in decoding non-verbal cues, Psychological Bulletin, 85:845–857

Hendrick C and Brown S R (1971) Introversion, extroversion and interpersonal attraction, Journal of Personality and Social Psychology, 20(1):31–35

Hill D (1974) Non-verbal behaviour in mental illness, British Journal of Psychiatry, 124:221–230

Keenan A and Wedderburn A A I (1975) Effect of the non-verbal behaviour of interviewers on candidates' impressions, Journal of Occupational Psychology, 48:129–132

La Russo L (1978) Sensitivity of paranoid patients to non-verbal cues, Journal of Abnormal Psychology, 87:463–471

Libet J M and Lewinsohn P M (1973) Concept of social skill with special reference to the behaviour of depressed persons, Journal of Consulting and Clinical Psychology, 40:403

Pilkonis P A (1977) The behavioural consequences of shyness, Journal of Personality, 45(4):596–611

Rosenthal R (Editor) (1979) Skill In Non-Verbal Communication, Pelgeschlager, Gunn and Hain

Rutter D R and Stephenson G M (1972) Visual interaction in a group of schizophrenic and depressive patients, British Journal of Social and Clinical Psychology, 11:57–65

Rutter D R (1976) Visual interaction in recently admitted and chronic long-stay schizophrenia patients, British Journal of Social and Clinical Psychology, 15:295–303

Silberschatz G (1978) Selective attention and changes in clinical state, Journal of Research in Personality, 12(2):197–204

Spivack G, Platt J J and Shure M B (1976) The Problem-Solving Approach to Adjustment, Joney-Bass

Tepper D T and Haase R F (1978) Verbal and non-verbal communication of facilitative conditions, Journal of Counselling Psychology, 25:35–44

Waxer P H (1977) Non-verbal cues of anxiety: An examination of emotional leakage, Journal of Abnormal Psychology, 86:306–314

Weiss T and Engel B T (1971) Voluntary control of premature ventricular contractions in patients, American Journal of Cardiology, 26:666

Wexley K N, Fugita S S and Malone M P (1975) An applicant's non-verbal behaviour and student-evaluations, judgements in a structured interview setting, Psychological Reports, 36:391–394

Zigler E and Phillips L (1961) Social competence and outcome in psychiatric disorder, Journal of Abnormal and Social Psychology, 63:264

Further Reading

Argyle M, Furnham A and Graham J (1981) Social Situations, Cambridge University Press

Hargie O, Saunders C and Dickson D (1981) Social Skills in Interpersonal Communication, Croom Helm

Mehrabian A (1972) Non Verbal Communication, Aldine Atherton

Trower P, Yardley K, Bryant B and Shaw P (1978) The treatment of social failure: A comparison of anxiety-reduction and skills acquisition procedures on two social problems, Behavioural Modification 2:41–60

Wing J K (Editor) (1978) Schizophrenia Towards a New Synthesis, Academic Press

CHAPTER 3

SOCIAL SKILLS TRAINING AND SCHIZOPHRENIA*

Social skills training with schizophrenics has developed rapidly over the past 10 years, as social learning techniques have been developed by behavioural therapists, thus improving the social competence of clients with a wide variety of psychiatric disorders. Many clinicians and researchers have been attracted to work in this field because of the well documented correlation between premorbid social adjustment and the course of schizophrenic illnesses. However, the early work, using either assertive or social skills training techniques with schizophrenics, met with mixed results. In general, these studies appeared to find that social skills training was effective during the training period, but that there was no clear evidence that the skills learnt generalised from the training period.

While the exact training techniques and assessment methods vary somewhat, most social skills trainers working with schizophrenics use highly structured methods, including instructions, prompts, modelling, role-play, positive feedback and homework assignments. Most training has tended to take place in hospitals or clinical settings, and has usually been given intensively for two to six sessions per week over a relatively brief period of up

---

* The author is aware that he can be accused of using imprecise terminology in this chapter. Practitioners should remember that it is necessary to precisely define individual difficulties. However, this chapter discusses general issues as opposed to any individual therapy, and it is considered that, at the present time, the concepts of schizophrenia, psychosis and so on effectively communicate the group of people and the problem to which the author is referring.

to 12 weeks. The goals of training are usually chosen from interpersonal situations that are viewed as being important for effective hospital, community and family adjustment. Assessment of training has, by and large, flowed from stylised role-playing tests, ratings and self-reports from client.

There is some indication that the early claims of the effectiveness of social skills training with this group of clients were vastly over-rated. In this chapter a number of developments in the field of schizophrenia will be reviewed and their conclusions applied to practical aspects of social skills training. They will be reviewed under five main headings:

1. Family factors;
2. Social and community factors;
3. Psychopathology;
4. Motivational deficits;
5. Cognitive deficits.

Family factors

A series of studies over the past two decades begun at the social psychology unit of the Institute of Psychiatry in London has highlighted the importance of the emotional climate in the family on the course of a schizophrenic illness in a family member. Evidence has accumulated that points to the interpersonal processes within the family as being one of the most powerful predictors of relapse in a person having an established schizophrenic illness.

These studies were begun in response to the changing patterns of mental health care for schizophrenics in the 1950s that were accompanied by increasing rates of discharge and matched by increasing rates of readmissions. They were based on the Camberwell Family Interview, an effective and reliable interview format conducted by a trained interviewer/rater with a single family member in a comfortable setting, usually the family home. It is semi-structured and lasts for about one and a half hours.

The interviewer obtains a relative's account of the recent interactions between the patient and family members, as well as an opinion of the patient's behaviour during the three months before admission. Circumstances surrounding the decision to hospitalise, acting out, frequency of quarrels, socialisation and symptoms shown by the patient are covered. Of even greater importance for the subsequent ratings of expressed emotion (EE), are the feelings and attitudes of the relative towards the patient, and the patient's relationship with other members of the family. In measuring the relative's EE, the interviewer/rater evaluates non-verbal elements as well as the verbal content of the relative's responses. Emphasis is placed on rating the vocal aspects that reflect emotional qualities such as tone, pitch, intensity, pace and fluency.

Five scales have been developed by Brown *et al.* (1972) that measure warmth, hostility, positive comments, critical comments and emotional over-involvement. With adequate training and supervision, interviewers/raters can reach acceptably high levels of reliability in scoring these scales. Unfortunately, the training requires a two-week full-time workshop, followed by two to three months of reliability checks on ratings of tape-recorded interviews. The two scales that have turned out to be the most predictive of relapse are the ones measuring critical comments and emotional over-involvement. Most relatives who show excessive criticism or marked emotional over-involvement do not appear abnormal or strikingly deviant in light of the extremely asocial, impaired and symptomatic behaviour of the "ill" family member.

The replicated results from three separate studies conducted in London over a 15-year period revealed that patients returning to families that were high on expressing criticism and emotional over-involvement, relapse four times as often as those returning to families that are low in these areas of EE. Of patients returning to homes where a family member was high in EE, 51 per cent relapsed during the first nine months after discharge, whereas only 13 per cent of those relapsed who returned to low EE families.

Another line of research has implicated dysfunctional communication patterns in families as potentially influencing the development of schizophrenia. Communication deviance has been described as vague amorphous statements, contradictory statements, disqualification of other people's comments, intrusiveness, failure to specify problems and perceptions, statements tangential to the issue at hand, and failure to resolve a problem. In several studies, parental communication deviance has correlated highly with the psychopathology of offspring. Certain patterns of parental affective communication, obtained in a direct interactional situation involving family members discussing differences of opinion, have been found to be significantly predictive of subsequent psychiatric breakdown in vulnerable adolescents. Factors such as parental criticism, intrusiveness and guilt inducement — especially in the context of low emotional supportiveness — were the key predictive factors. It has been suggested that critical and hostile parental behaviour contributes to deterioration in psychotic individuals.

Implications for social skills training

Of significance in the studies of EE is the fact that the vulnerable target group of schizophrenics can now be identified as being at high risk of relapse. The groups at highest risk are individuals with schizophrenia living at home with parents who are high on EE and communication deviance. More importantly, independent of chronicity, this vulnerable group can be identified at the time of hospital admission through the administration of a standardised interview. To date, the results point to the use of maintenance anti-psychotic drugs for these people, as well as a reduction in the amount of face-to-face contact between them and their relatives after discharge. However, side-effects and non-compliance limit the effectiveness of anti-psychotic drug preparations, and reducing the amount of face-to-face contact is often easier said than done.

Other techniques used have included reducing EE and communication deviance in relatives through family therapy techniques, strengthening the social and communication skills of the schizophrenic patient through a training programme aimed at enabling the patient to better cope with high EE from family members or to leave the family and become more autonomous. Clinicians employing behavioural therapies with schizophrenics can no longer ignore the areas of familial communication, affective expression and problem-solving. The strategies effectively used include education, teaching communication skills, modification of dependent relationships, and teaching problem-solving skills. In particular, social skills training has been used to role-play family conflicts and problems of communication.

The long-term community management of schizophrenics is at a relatively early stage of development. However, several major factors need to be considered:

1. Treatment may need to be lifelong for many people;
2. The provision of adequate vocational rehabilitation is often limited by the patient's learning ability and motivation, as well as by community resources and the economic climate, for example, unemployment levels and funding of sheltered employment programmes;
3. Residential care is seldom ideal for individuals suffering from psychosis, and while there is often greater tolerance of aberrant behaviour within these facilities, communities are usually less tolerant. A lack of personalised support often leads to a reduction in social functioning;
4. Despite apparently ideal community care conditions, compliance with all aspects of the programme is difficult to sustain for long periods, so that the people who need maximum support can usually receive very little.

A review of the family factors related to the course of schizophrenia suggests that an effective family intervention should educate the family and social networks about the nature and management of schizophrenia, so that the family members can more readily provide a caring, supportive environment and encourage treatment compliance, based on a clear understanding of the basic principles of primary care for schizophrenia. It should also teach more effective verbal and non-verbal communication (in particular the appropriate expression of dissatisfaction and concern), in order to decrease hostile criticism and over-involvement. Finally, family intervention should also teach more effective problem-solving skills so that family members can learn to identify and cope with stressful life events, as well as decrease family tension.

In a pilot study conducted at the Bethlem Royal and Maudsley Hospitals in London, Falloon, Liberman Lillie et al. (1981) devised a family therapy method that took as its theoretical basis the EE findings of the social psychiatry unit outlined above. The principle goal of this method was to decrease the level of EE in key relatives. Strategies were directed at changing the patterns of negative criticism and hostility towards the patient, and reducing over-dependent bonding between relatives and patients. This family therapy formed an integral part of a larger intervention approach that sought to increase social distance through teaching independent living skills during a 10-week inpatient social skills training programme. All patients were maintained on anti-psychotic medications. The programme consisted of three elements: family therapy, family education and communication training.

Family therapy programme   The goal of the family therapy programme was to provide comprehensive long-term community care for people suffering from schizophrenia by utilising natural support systems. This family intervention addressed the long-term difficulties of long-term drug therapy as well as teaching coping mechanisms that were effective at reducing environmental stress. Two major sources of stress were specifically addressed, namely, disturbed family relationships and life events.

Families who have severe deficits in their ability to cope with these stresses were selected for the programme. After detailed behavioural analysis of their assets and deficits, they began an intervention programme of two years' duration. The specific interventions included: education about the nature of schizophrenia; carefully monitored neuroleptic medications; communication training; problem-solving skills; and crisis intervention skills.

The family sessions were conducted in the home, since there are several advantages to this approach. Firstly, generalisation of behaviour from one setting to another is a problem that is seldom addressed adequately by clinic-based community treatment programmes. The problem is compounded in the treatment of schizophrenia by the evidence of low levels of transfer of learnt skills across settings with this population. *In vivo* family sessions not only enhance generalisation in the natural environment, but also take advantage of the family unit as a powerful agent for effecting social learning and reinforcement.

Second, failed appointments, that frequently frustrate therapists and reduce the effect of delivery of therapeutic programmes, are minimised. Poor compliance with clinic-based therapy programmes has been a major problem to date in the community care of schizophrenics that has not been effectively resolved.

Third, in the home setting, the therapist is able to gain a substantial knowledge of family behaviour problems and ideosyncratic aspects of the family's daily life, which may not be demonstrated in the clinic.

Finally, *in vivo* family therapy is able to involve family members, friends and neighbours in these therapy sessions who would otherwise be unlikely to attend clinic sessions.

The broad impact of family therapy on the social network provides greater opportunities to create community support systems outside the family. Over the two-year period, the frequency of therapy sessions is organised on the following basis: up to three months, one-hour sessions held weekly; three to six months, one-hour sessions held fortnightly; six to nine months, one-hour sessions held three-weekly.

The reason for this approach is related to some available evidence on risks of relapse that indicates that patients are most vulnerable to symptomatic relapses during the three months following an acute episode, and that although they remain at risk throughout the subsequent two-year period, few relapses occur after nine months post-discharge. Patients who have not relapsed within nine months post-discharge are relatively unlikely to relapse in the following 15 months.

Family education sessions The first two sessions of the family programme were educational in nature and attempted to provide the family and patient with information on the nature, course and treatment of schizophrenia. Hand-outs and visual aids were used to facilitate this. The family was asked to share its perceptions and experiences, and the patient was encouraged to discuss his individual symptomatology and inter-personal difficulties. The importance of neuroleptic medication was discussed in the second session.

Communication training   On the completion of the education of the two family sessions, the next 12 *in vivo* sessions were geared to the need for improvement in family patterns of communication. Specific training strategies were employed to shape effective expression of positive and negative feelings, reflective listening, request making and reciprocity of conversation. This was tailored to the family's unique communication deficits as ascertained during the assessment process. Week-to-week problems were pinpointed during a brief 10- to 25-minute individual session with the patient, while the co-therapist met with the rest of the family. The remainder of the session was spent with the entire family. The following elements of communication were specifically addressed:

1. Non-verbal behaviour, for example, voice, tone and volume, body language, eye contact, facial expression;
2. Verbal content and it's appropriateness;
3. Expression of individual statements and feelings;
4. Timing of responses and transitional statements.

Generalised expression of feelings was discouraged in favour of praise or criticism for specific behaviour. The importance of the immediacy of reinforcement was stressed.

One of the most powerful and important interventions is the repeated rehearsal of difficult family situations. Improved communication was shaped through rehearsal by using instruction, modelling, coaching, social reinforcement and performance feedback. Family tension was diffused or slowed down by this process. Role-reversal was another strategy that was used where one family member assumed the role of another. Role-play of extra familial situations was also of great value in preparing family members for anticipated stressors. Family members were trained to set up their own role rehearsal to model and to provide feedback and coaching. Families were encouraged to practice newly learnt communication techniques between sessions. Homework assignments were given which included rehearsal of specific skills on a daily basis. Reports of these efforts were kept on family worksheets, which were reviewed at the beginning of each session. Individual diaries were also kept as further evidence of generalisation. Family members were prompted to show retention of skills and therapists looked for spontaneous performance of new communication skills during the sessions.

The problem-solving model

When families showed some mastery of basic communication skills, the problem-solving model was introduced in an effort to reduce stress at family crisis points. Problem-solving was used to modify familial tension and extra familial stresses. Family members were taught to: *come to an agreement* on the specific definition of the problem; *generate* at least five possible solutions or alternatives to the problem without judging their relative merits; *evaluate* the positive and negative aspects of each alternative; *agree* about the best solution or combinations of solutions; *plan and carry out* the agreed solution; and *review and praise* efforts at implementing the solution.

Families were further encouraged to structure their efforts by writing down all suggestions. This maximised group participation and focused attention on the task. The therapist initially provided much active guidance which was generally withdrawn as the family mastered the technique. The problem-solving method tried to diffuse the burden of coping with the problem to all members of the family system, and to draw on the strengths and resources within the family. Homework assignments were given with the goal that eventually the family would utilise the problem-solving model at the time of major life events, as well as in planning strategies for dealing with individual and family goals.

Additional behavioural strategies

Few families have an adequate repertoire of coping skills for dealing with the behavioural disturbances often associated with schizophrenia. Specific problems such as medication compliance, reduction of side-effects, dealing with persistent delusions or hallucinations, or when to seek professional intervention, are commonly raised by families. Behavioural strategies that have been taught to families include: contingency contracting, token economy reinforcement schedules, shaping, time-out techniques, limit-setting and identification of warning signals of impending relapse.

Conclusion

There is extensive evidence which supports the view that the social competence of the family members with whom a person suffering from schizophrenia is living, has a significant role in determining the outcome of the individual's illness. In particular, deficits in emotional expression and problem-solving skills appear to be associated with a poor prognosis and a high risk of relapse. Furthermore, it is also probable that a lack of information about the nature and treatment of schizophrenia has contributed to this deficiency.

A family-orientated treatment approach has been developed over the last five years which has proved effective with families where there is a high degree of expressed emotion and an inadequate reserve of coping mechanisms to deal with the behavioural management of a chronic illness. Two methods based on social learning theory have been employed, which involve teaching the family and client communication skills and effective problem-solving techniques.

These techniques, coupled with continued family education about schizophrenia, carefully monitored neuroleptic medication and effective crisis intervention, have formed the basis of the family therapy programme. The goal is to maintain the person suffering from schizophrenia at their highest level of social functioning, while reducing stress and preventing further relapse.

The preliminary findings of a controlled outcome study that compares the *in vivo* family approach with an individual approach conducted in an inpatient setting, suggest that there are specific benefits associated with the family therapy approach. Behavioural observations indicate that measurable changes in family communication and problem-solving can be achieved by the third month of treatment in most families. However, this research is only preliminary and should be treated with caution.

Social and community factors

While in many cases the family provides the closest emotionally arousing social stimuli to schizophrenic patients, there are other life events that influence the onset and course of this illness. Much theoretical experimental evidence has pointed towards other interpersonal and socio-economic features of the environment that serve as antecedents or precipitants of acute schizophrenic reactions.

Brown and Birley (1968) ascertained the frequency of life events in schizo-phrenics during a three-month period preceding a psychotic breakdown that required hospitalisation. The patient and significant others were asked to describe disappointments, losses, damage and fulfilments that could be dated specifically. Life events were both pleasant (getting married, finding a new job, moving to a better house) and unpleasant (losing a friend, being made redundant), and included events that were outside of the control of the patient as well as those linked with the patient's behaviour. Comparisons were made for the same three-month interval with a sample of "normal" people. During the three-month reporting period, the proportion of "normal" people having life events remained constant; however, the proportion of schizophrenics experiencing life events increased markedly in the three-week period before the onset of symptoms. Of the schizophrenic cases, 60 per cent had an abrupt change in their social environment during this three-week pre-breakdown experience, compared to only 14 per cent of "normal" controls. Birley and Brown found that this concentration of life events occurred just before the first psychotic episode in young schizophrenics, as well as before exacerbations and repeated relapses in more chronic schizophrenics.

It is possible that schizophrenics could, because of their perceptual and cognitive impairments and increased psychological vulnerability, be stressed by mundane, small-scale and everyday life events that would not be upsetting to normal people. The Social Psychiatry Research Unit in London found that patients who relapse while taking neuroleptic drugs were more likely to have experienced major life events in the period immediately preceding the flare-up of symptoms than other relapsing schizophrenics who were not taking medication. The unit concluded that medication may protect vulnerable schizophrenic patients from the demands of everyday living, but not from stressful or large changes in their environment.

It has been found that patients experiencing close social relationships were more likely to remain in the community, irrespective of their living environment. In particular, socially isolated, unstimulating, deprived and custodial living environments tend to produce social breakdown or institutionalisation characterised by apathy, social withdrawal, loss of self-care skills and other negative symptoms of schizophrenia.

The concept of a social network describes the relationship between a patient and his/her inter-personal environment. The quality of this network can determine whether the environment has a positive or damaging effect on the patient. Tolsdorf conducted a study of social networks and their effects on psychiatric disability. He concluded that psychiatric clients reported fewer intimate relationships, fewer but more powerful figures in their network and fewer relationships with individuals other than family members. The schizophrenic patient had a much more pessimistic and negative view of their ability and lack of interest in their social networks, to assist them in times of need, a view that reportedly developed long before the onset of any schizophrenic symptoms. At the inter-personal level, the adaptive capacity of the individual is strengthened by the supportiveness, encouragement and reinforcement provided by primary relationships and figures in the social network.

Implications for social skills training

An increase or reappearance of symptoms in a person vulnerable to schizophrenia is the outcome of the balance or interaction between the amount of life stressors and the problem-solving skills of the individual. Social skills trainers have tended to assume that certain situations and events are critical to a schizophrenic's adjustment to survival in the community. Thus, there are the familiar range of situations inserted into behavioural rehearsals — positive and negative assertion, starting conversations, making an appointment with a doctor, dating and saying no to unreasonable requests. Wallace (1981) conducted a pilot project to assess situations relevant to successful living in residential care facilities in the community. Twenty-six potentially stressful scenes were integrated into a social skills training framework. Several of these were then selected at random and used in a role-playing assessment/training programme. The context of each situation was presented by the therapist and a role-model delivered to open the scene. The patient was then expected to respond spontaneously to the prompt and attempt to deal with the stressful situation. After the behaviour rehearsal was completed, the patient was asked to: identify his rights, duties and goals in the situation; generate a variety of alternative responses; predict the likely consequences of each of these responses; and evaluate each of these alternatives as a means of achieving the identified goals.

The goal of this project was to develop an individual problem-solving profile which could be extended to many dimensions of life outside residential care in the community. It was hypothesised that an individual might give an unskilled response because he did not accurately perceive the situation, did not generate a reasonably good alternative or did not have the behavioural repertoire to effectively deliver the response chosen.

A further step was planned for individualising the social skills assessment/training programme. The focus was on skill attainment for each patient, based upon specific inter-personal problems facing each client in the various settings of everyday life. Patients will enter the training sequence with a level commensurate with his/her skills, some requiring basic skills acquisition, while others may begin at higher levels of skills training. Each patient progresses at his own pace through a four-level hierarchy of skills development in areas such as peer and family relations, community living and symptom management.

The assessment/training programme, a personalised system of instruction, is designed to allow a person to progress at a different rate in each of these four areas of skill development. Thus some individuals will possess adequate independence skills for community life (for example, purchasing and preparing food, getting a flat), but will lack skills for socialising with peers and for obtaining a job. Alternatively, a person may have adequate employment skills but lack the know-how for coping with distracting and distressing symptoms (for example, how to obtain psychiatric consultation, how to request changes in medication or antedotes for side-effects).

The advantage of focusing separately on these various areas of skill development is that a person may reach a plateau in his progress in one area, while continuing to advance to higher levels in another area. By the end of training, patients should have an opportunity to maximise their assets, and move capably into the least restrictive environment consistent with their level of skills.

Wallace's social skills training technique

The aim of this research (Wallace et al. 1980, Wallace 1981) was to expand social skills training away from its usual focus on behaviour such as eye contact and voice volume, to focus on problem-solving skills. The design of the project was a comparison of the effects of nine weeks of intensive inpatient social skills training with a similar intensive nine weeks of a control therapy, designed on the basis of holistic health. The social skills training was conducted for five days a week, two to six hours daily. It consisted of:

1. Daily two-hour morning sessions designed to increase problem-solving skills;
2. Thrice-weekly afternoon sessions designed to generalise training to new persons and places;
3. Twice-weekly afternoon trips to the surrounding community to provide an opportunity to complete homework assignments;

4. Twice-weekly evening sessions designed to increase problem-solving skills in non-interpersonal areas;
5. Weekly meetings of patients and their families designed to increase family communication skills.

All patients were discharged to appropriate aftercare facilities after the nine weeks of inpatient treatment. They were provided with active aftercare treatment that began with five contacts per week, declining to two per month, and tapering out, with no contact being provided two years after discharge. A socially skilled response to a problem situation was presumed to be the outcome of a process that began with the accurate perception of the situation, moved on to flexible processing of the information to generate and evaluate possible responses, and ended with the effective sending of the chosen response.

Problem situations were differentiated into instrumental versus friendship/dating situations. Instrumental situations were defined as those in which the goal was community survival, such as using a post office or obtaining a flat. Friendship/dating situations were defined as those in which the goal was maintenance of or enhancement of the inter-personal interaction. Receiving, processing and sending skills were defined for each type of situation (Figures 3.1, 3.2).

Six scenes were scheduled to be role-played and reported each day. Scenes were grouped into those that portrayed situations dealing with peers and staff in the hospital setting; those that portrayed situations dealing with various community agents such as doctors, social workers, shopkeepers and landladies; and those that dealt with family difficulties. These were selected on the basis that the scenes were potentially important for adjustment from the hospital to the community.

The family scenes were different for each patient and were constructed on the basis of information provided by the family members during the Camberwell family interview and by the patient. The introduction and setting included a brief description of the context of the scene, the person with whom the role-player was to be interacting and the short- and long-term goals to be achieved.

One of the three patients was selected to be the role-player and one of the therapists was selected to be the role-play partner. The role-play began with the therapist reading the setting and starting the video recorder. Depending upon the instructions to the role-play partner, the interactions could stop after the patient's response or could continue for several

Figure 3.1 Hierarchy of Clinical Interventions for Community Living/Social Skills Training Programmes (Adapted from Wallace 1981)

Level	Type of Training	Components
1.	Basic social skills training	Sheltered living — training in house-keeping, personal hygiene, shopping, budgeting, cleaning, cooking, grooming
2.	Instrumental skills training	Community living with supportive room-mate. *Daily* staff visits. Basic interactional skills
3.	Conventional skills training	Community living with supportive room-mate. *Weekly* staff visits. Basic problem-solving skills.
4.	Generalising skills to special problem situations	Community living with supportive room-mate. *Monthly* staff visit. Cognitive skills in addition to the above

exchanges. Once the scene had ended, the video recorder was stopped and the patients were asked several questions designed to assess their accurate receiving.

After the four-and-a-half week training in instrumental situations, the focus of the sessions shifted to training problem-solving skills in friendship/dating situations. The first three days of training were designed to teach patients to recognise and generate three additional emotions, e.g. boredom, sadness, four non-verbal listening skills, e.g., head nods, leaning forward and three levels of self-disclosure, e.g., high, medium and low. The training was divided into five modules designed so that skills taught in the new modules were added to the ones taught in previous modules. The training method was similar to that used in the instrumental situations.

Module one   This module was designed to teach patients to learn to recognise possible topics and to use them in initiating conversations. Nine scenes were used to practice the skills. Each scene was introduced by the therapist and role-played for one or two exchanges. At the end of the role-play, the other patients were asked several questions.

Module two   The second module was designed to add the use of open and closed questions to the skills taught in the previous modules.

Module three   The third was designed to add to the skills learnt in the previous modules the use of active listening skills plus the recognition of the inter-personal partner's level of self-disclosure and comfort/discomfort. Nine scenes were used for the method that expanded the role-play from a few exchanges to three or four minutes of conversation.

Module four   This module was designed to add the skills of turn-taking and acting as the leader of conversation, to those skills taught in previous modules.

Module five   This module was designed to add the skills of changing topics and terminating conversations.

Afternoon sessions   The thrice-weekly afternoon sessions were designed to generalise the skills learnt in the morning sessions to new places and interpersonal partners. Scenes were selected from those that had been role-played in the morning, and each scene was played in several variations. First,

Figure 3.2   Weekly Schedule for Intensive Social Skills Training (Adapted from Wallace 1981)

Time	Monday	Tuesday	Wednesday	Thursday	Friday
7.00 9.00	Self-care Breakfast				→
9.00 10.30	Therapy Simple role-play				→
10.30 12.30	House- keeping		→		Trip to town
12.30 14.00	Lunch Assignment				→
14.00 15.30	Trip to town	Problem- solving	Trip to town	Simple con- versational skills	→
15.30 17.00	Trip to town	Problem- solving	Trip to town	Skills	Review
17.00 19.00	Dinner Assignment				→
19.00 21.00	Family therapy	Leisure training	Family therapy	Leisure training	Family therapy

the scene was enacted in the same manner as in the morning session. After the role-play, the two non-role-players were asked various questions about the scene. An incorrect answer resulted in the therapist providing the correct answer and prompting the patient to repeat it in response to the question. An inadequate role-play was corrected by the therapist using instructions, modelling or coaching as necessary to prompt an adequate performance. Second, the same scene was role-played with a new inter-personal partner, who responded in the same manner as in the original role-play. The same questions were asked of the two non-role-players. Third, the same scene was role-played with a new inter-personal partner responding in a different manner than that of the first two role-players. The same questions were asked after the role-play. The same general routine was followed for the friendship/dating modules. The duration of the role-play was longer, and fewer than three scenes were used since there might not have been three scenes role-played during the morning session.

Homework assignments The patients were requested to select and complete homework assignments designed to prompt them to use the skills developed in the morning and afternoon sessions, with new inter-personal partners and in new places and situations. Thirty-six assignments were developed: nine with hospital partners, for example, after receiving a cup of coffee patients had to ask someone to pass the milk; nine with community agents, for example, patients had to request change for a pound note at a shop without buying anything; nine with family members, for example, patients had to discuss their weekend arrangements with parents at the family therapy sessions; nine appropriate to the friendship/dating module, for example, patients had to approach a staff member that they liked and ask an open-ended question, expanding the topic by asking at least two other open-ended questions.

At the end of each Monday and Wednesday afternoon session, patients were asked to select two assignments. On Mondays patients were asked to select one each from the community and in-hospital assignments; on Tuesdays, one each from the friendship/dating and in-hospital assignments; on Wednesdays, one each from the family and community assignments; and on Thursdays, one each from the friendship/dating and family assignments. The chosen assignments were noted on information sheets and reviewed with patients at the beginning of the following morning session.

No reinforcers other than praise were arranged for the successful completion of these assignments. The opportunities to complete the community assignments were given on a Monday and Wednesday afternoon. All of the patients were driven to the surrounding community, dropped off at a common point and asked to rendezvous one hour later for coffee in a local restaurant.

The evening sessions were designed to provide information about solutions to non-interpersonal, community-survival problems. The formula was a group discussion of 10 topics consisting of subjects such as recreational planning, good social habits, food preparation, locating and moving into suitable accommodation, job interviews, transportation, maintenance of clothing, how to use local health centres and social services departments, and how to look after money and use post offices and banks. Additionally, there were tasks for each topic area that were to be completed during the session. For example, for the topic of transportation, the patients used a local map and bus timetable to plan their transportation to relevant destinations, and completed a worksheet on appropriate methods of transportation for different sessions.

The final evening session was designed to assist patients to cope with anger and anxiety. The formula consisted of a group discussion of topics such as passive, assertive, agressive behaviour, anger and stress control, and how to deal with them. Additionally, there was either role-play or tasks for each area that was to be completed during the session. For example, for the anger and stress control session, each patient selected a situation that was anger- or stress-provoking to them, and then role-played the situation with the therapist. The role-play was videotaped and the patient practised out loud while watching the videotape self-statements designed to control his anger. The patient then practised the statements covertly while the tape was replayed. Finally, the situation was again role-played with the patient practising the self-statements while experiencing the provocation directly.

This study has been quoted at length to give an indication of the comprehensive extent to which treatment for long-stay inpatients has developed. The implications for rehabilitation units trying to integrate people into the community are self-explanatory.

Psychopathology

To date, considerable difficulty has been experienced because of the lack of rigour that has been applied to the psychiatric diagnosis of people undertaking social skills training. This has led to problems in interpreting many of the research findings. The vast majority of reports in the social skills training literature have been based on mixed groups of psychiatric patients. This has made it difficult to reach any conclusions about the best approaches for different types of problems. The environment in which the person with schizophrenia exists has a profound impact on the course of the illness. There is some evidence that improvements in hospital and community treatment during the last 70 years has led to a corresponding improvement in symptoms, social functioning, and quality of life for people suffering from schizophrenia.

The setting in which social skills training takes place can interact with variables within the patient and with the training method to affect responsiveness and outcome. This interaction effect has been clearly documented by Paul and Lentz (1977) who showed that neuroleptic drug therapy slowed improvements in long-stay schizophrenics who were receiving psychosocial therapy in an intensive treatment ward, but did not produce this deleterious effect in patients who were randomly assigned to a custodial back ward.

The same interaction between patient and treatment variables can impinge upon the endeavours to apply social skills training. For example, among chronically institutionalised schizophrenics who view release into the community with a mixture of fear and confusion, the implementation of social skills training with implicit goals for discharge may bring into play various schedules of reinforcement that limit the effectiveness of the training programme.

Implications for social skills training

It is tremendously important to carefully diagnose patients who are to participate in social skills training. With clear definitions of characteristic symptoms, social adaptation, duration of illness and course of illness, results emanating from social skills training can be linked to specific types of patients and can be generalised and replicated. In addition, the major differences between acute, relapsing and chronic schizophrenics needs to be taken into account when interpreting outcomes of social skills training. There is very compelling evidence that schizophrenic patients with acute onset, brief psychotic episodes and who have good pre-morbid adjustment, are different to patients with chronic and sustained symptoms. The vast difference in the various courses of a schizophrenic illness points to the need to consider optimal timing for making psychosocial and social skills training interventions.

Obviously, social skills trainers will not make much headway if they attempt their procedures while the patient is still flagrantly psychotic. On the other hand, while experiencing continuing psychotic symptoms, including mild thought disorder, patients may improve, given the structure and positiveness of the social skills approach (Figure 3.3).

The degree of psychoticism may determine whether or not a schizophrenic can benefit from a social skills training course. Social skills training for patients with long histories of relapse or exacerbations, superimposed upon periods of remission or periods of moderate impairment, will be best timed when the patients are in their good periods.

Research has found that only after 18 months of weekly and biweekly sessions did sociotherapy lead to significant improvements in the social functioning of schizophrenic patients — and the results were even better after 24 months of therapy.

If the realistic responsibility of continuing care of schizophrenics is assumed, it will be feasible to intervene with social skills training when the time is right — for example, when symptoms are in remission and when a patient is about to take a step forward in rehabilitation or independence. It must also be learnt how to integrate social skills training with optimal doses of neuroleptic drugs — using sufficient medication to suppress symptoms, but not so much that the patient is unable to learn from the training.

Research has begun to show which schizophrenic patients improve without the use of drugs: in most schizophrenic patient samples, 15 to 20 per cent do as well on placebos or on no drugs whatever. Patients who are likely to benefit from social skills training without the addition of medication have had their onset of illness at a later age, and have had briefer psychotic episodes, shorter hospitalisations and better pre-morbid levels of adjustment.

An important part of psychosocial therapy will be teaching symptom management to patients so that they are better able to self-monitor their symptoms and seek earlier professional intervention. To encourage medication compliance, patients need to be educated about their illness, about the drugs they are taking, and about the ways in which they can arrange their environment to increase the regularity of medication-taking.

Certain elements of the psychopathology of deviant behaviour associated with schizophrenia may be beyond the scope of social skills training. These areas include unusual and bizarre symptomatic behaviours that frighten others. A number of studies have found that relapse and hospitalisation were

Figure 3.3 Courses of Symptoms and Social Adjustments in Schizophrenia

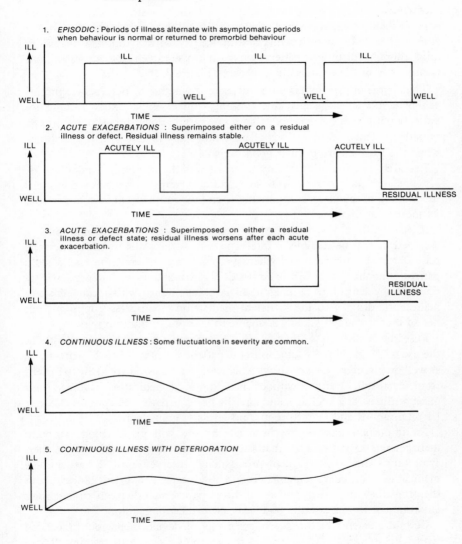

regularly preceded by increases in bizarre behaviour, including incoherent speech and aggression towards self or others. Ways to reduce the nuisance value of these bizarre, symptom-like behaviours need to be integrated with social skills training. For example, teaching the patient to talk to himself only in his own room may be an important first step in social skills acquisition.

Motivational deficits

Many schizophrenics, in addition to suffering from major inter-personal deficits, have a loss of affective expression and experience. Few reinforcers are available to strengthen their adaptive behaviour. Just as a schizophrenic's thought processes are often jumbled, fragmented and unconnected with reality, so is their quality and flow of emotions disrupted from real-life events. This apparent disruption of connectiveness of affect to external reality produces inappropriate affect, externally to the observation of others. This loss of affective responsiveness places a heavy burden on the family and professional help-givers who find that their attempts to engage in daily life are rebuffed or ignored. Active efforts to pull the withdrawn schizophrenic patient into social and recreational activities frequently have the effect of making worse the positive symptoms of the illness, delusions or hallucinations, and so on. The effect of social withdrawal, emotional dullness and resistance to inter-personal involvement leads to a vicious cycle of ever-increasing social isolation and increased negative symptoms of schizophrenia, such as apathy, slovenliness and withdrawal.

Not only are positive reinforcers lacking in the lives of many schizophrenics, but they are also troubled by aversive stimuli. Instead of experiencing social relationships as rewarding, schizophrenics may attempt to escape or avoid relationships that are viewed by them as stressful and unpleasant.

Implications for social skills training

It is understandable why many people involved in working with schizophrenics are subject to feelings of frustration, rejection, disappointment and even emptiness, and are reluctant to continue working therapeutically with them on a regular basis over a long period of time. Even though fear of relationships and flight from social reinforcers is a major feature of schizophrenia, a tolerant and demanding long-term, reliable and trusting relationship with a therapist is just what is needed for someone suffering from this illness.

One can sense the inadequacy of providing social skills training to schizophrenics for eight to twelve weeks, only to pat them on the shoulder and send them back into the real world, where they are likely to be victimised, ignored and excluded. On the basis of the long-term or intermittent nature of this disorder, one would assume that treatment needs to fit the timetable of the patient's dysfunctions. Six months is probably a minimum period of therapy, and perhaps even two to four years of treatment will be necessary to bring about a clinically significant and durable outcome in this client group. This is similar to maintaining a shaping attitude, starting with where the patient is at, and reinforcing small steps towards social reintegration; in this instance, there are a considerable number of small steps that need to be taken. One does not have to employ a non-directive, interpretive stance for effectively building a therapeutic relationship with the schizophrenic patient. By becoming a "real" person to the patient and accompanying him on expeditions into his real world, the therapist can both construct an effective relationship and teach the patient useful skills for community life.

The mainstreaming project

This is an interesting model for *in vivo* social skills training in which severely impaired schizophrenics were placed in their own flat in the community, surrounded by a number of ordinary people who did not suffer from any mental illness. Special support was provided to each schizophrenic by a team of three individuals who each spent up to four hours a day with the patient, shopping, cooking, housekeeping, taking exercise, looking for a job, going to work, using a bus, taking driving lessons, going to the doctors and visiting the family. Patients were encouraged to meet and spend their time with non-patients. They learnt to cope with crises of loneliness, failure, disability, fear and impulse control in a normal setting, and were given role-modelling by their team members (Mendel, Houle and Osman 1980).

As Brown and Birley (1968) suggested, it is time for social skills therapists to leave hospitals and move into the real world for *in vivo* training of social and community life skills for this group of clients. While schizophrenics are characterised by constriction in their range and potency of reinforcers, they can be motivated to participate in social skills training by the creative use of positive and negative reinforcers. Money — a widely accepted, highly normative, generalised reinforcer — has been found in America to be effective in reinforcing schizophrenic patient performance in role-playing and carrying out interpersonal assignments. Another unusual source of motivation for use in social skills training has come from the experimental literature on social censure. While criticism and negative feedback tend to be viewed as harmful by behaviour therapists, the studies conducted on laboratory tasks suggest that critical feedback helps schizophrenics improve their performance when clearly linked to incorrect responses.

Two recent studies have indicated that exposure to a censure can result in positive behavioural changes during social skills training (Hersen and Bellack 1976). It is likely that pairing praise for appropriate behaviour with censure for inappropriate behaviour can improve outcomes for schizophrenic patients. Important considerations are the quality of relationships between the patient and the therapist giving the criticism, the amount of psychopathology being experienced by the patient and the active perceiving and processing of the critical feedback (the patient will not benefit if he interprets the criticism in a delusionary fashion).

Cognitive deficits

The most intensively studied psychological aspects of schizophrenia have been cognitive and attentional deficits. Some of the major attentional and informational processing deficits that have been reported among schizophrenics include: deficiencies in sustaining focused attention; distractability; slowness in initial processing of information in sensory memory; impaired detection of relevant stimuli from background activity; and inefficient active organisation of information in short-term memory.

While the stage or level of information processing at which a schizophrenic has particular difficulty remains unclear, one common end-point of many of the individual deficits would appear to be a state of information overload. It has been suggested that some clinical phenomena in schizophrenics may represent attempts of the patient to cope with this state. Although the need to clarify the relationships between specific aspects of information processing and fluctuations in various schizophrenic clinical symptoms is clear, the global concept of information overload as an end-point of specific information-processing deficits gives rise to a useful model of schizophrenic symptomatic relapse.

British investigators have postulated two complementary processes linking social stimulation and schizophrenic symptomatology. On the one hand, schizophrenics living in understimulating environments such as large custodial institutions are prone to develop negative symptoms such as apathy, social withdrawal, inactivity and loss of self-care skills. These negative symptoms or deficits in adaptive behaviour have been termed the "social breakdown" or "clinical poverty syndrome". On the other hand, overstimulating environments such as highly critical or with emotionally over-involved relatives and suddenly introduced intensive treatment programmes can produce florid psychotic relapses. The primary handicap of many schizophrenics can be seen as an extraordinary vulnerability, like walking a tightrope, with the dangers of an understimulating social environment leading to the negative symptoms of social withdrawal and inactivity on the one side, and the dangers of overstimulation leading to florid symptoms and relapses on the other.

Implications for social skills training

If schizophrenics do indeed experience the cognitive dysfunctions described above, then much of the work to date in social skills training — emphasising verbal and non-verbal responses to social challenges — may bypass the more critical psychological processes that are closely linked with attention, perception and information-processing. Focusing only on the micro features of social skills — eye contact, gestures, voice volume and refusing unreasonable demands — may lead to limited generalisation, partly because the cognitive processes that facilitate the many different types of socially skilled behaviours in many different situations are not targeted for intervention. Thus, it may be more important to target the sensory input, selected focusing, and cognitive processing components relevant to verbal and non-verbal output.

Some of the relevant cognitive precursors of social skills have been identified by clinicians. They include problem recognition, problem definition, accurate perception of the relevant characteristics of the interpersonal situation, knowledge of social norms, information-processing capabilities, identifying short- and long-term goals, generating response alternatives, weighing the pros and cons of alternatives, evaluating and predicting potential consequences, choosing a reasonable alternative, and implementing alternatives and evaluating their effectiveness in achieving one's goals.

Among the skills taught through modelling, prompting and feedback have been: problem identification ("What is it I have to do?"); focusing attention ("Now carefully stop and repeat the instructions"); self-reinforcement ("Good, I'm doing fine"); and coping skills ("That's OK. Even if I make an error, I can still go on").

Such cognitive training is conducted across tasks, settings and people in order to ensure that people do not develop task-specific responses but instead develop a generalised response strategy.

Self-instructional and self-evaluative training with schizophrenics has been disappointing, to date. Most clinicians have reported that patients appear bored, have failed to attend or get too involved in the training procedures and do not reliably carry out assignments to practice their skills outside of the training sessions. To improve the results of cognitive training, investigators teaching problem-solving strategies to retarded clients have recommended alterations in the training programme, including: greater duration of training; increasing the use of cognitive strategies; fading of reinforcers from the therapist; and training across settings, problems and persons.

Additional tactics may be helpful in improving the learning of social skills by schizophrenics. These include such procedures as the use of brief, clearly focused tasks; prominent use of graphics that prompt patients to follow training procedures; repeated practice and overlearning; examining levels of autonomic responsiveness and potential for information overload through psycho-physiological cognitive tests; and allowing patients to escape temporarily or take time out from training when it becomes overstimulating. It could also be desirable for social skills trainers to recognise the diversity of the cognitive and attentional deficits and problems that schizophrenics demonstrate, since most studies indicate that only a subgroup of schizophrenics shows any given deficit.

This recognition of diversity will require a more personalised system of training that takes into account each individual's cognitive deficits, assets and needs (Figure 3.4).

Liberman, Lillie, Falloon et al. (1978) undertook research to assess whether social skills training used with schizophrenics was overstimulating and likely to cause symptomatic flare-ups in vulnerable people. They used fairly intensive skills training techniques and concluded that 10 out of 100 people had initially been reluctant to participate in the training. Their strategy was then to ease patients gently into the training and not to force them to proceed until a solid working alliance had been forged. Fewer than five patients dropped out of the training or absolutely refused to participate, even after a

Figure 3.4 Cognitive Skills and Schizophrenia

Cognitive deficit	Training programme
1. Associative intrusions in speech	— Mild censure for inappropriate response. Praise appropriate responding — Use thought-stopping or other intrusive stimulus to break pattern — Monitor thought processes by frequent questions and asking client to think aloud
2. Sustaining attention	— Keep training tasks brief and appropriate. Use frequent prompts to regain attention
3. Distractable	— Keep training setting uncluttered. Use graphics as reinforcement of verbal message
4. Overloading with complex tasks	— Break down tasks into sub-steps. Reduce novelty by many repetitions before moving on to new material
5. Being influenced by stimuli that are not relevant	— Give immediate feedback on performance; use overlearning, then gradually introduce delays into feedback and fade
6. Acute exacerbation imminent	— Pace training individually; keep performance demands low; allow time-out if necessary

gradual induction and relationship-building procedure. On rare occasions, patients have experienced anxiety or depression that has necessitated a brief period of time-out from the training — usually one to two days. However, much more common than symptomatic exacerbation has been boredom and impatience with the structure and repetition of the training procedures. Rather than overstimulation and symptom exacerbation, Liberman *et al*'s experience was that social skills training has been associated with reduction in psychopathology in over 90 per cent of the patients that were treated. They concluded that intensive social skills training does not produce exacerbations of schizophrenic symptoms.

Behaviour therapists have tended to target goals for schizophrenics aimed at equipping the patient to actively change his social environment. Thus, the social skills training curriculum for schizophrenics includes goals such as initiating and maintaining conversations; overcoming obstacles to obtaining appointments with care givers; getting satisfaction in shops, and so on, as well as using eye contact, hand gestures, leaning forward and a good tone of voice to express feelings.

Since these inter-personal goals are taught in a clear step-by-step structure with lots of positive feedback, there is little hazard of untowards overstimulation, arousal information overload or symptomatic exacerbation during the training period. However, once the patient has left the protective security of clinically sensitive trainers and the psychiatric setting, the "big bad world" may lead to frustration, disappointment, anxiety, arousal, information overload and symptomatic exacerbation. In most community aftercare programmes, trained personnel are not available on the spot to guide the ex-patient's social interactions, they are available only to pick up the pieces once relapse has occurred.

Social skills trainers must therefore consider how to develop coping strategies in their clients and what degree of support needs to be available for them in the community. When characteristic behaviours and persistent stressors have been identified in individual schizophrenics, it becomes possible to incorporate those stressor situations into a method that encourages the patient to identify the stressor (for example, critical comments by key relatives), to determine how continued engagement with the stressful situation might endanger short and long-term goals, to consider leaving the situation as a reasonable response option and to practise this option through role-play.

Conclusion

Because social skills training with schizophrenics has failed to produce generalisable and durable results, there is a need for rethinking the training methods. Therapists can no longer afford to ignore the family and its social processes. Social and community stressors, termed life events, have been tentatively implicated in the relapse of chronic schizophrenics. The modest correlations obtained by researchers between the occurrence of stressors and the onset of illness, suggests that recent life events alone are not sufficient to precipitate symptomatic flare-ups. The impact of life stressors is influenced by the individual's perception and cognitive processing, the coping skills and previous patterns of defence, and by the social network. Social skills trainers need to examine more closely the crucial events in the community that are related to relapse and breakdowns in social functioning.

Greater attention paid to psychiatric assessment reveals a variation in the course of schizophrenia and the need to tailor treatment programmes to the specific needs of a patient at a given point in the course of his illness. The timing of social skills training, preferably during periods of relative remission, becomes an important issue. Whether or not schizophrenics can benefit from social skills training while still experiencing psychotic symptoms may not be as relevant as how much benefit such patients can be expected to show. The next decade of experience with social skills training with severely impaired patient populations should be evaluated on much longer periods of training. Even within the group of patients who are characterised as schizophrenic, there is a great diversity in the responsiveness to tangible rewards and social reinforcers. This diversity and relative resistance to most incentives should encourage social skills trainers to go beyond the normal range of reinforcers to try to find incentives that are appropriate for the individual.

Social learning opportunities and supportive social networks in the environment, as well as social skills training, may cushion the full impact of social stressors on the vulnerable individual, or enable the individual to better cope with and resolve problems. Information overload and hyper-aroused physiological states, if they do endure past some critical time period, may contribute to the return of symptomatic symptomatology.

References

Brown G W, Birley J L and Wing J K (1972) Influences of family life on the course of schizophrenic disorders: A replication, British Journal of Psychiatry, 121 (562):241–258

Hersen M and Bellack A S (1976) Social skills training for chronic psychiatric patients: Rationale, research findings and future directions, Comprehensive Psychiatry, 17:559–580

Liberman R P, Lillie F, Falloon I R H, et al. (1978) Social Skills Training for Schizophrenic Patients and their Families, available from Clinical Research Centre, Box A, Camarillo, California, USA

Liberman R P, Wallace C J, Falloon I R and Vaughn C E (1981) Interpersonal problem-solving therapy for schizophrenics and their families, Comprehensive Psychiatry, 22(6):627–630

Mendel W, Houle J and Osman S (1980) Mainstreaming: An approach to the treatment of chronically and severely mentally ill patients in the community, Hillside Journal of Clinical Psychiatry, 2(1):95–178

Paul G L and Lentz R J (1977) Psychosocial Treatment of Chronic Mental Patients: Milviev VS Social Learning Programs, Harvard University Press

Wallace C J (1981) The social skills training project of the Mental Health Clinical Research Centre for the Study of Schizophrenia, in J S Strauss et al. (Editors), The Psychotherapy of Schizophrenia, Guildford Press

Wallace C J, Nelson C, Liberman R P et al. (1980) A review and critique of social skills training with schizophrenics, Schizophrenia Bulletin, 6:42–64

PART 2

PRACTICE

CHAPTER 4

ASSESSMENT

Accurate assessment is a major component of an effective social skills training programme. The assessment procedure depends on an individual assessment tailored to each client. In order to achieve this, the assessment procedure must focus on the individual's unique responses to the specific situations encountered. Although a number of complex inter-personal behaviour recording schemes exist, the emphasis will be on methods that are relatively economical in terms of cost and time.

Assessment methods in social skills training should always be regarded as a continuous process operating throughout training rather than as an isolated procedure undertaken before training. It is also important to remember that it is necessary to obtain information on all aspects of the client's social functioning. The therapist needs to consider various components in the assessment strategy to achieve this:

1. First, it is necessary to obtain a general impression of the client's behaviour. This leads to a judgement about whether or not the client is socially isolated, socially anxious or assertive. After this impression has been formulated, the assessment should focus on more specific aspects of the client's functioning;
2. Behavioural components;
3. Cognitive components;
4. Emotional components;
5. The effect of the social situation on overall performance.

Another purpose of the assessment procedure is to provide the client and therapist with a mutual understanding of the client's current social behaviour and the difficulties that the client is having.

General impression of the client's social functioning

The first aim of the assessment procedure is to obtain a general impression of the typical social behaviour pattern of the client. The intention is to focus on the major areas of skill deficits revealed by initial contact. The aim is to obtain a general impression of the client's typical methods of response in a variety of social situations. The therapist should attempt to obtain a general impression of these patterns and define the common elements. This will identify the areas that require detailed specification.

Specific components of client's social functioning

The second aim of the assessment procedure is to redefine the general impression that has been obtained into specific components, such as behaviour, cognition, emotion and situational specificity, which compose the client's social behaviour when recombined.

A general impression on initial assessment could be that someone was socially isolated. On further analysis, this impression could be broken down further into steps (Figure 4.1).

When the therapist has effectively broken down the general impression into a number of specific components, a suitable training programme can be conducted to alter each component. This should provide effective client social functioning when these altered elements are recombined.

Two major elements need to be considered when conducting assessments as part of social skills training: reliability and validity.

Reliability

A major concern of social skills assessment is reliability. In a general way, reliability refers to the degree of agreement among observers that they are observing and recording events in a similar way. The main problem is the use of general impressionistic terms, for example, shyness, aggression and

Figure 4.1 Molar—Molecular Analysis of Social Functioning

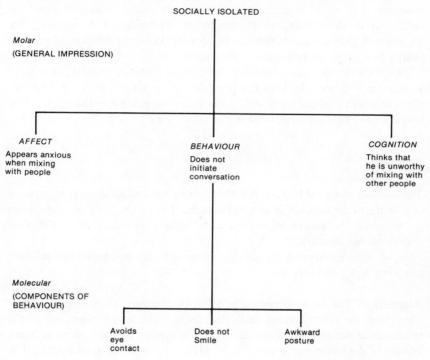

inadequacy. This is the language of the general public and many professionals, but it is an inaccurate way of trying to describe complex social behaviours.

For example, if 100 people were asked to assess whether a person "sounded confident" when speaking to a friend, it would be surprising if there was much agreement among the assessors. To increase the likelihood of getting agreement, the phrase "sounded confident" would have to be defined more clearly. The observers should therefore be told that to come to a conclusion that the person "sounded confident", the following criteria have to be met: that the person had to look at the person he was talking to, and that he had to speak in a loud and clear voice. Obviously, these criteria could be broken down even further to increase still further the reliability of the assessment. When an assessment commences, the client is likely to report his behaviour in general impressionistic terms. Therefore, it is necessary for the assessor to break down these initial descriptions into component parts to enable him to get more reliable information.

Two factors affect the reliability of the assessment, namely, length of assessment — since reliability has been shown to increase with the length of the assessment tool administered — and objective scoring — there should be no personal judgement required of the observers.

Validity

The assessor needs to be sure that the information collected is representative of how the client behaves in social situations. The validity of a measure refers to whether its values correlate with values obtained in a different (independent) measure.

Social skills assessment are usually concerned with two aspects of validity: sampling and predictiveness.

Sampling For an assessment to be valid, the measures used should produce samples of the client's social skills deficits that adequately represent all the situations in which the deficits occur. It is necessary to know about as many aspects of the behaviour as possible for effective treatment to take place. The task of assessment is to obtain a detailed picture of a representative sample of behaviours. For example, supposing a young woman is referred with social skills difficulties labelled as lack of assertion. On the initial interview the therapist forms the general opinion that her lack of assertion is restricted to her interactions with her husband. She has no apparent difficulty at work or with other members of her family. To obtain a more detailed picture of this woman's problems, it is necessary to sample how she behaves in more detail across a wide range of situations. One possible result of this sampling would be that the woman only lacks assertiveness when she is criticised, and that this is not specific to her husband.

Predictiveness The second question regarding validity is whether the assessment information obtained will be sufficient to predict how the individual will behave in real-life interactions. Very few assessments of inter-personal behaviour can be made in the client's natural environment.

Therefore, it is necessary that the assessment information — whether obtained from interview, role-play or by questionnaire — is predictive of how the client behaves in real-life situations. In the example above, the young woman could role-play an interaction with her husband. The validity question is whether the role-play interaction between the therapist and the woman will represent how she will actually interact with her husband. If it does, the validity requirement of the assessment has been met satisfactorily.

Factors affecting the accuracy of assessment techniques

1. Observer bias: the observer's own perception of the world can influence the way in which he interprets the client's social performance.
2. Observer drift: as time passes, assessors can become less meticulous and objective in their assessment techniques. This can lead to: forgetting some of the finer points of assessment; making changes in the assessment technique; missing episodes of behaviour due to distractibility or boredom; fabricating data; and adopting shortcut methods.
3. Measurement accuracy and observer agreement are higher when the assessors "know" that their data is being checked.
4. Assessors can shape data until it fits a favourite theoretical model.

What to assess

Social skills consist of relatively complex patterns of behaviour displayed in a great diversity of inter-personal situations. As outlined above, the preliminary objective of an assessment are to obtain a general description of the problem, usually from as many different viewpoints as possible. The problem should then be reduced to its component parts. An initial first step to achieve this is to look at the problem under the following headings:

1. Behavioural components;
2. Emotional components;
3. Cognitive components.

In addition, some attempts should be made to consider the effect of the particular situation on the problem. Any type of effective goal skill can be broken down into the behaviours that are felt to comprise it.

Problem definition

How does a therapist turn vague client problems into specific problem statements? The principle purpose of clear problem definition is to make an accurate decision regarding an effective social skills training programme for each client. It is necessary to define clearly the problem in order to:

1. Help the client and therapist to identify presenting problems and to determine whether they represent all or only part of a client's difficulties;
2. Structure training to a client's needs rather than to what the therapist feels to be appropriate;
3. Eliminate ambiguity and to clarify the client's requests for help;
4. Enable the client and the therapist to develop a consistent view of the problem.

Conceptualising Client Problems

Therapists can conceptualise people in different ways depending on their theoretical orientations. The information gained from an initial assessment can be used to label the client according to some pre-determined diagnostic category, that is, deviant neurotic or schizophrenic. Similarly, clients can also be labelled according to standardised tests, and be categorised as "introverted", "moody" or "withdrawn", for example. These approaches are not very useful for defining a client's problems because: diagnostic categories are not valid for all clients; the category assigned may bias the way that the client is treated; and labels such as "moody" and "disruptive" represent hypothetical constructs that are abstract and may overlook any relationship to overt behaviour patterns.

Clear definitions are essential

In social skills training a clear specification should be given of how the problem relates to the client, rather than simply defining him as being, for example, depressed. This should be attempted in terms of the behaviour, cognitions and emotions associated with the client's depression and of how they operate in specific situations.

One method of arriving at clear definitions of behaviour is the ABC model.

This suggests that behaviour (B) is influenced by the events that precede it, the antecendents (A), and by some types of events that follow behaviour, the consequences (C).

A is a cue or signal that can inform a person of how to behave in a situation. C is defined as an event that strengthens or weakens a person's behaviour. This technique can be a useful method of getting the client to look at his social performance in more detail. A simple ABC chart can be used for each situation (Figure 4.2).

Figure 4.2   A.B.C. Chart

Date and Time	Antecedent What happened just before?	Behaviour What happened?	Consequences What happened just after?

Assessing the behavioural components of social skills

The behavioural components of social skills refer to all observable behaviours that an individual exhibits when engaged in social behaviours. A simple clarification for assessment purposes is:

1. Verbal behaviour, for example, content of speech;
2. Non-verbal behaviour or behavioural attributes of speech, for example, volume:
3. Motor skills, for example, eye contact and facial expressions.

Verbal behaviour

This component is important as it transmits the client's intentions more directly than any other method. When evaluating the effectiveness of the verbal content used by a client, the therapist should be aware of both the client's *intent* and the *likely effect* if the client uses an alternative approach.

Commonly encountered difficulties, when recalling verbal behaviour, are that many people often find it difficult to remember what they have said, and have difficulty in being objective about what has occurred in social situations.

These difficulties make a client's verbal reports an unreliable source of clinical information and so more objective methods are usually used in

Figure 4.3   Some Verbal Components of Social Functioning

Verbal component	Definition	Example
1. Making an appropriate request	A direct statement of a person's requirements: not intimidating, threatening or grovelling	"I would appreciate it if you could tell me where the bus stop is"
2. Refusing a request	A clear, direct statement refusing the request, usually giving a reason	"I'm sorry I can't go to the pictures tonight. I've already made other arrangements"
3. Giving positive feedback	A direct statement approving something another person has done	"I think you dealt with that visit to the Job Centre very well"
4. Giving negative feedback	A clear, direct statement indicating disapproval of something someone has done. It usually includes a statement about how behaviour should alter	"I don't think you handled that meeting with your Father very well. You appeared very angry. Perhaps you could try talking about mundane issues initially when you meet"
5. Making empathic statements	A statement indicating understanding, but not necessarily agreement, with another person	"I understand that what I said made you feel unhappy, but my aim was to help you"

conjunction. The therapist must be aware of the likely consequences of the verbal behaviour used by clients in particular social situations. Figure 4.3 outlines an arbitary list of verbal components of social skills.

Non-verbal behaviour

The non-verbal behavioural attributes of speech such as voice volume, tone, pauses and so on accompany the verbal content of any conversation. In evaluating the behavioural components of social skills, attention should be focused on the non-verbal elements accompanying the verbal content. It is possible for non-verbal aspects of speech to convey messages that are widely divergent from the verbal message.

The co-ordination of the message between verbal and non-verbal elements of speech can either increase or decrease the impact of the message. There are numerous aspects of non-verbal behaviour, some of which are outlined in Figure 4.4, with some suggestions as to how they can be measured.

Motor skills

In addition to the verbal and non-verbal behaviours outlined above, other motor activities contribute to social behaviour. These include facial expressions, gestures, posture and so on. During social interactions, head nods, smiles, frowns and changes in posture can convey information not necessarily included in other channels. For example, leaning forward in one's chair can usually signal that the listener is attending closely (Figure 4.5).

Assessing the emotional components of social skill

Emotions

Central to an accurate assessment of a client's social interactions is a clear understanding of his emotional experiences and the cognitive components of these experiences. Outlined below are the major dysfunctional emotional states that clients undergoing social skills group training experience.

Figure 4.4   Some Non-Verbal Components of Social Functioning

Non-verbal component	Description	Method of measurement
1. Volume of speech	Degree of volume is appropriate to the conversation	*Rating scale* 1 Very soft 2 Soft 3 Appropriate 4 Loud 5 Very loud
2. Emotional tone	The person's voice reflects successfully the emotional meaning associated with his speech	*Rating scale* 1 Flat, unemotional 2 3 Appropriate 4 5 Over-emotional
3. Speech fluency	Is capable of speaking without too many inappropriate pauses or interruptions	*Frequency count* Measure the number of speech disruptions against the length of time spent talking
4. Eye contact	Can look directly and appropriately at another while engaging in social interaction	*Frequency count* Measure the number of glances and the total amount of time spent looking

Figure 4.5 Some Motor Components of Social Functioning

Motor components	Description	Method of measurement
1. Gestures	Appropriate use of hands and arms when speaking	*Rating scale* 1 — 3 — 5 Gestures absent / Gestures inappropriate / Gestures appropriate and/or frequency count
2. Head nods	Appropriate movements of the head, while listening, indicating attentiveness	*Rating scale* 1 — 3 — 5 Absence of head nods / Appropriate head nods and/or frequency count
3. Posture	Sits or stands appropriately. Appears open and relaxed	*Rating scale* 1 — 3 — 5 Tense, uncomfortable / Relaxed

Anxiety   according to rational emotive therapy, there are two forms of anxiety, ego anxiety and discomfort anxiety. Ego anxiety is based on a prediction that future events will occur that will result in the client making a global self-evaluation. Often associated with such negative self-evaluations are predictions of future events based on magnification and personalisation. Typically, clients in social skills groups predict harsh, negative responses from others, distorted in terms of the intensity and duration of the responses.

Discomfort anxiety stems from the client's belief that he must be comfortable, and that the experience of anxiety is intolerable. As a result, the client seeks a guarantee of comfort and in doing so often adds to his ego anxiety.

Ego and discomfort anxiety often interact. There are numerous techniques available for assessing a client's level of anxiety. One frequently used rating scale is the "fear scale" to assess the extent to which a client is experiencing anxiety. There are numerous adaptations of this scale but most are based on the format where the client is asked to indicate on the scale how he feels in a given situation:

0 = calm and relaxed;
1 = a little uneasy;
2 = feeling tense and aware of heart rate;
3 = sweaty, feels tight, heart rate fast;
4 = very tense, wants to run away;
5 = terrified, feels he is going to die.

Anger   This should be distinguished from annoyance. Both emotions stem from frustration. Annoyance stems from the rational preference that other people follow the same personally valued rule, and the following conclusions are typically made when transgression occurs:

1. It's annoying that this person has acted in such a way;
2. I really do not like his behaviour.

Anger results from the irrational demand that the other person should not break the client's rule.

Depression   Inferences that commonly lead to clients becoming depressed include negative interpretations of the clients' ongoing and future experiences. Evaluations that are made of these negative interpretations include negative self-ratings ("I am no good") and evaluations of the world ("Life is bad for letting this happen"). Another form of depression results from self-pity.

Shame   Shame is experienced when some weakness or undesirable behaviour is revealed in public which has incurred or might incur the disapproval of other people. The evaluation added to such an inference, so that shame is experienced, is: "I must have their approval; I am worthless if they disapprove of me." Clients involved in social skills training groups are particularly concerned about the public display of such weaknesses. Again, they imagine extremely harsh reactions to such a display.

Guilt   Guilt is distinguished from shame by the fact that the emotion is experienced in both public and private, whereas shame tends to be experienced only in public situations. Guilt is based on the client's inference that he has done something bad, stupid or wrong. However, guilt is experienced when the judgement "I am a failure for going against my principles" is added to the inference.

Assessing the cognitive components of social skill

Over the past few years there has been a considerable increase in the assessment of cognitive aspects of social skill. It is now widely recognised that the absence of socially skilled behaviour may be due to faulty or inappropriate thoughts that occur in social situations.

The assessment of cognitive components can help in the understanding of why someone performs certain types of behaviour. It has become increasingly clear that certain kinds of thought can improve the performance of socially skilled behaviour, whereas other kinds of thought can inhibit its performance. There are several specific areas where cognitive difficulties can occur.

Knowledge

Socially skilled individuals are usually aware of a wider range of alternate responses than those who are not perceived as being skilful. Some people are simply unaware of the appropriate response to make in a certain situation, and are unaware of how to improve their performance in a given situation.

A person's knowledge can be explored by questioning the awareness of alternative, and perhaps more appropriate, responses, and by exploring awareness of social norms. The lack of social skill exhibited by some individuals results almost entirely from deficits in their knowledge of appropriate responses for various situations.

Belief and attitudes

Socially unskilled behaviour can be brought about because a person's behavioural options are constructed by their beliefs or attitudes: for example, if someone believes that it is never appropriate to display anger or displeasure. The following kinds of questions posed during an interview can elicit information about clients' beliefs and attitudes:

1. Do you believe that you have the right to express various opinions, beliefs and ideas?
2. How do you feel about challenging the beliefs, attitudes and ideas of others?

No amount of behavioural training will have any impact if the client believes that there is something wrong about behaving in a way most other people consider to be appropriate.

Perception of others

To effectively employ social skills the client must have the ability to perceive accurately the intentions and motivations of others in social situations. Some people are not sensitive to these uses, for example, someone who carries on talking even though the host is yawning and saying that he has to get up early in the morning. In more generalised cases, clients may believe that people cannot be trusted — and that distorts the perception of the person with whom they are interacting. Assessment should be made to determine whether clients can "read" accurately different social situations.

Expectations of consequences

The fourth aspect of cognition that can affect social behaviour is the client's expectations of the probable consequences of engaging in particular social behaviours. Most people behave in ways that they believe will increase positive consequences and decrease negative ones. The therapist should assess the client's expectation of what is going to happen in social encounters. This often helps to clarify the client's objectives in more accurate terms.

Assessing the situational components of social skills

The behavioural, emotional and cognitive components of social skills are inextricably interwoven with an assessment of an individual's behaviour in specific social situations. Moreover, it is impossible to evaluate successfully social behaviours independently of the situation in which they occur.

The situational specificity of social skills can be approached in several ways. First, it is clear that different social situations have different requirements in terms of the response components deemed necessary for dealing with them skilfully. One of the major reasons for the assessment of social situations is to differentiate highly specific response deficits, that is, those behavioural problems that occur in particular kinds of encounters, from generalised response deficits or from those that occur only in particular social situations. In order to achieve this it is necessary to identify the kinds of situations in which the client exhibits problems. Thus the therapist may identify a number of situations that give rise to generalised social skill deficits.

For example, the client may have problems in expressing himself adequately in any situation which involves a group of more than three or four people. He may also have problems in a different kind of situation that require a fairly high degree of self-disclosure or expression of intimacy. The latter problem may be specific to one encounter. The problems of assessing the generality or specificity of the client's problem behaviour boils down to attempting some classification of situations that give rise to the response deficits. Does the problem occur with those with whom the client is unfamiliar, does it occur with friends and acquaintances, or does it involve those with whom the client has intimate personal attractions? Does it occur more often with males or females, or with those who are younger or older? Does it manifest itself only with those in authority, such as parents or employers? Does it occur in one-to-one situations or in social groups? Is the problem confined to marital interactions or is it operative in all opposite-sex relationships?

In assessing all the situations where the client exhibits skills deficits, a picture will begin to emerge in which either specific social behaviour problems are related to a specific class of interactions, or generalised deficits are found in the individual's ability to relate successfully to a variety of individuals.

Inferences

Inferences are non-evaluative interpretations of actual events. Inferences may be revealed if a therapist asks a client what situations triggered off their problem, for example, Mrs P became depressed when one of her colleagues at work criticised her. On further exploration, it transpired that the lecturer corrected one of the client's statements made in class. However Mrs P interpreted such a correction as criticism.

It is important to distinguish between specific inferences when assessing client inferences — e.g., interpretation of specific events and generalised inferences, e.g., habitual styles of information processing. It often transpires that inferences are hierarchically organised in the client's cognitive structure.

Inference chaining

With inference chaining, clinicians begin with the first inference expressed by the client, and then continue by asking detailed questions that reveal more deeply embedded inferences. This is usually done by asking open-ended questions and eliciting increasingly deeper inferences until the client states an evaluation.

Therapists often suggest that clients participate in the assessment of inferences outside therapy sessions. The general rule here is that the closer in time the clients record their thoughts, the better. As a result, therapists often suggest to clients that they keep a written record of thoughts that occur in particular situations.

Application of assessment procedures to stages of social skills training

How can such assessment procedures be employed at various stages of social skills training? Basically, there are three phases where clinicians need to conduct thorough analyses of client's inferences and beliefs. This is best done in conjunction with a behavioural analysis. The three phases are: prior, during and at the generalisation phase of training.

Assessment procedures before social skills training

Thorough behavioural analysis is usually conducted before social skills training is begun. Clinicians should use such an opportunity to assess the presence of any dysfunctional inferences or irrational beliefs that the client may hold. This may be difficult since, typically, clients may display a pattern of avoidance and withdrawal from social situations. Clinicians should use creative methods to obtain this information, for example, by setting up role-play situations in assessment interviews where clients are asked to portray themselves interacting in the social situation with another person, played by the therapist. Afterwards, clients should be asked to reflect on what thoughts were going through their minds at the time. Another method is to ask clients to imagine themselves approaching, and not avoiding, a particular social situation and staying in, and not withdrawing from, the situation. Particular emphasis should be placed on the client's emotional feelings and cognitions. The therapist should identify specific social situations that clients would like to approach and stay in, rather than general social situations that are employed as a diagnostic form for all clients.

One useful situation to employ as a stimulus for assessing problems is the client joining a social skills group. It is important to remember that such a group is, in fact, a social situation and, as such, is likely to activate a client's cognitions and emotions about entering social situations. In particular, therapists should pay attention to the client's anticipations of other people's reactions to them, and their anticipated reactions to such reactions. It is important for therapists to remember that clients have expectations about their abilities to benefit from such treatment procedures. Common thoughts expressed by clients at this stage are: "What you suggest to me won't work. I'll never be able to do the things that you have explained to me." At this stage it is important for the therapist to help the client modify such dysfunctional cognitions. They may interfere with skill learning if this does not occur.

Assessment procedures during social skills training

It is important to continue to assess the four components of the client's social behaviour during the process of social skills training. Clients should be helped to understand the effects of cognitions on emotional experiences and behaviours, and they should be encouraged to verbalise their thoughts, when appropriate.

Clinicians should pay particular attention to clients' thoughts about the skills they are being asked to learn. Because, typically, such clients have not enacted such skills, the learning of thoughts such as "This is silly — it's not me and I'll never be able to put this into practice", may interfere with skill learning.

Assessment procedures during generalisation from a social skills group to everyday life situations

At this stage it is assumed that clients have been helped to try and correct the negative inferences and irrational beliefs that give rise to dysfunctional emotional experiences such as anxiety and anger. Furthermore, it is assumed they have made progress in acquiring social skills as a result of practicing them in a group situation. It is at this stage when generalisation occurs that clinicians should be aware of the existence of beliefs derived from discomfort, anxiety or low frustration tolerance.

The generalisation stage is most important in determining the degree of therapeutic gain to be achieved by social skill group members. At this point, clients have developed social skills but are awkward in executing them and have not yet learnt the skill of correct timing in the enactment of such skills — a skill that is learnt only through social intercourse. As a result, clients may still be rejected because they come across awkwardly to other people. Discomfort-related beliefs will thus interfere with clients persisting in the face of adversity. They often do not persist in practising skills that would improve their chances of gaining what they want in life, precisely because at some point in the skill acquisition process they claim that they don't "feel like themselves". Therapists must be aware of such cognitions if they are to help clients persist in this crucial stage of therapy.

The structured interview

Interviewing is probably the most frequently used and most convenient method of evaluating a client's social behaviour. However, all interviews are subject to biases in reporting which limit the accuracy of some of the information obtained. In one sense, the client knows more about his behaviour in social situations than anyone else. The apparent paradox of this situation is that, although the individual is "always there" in every social situation, he is not necessarily the most accurate observer of his social behaviour.

Nevertheless, many clients can report on their behaviour and the behaviour of others with reasonable accuracy, and most clients can learn with practice to increase the accuracy of their self-observation. Another advantage of interviews is that the client is the absolute expert on the cognitive components of his social behaviour. In other words, the best source of information on the client's behaviour is the client himself. The client's biases, distortions or misconceptions can be important sources of data in assessing social skill deficits.

Focused interviewing can be conceptualised as consisting of several overlapping phases, each phase having one or more objectives. In addition, interviews can be conducted over several sessions to help clarify data from other sources, or even during training to assess progress.

During the first phase of the assessment interview, it is obviously necessary to establish a good working relationship with the client so that he will have confidence in revealing information to the interviewer. Therefore, the first step in the interview is listening in a non-judgemental way and communicating an empathic understanding of the client's situation.

Once a working relationship with the client has begun, the second step is to begin a survey of the client's problems in social interaction. The objectives are to obtain a thorough history of the client's difficulties. Most clients will begin by discussing their problems in vague terminology of personality, such as always having been excessively "shy" or "anxious". To help the client to specify the history of his social problems in behavioural terms, some direct questions can be asked about who the problems were with and what the client did in those situations. Towards the termination of this phase, the assessor should have arrived at some general picture of how the client has dealt with social relationships in the past, and about whether the difficulties remain in the present.

At the beginning of the third phase of the interview, the focus should shift more directly to the client's current inter-personal relationships with friends, spouse and employers — in short, anyone with whom the client has recurrent interactions on a day-to-day basis. A partial list of areas to be explored could be:

1. How does the client express opinions to others? Who are these people, and how successful is he?
2. Does the client initiate conversations with peers or with members of the opposite sex?
3. Can the client refuse unreasonable requests from friends and strangers?
4. Does the client have any problem offering compliments to another person or showing appreciation for what someone has done for him?
5. How does the client ask for help when he needs it? Are the client's requests usually successful?
6. Can the client resist pressure from others who want him to do something against his will? How effective is it?
7. Can the client typically express his angry feelings towards others? What does he usually say, and what happens?

Towards the conclusion of the third phase, the interviewer should have some concrete ideas about with whom the client is currently having difficulties, and over what sort of issues. In addition, the interviewer should have specific information on precisely what the client does in these difficult situations, described in specific behavioural terms. The cognitive style — how the client approaches people — should also be apparent and, in addition, the therapist should have some idea of how the client's emotional functioning is involved. Finally, the therapist should have formed some opinion as to whether the social skills deficits seem limited to one or two types of situation, or whether the skill deficits are general to a large number of social situations.

During the fourth and final stage of the interview, the therapist may want to give the client some general feedback about what he has learned. The feedback should be direct but, at this stage, not presented as firm conclusions. The therapist should start to draw some conclusions, albeit tentative ones, and should seek agreement or disagreement from the client. Finally, at the conclusion of the interview, the client should be informed about the next steps and whether future assessments will be necessary, or whether the training procedure will begin.

Structured inventories

A number of self-report inventories are available to assist individuals in reporting their responses to social situations. Most of these questionnaires have been developed for research purposes on fairly homogenous populations, such as college students, neurotic adults, and so on, so that their application to any particular client who does not have the characteristics of college students or neurotic adults needs to be made carefully.

Most of the self-report questionnaires developed to date assess only a few facets of social skills such as "assertiveness", "heterosexual skill" or general "social anxiety". Thus no single questionnaire or group of questionnaires can possibly assess all of the relevant dimensions of a particular client's social competence.

Despite these limitations, the measures that have been developed this far can provide the therapist with theories about the client's general areas of difficulty. These tentative ideas of general areas of difficulty can then be amplified through interviews and other assessment methods.

How do these self-report questionnaires operate? Most of the instruments sample a range of inter-personal situations that typically elicit responses of interest. For example, how does the client perform in situations that typically require assertive responses, or how much anxiety does the client feel in various social situations? The client is asked to indicate how true the statement is of him, or how typical of him is the behaviour described in the statement.

The Rathus Assertive Schedule (RAS) was designed to assess assertive behaviour. The RAS is a 30-item inventory (Figure 4.6) in which the respondent is asked how "characteristic" the statements are of his behaviour: for example, "I often have a hard time saying no", or "When I am given a compliment, I just don't know what to say." Two popularly employed self-report measures of social anxiety have been developed by Watson and Friend (1969). The social avoidance and distress scale was designed to assess the client's experience of discomfort and anxiety in social situations. The other measure, the fear of negative evaluation scale, was designed to evaluate the degree to which the client affirmed statements indicating a fear of social disapproval in inter-personal situations.

What are the uses of such structured inventories? They are economical of time; many questionnaires can be scored objectively; they can help to identify broad problem areas that can be analysed more thoroughly than other assessment methods; and the same measures can be administered more than once so that progress during training can be assessed.

There are, however, limitations also. It may be difficult for the client to remember how he behaved in certain situations; the client may not be motivated to report honestly; the structured inventories are usually phrased in general terms, for example, "Do you usually...", which make it difficult for a client to average his responses across situations.

Figure 4.6 Assessment Scale of Social Anxiety (Source: Rathus (1973) reproduced by permission of Academic Press)

Directions. Indicate how characteristic or descriptive each of the following statements is of you by using the code given below.

+ 3 very characteristic of me, extremely descriptive
+ 2 rather characteristic of me, quite descriptive
+ 1 somewhat characteristric of me, slightly descriptive
− 1 somewhat uncharacteristic of me, slightly nondescriptive
− 2 rather uncharacteristic of me, quite nondescriptive
− 3 very uncharacteristic of me, extremely nondescriptive

1. Most people seem to be more aggressive and assertive than I am.
2. I have hesitated to make or accept dates because of "shyness".
3. When the food served at a restaurant is not done to my satisfaction I complain about it to the waiter or waitress.
4. I am careful to avoid hurting other people's feelings, even when I feel that I have been injured.
5. If a salesman has gone to considerable trouble to show me merchandise which is not suitable, I have a difficult time saying "No".
6. When I am asked to do something, I insist upon knowing why.
7. There are times when I look for a good vigorous argument.
8. I strive to get ahead as well as most people in my position.
9. To be honest, people often take advantage of me.
10. I enjoy starting conversations with new acquaintances and strangers.
11. I often don't know what to say to attractive persons of the opposite sex.
12. I will hesitate to make phone calls to business establishments and institutions.
13. I would rather apply for a job or for admission to a college by writing them letters than by going through with personal interviews.
14. I find it embarrassing to return merchandise.
15. If a close and respected relative was annoying me, I would smother my feelings rather than express my annoyance.
16. I have avoided asking questions for fear of sounding stupid.
17. During an argument I am sometimes afraid that I will get so upset that I will shake all over.
18. If a famed and respected lecturer makes a statement which I think is incorrect, I will have the audience hear my point of view as well.
19. I avoid arguing over prices with clerks and salesman.
20. When I have done something important or worthwhile, I manage to let others know about it.
21. I am open and frank about my feelings.
22. If someone has been spreading false and bad stories about me, I see him (her) as soon as possible to "have a talk" about it.
23. I often have a hard time saying "No".
24. I tend to bottle up my emotions rather than make a scene.
25. I complain about poor service in a restaurant and elsewhere.
26. When I am given a compliment, I sometimes just don't know what to say.
27. If a couple near me in a theatre or at a lecture were conversing rather loudly, I would ask them to be quiet or to take their conversation elsewhere.
28. Anyone attempting to push ahead of me in a line is in for a good battle.
29. I am quick to express an opinion.
30. There are times when I just can't say anything.

Self-monitoring

Self-monitoring is an extremely useful assessment technique. It can be used to assess both the client's overt social behaviours and his thoughts in social interaction. It enables clients to observe, record and report on their inter-personal encounters in more detail and in a systematic manner. It has an important additional benefit in that it teaches the process of self-assessment — an important objective of social skills training. The client must learn what to observe and then systematically record when and under what circumstances it occurs.

For example, clients may be asked to record specific social situations in which they feel anxious. The information provided by this method can be extremely comprehensive. Self-monitoring procedures can be used repeatedly throughout assessment and training.

Developing self-monitoring procedures

Some clients provide more useful data from self-monitoring than others. Information is likely to be more accurate from people who are highly motivated and have some understanding of their skill deficits. It is often useful to conduct some preliminary training in self-monitoring using simple behaviours. In addition, the target behaviours to be assessed by the client should be defined as unambiguously as possible using several examples.

Clients should also be prepared by teaching basic behavioural assessment before beginning self-monitoring procedures. The observation and record-keeping planned in advance should be the simplest possible. Attempting to obtain too much information will lead to unnecessary confusion and incomplete data collection.

The client should be advised to record data immediately after the event if at all possible. If not, then two to three periods a day should be set aside.

Self-monitoring has been defined as a "process in which clients observe and record specific things about themselves and their interactions with environmental situations." A simple behaviour analysis for use in self-monitoring is the ABC method. The client is taught to record data about:

A — Antecedents (what happended immediately beforehand)
B — Behaviour
C — The Consequences of B.

Some researchers have noted that the mere act of observing oneself can influence and change one's behaviour. However, this is usually only a mild effect and other therapies are needed in conjunction to bring about lasting change.

Factors affecting self-monitoring

Reliability, the accuracy of the recorded data, is one of the most important factors affecting self-monitoring. Reliability of information is important if treatment decisions are being based on this information. Adequate training therefore has to be undertaken.

Effectiveness is also crucial. Self-monitoring has been shown to be most effective when clients monitor a small number of positively valued target behaviours. It is made even more effective when performance feedback and goals or standards are made available and unambiguous, and when the monitoring act is both pertinent and closely related in time to the target behaviours.

Several variables have been identified that seem to affect self-monitoring programmes:

1. Clients who are well motivated are more likely to benefit;
2. Behaviours valued positively are likely to increase with self-monitoring, whereas negatively valued behaviours are likely to decrease;
3. There is a good chance of adequate monitoring if only one target response is monitored. This declines rapidly as the number of target responses increases;
4. Continuous self-monitoring may result in more accurate results than occasional monitoring (Figure 4.7).

Steps to self-monitoring

There are four basic steps to a self-monitoring programme:

1. Selection of target response to monitor;
2. Recording of target response;
3. Charting response;
4. Analysis.

Figure 4.7 Self Monitoring Form — Social Behaviour Situations

NAME:

DATE:

When occurred	Situation	Anxiety rating Low–High 1–5	Thoughts	Social behaviour observed	Others' responses	Satisfaction with outcome 1–5
8.30	On bus, saw girl from office down the road	3	I'd like to talk to her. She won't know who I am	Sat next to her and smiled but didn't say anything	After 10 mins she asked me if I worked up the road	(2) Should have started conversation
10.00	Went to the staff canteen for coffee. Sat on my own. Group of people sat at other table	5	Wanted to ask if I could join them. Afraid they might say no	Looked at their table but did not go over	They ignored me	(1) Felt they should have asked me to join them

Selection of target response The therapist has to help the client identify what to monitor. Usually it is a good idea to limit monitoring initially to one response. Another can be added later if the client copes easily with this. The response to be monitored should be clearly identified and clearly understood by both parties.

Recording It is important that behaviour is reported systematically. Therefore, the client must have instructions on when to record, how to record, and have devices for recording:

1. When?
   (a) If the client is using monitoring as a way to *decrease* an undesired behaviour, then pre-behaviour monitoring may be more effective, as this seems to interrupt the response chain early. Here, the client records the desire to do something before actually doing it;
   (b) If the client is using monitoring as a way to increase a desired response, then post-behaviour monitoring may be more helpful;
   (c) Recording instances of desired behaviour immediately it occurs or immediately after is usually most helpful. If the wait is too long then the impact of recording may be lost;
   (d) The client should be encouraged to record the response when not distracted by other influences.

2. How?
   The therapist must tell the client how to record the target response. The method of recording can vary in a number of ways:
   (a) Informal — for example, the client is instructed to make mental notes of any event that seems related to changes;
   (b) Formal — the client is asked to fill out a rating sheet according to a time-sampling schedule;
   (c) Simple — the client is asked how many times he felt uncomfortable in a social interaction.
   (d) Complex — the time, place, circumstance, the effects of each response, plus cognitive and behavioural responses are recorded;
   (e) Objective — the client is asked how many times he carried out the target response;
   (f) Subjective — time sampling.

3. Devices for recording
   The client has to be given a device for recording his behaviour. A

variety of devices have been developed to help keep an accurate record, for example, daily record sheets and diaries, anything that records frequency (beads, tokens, calculators), and duration can be measured by watches and clocks. In addition, the device should be portable and accessible, easy and convenient to use, economical, and unobtrusive but noticeable by the client so that it will stimulate him to self-monitor.

4. Practice
The client must be thoroughly familiar with what is expected before starting to record data.

Charting responses   When the client has recorded the data it must be transferred to a more permanent record so that it can be stored for future use. The client should receive instructions on how to chart the information and the frequency of when to chart.

Analysis of data   There is some evidence that people who receive feedback change more than those who do not. The recorded data should be used to draw up target behaviours for social skills training. These self-monitoring techniques should continue to be used throughout training if they are adopted, and the client should bring his data on a regular basis to be evaluated with the therapist. The client can use the data for self-evaluation and, with the therapist, to modify targets or achieve goals. The therapist's role is to help the client to interpret the information correctly (Figure 4.8).

Figure 4.8   Self-Monitoring Chart

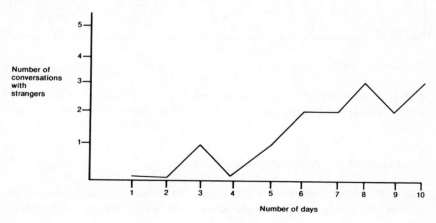

Daily record sheet

In the initial stages of assessment, a simple descriptive chart can be used to find out, in broad terms, what the client feels about a problem. This is useful if the client is having difficulty identifying problem situations. The client is asked to keep a simple record of his activities on a sheet such as the one shown in Figure 4.9. Once problem concerns have been identified, a more detailed assessment will be necessary.

Figure 4.9   Daily Record

NAME:			DATE:	
Time	Place	Activity	Who else was there?	How I acted

Behaviour chart

This is an extension of a daily record sheet. Here, a client is asked to observe and record targeted behaviours so that a baseline can be established (Figure 4.10).

Assessment by role-play techniques

Role-play interactions involve the simulation of social interactions in the natural environment. This method is used frequently in social skills

Figure 4.10 Behaviour Chart

NAME   DATE:

Problem behaviour	Date	Time	Place	Frequency/ duration	Antecedents (what preceeds them?)	Consequences (what follows behaviour?)

assessment because it is usually easier to observe a client's behaviour in a simulated encounter than in the natural environment.

Role-play observations are usually utilised after an initial interview or structured inventory has identified general areas of difficulty for a client in social situations. The purpose of the initial client contact is to build up a general picture of the type of social situations that lead to the client's ineffective social behaviour.

Role-play then helps to pin down the specific behavioural components of the client's responses (for example, non-verbal behaviour, cognitive aspects), which are to be the target of social skills training.

Following the assessment of general areas of client difficulty, the therapist should select specific social interactions for the client to role-play. Usually, three to six scenes are used to assess each skill deficit. The objective of the role-play is to more clearly define specific target problem areas at which specific social skills training can be aimed.

Client preparation

Clients must be introduced to the procedure in order to obtain maximum benefit from role-play assessment. A simple explanation of the ideas behind role-play and how it will improve the assessment procedure is usually helpful. Some people may be resistant to the idea or feel that it is silly or unnatural. It should be explained that much more relevant information can be collected by this method than by simply talking.

If the client can be encouraged to try out the most simple role-play, then it is usually possible to gain co-operation for future attempts. Most people soon feel comfortable with this technique.

It is important that the client understands the nature and purpose of any role-play assessment. He should be instructed to imagine that he is actually in the situation described and that his partner is actually the person involved.

Another clear instruction should be given to the client that he is not to involve the therapist in the interaction, and that he should behave in the role-play as if it was genuinely occurring.

Role-play techniques

Most role-plays used in social skills assessment consist of three parts. First, a narrated background description of the particular situation in which the client finds himself. Second, comments made by a role-play partner directed towards the client and, third, the client's response to the partner.

The material chosen for the role-play is derived by the client on troublesome problems. Role-play assessments ideally require the presence of three people — the client, the therapist and a co-therapist who engages in directed role-play with the client.

The therapist/assessor is not normally involved in the role-play and should be positioned in such a way as to observe the interaction unobtrusively. Video-recordings are often useful tools to help in the assessment.

Role-plays can easily take place in an office, as long as there is sufficient room for the interaction, that is, two chairs placed opposite each other for conversational exchanges. More complex exchanges, such as those involving simulated environments, may require more formal settings, but usually any medium-sized room will be adequate.

Role-play assessments usually sample the client's behaviour across a variety of social situations requiring a particular social skill to examine the extent of the deficit.

Co-therapist's role

In most cases the role-play partner's behaviour should be structured and planned before the assessment. The co-therapist may follow a written script which will guide the assessment. Alternatively, in more extended role-plays, guidelines of desired responses for the co-therapist to follow should be constructed.

The co-therapist should deliver standardised replies to the client for research purposes. However, this can create a somewhat artificial atmosphere and it is more acceptable for clinical purposes that the co-therapist responds as he feels someone would do in the actual encounter.

Several steps can be taken to maximise the validity of the role-play assessments:

1. All role-play scenes should be individualised to a client's own needs. This is preferable to having a standardised set of role-play scenes;
2. Role-play scenes must be presented as realistically as possible. For example, the role-play partner should be a member of the opposite sex if a client has a particular difficulty interacting with people of the opposite sex;

3. Some people adjust quickly to the idea of role-play, others have great difficulty and feel self-conscious. One would not expect clients deficient in social skills to handle role-plays of troublesome situations effectively, since they presumably do not handle these well in the natural environment. Thus, feelings of embarrassment or of not knowing what to say in a situation may be the client's usual response.

It is useful to repeat the same role-play on several different occasions before training is initiated since a more stable baseline behaviour is likely to emerge as the client becomes more acclimatised to the role-play.

Role-play interactions should be recreated as vividly as possible. Particular attention should be paid to the factors leading up to the situation, and the environmental surroundings. After interaction, the client should be questioned about how he felt during it and how he thought the other person was feeling.

Sometimes it helps if the client takes the role of the other person to enable him to gain more insight into his feelings. It is possible sometimes for the therapist to forego a co-therapist and undertake the role-play himself with the client. This may affect the therapist's ability to undertake the assessment but, even if a co-therapist is not available, this method can still provide considerably more information than the interview format.

Behavioural assessment through direct observation

Theoretically, the most accurate way to assess a client's social skills is by having the therapist observe the client in his social environment. Although this is potentially the most objective method, free from possible biases and distortions inherent in the client's self-report, it is often not feasible from a practical standpoint. The observer usually cannot follow the client around all day to make observations in critical inter-personal situations. In addition, the presence of the observer would probably change the nature of the social situations so that they would not be representative samples of the client's "true" behaviour anyway.

There are, however, several methods of directly observing social behaviours without having to escort clients to a variety of social events. None of these methods are perfect, but they can provide fairly accurate and representative samples of client social behaviours close to what might be obtained in the natural environment. One obvious method is to observe the social behaviour displayed toward the therapist during the interviews. Although the interview might not be representative of all social situations, it is an inter-personal encounter. The way in which the client behaves in the interview is a source of information that should not be neglected.

There are additional methods of creating the sort of inter-personal situations that the client encounters in everyday life. First, in certain situations, the client's real-life interactional partners can be invited to participate in the assessment by taking part in planned interactions with the client and relevant others while the therapist is present. This method is often feasible for observing the client interacting with a spouse or peers. It is more difficult to obtain the necessary co-operation from social partners who have no particular stake in the client's behaviour, or from those whose involvement in the assessment might jeopardize the relationship with the client. Despite these limitations, it is useful to involve the client's significant social partners in direct observational assessments whenever possible.

The most feasible method of obtaining direct observations of the client's social behaviour is probably through simulated interactions involving role-playing. In this method, the client and the therapist role-play, or simulate the interaction that the client has had with his natural environment partners, exceedingly well.

Assessing social skills in the natural environment

Direct observation of social behaviour in the natural environment may be possible when the client's difficulties involve interactions with other people in the natural environment, when the client spends a substantial amount of time in a particular setting and can be observed closely while in it, and when the particular interactions of interest to the therapist occur relatively frequently or predictably.

Direct client observation is the most accurate representation of a client's behaviour in a social situation, however, there are limitations to its use. For example, cost-effectiveness could be a problem in that the therapist may not have sufficient time to carry out detailed assessment. Also, it is often difficult in a natural setting to observe unobtrusively the interactions. Finally, the therapist has no control over the interaction, and so it may be necessary to observe clients for a considerable period of time before noting the troublesome interaction.

Checklists and rating scales

When a client's social skill behaviour sample is analysed, whether from a role-play, semi-structured or unstructured interaction, the aim is to locate inadequacies of performance, which can be targeted for later training (Figure 4.11).

Figure 4.11 Analysing a Client's Social Skill Behaviour

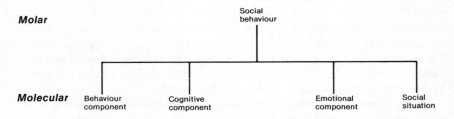

If each identified component of behaviour is a necessary part of that skill, it is then possible to observe whether clients exhibit each of these components in the assessment procedure. An absent component will need to be made a focus for skills training. In order to achieve this analysis, a therapist can rate objectively the client's performance on each of the component behaviours that require an effective skill. Most social skills have many components and it can be difficult during assessment to attend to all of these. Therefore, a range of tools has been developed to help systematise the assessment. In its simplest form, this consists of video-taping or audio-taping an interaction so that the therapist has more time to consider different components at a later date. Additionally, a number of tools have been developed to ensure a comprehensive assessment.

Rating scales

Originally from the Latin word *scala*, meaning a ladder or flight of steps, a scale represents a series of ordered steps at fixed intervals used as a standard of measurement. In order to fully evaluate the client's baseline skills in handling the situations presented, it is necessary to compare the components present in the client's behaviour with those behavioural components that will be present in skilled responses. Therefore, a first skill in the rating procedure is to organise and list the components that the therapist will look for in the client's assessment interactions.

Types of rating scales   The first type is the *graphic rating scales*. The therapist places a mark along a continuous line. The ends and perhaps the midpoint of the line are named but not the intervening points. The client can make his assessed point at any place along the line.

The second type is the *interval scale* which requires the rater to select one of a series of steps. Intermediate points are not used and the steps are usually numbered. Finally, *comparative scales* are used in which the rater compares the person with others in the same category.

Rating scales are used to rank people's judgement of objects, events, people and so on. They provide numerical scores that can be used to compare individuals and groups. Scales are a special type of questionnaire, designed to produce scores indicating the overall degree of a person's attitude to a particular topic.

A Thurstone-type scale consists of statements expressing a full range of opinions on a subject. The rater marks all the statements with which they agree. A Likart-type scale contains only statements that are clearly favourable or unfavourable. No neutral questions are included.

Checklists

Checklists differ from rating scales in that there are no grades of response, the answer to the question is either "yes" or "no". The self-rating form is used to evaluate for example, each separate assertive response made by the client. Thus, if the client role-plays six different situations in which assertion skills are required, the form would be completed six times.

This type of rating can identify specific verbal and non-verbal deficits in the client's performance. For example, if it was observed that a client maintains eye contact for 25 per cent of the time, speaks in a soft monotone, fails to state his options, does not offer a solution and punctuates responses with dysfluencies, then it would be necessary to use each of these components as a target for future training.

Consistent deficits across role-plays should be determined, plus the factors that lead deficiencies to occur in one role-play and not another. For example, a client may be able to behave assertively with men but not with women.

Devising a checklist or rating scale

The most basic record of behaviour is a straight count of the number of times a given event occurs during a given time. A checklist is a simple measure of whether the behaviour did or did not occur. A five- or seven-point scale is used to translate a checklist to a rating scale. The additions of the rating scale makes the measurement more precise (Figures 4.12, 4.13, 4.14 and 4.15).

Figure 4.12   Sample Rating Form for Conversational Skills

Name: ....

Date of this Interaction: ....

Type of Interaction:
— Pretraining assessment
— Session practice (training focused on what component)
— Follow-up

Description of this role-play scene ....
....
....

Component behaviours

1. *Eye contact* (approximate ratio of eye contact to total time the client was actually conversing)

   0%   25%   50%   75%   100%

   Eye contact   Eye contact made
   never made   entire time.

2. *Affect* (emotional appropriateness/responses)

   1   2   3   4   5   6   7

   Extremely   Totally appropriate
   inappropriate/
   absent

3. *Client speech duration* (measured in .... throughout)

   .... seconds

4. *Conversational questions* (total number of times that client directed a conversational question to partner)

   .... = total ....

5. *Self-diagnosing statements*

   .... = total ....

6. *Reinforcing/complementary comments*

   .... = total ....

Figure 4.13   Rating Form for Client's Refusal-Assertion Role-Play

Name: ....

Date of this Interaction: ....

Type of Interaction:
    — Pretraining assessment
    — Session practice (training focused on what component)
    — Follow-up

Description of this role-play scene ....
....

Component behaviours

1. Eye contact (approximate ratio of eye contact with partner to
          total speaking time)

   0%   25%   50%   75%   100%
Eye contact   Eye contact
never made   made whole time

2. Affect (emotional appropriateness/responsiveness)

    1   2   3   4   5   6   7
Extremely   Firm,   Became angry
passive,   convincing
unconvincing   appropriate
                      to interaction

3. Speech loudness

    1   2   3   4   5   6   7
Extremely   Appropriate   Too loud,
soft spoken   loudness and   overbearing
so as to be   clarity
inaudible

4. Gestures (did the client use any observable arm or hand
          gestures to add emphasis to his/her response?)

          — Absent   (tick)
          — Present

(continued)

Figure 4.13   (continued)

5. Statement of problem (did the client include in the role-play
                         response a statement conveying the
                         nature of the conflict problem?)

   — Absent
   — Present

6. Verbal non-compliance (did the client include in the role-play
                         response a statement explicitly
                         disagreeing or non-complying with the
                         antagonist's unreasonable behaviour?)

   — Absent
   — Present

7. Request/solution to resolve problem (did the client make a
                         statement specifically
                         requesting that the
                         antagonist behave
                         differently in the future,
                         or a statement proposing
                         some more acceptable
                         solution to the conflict?)

   — Absent
   — Present

8. Speech duration (length of client's role-play verbal responses
                   in seconds)

   —   seconds

9. Other components being rated (or any undesirable,
                         inappropriate behaviour being
                         examined)

   Definition/description of behaviour ....

   ....

   Frequency count or rating ....

Figure 4.14   Public Speaking Rating Scale

Name: Date:	Therapist:

Please circle appropriate answer

1. I appeared anxious before
   the start

   1   2   3   4   5

   Very   Calm
   anxious

2. I used a clear introduction

   1   2   3   4   5

   Incomprehensible   Clear

3. My voice could be clearly
   heard

   1   2   3   4   5

   Inaudible   Clear   Shouting

4. My body posture was appropriate

   1   2   3   4   5

   Inappropriate   Appropriate

5. I involved the audience

   1   2   3   4   5

   Not   Well
   involved   involved

6. I kept people's attention

   1   2   3   4   5

   Not at all   All the time

7. My voice wavered at times

   1   2   3   4   5

   Inaudible most   Clear all
   of the time   the time

8. I appeared confident

   1   2   3   4   5

   Not at all   All the time

9. I managed to get my message
   across

   1   2   3   4   5

   Not at all   Completely

10. I allowed adequate time for
    questions

    1   2   3   4   5

    None   Adequate

11. I kept reasonably within the time
    allowed

    1   2   3   4   5

    Hopeless   Effective

Note: This is an example of a rating scale that can be used to assess competence at public speaking. It is designed to be used by clients for self-assessment of a video-taped performance of themselves speaking in public.

Figure 4.15   Social Skills Assessment Check List

Please indicate with a tick (✓) for YES or a cross (×) for NO if you have any difficulty with the following situations

1. Walking down the street   ....
2. Going into shops   ....
3. Going on public transport ....
4. Going to parties   ....
5. Going to work   ....
6. Meeting people at work   ....
7. Meeting people generally ....
8. Meeting strangers   ....
9. Meeting friends   ....
10. Meeting people of the same sex   ....
11. Meeting people of the opposite sex   ....
12. Meeting younger people   ....
13. Meeting older people   ....
14. Being with one person   ....
15. Being with a group of people   ....
16. Going into a room full of people   ....
17. Introducing yourself   ....
18. Starting a conversation   ....
19. Starting friendships   ....
20. Going out with someone you are sexually attracted to   ....

21. Making decisions concerning other people   ....
22. Deciding what to do   ....
23. Putting across your point of view   ....
24. Listening to other people ....
25. Other people listening to you   ....
26. Is what other people think important to you   ....
27. Do you feel anxious in social situations   ....
28. Do other people criticize you   ....
29. Looking someone in the eyes   ....
30. Making decisions and sticking to them   ....
31. Saying no to someone who wants you to do something you don't want to.   ....
32. Dealing with personal criticism   ....

Further reading

Bandura A (1969) Principles of behaviour modification, Holt, Rinehart and Winston

Bellack A S (1979) A critical appraisal of strategies for assessing social skills, Behavioural Assessment, 1:157–176

Bellack A S, Hersen M and Lamparski D (1979) Role-play tests for assessing social skills: Are they valid? Are they useful? Journal of Consulting and Clinical Psychology, 47:335–342

Cone J D and Hawkins R P (Editors) (1977) Behavioural Assessment: New Directions in Clinical Psychology, Brunner/Mazel

Curran J P and Mariotto M J (1980) A conceptual structure for the assessment of social skills, in M Hersen, D Eisler, and P Miller (Editors), Progress in Behaviour Modification, Academic Press

Fenwick A M (1979) An interdisciplinary tool for assessing patients' readiness for discharge in the rehabilitation setting, Journal of Advanced Nursing, 4:9–21

Gambrill E (1977) Behaviour Modification: A Handbook of Assessment, Intervention and Evaluation, Jossey-Bass

Hersen M and Bellack A (Editors) (1976) Behavioural Assessment: A Practical Handbook, Pergamon Press

Lowe M R and Cautela J R (1978) A self-report measure of social skills, Behavioural Assessment, 1:157–176

Rathus (1973) Schedule for assessing assertive behaviour, Behaviour Therapy, 4:398–406

Robertson J M (1978) Ideas for materials for social skills assessment, Occupational Therapy, November

Stuart R B (Editor) (1977) Behavioral Self-Management: Strategies, Techniques and Outcomes, Brunner/Mazel

Trower P et al. (1969) Social Skills and Mental Health, Methuen

Watson D and Friend R (1976) Measurement of social-evaluative anxiety, Journal of Consulting and Clinical Psychology, 33:448–457

CHAPTER 5

ROLE-PLAY

Role-play has been developed as part of a broader group of techniques known as simulation/gaming, which attempts to provide a simplified reproduction of a real or imaginary world. These techniques have been in existence for a large part of history, early evidence for which can be found in the Japanese game of GO and in chess. Additionally, war gaming has been used in various guises to simulate battles.

Over the past 20 years the use of this group of techniques has undergone a rapid expansion and today they are used in many areas of training, especially as part of staff development in industry, management, teaching and in the helping professions. Role-play is one particular type of simulation that focuses attention on the interaction of people with one another. It emphasises the roles performed by different people and the various situations in which they can occur.

The basic principle of role-play is to ask someone to imagine that they are either themselves or another person in a particular situation. They are then asked to behave exactly as they feel that person would. As a result, they learn something about that person and the situation. A large number of alternative techniques have been developed based on this simple concept.

Confusion frequently occurs about the difference between role-play and acting, and this is an important distinction to make. Role-play attempts to enable individuals to *experience* the consequences of certain situations in a relatively safe environment so that they can cope more skilfully with social situations. Acting attempts to bring to life an author's ideas to entertain an audience.

Role-play has been found to be a very powerful technique. It has been well documented to be an effective change agent and it has been widely used in a variety of clinical settings to deal with all aspects of communication skills.

Types of role-play

Several types of role-play have evolved to meet different requirements. It is important for the clinician to be clear about the type of role-play he is using. It is easy for the client to become confused and receive the wrong training if different approaches are used for the wrong types of problem.

The major distinction that needs to be made is between role-plays dealing with the practice of skills and those dealing with changes in feelings and attitudes. In skills acquisition role-play, the therapist has to ensure that the client has been given an outline of the correct skill he is to acquire. The location is chosen as an example of a situation in which the skill is likely to be needed, and the role-plays are likely to be organised into a hierarchy of increasingly more difficult problems to facilitate skill acquisition. When the client has role-played the skill, the therapist will feed back information to the client about how effective the client's performance was, and use techniques such as modelling to alter his/her performance. The client is usually given repeated opportunities to practise each skill until he successfully masters it.

Role-plays involved in changing feelings and attitudes have a different emphasis, and this type of simulation is much less structured. It is usually based around a common problem and each client is encouraged to use his own emotions, thoughts and behaviours. Considerable effort is put into exploring feelings and emotions. The therapist's role is to maintain a safe environment and to make sure that the boundaries between role-play and reality are maintained. Each of these two main groups can be further subdivided as follows.

Skills acquisition

Scene description   This is a simple type of role-play used to give a description of social situations. The roles tend to be undemanding on the client and it is a useful method of introducing people to role-play practice. The therapist provides a description of the scene to be enacted and there is usually little improvisation allowed. The purpose is for the client to have an understanding of the situation. This type of role-play is useful for setting the scene before using other techniques. The only feedback necessary is for the therapist to correct any errors that occur.

Demonstration This is similar to scene description, but the goal here is to provide a model that can be copied by the client. The focus is on the behaviour being modelled and the preparation necessary for the role-play revolves around the points relevant to skills acquisition. The therapist or co-therapist frequently models the desired behaviour in this technique, and the client's role is then one of being an observer.

Skills practice The purpose of this type of role-play is for the client to acquire a specific behaviour. It is usually highly structured, the client being given clear instructions by the therapists about the behavioural components he/she is expected to acquire. This is often achieved by means of skill cards which define the essential steps to successfully complete the skill. Other members of the group are used to provide feedback on how the client has performed in the role-play and about any specific aspects of the skill he/she has achieved or failed to successfully complete.

This is a more difficult type of role-play for the client, as he is expected to behave in front of other people who are observing and criticising the performance. It is essential that the therapist controls closely how people respond and keeps unexpected events to a minimum. The client is then given repeated opportunities to practise the skill, each time receiving feedback which gradually improves performance. This type of technique is now extensively used for skills acquisition. In addition to using social skills training, it has been used in training professionals such as nurses, doctors, social workers and teachers. It has been found to be a highly effective method of acquiring skilled behaviour.

Feelings and attitudes

Reflection The purpose of this type of role-play is to show clearly to a person how his behaviour appears to other people. It is often similar to skills acquisition. Reflecting to the client how he appears to other people can be achieved either through imitation or video-tape techniques, or through both. The client needs to be more aware of his behaviour and why he is doing certain things. The aim is for the client to be introspective and to consider why he behaves in certain ways. In the role-play analysis, more emphasis is spent on the reasons why the client behaves in a certain way, although the effects of his actions also have to be considered. The therapist's role is largely one in which he provides a safe environment for the client; he will intervene only if absolutely necessary. The role-play analysis usually involves much more of a discussion between the client and therapist about the reasons for certain actions than in any of the previous role-play types.

Sensitisation Here the therapist attempts to create an environment in which the client can express any emotional feelings that are brought about by the interaction. This is a difficult area for therapists, and one into which they should tread with caution unless they are clear about what they are doing.

The area covered can range from sensitising someone to another person's feelings, to potentially dangerous areas involving highly charged emotional involvement. Whenever a therapist starts to explore people's reactions and feelings in analysing role-plays, he should be aware that he is entering emotionally laden areas that may be difficult to control unless considerable skill and expertise are used.

The key factor is the extent to which the pre-role-play instruction and post-role-play analysis focus on the actual personality of the role-player. The therapist must limit the amount of probing that is anticipated or allowed to take place in the analysis if he wants to keep the role-play restricted to educational or instructional elements. On the other hand, if the emphasis is on the role-player's personality and the emotional consequences, then the intent is to explore the change in the client's personality. This therapeutic situation requires close questioning by the therapist and other members of the group on the emotional or hidden reasons of the client's actions.

Two other types of role-play classification are frequently encountered, as follows.

Shaw — structured role-play

Shaw, Corsini, Blake *et al.* (1980) considered that there are two basic types of role-play.

Structured role-play   This type of role-play is constructed so as to explore a particular situation. It is constructed along problem-solving lines with the emphasis on finding a solution to a particular problem. Fairly strict guidelines are given indicating a beginning, middle and end to the role-play. The purpose of this type of role-play is to resolve conflict or arrive at a compromised solution.

Unstructured role-play   This type of role-play allows clients to present their own situations or problems. There is little structure and the role-play develops according to the requirements of the role-players. Therapist involvement is minimal and the clients continue until they feel that it is appropriate to stop.

Wohlking — method-centred role-play

Wohlking and Gill's (1980) categories are broadly similar to those of Shaw.

Method-centred role-play   This technique is similar to Shaw's structured role-play. Its purpose is to develop specific skills. The role-play sessions comprise of a series of short problems for which the therapist provides guidelines for effective performance. Facilities are available for the client to repeat these behaviours several times in order to gradually improve them. The method is particularly applicable to social skills training and can be used for various situations such as initiating a conversation, and for more specific situations such as buying a pair of shoes.

Developmental type of role-play   This is similar to Shaw's unstructured category and is more concerned with learning about attitudes and feelings. It deals with relatively complex situations and is a process of integrating and applying learning from a variety of sources, including the client's own background and experience. Role-play is more spontaneous and is not modelled on guidelines provided by the therapist. It can be used to teach communication skills and to develop skills of group participation, providing an environment in which clients can experiment with different approaches.

A framework for role-play

Roles can be assigned to clients that provide boundaries on the behaviour they can perform. There are some important factors involved when assigning roles to provide these boundaries, as follows.

Status

Roles can be given to people — shopkeeper, bank manager, father — to establish their position within an overall structure and clarify their relationship to others. This can be done in an overt fashion, as with the examples above, or in a covert way, for example, by allocating roles such as being "female", which, in some societies, can affect the behaviour allowed.

One of the ways in which roles are defined in real life is by the expectations that the role title produces in others. The same mechanism may be used in role-play, for example, if the client is told he is to be a car salesman or a fireman, then this will define his role in society. Sometimes care has to be taken with these roles as there are often considerable societal preconceptions and myths surrounding some of the roles — not all nurses are females, for example.

Background

Sometimes it is sufficient to describe the situation in which the role-play is to take place — in a shop, watching a cricket match, and so on. The assumptions implicit in the descriptions can provide material within which the role-play can develop.

Skills

The part played by each individual may be defined by their particular knowledge, ability or skill. This may be indicated in the role description by the therapist saying to the client: "You are an expert on something." Alternatively, ability may be indicated by a description of the role-player's age, background or experience. This relies on the role-player's imagination or experience to fill in the appropriate details.

Personality

This type of framework has been widely used in role-play. A typical description under this heading would be: "You are a man of about 30, who is rather passive towards other people. You are fond of animals but would rather keep your own company."

Although this type of framework is still frequently used, every effort should be made to prevent the framework from being too restrictive. One of the common causes of role-play failure is to make them too complex. Similarly, the role-play framework should be designed to achieve clear and simple steps.

Advantages of role-play

It is an effective method of acquiring new skills in a safe setting. The client can practise these skills in a positive and safe situation. Because he adopts a role, it is possible for the client to explore aspects of his own behaviour that he would normally have found to be threatening.

Another advantage is that the role-play situations can have a close proximity to everyday life. They can explore behavioural patterns that the client will need to use in the everyday world, and they allow people to practise the skills they will need to use in their lives without having to immediately accept the consequences. By exploring these responses in a variety of different situations, it is possible for someone to acquire social skills that will generalise to a variety of social situations.

Clients also receive accurate and rapid feedback on their performance in the role-play, thus ensuring that they do not learn maladaptive behaviours.

In addition, role-play is enjoyable for clients if it is well organised and operated. Thus they usually become involved in role-plays, and this can be an effective form of learning.

Disadvantages of role-play

Role-play sessions usually require amounts of time that may not be required in other therapies. Thus clients must be prepared adequately to use role-play, and the sessions usually need adequate time for each client to participate. Sufficient time is also needed for effective analysis after role-play.

Role-play exercises can be run successfully by a single therapist but, generally, as the group is complex, they require an additional therapist. Additionally, there is often a need for observer participation to feed back information.

The minimum requirement for role-play is two clients, with a maximum of

12. This obviously sets limits that may not be compatible with the situation's needs. Role-play techniques can be used effectively over an extremely wide range of ages — even children use these techniques naturally as part of their games. However, there are particular problems with each age group that need to be borne in mind when the therapist is involved in therapy.

In the 5 to 14-year age group the major problems are caused by lack of life experience. Additionally, it may be difficult for the client to move from emotional involvement to objective analysis, and cognitive capacities may not yet be fully developed.

In some ways the 14 to 21-year age group is the most difficult group of clients to work with, and in other ways it is the most rewarding. The clients are likely to suffer from embarrassment and it may be necessary to carry out extensive warm-up exercises until self-consciousness can be overcome. The best role-plays for this group are tied into real problems that the group can recognise and identify with.

The relationship with the therapist can be important to the 21 to 40-year age group, because the boundaries of authority are not at all clear in an unconventional setting like role-play, and the client needs to feel trust on both sides. There is considerable scope for creativity. One potential difficulty is that the exercises are not taken seriously and trivialised.

The 40 to 65-year group often shows a division between those that take a conservative attitude and those who are eager and willing to try new methods. It is helpful to have a balance so that the group is not dominated by either type.

The over-65s do not present as many difficulties as one might expect. However, it is important to take into account the general slowing-up of reactions. More time should be taken to introduce ideas and to prepare roles. It may be wise to use teaching aids such as blackboard notes or flipcharts to record ideas and to reinforce memory.

Practical aspects of role-play

Role-play is a relatively straightforward technique that depends for success on the correct application of simple principles. There are a number of basic factors that need to be considered by a therapist to ensure that a role-play session is well planned and smoothly run, and that the clients will benefit most from the experience. The basic components that make up an effective role-play can be divided into three main factors:

1. Preparation;
2. Running the role-play;
3. Analysing the role-play.

Preparation

As in any effective therapy, a therapist must prepare for what may happen in the therapy session as far as is practical. This section will consider preparation in two parts:

1. Preparation before therapy begins;
2. Preparing clients to participate in role-play.

Preparation for role-play   The therapist should always ask himself what he is trying to achieve with therapy, and whether role-play is the best method of achieving these objectives. This should be a broad consideration as it is not always clear what the learning objectives are. Role-play techniques can be used effectively at a number of different points of therapy, often for different purposes. Currently, role-play is commonly used for assessment, warm-up exercises, and as a central feature of therapy.

Additionally, it can be used occasionally for summing up and for revising points previously covered. The therapist should have a general idea of how a particular role-play will connect with assessment techniques, and of any therapy sessions that have taken place before the role-play. In general, he should also know how the role-play will connect to the therapy sessions that follow.

Before the role-play session starts, it is prudent for the therapist to consider any factors that may affect its smooth and effective running. For example, where is the role-play to be held? Is the room adequate? Is the room available when required? The most suitable room for role-play is usually medium-sized and relatively square. There should not be any awkward projections into the room. Ceiling height is only important at the extremes, that is, if it is very high or very low. Furniture, if any, should be easy to move and stack. There should be adequate seating for all clients and if anything specific is required for the role-play, such as a desk, then it should be made available before the role-play starts.

Time is also important. There must be sufficient time available to warm-up and brief the role-players, run the role-play and then analyse what has happened. It is also often desirable to have enough time to repeat all or part of the role-play, with variations. A simple role-play may last for five to 10 minutes; most last between 10 and 20 minutes, although some may require longer.

Another important consideration in planning any role-play is whether or not a co-therapist is required to work with the therapist. It is usually recommended that one does work with the therapist throughout the role-play sessions, and that two partners build up some experience of working together.

Is there any need for other clients to play the roles of observers while the role-play is taking place? If so, is general observation adequate or will the clients be using rating scales? If so, has the therapist developed appropriate rating scales? Each of these considerations is important.

The therapist must also be clear about the type of role-play to be used, since the requirements for each different role-play can have considerable impact on the way in which it is run. In particular, the distinction is crucial between open role-plays, where there is considerable discussion, and structured role-plays. The therapist can consider preparing the clients only when each of these factors has been dealt with.

Preparing clients for role-play   The term "role-play" seems to be regarded with suspicion by many adults. When the therapist announces bluntly that he is going to run a role-play, considerable damage to the cohesiveness of the group can be caused. This can take considerable time to remedy. There are thus two main ways of approaching role-play for the first time, the choice of which will depend largely on the clients' age group and their motivation. The first way, most successful with adults and those who have a strong motivation, is to use the subject itself as a lead-in. The alternative, best used with children or adults whose objectives are less clearly established, is to use a class of activities known as ice-breakers.

1. Graduated lead-in. The key to this approach is to not force a role-play on the client, but to let it arise naturally as a result of exploring the problems in which the client is interested. A therapist can start with a general problem from which he gradually separates out the inter-personal elements he wishes to deal with at that particular session. From there, it should be possible to get an example and hence develop a role-play.

    Problems or difficulties should be presented in situational rather than behavioural terms whenever possible; for example, it is important to explore what is happening rather than the behaviour that appears to be causing it. The therapist should also resist the temptation to pose the problem in such a way as to indicate his own solution — the outcome should be left to the clients.

There are many other ways to start these simple introductory role-plays. The therapist can ask for an indication of a problem area, for example, by asking how to get a refund if one is sold shoddy goods. Alternatively, the therapist may have already prepared a very simple example with the first four or five lines of a dialogue. Using this method, the therapist can either ask the role-players to say the lines and then continue, or he may ask them to discuss what should have been said, re-write the first few lines, and then use them once again as a lead-in.

An interesting variation of this concept is the use of a short pre-recorded video scene. These are known as *prompts* or *trigger scenes* and consist of brief presentations of situations by actors. In some cases, the actors act to one another; in other cases, they act towards the viewer as if he is part of the action. The scene lasts only for a minute or two and finishes at a point at which a decision or reaction needs to be made. A typical finishing remark might be: "I can't see anyway out of this, can you?" or "It seems that the ball is in your court." This can be used to stimulate role-players to continue the scene between themselves.

There are other ways to get clients to start thinking about the subject of role-play, for example, asking them to study a text and make notes on it, asking them to write a letter or memo to act as a starting point from which the role-play can be developed, or showing them diagrams, charts or pictures and asking for a discussion about them. Additionally, questionnaires can be used as a way of introducing a subject, or the class can split up into pairs, with every pair talking, arguing or discussing similar topics. Each pair can role-play a part of the problem, working at the same time. Alternatively, the pairs may work at the same part, or on different parts. After 10 minutes or so, the group will be in a more informed or receptive mood to develop the main role-play. If role-playing in pairs is regarded as too threatening, then another effective starter is to encourage clients to interview each other about the subject.

2. Ice-breakers. Sometimes it is more appropriate to concentrate on generating a relaxed atmosphere than to start with the subject of the session. Ice-breakers or warm-up exercises are an excellent way of doing this. They are quick, simple and require little knowledge. There are many exercises of this type, most of them handed down by word-of-mouth and by demonstration from one therapist to another. There are also a number of books in which these exercises are collected (see further reading).

One example group exercise is the word-go-round. This exercise should be carried out in larger groups of four or more and can be used for a whole group of up to 12 people. The idea is to tell a story but with each person contributing a word at a time in succession. There should be some pressure to keep up the speed as the story goes around the group: beating a rhythm is one way of doing this. The story topic can be left completely open or the therapist can suggest a topic such as sport or hobbies. The therapist must exercise caution using these exercises: it is important not to get "carried away" by the fun and excitement such activities can generate. It should always be remembered that it is acting only as an introduction. It must be emphasised to clients that the purpose of the exercise is to help them prepare for role-play. Consequently, icebreaker exercises should be kept to a relatively small proportion of the total time.

Practical preparation for role-play   The therapist must undertake practical steps to ensure that the role-play proceeds smoothly while the session is underway. He should devise a background for the role-play that is simple and easy for the client to remember, bearing in mind the purpose of the role-play and the capabilities of the clients. The description should be concise, consisting of a few sentences, and should describe clearly the social situation the therapist intends to use.

Three types of role need to be created: key roles, subsidiary roles and spare roles. Key roles are the main players, between whom the principle interactions will occur. It is usually wise to keep the number of principal players down to two, with a maximum of three, as it can become difficult for clients to concentrate if too much detail is expected of them. Subsidiary roles support the key roles and may act as information givers, moral supporters or adjudicaters. They should not have too large an influence in the exchanges between the principle interactors.

In many cases the role-play may need to be used with a variety of groups of different sizes and different abilities. Although some participants may be needed as observers, it is often useful to have extra roles — spare roles — that can interest and occupy certain participants. These roles must be carefully thought out beforehand, otherwise it can lead to a situation where the extra role-players have little to do. It is usually possible to involve these roles as part of the observation process, thus providing interest for the participants.

It is unlikely that the role-players' sex, age and physical build will exactly match the roles that are being developed and so the therapist must decide how to handle this. Possible alternatives are to use neutral roles, design the roles to fit the client (this is a dangerous practice because it may reveal in public how the therapist perceives the client), or ignore the overt problem and use role-players irrespective of these factors.

Developing specific roles   This is usually done in two stages, incorporating key features of the roles and the intended actions of the role-players. The key features of the specific role need to be broadly defined by the therapist. In particular, the following aspects need to be stated:

1. The *skill* the role-player has;
2. The constraints he is under;
3. The *authority* that he has;
4. The situation in which he is expected to act.

As far as intended actions are concerned, the therapist should define who the role-player will meet, under what circumstances, the purpose of their meeting, and for how long they will meet.

It is usually better to write in the second person, and names should be simple, not jokey and generally not those of celebrities. It is usually best to avoid descriptions of an emotional state. The role briefings outlines should be kept as short as possible and should be either recorded on cards or video. It should not be necessary for the client to consult the role card after the role-play has started.

Allocating roles   Roles can be allocated in a variety of ways: randomly; allocating the key participants and distributing the remainder randomly; assigning clients to roles that fit them closely; deliberately choosing clients with characteristics opposite to the role; letting the group itself decide the allocation of roles; or rotating roles among all the clients.

To some extent, the choice of method depends upon the purpose of the role-play and the particular group with which the therapist is working. Clients should be given roles similar to their own characteristics if the purpose of the exercise is to obtain maximum realism. However, if the objectives are to give the players an opportunity to experiment with a behaviour and become more sensitive to the attitudes and feelings of others, it is usually more effective to give them roles that are different from the ones they would normally adopt.

When asking clients to participate in role-playing, it is advisable to wait for at least 20 seconds after asking for volunteers before giving up. The next best choices are those people who maintain eye contact with the therapist;

otherwise it is best to choose those who are verbal, animated, articulate and not excessively anxious.

Observers   Observers are most useful in role-play for social skills training. They may take part as actors in the role-play or they may sit or stand apart from the role-players, either in the room as participant observers or observing via a one-way screen. Careful attention is necessary to the observation methods and the observers must be fully briefed. Whatever preparation for observation is made, the therapist should ensure that observation relates to what actually happens within the role-play and how or why it happens.

The observation of role-plays can be carried out at different levels. Two simple types are frequently used: physically observable acts, including movement and speech, can be noted, or more complicated, abstract qualities such as sincerity and aggression can be recorded. Ideally, however, this requires trained and experienced observers if their conclusions are to be relied upon. Many observation schemes have been devised for carrying out this type of interactional analysis, However, many of them are often very specific and not suitable for practical use. Thus it is often more beneficial for therapists to develop their own observation methods. Useful guidelines are to use broad categories and a problem-orientated approach. Two simple methods that can be easily used by most observers are observer grids and key items of interest.

1. Observer grids. Here, the observer is asked to make a mark (such as a tick) every time a particular event occurs. It is usually best to keep the amount or type of recordings as simple as possible. So, for example, every time the observer sees a looked-for behaviour occurring, such as eye contact while speaking, he will put a tick in the box.
2. Key items of interest. This usually consists of a series of closed questions for the observer to rate. Examples of the types of questions commonly asked are: Who spoke the most/least? Did anyone interrupt before other people had finished? Did the speaker maintain eye contact? Did you feel that the person was listening?

Other preparations the therapist needs to make will depend on the way in which the role-play is to be organised. Many therapists like to use props during role-play, while others like to keep additional material to a minimum. A few props can create the right atmosphere while too many can create the impression of a theatrical performance. As with any other activity, the actual running of the role-play should not present any difficulties if the preparation has been done thoroughly and efficiently.

Running the role-play

Ideally, the therapist should try out any new material he is going to use before using it on clients. In practice, this can often be difficult to achieve and the best that can be attained is to discuss it with colleagues. This is better than nothing at all. Once the material has been prepared, the running of the role-play with clients normally follows the following sequence:

1. Introduction;
2. Warm-up exercises;
3. Running the role-play;
4. Analysing the role-play.

The main problem for the therapist at this point is the timing of each segment. In particular, the ending of the role-play must be timed in such a way that it fits into the whole programme. This can be done by writing the mechanism into the script for the role-play, using methods such as: "I'm sorry to disturb you, but something's happened" or "Somebody's called to see you."

By this stage the therapist will have decided on the objectives and how the role-play will fit into the overall training package. He will also have looked at the constraints and factors affecting his choice and he will have written or obtained materials for running the role-play.

Basic techniques There are many ways of organising a role-play, depending on its purpose and the type of client involved. Two basic techniques will be described here.

1. Fish bowl. The fish bowl technique is the one that is frequently encountered in role-play. The principal players meet each other in the centre of the room and are observed by the other members of the session who sit in a rough circle around them. Subsidiary characters, if any, enter from the periphery of the room and return there when their part is done. Whatever the actual physical layout, the term "fish bowl" denotes the idea of one group portraying the action while another group observes. This technique has some fairly clearcut advantages and disadvantages.
   It differentiates very clearly between the role-players and the observers; it allows clients who do not want to take part to detach themselves from the action; and detailed observation can take place, since all the observers

can get a good view of what is going on. However, there are disadvantages with the fish bowl technique: the setting of the fish bowl stresses the artificiality of the situation; the whole arrangement puts a strain on the role-players and introduces pressures that arise from outside the enacted situation (particularly when the group is larger than eight or 12 people); the pressures can distort the actions of the players who, from time to time, will be conscious of the presence of an audience: it tends to restrict the enactment of each role to one person, thus denying others the opportunity of trying out how it feels.

2. The multiple technique. In this technique the group is split up into a number of small groups, each of two to three clients. Each group enacts the role-play at the same time. In other words, a number of identical role-plays take place in parallel. Observers can be included. The classic situation for using this method is where the class wants to explore the interaction between two people, in either formal or informal settings; therefore, there may be two players and one observer in each group.

What are the advantages of this technique? The clients tend to feel less embarrassed and exposed and can come to terms with the interaction, seen only by one or possibly two colleagues. It enables a number of different interpretations to be tried out simultaneously and can, therefore, take up less time. Finally, after everyone's role-play has finished, the different groups can meet together to exchange experiences and draw on the range of things that have taken place.

The disadvantages include the fact that: no two people will have observed the same role-play and it is difficult to check on exactly what happened and why; and it is difficult for the therapist to observe more than one interaction at a time. Thus he is likely to miss some of the crucial occurrences that take place, although this is reduced if a co-therapist is present.

Special techniques   The point of many of these techniques is to enable the role-player to explore the implications of a role more deeply than he would using more straightforward techniques. Many of these techniques originate in Mareno's development of psychodrama:

1. Role rotation. In this technique, the role of protaganist is rotated between a number of clients. Sometimes it may be rotated across all clients so that they all have experience of playing that part. The rotation is usually done fairly rapidly with each client playing the part only for a few minutes.

It is useful for getting different approaches to the same problem, and it overcomes the problem of other members of the group saying that they could have done the role better. Also, it gives each client the time to consider his approach as the individual time spent role-playing is short and the client is less likely to dry up.

Another type of procedure also known as role rotation is where a number or all of the roles are rotated simultaneously; this is less commonly used because of the obvious complications.

There are some disadvantages with role rotation: there is a potential danger of highlighting the fact that one person is clearly the worst at handling the problem. This technique is also not usually suitable for role-plays using large numbers of people.

2. Role reversal. There are a number of different ways in which role reversal can be achieved:

(a)   The two principal role-players exchange their roles;

(b)   A client who is playing himself is replaced by another client, and the first person may take some other role;

(c)   The client is asked to take a part outside his normal range of experience because of non-behavioural characteristics such as sex, race and so on.

There are some circumstances ideally suited to using role reversal techniques. One of these is the exploration and clarification of communication between men and women. One of the most dramatic ways in which role reversal can be used is at the climax of a role-play when each client is emotionally committed to a particular point of view. The effect of having to change this viewpoint can give a powerful impetus to learning about other people's attitudes and the way that a particular situation is seen from both sides.

3. Alter ego and doubling. These techniques depend on the use of other clients to reveal aspects of the protagonist that are normally hidden. In the doubling technique, the protagonist and antagonist play their parts as normal, but an extra player is brought in to speak feelings which he attributes to the clients. It goes without saying that the person playing the double must be sensitive enough to provide feedback without undermining the confidence of the player whom he is doubling. It is usually most appropriate that this is done by a co-therapist. It is most often used when the role-play is short or episodic and when there are opportunities for the protagonist and the double to discuss between themselves how accurately the double is portraying the protagonist's feelings.

4. Mirroring. This is another technique that requires the use of other clients. The idea here is to get another player to re-enact the scene, playing the role of the protagonist, while the original protagonist watches. In the therapeutic environment this can be a powerful way of showing clients how they appear to others.

5. Supporter. This technique is designed to help in those situations where either the client dries up or other members of the group feel that the scene is not going well. The supporter role is that of a person who comes and stands behind the original client and speaks for him. The supporter speaks in the first person, just as the protagonist, and comes in at a break point when there is a pause in the speech of the protagonist. The supporter can either help fill in the gap or give the role-play new direction, and his contribution can take the form of a single sentence or he may remain in role for several minutes.

   There must be a considerable rapport between the client and his supporter, but it provides a useful alternative to stopping a role-play when the life and direction seem to have gone out of it, yet when there is clearly much left to be explored. The person best placed to adopt this role is usually the co-therapist.

6. Consultant group. This technique can be used if the role is complex or difficult, and where there are a number of ways in which decision-making may be approached. It consists of having a special support group, whose function is to act as a consultant and to advise the protagonist on how to proceed.

   The protagonist meets with his consultant group before the role-play begins and discusses the whole background to the role-play and the way in which they think it should be handled. During the role-play, the therapist either arranges for there to be periodic breaks for meetings to take place or writes the role-play in such a way that the meetings arise as a natural part of the action. One of the great virtues of this technique is its closeness to real-life.

7. Positioning. A role-play would normally be set up to represent as accurately as possible the physical setting of the scene to be played. In some circumstances, however, it can be advantageous to upset preconceived notions of spatial relationships by changing the physical positions in which the scene is played. For example, the boss may be standing while the employee is behind a desk, or two role-players may be asked to talk very closely to each other to emphasise problems of inter-personal communication. This method can be used to isolate specific

aspects of communication such as facial expression, tone of voice and so on. This deliberate inversion of the form forces role-players to reappraise what they are doing.

8. Replays. If role-play is designed to teach simple inter-personal skills, then repetition is of the essence. Usually there is too little rather than too much use of replay, as time can be short and there may be some fear of boring the participants. It would be better in many cases to use shorter role-plays and repeat them, or parts of them, rather than use longer and more elaborate ones once only. Replays can take many forms as they are themselves forms of role-play. Roles may be reversed or rotated, additional players can be used, new instructions issued, the physical layout altered or the observers' brief changed. On the other hand, it may be sufficient to repeat the role-play under exactly the same conditions as before. The only important point is that the therapist should consider the use of replay and the possibility of changing the format of the role-play for the replay.

Role-play analysis

When the role-play has been performed it is essential for the therapist to ensure that each client returns to reality. This is usually a gradual process consisting of several stages. It should take place as soon as possible after the role-play has finished and usually takes at least as long as the role-play, and often two to three times longer.

Stage one The therapist should ask the principal role-play actor for his understanding of what happened. The main purpose is to get the reaction before it is influenced by anyone else's comments. The therapist usually asks the client the following types of questions: Did you achieve your target behaviour? Did you feel comfortable? How do you think Player A interpreted what you were doing? What did you feel about the way Player B reacted?

The questions are specific and do not allow much room for the client to expand. Frequently, the therapist will allow the client to answer in role.

The other principal role-play actor should be asked for his response to the performance. Again, the questions should be specific: Were you clear about what Player C wanted? Did you feel uncomfortable about anything that occurred? Did Player D look at you?

Observers, if used, should then be asked to feed back their information.

This should be in specific form, according to the type of information that was to be recorded, for example, you only looked at Player E twice; your voice was inaudible for half of the role-play.

Video recordings can also be replayed at this stage. At the end of this process the therapist has two options: to repeat the role-play with modifications, or to go on to stage two.

Stage two   The therapist can broaden the discussion to analyse the causes of the behaviour. He can use discussion, modelling techniques, handouts and small groups as well as other techniques to explore the group's understanding and to devise effective methods of altering behaviour. The major change in this stage is that the clients should clearly come out of role and be themselves. Every effort should be made to apply the learning from the role-play to the client's everyday situation. According to the type of role-play being used, the therapist can keep the analysis to specific skills acquisition and their application to social situations, or he can explore individual attitudes and feelings.

The therapist should link the lessons learnt from the role-play with the rest of the training programme and set effective homework, which will apply the skills learnt to the client's social situation. This is also an opportunity for the therapist to revise and reinforce skills that have been learnt in previous sessions. The role of the therapist should be to keep the environment safe for clients to explore their reactions, to summarise points made, to stimulate further discussion and to get agreement from the group as to what should happen next. In this section it is usually wise for the therapist to stay in the background, using open-ended questions to stimulate discussion and to intervene only when necessary.

Problem areas   The role-player may depart from the role. A problem frequently encountered with anxious clients is that they cannot easily settle into the role, and they often come out of role to explain what they are doing. If this does occur, the therapist should stop the role-play and discuss the problem. If the problem persists, it may be necessary for the therapist to rotate roles and to give the client an easier role. In addition, any of the support methods previously outlined should be used.

Over-acting is another problem area. This is the equivalent of someone "acting the fool", but it is a little more subtle because of the thin borderline between strongly involved behaviour and over-acting. The role-play should be stopped if the client seems to be over-acting, mainly for the sake of the other clients. Whether or not this is easy to deal with depends on the motivation of the client and whether he is over-acting because of genuine over-enthusiasm or misunderstanding. A change of role is clearly called for if the overacting is deliberate. Similarly, a change of environment may help: the physical environment (furniture and equipment) can be altered to encourage a more realistic setting and to remove any signs of a clinical atmosphere that may have developed. Additionally, it may be beneficial to provide the client with more work to do in the course of the role-play.

The best solution to poor performance, if this is a problem — apart from changing the role-player, which carries a potential loss of face — is to use the supporter idea, where the role-player has another person with him to help at awkward moments. Sometimes it is even possible to change the role so as to share it between two or more characters who act as a group. Other possible ways of dealing with this problem are to use multiple role-playing or to stop the role-play for a while to explore the reasons behind the "drying up". It may be possible that the role-player does not understand the role or lacks the necessary information. Alternatively, the occurrence of a problem in the role-play may be an indicator of a difficult area.

Lack of insight can be difficult to deal with if it indicates a general lack of sensitivity on the part of the role-player. One way of trying to increase sensitivity is to use role-reversal, putting the client in the opposite part so that he can see the situation from the other point of view.

Repetition and boredom can also be a problem. When it becomes evident, the therapist should either change the format or stop it all together. It is an indication that the role-play has run its natural course and is no longer a challenge.

Emotion may be generated during the role-play or in the course of the analysis, and the two situations require different approaches. If the emotional level arises during the role-play, then the greatest safeguard is for the therapist to be aware of the potential emotional escalation and to be sensitive to the way in which things are developing. Clients who begin to get agitated are likely to be carried away in their parts to such an extent that either they or their colleagues will suffer. In this case the role-play should be stopped and time allowed for diffusing the situation.

The point at which this becomes necessary is a matter of judgement and will depend on the therapist's knowledge of the client and his behaviour. Alternatively, roles may be switched or the clients re-briefed for the discussion on the purpose of the role-play and the place of emotion within it.

It should be bourne in mind that the display of emotion is rarely damaging in itself: it is the potential loss of dignity or the partly worked-out emotional feeling that can cause the damage. In analysis it is relatively easy to control the emotional climate by moderating the amount of negative criticism, and directing it at the character rather than at the client. The important thing is for the therapist to be aware of the temptation to go deeper than he had at first intended, and to resist the temptation in the interests of the client and the group.

As a general rule, many therapists try to deal with problems that occur by entering into the role-play themselves and dealing with the problem from within a role. Although this has the undoubted advantage of keeping the role-play going and demonstrating the therapist's belief in the seriousness and importance of the role-play, the inexperienced therapist may find this difficult to do.

References

Shaw M E, Corsini R J, Blake R and Mouton J S (1980) Role Playing: A Practical Manual for Group Facilitators, University Associates, La Jolla

Wholking W and Gill P J (1980) Role Playing, The Instructional Design Library, volume 32, Equalational Technology Publications, Englewood Cliffs

Further reading

Flowers J V (1975) Simulation and role-playing methods, in F H Kanfer and A P Goldstein (Editors), Helping People Change, Pergamon

Van Ments M (1983) The Effective Use of Role-Play, Kogan Page

CHAPTER 6

MODELLING

Modelling uses the principle that "a picture is worth a thousand words". It is a well researched and effective technique for acquiring new behaviours, based on social imitation. Other names commonly used for the same process include copying, mimicking, vicarious learning and observational learning.

Modelling is the process by which the behaviour of one individual or group (the model) acts as a stimulus for another individual, who observes the behaviour. Behaviours are acquired not through direct personal experience but by observing how others act in particular circumstances and the effects their actions have.

The technique has been found to be effective in bringing about changes in behaviour in a wide range of clients. The therapeutic use of modelling involves the client observing an individual or individuals (the model), who actually demonstrates the appropriate behaviour to be learnt by the client. Various methods can be used to present the model to the client, several of which will be described later.

Socialisation

A large proportion of each person's behavioural repertoire is developed not by personal experience, but by observation of the behaviour of others acting in particular situations, and observing how they are as a consequence. Through modelling behaviour on others, and by imitating elements of their performance, people can see how to perform in social situations. Modelling is a powerful influence in the socialisation of individuals in society.

Socialisation is the process by which individuals learn the culture of their society, as experience gradually shapes their behaviour. It consists of two principle components:

1. Primary socialisation, the process by which children learn the rules of living, including language, from a few significant others, usually their family;
2. Secondary socialisation. The process of socialisation does not end in childhood but continues throughout life. Secondary socialisation occurs when there is increasing contact with others and the influence of widening social contacts. It can operate at all levels, including political and social.

Socialisation is not a passive process as it is shaped, to a certain extent, by the individual — although much of this is unconscious and there may be considerable conflict between the roles that the person being socialised is expected to play. A large part of socialisation is unplanned and arises out of day-to-day activities. However, the development of the individual is inhibited if socialisation does not progress normally.

Several anecdotal instances serve to illustrate the effects of socialisation. An Indian emperor called Akbar, in the sixteenth century, ordered that a group of children be brought up in an environment in which the only communication was by gestures. They were looked after solely by deaf mutes. The purpose of this was to test Akbar's belief that Hebrew was the language of God and would be naturally developed by these children. Unfortunately, they were able to communicate only by gestures and developed no spoken language.

Similar instances have been reported of children brought up by animals: the children have tended to develop the behavioural patterns of the animals with which they have been raised. Such examples tend to indicate that socialisation involving prolonged interaction with adults is essential for individuals to develop the skills of social interaction.

Cognitive-mediational theories of modelling

Theoretically, modelling is derived from classical conditioning, the method by which new responses are generated through stimulus association, and operant conditioning, the method by which responses are established in a person's behavioural repertoire as a result of the consequences they produce.

Bandura (1975, 1976, 1977) has argued that if operant conditioning was the only method by which individuals could acquire a behavioural repertoire, then the human race would probably be erradicated because any learning technique, such as trial and error or successive approximation, would have dire consequences when applied to learning such skills as driving a car, swimming or operating dangerous industrial machinery.

Bandura developed a four-stage theory that explains the process that occurs between the modelled behaviour and the imitation response. These are the cognitive-mediational theories. Bandura suggests that the following four stages must be followed through for the modelled behaviour to become an imitated response:

1. The observer must *attend* to the modelled behaviour;
2. The observer must *retain* what he has seen, using his imagination or word symbols to store the information in his memory;
3. He or she must *reproduce* the observed behaviour;
4. He or she must have the *motivation* to copy this modelled behaviour.

As is the case with other forms of learning, it is possible to acquire both useful or destructive responses through learning by observing other people's behaviour.

Uses of modelling

Modelling techniques have been applied successfully in a wide variety of therapeutic situations. In particular, these techniques can be applied to the following situations:

1. Teaching the behavioural skills lacking due to behavioural deficits;
2. To reduce social anxiety by modelling adequate coping behaviours;
3. For allowing the client to see the entire behavioural repertoire if complex behaviours are being taught (verbal instructions may be adequate for simpler behaviours);

4. For teaching non-verbal behaviours such as eye contact, tone of voice and gestures;
5. Giving a new member an idea of the behaviours expected of him within the social situation in which he finds himself.

A thorough assessment of the client's behavioural deficits should be undertaken before modelling begins. An agreement should be reached with the client about the goals and aims of the therapy. The target behaviours should be broken down into the simplest components and the model should demonstrate to the client what a competent performance looks like. Next, the therapist encourages the client to imitate this sequence, while the therapist shapes and corrects the client's behaviour, as necessary. More complex behaviours are developed by chaining together different sequences. Any artificial reinforcers used in the initial stages should be gradually faded. Situations should be developed which will aid the generalisation of the learnt behaviours to the client's everyday situation, including the use of homework.

Modelling techniques are usually used in conjunction with behavioural rehearsal and feedback. A commonly used technique for a modelling session with a client who is aiming to learn a new behaviour is as follows:

1. A dry run. The client is asked to perform the skill so that the degree of behavioural deficit can be assessed;
2. Modelling. The model demonstrates the behaviour to the client;
3. Behavioural rehearsal. The client performs the behaviour while the therapist uses appropriate techniques such as shaping and prompting to rectify the client's deficits;
4. Re-run. The client performs the appropriate skill again while the therapist uses positive reinforcements to help the client make the desired improvement.

In general, modelling techniques are not employed as a sole clinical technique: instead, they usually form part of a more comprehensive intervention programme.

Model characteristics that affect client learning

If the above mechanisms of learning are true, why do people not imitate all the behaviours that they observe in everyday life and at all times? In fact, most observed behaviours are *not* imitated. Apparently, people learn by modelling under some circumstances but not under others, that is, they learn selectively. The following characteristics have been found to be important in the presentation of models for effective learning by the client.

Characteristics of the modelled performance

The model should be of high status in the observer's eyes, and he should also be of the same sex, approximately the same age and of the same race, as the client. In addition, the model should be clearly rewarded for engaging in the behaviour being displayed.

The model should be able to capture easily the observer's attention; the performance needs to be credible and not too "wooden", with appropriate emotional expression. The use of multiple models for the client to observe will prevent stereotyping and will increase the likelihood of generalisation. Finally, the model should be able to effectively display the desired behaviour.

Model presentation characteristics

The modelled behaviour should be displayed in a clear and detailed manner. It should be presented in the order of the least to the most difficult, and should be repeated sufficiently so that over-learning is likely to occur.

There should be as little irrelevant (not-to-be-learned) material as possible. The client should be able to clearly see the behaviour, and as much extraneous distraction as possible should be removed. The behaviour should be broken down into manageable components, feedback techniques should always be positive, and modelling should always take place in an environment in which the client feels safe. Finally, the first skill taught should be one that the client can master with relative ease.

Observer characteristics

Effective learning is more likely to occur when the client is: told to imitate the model; similar in background and so on to the model; friendly towards or likes the model; rewarded for performing the modelled behaviour or any approximations of it; instructed clearly and specifically on the importance of the model's behaviour.

An important differentiation concerns whether the modelled behaviour should display a "coping" or "mastery" behaviour. It has been clearly found that the "coping" model, where the model initially demonstrates apprehension but subsequently overcomes this fear and performs the skill effectively, is much superior to the "mastery" model in which the model demonstrates ideal behaviour.

Modelling techniques

Participant modelling

Participant modelling assumes that a person's successful performance is an effective means of producing change. A person can achieve potentially enduring changes in behaviour by performing successfully a formerly difficult response. It is a widely used technique for people with social communication difficulties, and has three major components: a modelled demonstration of the target behaviour; guided participation; and homework.

After the therapist and client have assessed and agreed the problem behaviours, the therapist should present the client with a brief explanation of the techniques to be used and explain clearly what is going to happen and what the client is expected to do.

Modelling   If the target behaviours are complex they should be divided into a series of sub-skills so that the programme can begin with a skill that the client is highly likely to suceed at. It is crucial that the client experiences success in performing what is modelled, and it is essential that the therapy begins with a successful response.

These divided skills should be arranged into a hierarchy, with the first situation in the hierarchy being the least difficult to achieve. Successively graded tasks according to degrees of difficulty then follow, ending with the most difficult skill at the top of the hierarchy. After each of the tasks has been successfully practised one at a time, the client should practice combinations of tasks until the whole behaviour can be performed.

An appropriate model should be selected using the criteria outlined above. Immediately before modelling, the therapist should instruct the client about what will be modelled. The model should demonstrate each successive component, with as many repetitions as necessary. It should be pointed out to the client that the model is participating in certain situations without experiencing any adverse consequences. Multiple models can be advantageous as they can lend variety to the way in which the activity is performed, and aid the effects of generalisation.

Guided participation After viewing the modelled behaviour, the client is provided with the opportunity to perform the target behaviour. This is one of the most important components of learning to cope and to acquire new behaviours. It is essential that the client should experience success in what he is trying to imitate, and so the session should be non-threatening and aim at fostering new competencies rather than exposing deficiencies. This section of the procedure consists of four steps:

1. Client practice. After the model has demonstrated the desired behaviour, the client is asked to imitate what has been modelled.
2. Therapist feedback. After each attempt by the client to imitate the desired behaviour, the therapist should provide verbal feedback to the client about the performance. This should consist of two parts: positive encouragement for successful practice; and suggestions for correcting or modifying errors.
3. Various techniques can be used to help the client perform a response if he is finding it difficult, for example: using very *short time periods* of exposure to the undesired behaviour; *verbal cues* from the therapist to help the client; and having the therapist *imitating* the desired behaviour with the client. These aids should be withdrawn gradually as the client becomes more comfortable in the social situation.
4. Client self-directed practice. The client should practise each behaviour until he can perform it skilfully and competently without any input from the therapist. A period of client self-practice should be encouraged to reinforce the learnt behaviour. Ideally, this would occur both within the therapy session and the client's natural environment, but generalisation should be encouraged by making the situations used in the therapy sessions as realistic as possible.

Homework The final component of the participant modelling technique is the attainment of successful or reinforcing experiences. Changes are unlikely to prove effective and continuing unless they are put into practice in the client's everyday life. To encourage this generalisation of the learnt skills, the client should first practise the newly acquired skills in low-risk situations in his natural environment. Gradually, he should extend the application of these skills to more and more unpredictable and threatening situations.

An effective generalisation programme for participant modelling should include the following steps:

1. The therapist and client identify situations in the client's environment, which they agree are targets;
2. These situations are arranged into a hierarchy, starting with easy, safe situations in which the client is likely to succeed, and ending with much more unpredictable and risky situations;
3. The therapist can accompany the client into the environment and work with him in each situation using modelling and guided participation. Gradually, therapist participation is withdrawn;
4. Finally, the client is given a series of situations to deal with in a self-directed manner.

The advantages of participant modelling are that it can help clients to learn new responses in fairly life-like conditions. It is also possible to use a broad range of people as models. The therapist is able to structure the environment in such a way that, despite clients' incapacities, it is possible for them to perform successfully.

Symbolic modelling

In this method the model is presented through written materials, slides, or audio or video tapes. The technique can be used for individual clients or it can be standardised for a group of similar clients. It is possible for a therapist to develop a series of standardised models to use with commonly occurring skills deficits.

A self-instructional technique for symbolic modelling is often used. It is composed of three steps: a *demonstration* of the target behaviour; opportunities for client *practice*; and *feedback*.

In developing a treatment package based on these steps, there are certain elements that need to be considered. First, the characteristics of the client must be taken into account to ensure effective model presentation. Second, the goal behaviours to be modelled need consideration. The normal assessment procedure should be used to ascertain the skill deficits that need working on. It may be possible for a therapist to develop standardised techniques for commonly used areas such as job interviews, simple interaction problems and assertion difficulties. Third, the therapist must consider the media to be used. The choice will depend on where, with whom and how symbolic modelling will be used. The main advantage of written and audio tape models is that they can be used independently at home and they are extremely economical and versatile.

Content of the treatment programme is also important. Regardless of the media to be used, the therapist should develop a programme that clearly demonstrates to the client what is expected. This programme should incorporate five parts:

1. Instruction — this should be included for each behaviour or sequence of behaviour to be demonstrated. Brief but specific and detailed instructions will help the client to identify the necessary components in the model;
2. Modelling — this should include a description of the behaviour to be modelled, as well as examples of models engaging in the desired behaviour;
3. Practice — modelling effects are likely to be increased when presentation of the modelled behaviour is followed by opportunities to practice. In symbolic modelling there should be opportunities for clients to practise what has been demonstrated;
4. Feedback — after the client has been instructed to practice and sufficient time has been allowed, feedback — in the form of a description of the behaviour or activity — should be included. The client should be instructed to repeat the modelling and practise portions of the programme again if the feedback indicates some trouble areas;
5. Summary — at the conclusion of a particular section, the programme should include a summary of what has been modelled and the importance for the client of acquiring these behaviours.

It is recommended that a symbolic modelling programme should be tested before it is implemented with a client group. This is usually best achieved by using colleagues, who should be asked to comment on the language, sequencing of the modelling, practice time and feedback, particularly with respect to their effectiveness and clarity of presentation.

Self-as-a-model

This technique uses the client himself as a model, and has been developed principally by Hosford, Moss and Morrell (1976) in the United States. Some clients find that observing other people as models can produce negative results, even if the models have similar characteristics to themselves. Some people seem to change their behaviours more effectively when they see or listen to themselves. The purpose of this technique is for the client to see himself as the model performing the target behaviour in the desired manner.

There are four major components to this method. As usual, the client and therapist should review the client's problem behaviours and identify target behaviours. Only then should the therapist give the client a thorough explanation of the technique to be used.

Recording the behaviour   A "dry run" can be held to assess the client's performance. Audio or video tape can be used to record the client's behaviour but, either way, the tapes should be of sufficient duration so that later, after editing, the client may be able to observe his behaviour over a reasonable period of time.

The recording is usually repeated until a sample of the desired behaviour is obtained. The therapist may have to coach the client so that at least some portion of the recording demonstrates the desired modelled behaviour.

Edit tape   The tape is edited by the therapist so that the client will see or hear only the appropriate behaviour. Recordings of the inappropriate behaviour are deleted so that only a positive model is provided for the client.

Modelled behaviour   The therapist plays the edited tape to the client. He instructs the client about what to observe on the tape, and encourages him to practise the desired behaviour. Feedback is then given, as appropriate, using coping, shaping and other techniques to correct errors, while rewarding successful imitations.

Homework   The client may benefit more from the self-as-a-model strategy when the edited tape is used in conjunction with practice outside the treatment session. Typical homework instructions may be: to play the recorded tape daily; to practise either covertly or overtly the target behaviour; gradually (this would need to be specified by means of, for example, hierarchical techniques), to use the desired responses in actual instances; and the client rewarding himself for successful experiences, keeping a record of success or failure, using one of the evaluative techniques.

Covert modelling

With some client problems a therapist may find that it is impossible or unrealistic to provide live or symbolic models, or to have the client engage in overt practice of the goal behaviour. In these cases, it may be more practical to employ strategies that use the client's imagination for the modelling and rehearsal. In covert modelling the client imagines a model performing various behaviours while being directed.

There are several advantages to this procedure: it does not require elaborate resources; situations can be developed to deal with a variety of problems; situations can be individualised to fit each client; the client can practise the imagery scenes alone; and the client can use the imagery scenes as a self-control procedure in problem situations.

There are four major components to this method: practice scenes; developing treatment scenes; applying treatment scenes; and homework. As usual, an explanation of the procedure should be given to the client after mutual exploration of the target behaviours.

Practice scenes   Imagining a scene may be a new experience and may at first seem alien for most clients. Practice scenes can help to familiarise clients with the procedure and sensitise them to focus on specific details. This is also an opportunity for the therapist to assess the client.

Practice scenes usually consist of simple, straightforward situations that are unrelated to the client's behavioural problems. They usually consist of six steps. First, the therapist instructs the client to close his eyes and to sit back and relax. The therapist then asks the client to tell him when he feels relaxed. If the client is unable to feel relaxed, then the therapist should assess if the client needs relaxation training. Second, the therapist describes the practice scene and instructs the client to imagine it. At this point, the client should indicate in some appropriate manner, for example, raising an index finger.

The therapist then instructs the client to open his eyes after the scene and to describe the scene or to narrate the imagined events. Next, the therapist probes for greater detail about the scene, asking what clothes a particular person was wearing or for a description of a particular place in the scene.

The therapist may suggest additional details for the client to imagine during a subsequent practice. Usually, each practice scene is presented several times before moving on to developing and applying treatment scenes, the number of which will depend on several factors such as whether the client feels comfortable with the imagined scenes, and whether, after several practice scenes, he can provide a fairly detailed description using imagery. If the client can do this fairly easily, it is usually a good indicator to start developing treatment scenes.

The following are possible examples to use as practice scenes: lying on a beach; eating a delicious meal with a friend; going to a library to borrow a book.

Two problems are likely to occur with covert modelling practice scenes: the client can have difficulty in relaxing — if this occurs it should be dealt with using relaxation techniques; or the client may have difficulty in generating an image. It may be necessary to use another technique if this persists.

Developing treatment scenes   Treatment scenes are developed in conjunction with the client, and devised out of the treatment goals. The scenes consist of a variety of situations in which the client wants to perform the target responses in real-life environments.

Five factors need to be considered in the development of treatment scenes:

1. Model characteristics. Kazdin (1974, 1975) has undertaken a considerable amount of research into the model characteristics that are most effective for covert modelling. He concluded that the following are more likely to lead to effective modelling: the imagined model should be of the same sex and similar age as the client; multiple models should be used; a coping model should be presented rather than a mastery model.
2. Individualised versus standardised scenes. Standardised scenes cover different situations in everyday life and can be presented to a group of clients with similar target responses. Individualised scenes are tailored to an individual client's needs. In general terms, scenes should be individualised for clients with unique or unusual problems, otherwise there is no reason why this technique cannot be used for group practice.
3. Degree of specificity of scenes. Some clients benefit from being given detailed instructions about what to imagine. Other clients may benefit if the scenes are more general. One risk of not giving detailed instructions is that some clients will introduce material that is irrelevant or negative. The degree of specificity of each scene will depend largely on the client, the concern of the problem and the goal for treatment.
4. Scene composition. Three principle factors are required: first, a description of the situational context in which the behaviour is likely to occur; second, a description of the model demonstrating the behaviour to

be acquired; and third, a depiction of some favourable outcome or result of the desired behaviour.

5. Number of scenes. The therapist and client can develop different scenes that portray the context or situation in which the client experiences difficulty. This is usually helpful in developing generalisation of the behaviour from specific scenes.

Applying treatment scenes After the scene has been developed, the therapist can apply the treatment scenes by getting the client to imagine each situation. There are several steps the therapist can use to help the client to successfully imagine the model, as follows: arrange the situations in a hierarchy of difficulty; instruct the client about how he should use the imagery techniques; present one scene at a time from the hierarchy; present the scene for a specific duration; obtain client reactions to the imagined scene; present each scene at least twice; have the client imagine each scene at least twice; and finally, present scenes from the hierarchy at random.

There are specific areas that need to be looked at and these can be divided into five areas:

1. Duration of scenes. A common duration for presentation of a scene is 15 to 30 seconds. A general rule is that the effective length of presentation should be worked out with the client. The basis is that a scene should be held long enough for the client to imagine the scene ingredients without rushing.
2. Client reaction. This should enable the therapist to maintain the various elements to gain the most effective approach. It may be necessary at times to revise the scene content, manner of presentation or hierarchy. After each scene presentation the therapist should assess whether the scene is being delivered correctly, the clarity of the image, and the degree of pleasantness of the scene for the client.
3. Trainer-directed scene repetitions. The number of scene repetitions may be dictated by the degree of comfort the client experiences while imagining the scene and the complexities of the behaviours the client is to acquire.
4. Client-directed scene repetition. Again, this is somewhat arbitrary, although two repetitions are the minimum. In general terms, the client should carry on imagining the scenes until he feels comfortable.
5. Random presentation of scenes. After all the scenes in the hierarchy have been presented adequately, the therapist can check the client's readiness

for self-directed homework practice by presenting some of the scenes in random order.

Homework   Again, this is probably the most important ingredient in helping generalisation. Some practitioners have recommended that the client should practise covert modelling techniques at least 10 times a day at home; others recommend less frequent use. However, the technique should be practised at least on a daily basis.

Two possible techniques have been used to encourage frequent home practice, namely, tape recording and a "telephone mate". For the first technique, a tape is designed to take the client through the various stages of the covert modelling techniques. A "phone mate" is someone whom the client can call to practise their covert modelling techniques over the telephone.

In arranging homework, the therapist and client should — together — agree how often, for how long, at what time during the day, and where training should take place.

The client should keep a record of his use of the covert modelling techniques, by means of one of the evaluation methods. The therapist should verify that the client understands the homework assignment and a follow-up appointment should be arranged after an agreed part of the homework is completed.

Cognitive modelling

Cognitive modelling is based on the basic assumption that a client's thoughts and beliefs can contribute to maladaptive behaviour, and that maladaptive behaviour can be altered by dealing directly with a person's beliefs, attitudes or thoughts.

In many instances, a client's unreasonable self-standards and negative self-thoughts can diminish the power of a treatment programme and it may be necessary to alter the client's beliefs and expectations so that other therapeutic strategies can be successful.

There are many ways of conceptualising cognitive problems. One common way of considering them is under the following areas:

1. Selective inattention — the client attends to irrelevant cues while ignoring relevant ones;

2. Misperception — the client mislabels either internal or external cues;
3. Maladaptive focusing — the client focuses on irrelevant external stimuli or events;
4. Maladaptive self-arousal — the client focuses on irrelevant internal stimuli or cues;
5. Repertory deficiencies — the client displays limited or inadequate behaviour due to a deficit in cognitive skills.

It is common for clients to have difficulties in more than one of these areas. Cognitive modelling is a procedure in which the therapist shows a person what to say to himself while performing a particular behaviour.

The procedure consists of six basic steps. They are undertaken after the client and therapist have explored the behavioural deficits and the procedures of the therapy have been explained.

Therapist model   The therapist instructs the client to listen to what he is saying while he exhibits a particular behaviour. Next, the therapist models performing a specific task while talking aloud. This performance should consist of five parts. The first part of the therapist's verbalisation should ask a question about the nature of, and the demands of, the task to be performed. The purpose of the questions are to compensate for a possible deficiency in the client's understanding of what he has to do, and to provide a general orientation to the technique.

The second part of the verbalisation answers the question about what to do or perform. The answer is designed to model cognitive rehearsal and planning in order to focus the client's attention on relevant aspects of the performance. Next, the therapist gives himself instruction in the form of self-guidance while exhibiting the behaviour.

The therapist then models self-reinforcement, which is designed to maintain the performance of the behaviour and to reinforce success. Finally, the therapist should demonstrate coping self-statements designed to handle errors and frustrations.

Overt external guidance   After the therapist has modelled these cognitive components of behaviour, the client is instructed to perform the tasks while the therapist instructs or coaches him. The therapist should ensure that the coaching contains the same five parts of self-guidance, as outlined above.

Overt self-guidance   The therapist instructs the client to perform the specified behaviour while instructing himself aloud. The purpose of this is to have the client practise the kind of "self-talk" that will strengthen attention to the demands of the behaviour, and minimise distractions. The therapist should attend closely to the contents of the client's self-talk, which should include the five component parts. If necessary, the therapist can return to any one of these steps. After the client has completed these steps, the therapist should provide feedback about those parts of the practice that the client has completed effectively. He should also provide further guidance about any errors or omissions.

Faded overt self-guidance   The client goes through the same procedure as above, while whispering the instructions to himself. This is an intermediary step between overt and covert self-guidance. However, it is usually best to repeat the overt self-guidance stage if the client finds this step difficult.

Covert self-guidance   In this step, the client performs the task while instructing himself covertly, that is, "in his head". It is useful after the practice to ask the client to describe his covert self-instructions to the therapist. If distracting or inhibiting self-talk has occurred, the therapist can offer suggestions for more appropriate "self-talk" and an additional practice can be arranged. Otherwise, the client is ready to use the procedure outside the therapy session.

Homework   Assigning the client homework is essential for generalisation to occur. The therapist should instruct the client to use the covert "self-talk" while performing the desired behaviours alone. The homework assignment should specify what the client will do, and when, where and how often he will do it.

References

Bandura A *et al.* (1975) Generalising change through participant modelling with self-directed mastery, Behaviour Research and Therapy 13:141–152

Bandura A (1976) Effecting change through participant modelling, in J D Krumboltz and C E Thoreson (Editors), Counselling Methods, Holt, Rinehart and Winston

Bandura A (1977) Social Learning Theory, Prentice Hall

Cautela J R (1976) The present status of covert modelling, Journal of Behaviour Therapy and Experimental Psychiatry 6:323–326

Hosford R, Moss C and Morrell G (1976) The self as a model technique: Helping prison inmates change, in Krumboltz and Thoreson (Editors), Counselling Methods, Holt, Rinehart and Winston

Kazdin A E (1974) The effect of model identity and fear relevant similarity of covert modelling, Behaviour Therapy, 5:624-635

Kazdin A E (1975) Comparative effects of some variations of covert modelling, Journal of Behaviour Therapy and Experimental Psychiatry, 5:225-231

Meichenbaum D H (1971) Examination of Model Characteristics in reducing avoidance behaviour, Journal of Personality and Social Psychology, 17:243-307

CHAPTER 7

FEEDBACK/GENERALISATION

Feedback

Although practice is necessary for skill acquisition, skills are not learnt by practice alone. In order to develop an improved skill behaviour, individuals must receive information about the consequences of their actions. It is a well known psychological fact that behaviour can be influenced by events which are made consequent upon it. When such events take the form of reinforcing stimuli, the effect is an increase in the frequency of occurrence of the preceeding behaviour. These reinforcing stimuli can take a variety of forms, but are of two principle types, namely, intrinsic and extrinsic feedback.

Intrinsic feedback is part of a particular behaviour, for example, the muscular movements involved in throwing a ball. With extrinsic feedback, however, information is received that is external to the behaviour being performed, for example, a person encouraging someone on to greater efforts can enable that person to achieve more than if they were not there. Research has shown that extrinsic feedback can help the development of skilled performance, but that it should be faded out as the person's performance improves, to prevent them becoming dependent on the feedback.

Feedback is usually more effective if it is given immediately after the behaviour, although there is some evidence that, if no other response intervenes, feedback can be delayed for up to 24 hours and still be effective. The intervention of other responses clearly prevents the individual from using the information to improve his performance.

Holding and Macrae (1965) differentiated between two types of feedback: concurrent feedback, where information is provided during the task; and terminal feedback, where information is presented on completion of the task.

Terminal feedback forces clients to attend to the intrinsic cues in the task during its performance and presents information in a concise form at the end of the task. Verbal comments, for instance, can be used as terminal feedback to present a considerable amount of information to clients in a brief and succinct form.

It appears that extrinsic feedback is most successful when given at the end of a response and presented in such a way as to highlight the intrinsic feedback in the task. Extrinsic feedback presented concurrently may produce initial improvements in the performance but may also obscure the feedback in the task itself, resulting in poor skills acquisition in the longer term. The therapist should praise the good aspects of the performance, focusing on the task and guidepoints, rather than the person. This can be followed by audio or video feedback and an invitation to the client to comment on his own performance. In a group setting, other group members can also be asked to contribute feedback at this stage, in particular, focusing on the impact the client's behaviour has had on them.

Evidence from experiments has shown that one of the most important factors in feedback is the amount of positive as opposed to negative feedback. Several elements have been shown to contribute effectively to successful feedback for skills acquisition.

Characteristics of effective feedback

Several characteristics have been found to be especially pertinent for effective client feedback. For example the therapist's comments should be focused, dealing only with those aspects relevant to learning the skill required. Second, the feedback should be detailed, referring to specific verbal or non-verbal behaviour that has been displayed by the client. In addition, the feedback should describe the impact the client's behaviour has had on other people, rather than be interpretive, for example, the therapist should say, "You made me feel that you were not interested by looking away", rather than, "You look bored."

Conciseness is also important: the therapist's feedback should be easily understood and given in nontechnical language. It should also be given on behaviour over which the client has some control and over which he has the opportunity to correct. Feedback is likely to lead to a feeling of frustration if the client has little control over the behaviour.

Feedback is much more effective if it is given promptly and immediately after the behaviour is carried out. In addition, feedback is likely to have more impact if: the client is well motivated and requests the feedback; the therapist checks that the client has understood the feedback; it is given by more than one person; it is given on the behaviour rather than on the person; it concentrates on no more than two to three areas at any one time; it is directed specifically, at the client's behaviour, rather than through other people.

There should be a period of feedback after any social skills training to enable the client to receive information about the effectiveness of his performance and the steps he needs to take to remedy any deficits. When approval or positive feedback increases the frequency of a desired behaviour, it is called social reinforcement.

An important feature of social reinforcement is shaping. This occurs when any improvement in acquiring a desired behaviour is reinforced by giving approval for successively better attempts. Any sign of improvement is clearly, immediately and specifically rewarded.

Guidelines for using positive reinforcement in social skills training

1. Provide reinforcement at the earliest appropriate opportunity after the client has performed the behaviour;
2. Provide reinforcement to the co-therapist for being helpful and co-operative;
3. Provide reinforcement *only* after behaviour that follows the designated steps;
4. Vary the specific content of the reinforcement offered;
5. Provide *no* reinforcement if the role-play departs significantly from the behavioural steps. It may be necessary to reinforce clients for "trying" during the initial stages of therapy;
6. Provide gradual reinforcement if an individual's performance improves over the previous performance.

Observer reinforcement

Group techniques are used in many of the techniques described in this book.

Other clients are often involved in giving feedback to individual clients about their performance. This provides interest for them as well as giving a wider variety of feedback. One effective method is to use rating scales: for example, each observer is asked to indicate for each of the components how he felt the client performed, on a scale of 1 to 5. Any aspects of the performance being taught can be utilised, and not just the examples used in this rating scale:

1. Verbal behaviour
    (a) Volume — Could I hear clearly?
    (b) Tone — Was his speech boring/interesting?
    (c) Pitch — Was his voice high/low?
    (d) Clarity — Was his speech clear/inaudible?
    (e) Pace — Did he speak too fast/too slow?
2. Non-verbal behaviour
    (a) Proximity — Was he too close/too far from the person?
    (b) Gaze — Did he look at the person for an appropriate length of time?

For each of these behaviours seen during the social interaction, the observers are asked to rate on the following scale how they felt the subject performed: 1 = very poor (desirable behaviour is lacking); 2 = fair (needs much improvement); 3 = average (could still improve); 4 = good (could improve, but really only needs to polish up); 5 = excellent (little or no room for improvement).

This type of rating scale can be drawn onto a blackboard or the therapist can devise his own rating scale form. If several clients are being rated successively they can be rated on the same form, but care should be taken not to isolate one client whose performance is markedly inferior to the others. Therefore, the scale should be adapted to each client. In addition, the ratings should tend towards positive feedback rather than negative feedback, and a slight positive bias is advised. A benefit of this system is the active involvement it generates in the group, which aids the development of group cohesiveness. If one of the raters' scores deviates markedly from the average rating, they should be asked to explain how they came to their conclusions.

Video feedback

This is an extremely effective method for maintaining involvement and active participation in groups. However, it can be cumbersome and requires more time to be spent with each client. The following guidelines can be used to provide effective video feedback: short examples of interaction should be taped, usually around 30 seconds is adequate; feedback should be provided after each scene; the therapist should highlight examples of desired behaviour by using the freeze-frame technique or other techniques (see Chapter 8); the therapist should focus on improved performance. Every effort should be made to ensure that the therapist does not focus on examples of poor performance. This is often difficult, as people's mistakes are so clearly demonstrated on video-tape, and there is an opportunity to use freeze-frame techniques to emphasise especially inept actions.

When to give feedback

Feedback should be given when the client has performed well and when the feedback will not interrupt the scene. It is usually better to wait until the end of a scene to reward a client than to risk distracting him. However, there are a few exceptions to this rule: for example, when the client seems unsure of himself and needs encouragement to continue in the role-play, then he should be reinforced immediately; a client who has repeatedly attempted a behaviour and finally gets it right should also be reinforced immediately; some types of non-verbal positive feedback can be provided without causing interruption to the flow of the situation, such as, smiling or nodding the head.

Style of feedback

"Subjective" versus "objective" feedback

Subjective feedback can be given by the therapist without any claim to be scientific. The advantage of this type of therapist feedback is that it allows the client to receive information without feeling judged.

Objective feedback is provided by the therapist being prepared to back up statements with supporting reasons. It is a stronger form of feedback than the subjective type, but is not necessarily more effective. The therapist has to be especially careful that he does not project his own opinions using this technique.

"Descriptive" versus "attributive" feedback

Descriptive feedback simply means describing the events that have occurred, for example, "Your left arm didn't move", or "You looked into his eyes on two occasions."

Attributive feedback conveys meanings to human behaviour that can be based on a variety of psychological mechanisms. These can be conveyed by using terms such as "motivation" or they can come from a particular school of thought, such as the social learning model.

Reinforcers

There are numerous types of reinforcer available to the therapist, although it must be stressed that only positive reinforcers are used for social skills training. Several types of reinforcers are commonly used, for example, verbal prompts, in which several types of utterances can be used to acknowledge and/or confirm what has been said by the other person. These can be effective in conveying that the therapist is paying attention to what is going on, and also as a sign to the client that he is heading in the right direction. Commonly used types of verbal prompts are: "OK", "Mmm", "Hmm", and "Yes".

Another type of reforcer is the use of positive statements. Statements which praise and support the client have been found to be effective reinforcing stimuli and can be of two types, verbal and non-verbal. Verbal positive statements include simple statements such as "Well done" and "Keep going".

There are several commonly used non-verbal reinforcers that can be used to encourage clients, such as smiling, eye contact, head nods, and certain gestures, for example, a "thumbs up" sign. In addition, a forward-leaning posture also seems to have some reinforcing potential.

A third type of reinforcer is the use of self-rewards. Clients can be encouraged to develop their own reinforcers for achieving desired behaviours, such as a trip to the cinema or buying a new coat. These should be considered carefully so that they have a full impact, as it is possible that the reinforcers will not have the required effect unless implemented correctly.

Group reinforcers can be built-in for successful accomplishments in group training. It should be stressed that reinforcement should be given only for successful completion. Every effort should be made to ensure that individuals are not "scapegoated" for ineffective performance, thus preventing the group achieving a goal, although this can be a powerful social pressure.

The therapist should use these components either alone or in combination to provide encouragement and reinforcement for the client's successful behaviour. The skill of reinforcement is used to its best when the selected reinforcing stimulus is appropriate for the situation, the person involved and the particular target response. Generally, it is also more advantageous to employ a variety of reinforcers rather than to rely upon the constant, repetitive use of any particular one since constant use of a reinforcer can result in the stimulus losing its reinforcing properties.

Frequency and timing are features of the skill that also play an important part in its successful implementation. While frequent reinforcement of the responses under focus is necessary in the initial stages, it has been found that, once the response has been established, the rate of reinforcement can be reduced without a decrease in the response rate. It is also possible to reinforce certain elements of a response by partial reinforcement, without necessarily reinforcing it in total.

Generalisation

Once social skills deficits have been assessed and the desired behaviour has been successfully taught, the remaining goal for the therapist is to ensure that the client is able to use these skills when and wherever it is appropriate for him to do so. The term "generalisation" describes the extension or transfer of improvement beyond the immediate treatment session.

Progress made in treatment sessions have a low probability of being maintained if they are not overlearned. Considerable research evidence shows that newly acquired skills can be extinguished under stress, to be replaced by previously well established patterns of behaviour. Generalisation does not automatically occur, but needs to be planned and programmed as part of the training process. There are three principle areas where it has to occur: the skills learnt have to be transferred to different situations; they have to be applied to different people; and they have to be maintained over a period of time.

Factors affecting generalisation

Considerable research has been undertaken into the factors that appear to influence whether or not skills are generalised into a person's behaviour, remain specific to the learnt behaviour, or are extinguished. For example, one important aspect is how social skills are taught. The way in which social behaviours are learnt appears to influence whether the new behaviour will occur in a variety of settings, and whether they will occur with people other than the therapist. A frequent occurrence in behaviour change programmes is that newly acquired behaviours are maintained only within the settings where the client is instructed, and they are not transferred to other environments. Ideally, social skills instruction should take place in the setting where the behaviour is to occur. If this is impossible, the therapist should try to replicate the natural environment in which the behaviour would occur. It has been found that the more closely the training environment resembles the natural environment, the more likely the client's behaviour is to generalise.

However, if training cannot take place in the natural environment, it has also been found to be desirable that the training should replicate more than one setting. It may not be necessary to provide social skills instruction in every setting, but the following procedure may be helpful. Role-plays should be set up in which the client can demonstrate how he will perform the behaviour in other settings. Hence, the therapist might say: "Let's role-play how you would go into a cafe and order yourself a cup of coffee." The client should then be encouraged to keep a record of how he performs in various settings, while attempting target behaviours as part of his homework.

It must be remembered that some responses are situation-specific, and do not generalise easily. The client needs to learn the responses appropriate to a particular setting, for example, which greetings are appropriate for different people. Additionally, the therapist should structure the training sessions to ensure that the client's behaviour is controlled by explicit aspects of the training and not by incidental factors. It appears that the most effective training conditions for individuals or groups are dictated primarily by the behaviours to be learnt, the client's skills level and the conditions under which the client will have to perform the behaviour under natural circumstances.

Training with different people is another important factor affecting generalisation. If two therapists are undertaking a social skills course, it is possible for them to alternate from week to week so that the new behaviours being learnt do not remain under the control of one therapist. Alternatively, members of the client's environment can be trained to instruct, prompt and reinforce the desired social behaviour. This approach can certainly be applied in a setting such as in a hospital, where the elements can be strictly controlled; it can also be applied to family settings if the other factors involved are appropriate.

Training relevant others to aid generalisation

The following is a simple programme for use with other relevant members of a client's environment to help aid generalisation:

1. Outline the overall programme;
2. Provide them with a written description of how the training is to be undertaken, and allow them to observe a training session;
3. Discuss in detail the role they will play;
4. If necessary, provide for additional observation;
5. Rehearse the training session through role-play, with the relevant person providing instruction to the client;
6. Provide corrective feedback either during or after the session;
7. Provide tape recordings of the training sessions for the other person to listen to and practise with;
8. Ensure that both the client and the person who will be providing the training are clear about how they will implement the training programme at home;
9. Provide a follow-up at an early date to ensure that the programme is being implemented effectively.

Peer groups can also be used to provide this type of generalisation training but certain precautions should be taken. For example, reasonably attainable goals should be established and gradually raised as the client progresses. It should also be ensured that the peer group uses only positive reinforcement and that the client does not receive punishment or negative reinforcement for inadequate responses. The peer group should be clear as to how exactly to provide support and encouragement; instruction sessions will probably be necessary. The positive reinforcements to be used should have a high standing within the group; they should be faded gradually as the behaviours become stabilised and maintained, and social or other natural reinforcers should be used.

Cognitive factors

Another approach to generalisation is to develop cognitive mediators to assist the client in generalising and maintaining appropriate behaviours in settings and conditions beyond those explicitly involved in training. According to

Bandura (1977), response patterns can be represented in memory, and retained in symbolic form primarily through imagery and verbalisation. There is some evidence that behaviour learnt through observation is acquired and retained more effectively if mental and verbal rehearsal is used in addition to behavioural rehearsal. Several cognitive techniques can be used to encourage generalisation, namely, language, imagery and expectation.

Language is the medium most often used when trying to develop generalisation. A simple method is to ask the client to state what he did or did not do while engaging in social behaviour. Self-instruction and problem-solving cognitive approaches are also potentially useful for behavioural generalisation.

Visual imagery is especially important if verbal skills are lacking. A common technique is to provide visual stimuli in the form of drawings and photographs and ask the client to close his eyes and to imagine himself in the depicted situation.

Generalisation is more likely to occur if the client *expects it to happen.* This element can be developed by emphasising the client's successful performances, by using coping skills and by having the ability to apply various means of controlling emotions in stressful situations.

Applying some of these factors to the generalisation of social skills can allow the therapist to enhance the client's future expectations of success. A client can develop feelings of competence to cope with any stressful inter-personal situations by receiving training in actual skills, by being provided with examples of successful models, or by suggestions being made, through discussion, about how the learning of social behaviours will be helpful in the future.

Varying aspects of reinforcement

The principal factor that maintains social skills over time is reinforcement and the types operating in the settings in which the social skills are to be used. The nature of reinforcement must be changed for generalisation to occur; for example, changing from extrinsic to intrinsic sources of reward, altering the ways in which reinforcement is given, and changing the kinds of rewards provided.

1. Changing the source of reinforcement. Although many social skills may, by their very nature, evoke maintaining responses from the external

environment, some planning and programming for generalisation and maintenance through altered reinforcements may be necessary. Two possible ways of doing this are: to alter the focus of reinforcement from the therapist to people in the client's larger environment, and to provide the client with the skills necessary to elicit reinforcement from the environment.

2. Changing the timing of reinforcement. In the process of teaching new social behaviours, reinforcement needs to be provided immediately on a continuous basis for correct responses. Once behaviours have been learnt, they are more likely to persist over time if the timing or schedule for reinforcement is faded to occasional reinforcement, provided on an intermittent or unpredictable basis.

    Contingency contracts provide one means of delaying rewards and enabling the source of reinforcement to be transferred from one person to another. A contingency contract should usually have the following components: the social behaviour should be clearly defined so that all concerned can agree when it has occurred; the performance criteria for the behaviour should be clearly stated, that is, how much of the behaviour has occurred to earn the reward and under what circumstances it should occur; the reward to be provided when criteria are met and who should provide the reward should also be clearly stated; a means of determining whether the reward has been earnt or not should also be incorporated.

3. Changing the nature of reinforcement. The types of external reinforcement can vary from social reinforcement (praise, smiles, positive attention) to various forms of tangible reinforcers (food, cigarettes). Alternatively, generalised conditioned reinforcers such as tokens or points can be used for a wide variety of reinforcing events, with the schedules being altered as the clients acquire proficiency.

    It has been clearly established that almost any high rate, more preferred activity can serve as a reinforcer for a low rate, less preferred activity. Since reinforcement is defined by its positive effects on behaviour, effective reinforcers cannot always be predicted. However, if social skills instruction begins with tangible reinforcers, then maintenance over time is likely to be enhanced if the therapist moves towards social reinforcement, since praises, smiles and attention are potentially available in most settings. If social rewards do not initially serve as reinforcers, they can take on reinforcing values if they are paired with whatever the client finds to be reinforcing.

4. Using reinforcement skills. This appears to be one of the most promising

means by which behaviour can be maintained over time. Bandura (1977) regarded self-reinforcement, or the ability to regulate one's own behaviour by self-produced consequences, as the highest level of development in the mental hierarchy of incentives. The ability to self-reinforce can be regarded itself as a social skill, with the following components: the adopting of standards by which performance is to be evaluated; the ability to monitor one's own behaviour; the ability to evaluate one's own performance according to the standards set; and the ability to provide self-reinforcement based on the degree to which the behaviour meets the performance standards.

Teaching self-reinforcement skills The following stages can usefully apply to many social skills training sessions, thus enabling the client to develop self-reinforcement skills to use when he has completed social skills training so that generalisation is encouraged:

1. The therapist controls both the behaviour being learnt and the reinforcers to be used;
2. The client assumes joint control with the therapist over either the amount of reinforcement or the behaviour to be performed;
3. The therapist and client share equally in determining both the reinforcer and the behaviour to be performed.
4. The client assumes full control of either the behaviour to be performed or the reinforcer, and shares joint responsibility with the therapist for the control of the other variable;
5. The client takes full control of both the amount of reinforcement and the behaviour to be performed.

Taking a client from extrinsic rewards to self-administered intrinsic rewards There are several steps in this technique to vary reinforcement:

1. The therapist should establish with the client a specific behaviour to be rewarded, the criteria for reinforcement, and the rewards that the client will provide for himself, beginning with tangible rewards if necessary;
2. Practise in self-monitoring should be provided, with rewards for accuracy;
3. Self-reinforcement should be initiated, with verbal reinforcement being provided by the therapist for effective social behaviour and the appropriate delivery of self-reinforcement;

4. The client should accompany self-reinforcement with a verbal description of what he did to gain the reward;
5. The client should be asked to say silently to himself what he did to earn the reward before he made the statement;
6. There should be a move to less frequently self-administered tangible rewards, and the client should delay reinforcement for longer periods;
7. The use of self-administered tangible rewards should be discontinued, using instead verbal reports reinforced by external praise;
8. Regular verbal reports should be discontinued. Regular reviews should be provided to ensure that the skill has been reinforced effectively.

Although, theoretically, social skills may be generalised across settings and across people, realistically it may be necessary to provide additional training periodically. Periodic booster sessions provide one way of maintaining behaviour change. They should be timed to occur before a behaviour has had time to deteriorate.

Homework

Homework assignments have become a standard part of many social skills training techniques in an attempt to aid generalisation. Initially, homework assignments should be structured to be as similar as possible to the therapy sessions. One way of doing this is to record practice sessions on audio-cassettes as a way of extending the therapist's influence into the home. Gradually, any reinforcers used are faded so that increasing self-control is promoted. The client should be given a homework assignment at the end of each session, beginning with the second session of a social skills training programme. The assignment should be based on the skills learnt during that particular session. It should be worked out jointly between the client and the therapist to encourage the former.

The homework instructions should be specific. It is not enough to tell someone to be more assertive in their everyday life: a specific description of the behaviours to be undertaken should be given to the client, for example, the therapist might say: "You should go into a cafe three times in the next week and order yourself a cup of coffee. You should have done this at least once by Tuesday and at least twice by Thursday. You should pay specific attention to..."

In addition, the client should be able to perform the assignment adequately. The assignment should be at a skill level at which the client has already achieved a degree of competence. The aim of homework is not to provide basic instruction but to provide overt training. Initial assignments should not demand substantial behaviour changes, even if the client has learnt the specific social skills responses needed.

The homework assignment should also have a high probability of leading to reinforcement. There should be every likelihood that the client can effectively carry out the desired behaviour and achieve reinforcement. The client should not be given difficult situations to deal with early on in his homework assignments. One way of monitoring homework performance is for the client to keep a diary and to record information on how effective he is being in carrying out the assignments. It is also possible to use this information at the next training session to find out about the client's social behaviour and how he is functioning.

The homework assignment should be seen as an integral part of the social skills training, and an opportunity for the client to put into practice the skills learnt during the therapy sessions.

Generalisation and psychiatric illness

Although the generalisation issue is relevant to the evaluation of therapy for all clients, it is most critical when working with chronically impaired psychotics. Since the social environment of chronically disabled schizophrenics living in the community has been shown to affect relapse rates, behaviour therapy approaches — with the emphasis on consistent use of reinforcement and ongoing monitoring of behaviour — have been found to be effective in acquiring behaviour change. Generalisation of skills acquired during training with chronic psychotics has been found to be effectively maintained by using the following methods:

1. Select as target behaviours those that will continue to be reinforced in the natural environment;
2. Use praise, acknowledgement, approval and other social reinforcers with tangible reinforcers such as tokens. In this manner, naturally occurring reinforcers will maintain behavioural gains after discharge if the tangible reinforcers are gradually withdrawn;
3. Gradually fade out these tangible reinforcers, eventually relying solely on the more naturally occurring social reinforcers;
4. Simulate the natural environment with its stimulus characteristics in the treatment environment, and reinforce adaptive behaviour under the simulated conditions. Examples of simulating the real world in a hospital setting are having the facilities for clients to cook their own

meals, perform meaningful work, wash their own clothes, and use telephones and public transport;

5. Gradually use the natural environment for training. Clients can increasingly begin to use more time in the community as they start to approach discharge;

6. Train relatives and other relevant people to carry out the reinforcement programme begun in hospital. This brings an element of the treatment situation into the aftercare. Family therapy and education of community agents are opportunities to emphasise and strengthen the skills of everyday living;

7. Teach clients 'to provide self-reinforcement for their own behavioural goals. Clients should be encouraged to develop control techniques and coping behaviours, which help to prevent new problems, stresses and difficulties from mounting to the point where they require professional intervention;

8. Use intermittent and delayed schedules of reinforcement as the treatment proceeds. The gradual building-in of uncertainty of reward helps to free the client from dependence on the hospital setting and the people within the environment, and increases the likelihood of the behaviour being generalised to the community;

9. Use over-training techniques, including homework, to strengthen the desired behaviours. In addition to homework, large numbers of training sessions can be used. This is particularly important with clients who start with minimal social skills or who have been behaviourally impoverished through long years of residence in institutions;

10. Involve each client in setting the goals of treatment, and in choosing from among alternative treatment methods. This helps to shift the reinforcement from external to internal factors, and ensures that the client begins to take more responsibility for his own actions. It is important in maintaining generalisation that the client attributes some responsibility for his success to his own efforts rather than to the efforts of others.

References

Bandura A (1977) Social Learning Theory, Prentice Hall

Holding D M and Macrae A W (1965) Guidance restriction and knowledge of results, Ergonomics 7(3): 289–295

Premack D (1962) Reversibility of the reinforcement relationship, science, 136: 235–237

CHAPTER 8

VIDEO TECHNIQUES

Over the past 10 to 20 years the use of video-tape equipment has expanded rapidly. This growth has been widespread, and the well known availability of "video nasties" and cinema films to view in one's home has been paralleled by the development of video equipment for use, with clients, by the helping professions. In some ways, the use of video-tape has had a similar history to social skills training itself, in that it has been characterised by an initial euphoria regarding its capabilities and potential uses, now replaced by a more professional approach. Adequate training and effective evaluation of practice now play an increasingly prominent role. This has led to video-tape being used much more specifically and more effectively in therapy sessions. This chapter will briefly examine some of the basic concepts behind the use of video recording before considering potential clinical techniques. Several practical issues relating to the use of video will then be analysed before some ethical problems are explored.

Introduction

The first use of techniques similar to those used in video recording are reputed to have been developed by Kraeplin who used film recording to present examples of psychopathology to medical staff learning psychiatry. It was not until the early 1950s, however, that experiments with film techniques were used for therapeutic purposes. Film techniques have been used in psychiatry to give both clients and professionals the opportunity to view the client's behaviour. Video-tape techniques have one major effect for the observer in that it tends to magnify behaviour. It allows an individual to examine aspects of behaviour of which he would normally be unaware. This is especially true of non-verbal communication.

The use of video went through a rapid period of expansion in the late 1960s and 1970s. This was largely due to considerable technological development that reduced the cost of the basic equipment, making it easily more available. Clinically, this meant that even small departments could consider using video-tape techniques. At about the same time, there was a considerable amount of research verifying the effects of video use. Through this period, clinical programmes using video equipment have been devised to treat such varied disorders as sexual dysfunction, disruptive behaviour, anorexia nervosa, phobias, alcoholism, drug addiction and a whole range of social skills deficits. Many theories have been produced to explain why video-tape techniques work as a therapeutic tool:

1. Psychotherapeutic. Some people have a distorted self-image because they are never confronted with a real picture of themselves. Video recording enables the observer to cut through these layers of denial, since it is difficult not to accept that the image on the screen is a real one. The technique is thus a form of self-confrontation.
2. Cognitive restructuring. Each person carries an "internal standard" of themselves. When they view a recording of themselves on video, there may well be a discrepancy between the image they carry of themselves and the image they actually see on the screen. This is often painful to the individual and behaviour can be altered in an attempt to reduce this pain, so that the individual's internal standards are conformed with.
3. Behavioural. Behavioural theories view video techniques as part of the feedback mechanism, which is itself regarded as a powerful part of the learning process. By viewing this behaviour more objectively, the individual is given the opportunity to modify his habitual behaviour.

Research findings concerning the efficacy of video-tape techniques and social skill training are still at an early stage. In general, the research concerning the use of video-tape in interaction with clients is positive, although there have been several research reports where no benefit has been found. More detailed research is being undertaken to try to clarify the particular components of video-tape recordings that are important in clinical practice. Some of this research will be reviewed later in this chapter.

Advantages and disadvantages of video techniques

The advantages and disadvantages of the use of video-tapes in practical situations can be summarised as follows:

Advantages

1. The equipment is now relatively cheap to buy and is usually easily available in most clinical areas.
2. Video-tapes used are re-usable, relatively easy to transport and can be used in various situations.
3. Relatively little training is involved in how to use video-tape equipment in a straightforward manner.
4. The video user has control over the playback speed, and is able to speed up or slow down particular items of interest.
5. It is relatively easy to edit video-tapes so that they can be used for clinical purposes.
6. It is easy to take recordings of different situations, because of the ease of editing, or use different people and then to show them consecutively to highlight specific points.
7. This ability to replay behavioural sequences means it is possible to develop measurement techniques that can be used for analysis and research purposes.

Disadvantages

1. In certain cases, an individual's behaviour may be affected by the presence of the video equipment, and therefore a representative sample of his behaviour cannot be recorded.
2. The video-tape recording is always more poorly defined than the observer's view of the original behaviour.
3. Three-dimensional cues are absent from the video record and so there is a lack of depth; similarly, movement towards the camera can produce an enlarged image on the video screen that is not apparent in real life.
4. There is not the same flexibility that a natural observer has because the camera angle is usually fixed.
5. Some people regard video-tape techniques as a panacea for all occasions, and it can often be used when it is not necessary.

Self-image and person perception

The self-image is an extremely strong influence on the way in which a person views the world. Self-image has been defined as the way in which a person sees himself as a separate, objective being. There has been considerable controversy in the psychological literature about the way in which a person sees himself and the way he is perceived by other people.

Kelly (1955) described the concept of person perception in which one person sees another. He suggested four criteria for successful person perception:

1. Distinctiveness. The person's behaviour is different from other people's behaviour, for example, if one person in a group is aggressive and the others are not, this may indicate that aggressiveness is a characteristic of that person's personality.
2. Consistency over time. To judge that a certain behaviour is caused by a particular person, it must be observed at various times, and not just once.
3. Consistency over place. The observed characteristic should be observed in various places.
4. Consensus. There should be some agreement with other people on the person's characteristics.

Bias

Bias can occur if the above criteria for perceiving another person are not met. This can take several forms, for example, *actor/observer difference*. The way in which someone perceives themself is different from the way in which that person observes other people doing exactly the same thing. If one describes oneself in a situation, one tends to attribute one's behaviour to the *situation*. However, if one is observing someone else's behaviour, one tends to attribute their actions to their *personality*, not the situation. In judging others, people often fail to take into account the situation, and ascribe their behaviour to their personality. This is sometimes called *attributional bias*.

People rarely bother to analyse behaviour over time, and this can lead to two principle biases, namely, first impressions and recency effects. *First impressions* tend to colour how one sees people on future occasions. One tends only to see behaviour that is consistent with one's original diagnosis. In the case of *recency effects*, judgement is affected, more unusually, by the way in which people last behaved.

A fourth type of bias is that of *generalisation* from one situation, in which a behaviour has been seen to another. Thus it is difficult to assess a person's personality in various situations.

Fallacy of pluralistic ignorance is another form of bias. There is a tendency to assume the attitude, "I'm right and everyone else is wrong." It is easy not to ask for other people's opinions. When someone looks at a person, he affects how that person behaves. However, different people can affect a person in many different ways.

Stereotyping or labelling is another bias in which there is a strong inbuilt mechanism that classifies people according to stereotypes. Category labels are applied to groups of people, such as social class, skin colour, age, race and dress.

When these category labels are applied, a systematic distortion is imposed that:

1. Over-emphasises inter-group differences.
2. Under-emphasises intra-group differences.

It is not allowed for that people might be different within each category.

The implicit personality theory of bias tends to assume that certain personality characteristics go together, for example, kindness, humorousness and intelligence. People also tend to fill in gaps, for example, someone is seen for a short time, a limited amount of knowledge about them is gained, and then a personality is built up from this limited information.

From these biases it is easy to see that the way in which people are judged is susceptible to all types of errors and can lead to all types of disagreement. These influences have a considerable effect on the way in which video recordings are perceived, and these biases should be remembered when using video for assessment purposes.

Factors influencing assessment of video recordings

The following factors have been found to influence the accuracy of assessments of video recordings:

1. People from different social backgrounds, countries and educational abilities have been found to make substantially different judgements of video recordings.
2. The time at which the judgement is made, and in particular the amount of time that has elapsed since the recording can alter reliability.

3. Observer characteristics, such as whether male or female, experienced or naive of psychological theories, similar or dissimilar to the subject in terms of culture, have all been found to effect reliability.
4. Observer drift. The standards an observer uses can change over time. The observer's criteria used for assessment may not be the same at the end of a series of assessments as at the beginning.
5. The order of presentation of recordings can effect the reliability of assessments, as previous recordings can effect the way later ones are assessed.
6. Fatigue has been clearly found to effect reliability if the assessment sessions are lengthy.
7. The accuracy of assessment of video recordings is also effected if the observer has any background information on the person being recorded.
8. The assessors need adequate time to make their assessment.
9. The accuracy of assessments are affected if the assessors making the analysis do not clearly understand the method of analysis being used.

Clinical issues

The practical usefulness of video is that it can provide an exact, immediate record of a person's interaction. Since much of social behaviour is automatic, the opportunity to get feedback on one's performance is an important component of a behaviour change programme. However, recent reviews of literature relating to the clinical use of video feedback have struck a cautious note regarding its therapeutic efficacy, and there appears to be an increasing awareness that video feedback is not inevitably therapeutic.

Client reactivity

One of the commonest recorded consequences of the interaction between people and video equipment is that a wide range of clients find it anxiety-provoking. Consequently, a worsening of symptoms has been reported, for example, schizophrenics have been known to become more bizarre in their behaviour. In these literature reviews, one can find an increasing diversity of the effects of video feedback. This is a complex area beyond the scope of this book (the reader is advised to see Trower and Kiely (1983) for an enlightening explanation of the cognitive processes involved, including the classic attribution and self-awareness theories, and for a general review of the research in this area).

The effect of video recording on an individual is a crucial consideration if the technique is to be considered for use. Client reactivity does not always occur but the effect of video on the participants should be considered closely. Reactivity has been noted in many diverse ways, such as change of voice tone, gestures, or the client referring directly to the camera. Research seems to point to children adapting more quickly than adults to being recorded. Also, there seems to be less reactivity among people in larger groups than among individuals participating in smaller ones. Other factors possibly associated with client reactivity include social and economic status.

Randall (1976) in his study of middle- and working-class mothers found that working-class mothers verbalised significantly less with their children during observation, while there was no effect noticed with middle-class mothers. It has been found with psychiatric clients that people with compulsive traits are more likely to report feeling inhibited when they are being recorded than people without those traits. However, client reactivity to video recording tends to be individually specific and it is difficult to be precise about how any individual will respond.

Reactive responses can often be clustered together and labelled as nervousness, for example, but it is possible that reactivity could intensify the characteristics that have brought the individual to the therapy session. It may be necessary to exclude someone from video recording sessions if client reactivity is too severe.

It should be stressed that this reactivity to the use of video techniques does not always occur and that some research has reported no change. Assessment of an individual's reactivity should be undertaken to decide whether someone is unable to benefit from the use of video techniques. Clients should not be excluded from the potential benefits of using video because of labels such as being "paranoid" or having "brain damage". The decision to include a potentially reactive client will depend on an assessment of: the *expected degree of reactivity*, the *client's level of co-operation*, and the *ability of the therapist to provide effective support*.

Methods of reducing client reactivity

Preparation Preparation of all the prospective participants should begin with an attempt to obtain their informed consent to participation. This serves two purposes: it educates the prospective client about what they are going to experience; and it provides an opportunity to gain information about their potential reactivity to video recording.

Familiarisation activities   The participant should be acquainted with the equipment, place of use and the people who will use the equipment before the video session commences. Thus the clients can be allowed to handle the equipment and observe it in operation, although this familiarisation should not automatically include the clients viewing recorded tapes, since in some cases this could increase reactivity.

Adaptation   It has been noted by several researchers that a change in the level of reactivity occurs over time and that a certain amount of time should be allowed after recording has begun to allow the client to get used to his surroundings. This technique is not used with all clients, but it can be helpful.

Minimisation of input of the recording process   Placing the camera, microphone and technician out of the direct view of the client is extremely important. Whenever possible, the camera should be operated from behind a one-way screen. Microphones should be sited as inconspicuously as possible.

If the presence of the camera and operator cannot be avoided, additional precautions are necessary to minimise their influence. All movements should be kept to a minimum through planning the therapy session beforehand. Clients should not be involved in any responsibility for organising the recording session.

Programming strategies   There are two commonly used techniques. The first is that of delay, in which the therapist does not begin actual recording until some time after the clients believe that recording has started. Second, the therapist discards the initial video recordings taken of the therapy session.

Attention management   Here, the therapist increases the amount of information the client is receiving so that his attention is focused away from the operation of the equipment involved.

Direct influence   The therapist can use techniques such as active listening, discussion, reassurance and feedback to reduce the clients' reactivity to the video equipment. Counselling techniques may be necessary for very reactive clients.

Body image

A very strong factor, possibly the most influential affecting a person's view of the world and his own behaviour, is his self-image, or his awareness of and perceptions of himself as a separate objective being. Despite the importance individuals attach to their body image, it appears that many people have surprisingly inaccurate perceptions. Confrontation, the reflection of information about the self from outside sources, has long been used as a technique in psychological interventions. Video-tape recordings provide people with an opportunity to observe how they appear to others.

   This can have a potentially profound impact on an individual's perception of himself and the therapist should be aware that the client can undergo severe personal stress as a result.

Introducing clients to the use of video

Berger (1978) listed four ways to introduce clients to therapy sessions involving the use of video equipment.

"The thing speaks for itself"

The very presence of video equipment usually illicits a question from the client to which the therapist can honestly respond. The client who does not immediately have anything to say can be queried for his reactions to the presence of the equipment in an attempt to relieve his fears, and to work through any anxiety he may have.

"Fait accompli"

The video equipment is turned on just before the client enters the session. When the client enters the room, the therapist says something which indicates that he feels the client is ready to use video equipment.

Advance notice

The therapist asks the client to agree to use video in a following session. In doing this, the therapist stresses the therapeutic value of the technique.

Although most clients readily agree, the therapist can use the client's reaction, whether it be negative or positive, as material for further exploration.

Seduction

Over a period of time the therapist may make suggestions regarding the use of video in the therapy sessions. This gives the client the opportunity to work through his anxieties while maintaining some sense of control.

Most clients soon become accustomed to the equipment once video is introduced into the therapy session, though it is essential to remember the likelihood of any individual reacting to the video session.

Therapist's role in video feedback sessions

The first major role is to *direct attention* to cues which the therapist feels are important in the client's performance. This can be achieved in a variety of ways. First, by a non-committal statement to open up discussion, such as, "I notice you didn't look at me when you were talking". Second, comparison to indicate possible motivation can be used, for example, "Whenever you walked into a room and met someone you averted eye contact and shuffled nervously".

Direct interpretation can also be used by the therapist, who might say: "It appears to me that whenever we talk about your family you get agitated and abusive. What is it that makes you react in this way?"

A wide range of therapeutic interventions are available to the therapist within this framework for use at this stage.

The second major role of the therapist is that of *educator*. Besides directing the client's attention to relevant cues, the therapist has an educative function, which consists of the therapist teaching the client to self-reflect on his behaviour and to consider how his social behaviour can become more effective. This is done primarily through modelling as well as by the simple act of observing his own behaviour.

Care should be taken with clients who are extremely depressed, or those who have had a history of depression and/or suicide attempts. It is possible that these clients may use their reflected image to validate their extremely poor self-image, and their desire to kill themselves *could* increase.

In the case of psychotic clients, the therapist should be reasonably certain that the acute phase of the episode has subsided before using video. It has also been found that paranoid or acutely depressed clients should not be given a lot of time of mull over the idea of being video-taped in order to avoid excessive anxiety or paranoia. When introduced promptly and in a manner which emphasises the likelihood that it will be a pleasant and therapeutic experience, most clients look forward to being video-taped. They should then be involved rapidly to quell any budding suspicions.

The first feedback session should incorporate a host of positive (but realistic) feedback which will result in an increased desire for further involvement.

Video techniques and social skills training

The client's emotional, behavioural and cognitive systems need to be assessed before beginning any video-based social skills training programmes. Video-tape can be used not just to diagnose a client's overall social skills deficits, but it is especially beneficial in pinpointing the specific skills in which the client is deficient. Many assessment procedures have been developed using video for this purpose.

After the assessment procedure is complete, a video-based social skills training programme usually involves several specific intervention procedures. This procedure is along the lines of the techniques previously discussed, including the reduction of the client's social anxiety, the demonstration of effective social performance, and altering the client's cognitions.

However, within this general framework, there is considerable opportunity for therapists to implement specific and sometimes quite innovative techniques that are applicable to each individual client.

Video techniques and social anxiety

When anxiety is inhibiting or interfering with the expression of inter-personal skills, therapy usually involves a variation of systematic desensitisation.

Technique 1 Scenes involving inter-personal situations are typed onto cards that can be sorted into hierarchy from the least to most threatening situation. These scenes can be tailored to reflect the areas in which the client is experiencing difficulty.

Beginning with the least threatening scenes, the client observes video models behaving effectively in each of the social situations. Afterwards, the client rehearses each of the scenes while being coached, video-taped and reinforced by the therapist. As he begins to feel more relaxed and is responding more effectively to some of the easiest scenes, progressively more difficult situations are attempted. The client will move on to progressively more difficult scenes only when he has successfully completed each scene.

Another method of reducing the client's social anxiety is to present models on video-tape whose behaviour is clearly shown to be reinforced after engaging in the anxiety-provoking behaviour. Observing other people engaging and being rewarded in certain social behaviours often makes clients feel less anxious about performing the behaviour themselves. Many clients have been taught to overcome various phobias using video-taped self-desensitisation programmes.

Simple treatment of anxieties is insufficient when clients demonstrate true deficits of social skills. Teaching new social skills utilises one of a combination of strategies and techniques broadly based on modelling. Currently, there are few commercial videos available in Britain that provide appropriate models of social behaviour. Therefore, therapists must rely on their own resources to develop video-taped models behaving appropriately in particular social situations.

In developing such programmes, a number of variables converge to enhance the effectiveness of the video modelling procedures: only *appropriate* social behaviour should be presented; the most *relevant* aspects of the modelled behaviour should be emphasised, for example, by using freeze-frame, close-ups, zoom lens shots, etc., to emphasise the appropriate components of the desired behaviour; third, in choosing models, the characteristics previously outlined affecting model effectiveness should be considered; and, finally, coping models should be presented if clients are especially anxious.

Technique 2: The job interview This technique has been used effectively with many client groups, for example, it has been used as part of vocational rehabilitation programmes for prisoners and psychiatric clients. It provides an example of the type of use to which video techniques can be put as part of social skills training.

Learning interview skills in this setting gives feedback to each client about how they are perceived by a specific group of people in their environment. Video feedback to the interviewees of their performance maximises the effectiveness of this procedure. Job interviews are a frequent problem when rehabilitating people into the community, and this type of social interaction can be applied to many client groups. The job interview is also a revealing role play even for these clients who are not contemplating job change or who are still unemployed, since it can portray feelings of alienation, frustration and impotence.

Speas (1979) used four instructional techniques to teach interviewing skills to former prison inmates. The most effective of her four techniques was a combined technique using modelling, role play and video feedback. The areas she focused on in the interview were: explaining oneself, answering problem questions, enthusiasm, appropriate appearance and mannerisms, and opening and closing the interview.

A commonly used technique for the job interview is as follows: each client completes a generalised application for employment; a 20-minute video of an interview is presented to the client; interviews are modelled demonstrating desirable interview behaviour; the client group is divided into dyads for role plays; for the first 10 to 15 minutes one client plays the interviewer, the other the interviewee; they swop roles for an equivalent time; after the role play, both therapist and peers provide feedback during a one-hour session while reshowing video-taped recordings of the simulated interview; the group meets for six- to eight-weekly sessions focusing on various aspects of the interview at each session, such as non-verbal behaviour, level of assertion, body posture, and open and closed questions; at the end of the six or eight sessions, a final winding up session explores the change in behaviour during the therapy, and follow-up programmes are established.

All members of the group are encouraged to comment on and make constructive criticism of all members of the group performance, including their own. In addition, homework is provided for each client at the end of each session to facilitate generalisation of learning.

Video techniques to accentuate aspects of client behaviour

With a little technical "magic" and imagination, variations in the presentation of video models and the client's self-observation can achieve additional therapeutic effects.

Printed overlays and audio-dubbing   Printed video subtitles and narration added to the audio track can help to focus the client's attention on relevant aspects of the desired behaviour. Audio-dubbing is more appropriate when dealing with visual behaviour.

Video vignettes   These are developed by the therapist to illustrate difficult social situations. After watching the vignette, the clients are asked to respond as if they were actually in the situation. Combined with coaching, instruction and reinforcement, these vignettes provide an extremely effective behavioural change method, principally because the client's level of self-belief increases as they realise they are performing successfully in difficult (although simulated) social situations. Therapists should develop a variety of vignettes suitable for the most commonly occurring social difficulties they encounter.

Accelerated or decelerated playback   By observing video feedback in slow motion, clients can more readily see, for instance, their subtle non-verbal cues, and the reactions of others. Alternatively, accelerated playback is especially helpful in demonstrating fidgeting and nervous or repetitive body actions, as well as the use of gestures.

Freeze frame   The pause mode on most recorders can isolate a specific expression, for example, for analysis.

Serial viewing   It may not always be apparent to clients that change has occurred during a social skills training programme. Such improvements can be demonstrated dramatically by editing together small segments of video tape of the client over a period of time.

Inter-personal process recall   This technique improves the effectiveness of video self-confrontation, and clients are video-taped interacting in a simulated social interaction with another person. During playback, the therapist asks the client to verbalise what they were thinking, feeling or imagining at various points of the interaction. The objective is to make the client conscious of their covert and overt behaviour during the social interactions, and to analyse whether such behaviours are functional or dysfunctional (Figure 8.1).

Practical issues

Contrary to the worldwide standardisation of cinema and audio-tape equipment, video recording equipment is characterised by a remarkable lack

Figure 8.1   Techniques Highlighting Aspects of Client Behaviour

Desired outcome	Technique
1. Focus client's attention on desired behaviour	Printed overlay, audio dubbing
2. Illustrate difficult social situations	Video vignettes
3. Focus client's attention on special non-verbal behaviour	Accelerated or decelerated playback
4. Isolate specific client response for analysis	Freeze frame
5. Demonstrate behavioural change over time	Serial viewing
6. Give the client increased awareness of covert and overt behaviour	Inter-personal process recall

of standardisation. A number of different systems and standards exist that are usually incompatible. This is obviously important for video users who want to exchange or circulate tapes, and should be considered when purchasing video equipment. This section will review a number of technical aspects of video operation which should be borne in mind when using video techniques as part of social skills training.

Lighting

Adequate lighting is essential for video recording. Video cameras are extremely light-sensitive. Even under poor lighting conditions, acceptable black and white recordings are possible. In fact, too much light may result in "flat" recordings with poor contrast. A smaller f-stop and the normal/low light switch provided by most cameras can be used in poor light conditions. Unfortunately, both options have severe drawbacks. When using the low light switch, the light reaching the video tube inside the camera is electronically amplified. This often results in a "grainy" picture and it can distort the colours when recording in colour. Small f-stops have their problems too.

The f-stop affects the amount of light reaching a sensitive device in the camera and also the depth of field and the depth of focus. If an object moves towards and away from the camera, the distance it can move while staying in focus becomes smaller with each small f-stop chosen. Thus, in these situations, the focus must be adjusted constantly. This makes recording difficult, if not impossible, in a therapeutic situation.

Generally, the depth of field becomes larger with larger f-stops, and smaller with smaller f-stops. Factors such as the focal length, and the light-sensitivity of the lens system affect this. Larger f-stops tend to reduce the contrast of the picture. It is usually advisable to adjust the amount of light so that medium f-stops can be chosen and the low-light switch does not have to be used.

Wrongly placed lighting can result in recordings in which the important features, such as the client's face, are covered by shadows and hence largely invisible. Too much light or shadow may be quite unsatisfactory if a person is unable to recognise himself. Proper placement of lighting is not usually a severe problem if a prepared room is available. Care should be taken from the earliest stage if such a room has to be designed for video recording, so that it is equipped with appropriate facilities such as movable spotlights and carefully arranged ceiling lights, if possible with dimmers that allow control of the amount of light at any one time.

Appropriate lighting is especially important if further analysis of the recording is planned, for example, analysis of eye contact and facial expressions.

Sound recording

This is a difficult area in video recording since microphones tend to record disturbing sounds such as moving furniture or street noise. As a first step to good sound recording, it is advisable not to use the built-in camera microphone, since they tend to record noises when the focal length of the camera is manipulated. Furthermore, the microphones are not usually of a superior quality. While it is possible to zoom a far-away scene optically nearer to the viewer, it cannot be sound-recorded with a built-in microphone.

An external microphone may be placed near the sound source, independently of the location of the video camera or recording equipment, and it is often better to use one if high sound quality is required. There are several different types of external microphones: high or low impedence, condensor or dynamic, and levalier or stationary. In addition, different microphones can have different directional characteristics.

High/low impedence Generally, low impedence microphones are preferred as they allow for long cable connections, up to 200 metres or more. They are also usually of superior recording quality. Humming can occur with high impedence microphones, even when used with very short cables.

Dynamic/condensor The basic difference between these two types of microphone is that dynamic microphones use a "mechanical" basis for the transfer of sound energy into electrical signals, and condensor microphones use an electrical system. The comparison between them is often difficult to assess. Dynamic microphones are usually less expensive and more robust. On the other hand, condensor microphones are more sensitive to dust, humidity and being dropped, although sound quality is usually superior. Unfortunately, this high sensitivity may lead to overload and damage when exposing the microphone to very intense sounds or noise. Finally, condensor microphones need an external power supply via a battery or external power supply unit.

Dynamic microphones are usually preferred in situations in which the microphone is exposed to problematic or extreme surroundings, while condensor microphones are more useful in situations where high sound quality is needed.

Levalier/stationary Both dynamic and condensor microphones are available as levalier or "collar" microphones and as stationary microphones. The decision of which type to use will depend on the recording situation, the person to be recorded, and the purpose of recording.

Levalier microphones are attached to the clothes of the person, near his mouth. Sound quality is usually good if people are sitting down for an interview or discussion, and, to a large extent, free of disturbance. However, some people have a tendency to fiddle with the microphone or the cable when speaking or listening, which can result in recording distortion. This is a problem if people are nervous or if children are likely to walk around a lot. These have the advantage that, whatever happens, they are near the speaker and guarantee high quality sound. Portable transmitters have been developed to replace the need for cables but this transmitting process is usually quite sensitive to external influences, such as nearby radio stations and unshielded cables. Transmitters have to be attached to the person and this can lead to problems of obtrusiveness.

In many situations, stationary microphones are to be preferred. They can often be placed unobtrusively near the interaction. The crucial factor then becomes the directional characteristics of the microphone. Directional characteristics influence the sensitivity of the microphone to sounds coming from different directions. A distinction can be made between the following characteristics: spheric, cardioid, super-cardioid, eight, super uni-directional (Figure 8.2).

Spheric or cardioid characteristics might be used for group discussion if it is possible to place the microphone above or between the speakers. Cardioid or super-cardioid may be selected if a single speaker is to be recorded who is not too far away from the microphone (under five metres). A uni-directional microphone can be used for a speaker who is further away than five metres. A microphone with "eight" characteristics can be used for recording two speakers facing each other in an interview situation.

Uni-directional microphones have the major advantage that high quality recording of a single person can be obtained even if he is quite a distance away from the microphone, but there are severe problems if the speaker moves around and gets lost by the microphone. Therefore, uni-directional microphones should be used only if it can be ensured that the speaker will not move around much, or if an assistant is available who can follow the speaker with the microphone.

Some practical precautions for high quality sound can be taken independently of the choice of microphone. First, microphones should be placed as near as possible to the sound source. A windshield is mandatory when recording in the open air, and furthermore, a solid tripod should carry the microphone whenever possible, or at least it should be placed on a felt pad to prevent vibration or floor noise.

Manual gain control should be preferred rather than automatic gain control whenever possible, since automatic gain control is not able to distinguish between noise and the signal to be recorded. In silent passages, automatic gain control tries to amplify the arriving signal which, in speech pauses, tends to be pure noise or simply humming. During pauses, this noise will become louder as the automatic control adjusts amplification. Then, when someone starts to speak again, it will be too loud for the automatic gain control level set during the pause. Thus, the signal is amplified only after some seconds, which means that, initially, the speech will be recorded at too high a level. The reverse also applies.

Figure 8.2   Directional Characteristics of Microphones (Adapted from Figure 7.2 by H.G. Wallblot in Dowrick & Biggs (1983) and reprinted by permission of John Wiley & Sons Ltd)

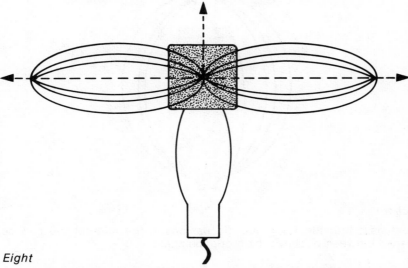

Eight

Best use: To record two speakers when both people's speech is to be recorded, eg an interview

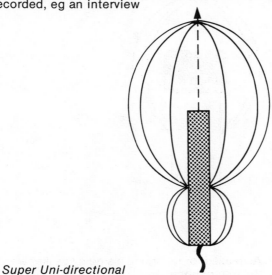

Super Uni-directional

Best use: Recording a single person who is more than 6 metres away. High quality recording possible. Difficulty in recording if person moves about, as 'lost' by microphone

Figure 8.2   (continued)

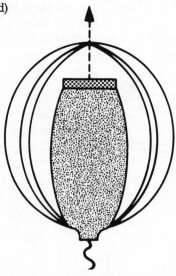

Spheric

Best use: Suitable for group discussions if the microphone can be placed between or above the group members

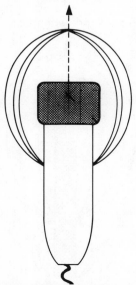

Cardioid

Best use: As for spheric. Also used for recording a single speaker who is less than 6 metres from the microphone

(continued)

Figure 8.2   (continued)

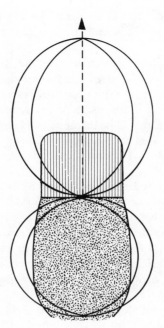

Super-cardioid

Best use: Single speaker who is less than 6 metres away from the microphone

A test recording can be taken with manual gain control to obtain the optimum level. Too low a level results in humming, while too high a level results in a distortion of the signal to be recorded. Unfortunately, some video recorders do not have a manual gain control and this is an important consideration when purchasing a recorder, if high sound quality is required.

Using a camera

A camera should always be placed as unobtrusively as possible. Several factors influence camera placement, for example, if the client's facial expression is important then the camera has to face the person, but tele- or zoom lenses can be employed so that the camera is placed a reasonable distance away.

In the case of dyadic interaction, the therapist must consider whether only the client is to be recorded or both people are involved in the interaction.

Obviously, the camera placement will be affected by this decision. If only one camera is available the choice is limited, especially if both members are to be recorded.

The camera can be placed in various positions, for example, on a tripod, wall-mounted in a corner of a room or mounted on a ceiling. Some of these placements require the use of remote control devices to operate the camera.

Zoom lenses can cause problems, as someone other than the therapist is needed to operate the camera. The therapist will know best what to record but it will be difficult for him to communicate during the recording, if he is involved in the interaction. Important information about the interaction can be lost in this way.

It should always be considered how changes in the camera angle or zooming can alter the interpretation of events. For example, it is a well known fact in cinema and television that a person will appear larger, more important and more powerful if the camera looks up at the person, instead of facing him directly. In most cases, a fixed camera should be preferred to minimise this distortion. This is especially true if scientific behavioural analysis from the recordings is planned, or if research is being conducted on the information collected.

There are several technical methods of making the camera position unobtrusive, one of which is the one-way mirror. These are usually found in specially built studios. The amount of light is an important consideration when using these mirrors and consequently the cameras used have to be fairly light-sensitive. This is especially important with colour recording in order to prevent wrong colours and colour distortion.

Even without one-way mirrors it is usually easy to camouflage a camera by using the natural environment, for example hiding it in a bookshelf. When taking recordings in the open air, there are numerous opportunities to hide the camera and equipment, especially if powerful zoom lenses are used. Specially designed angle lenses are also available for certain purposes.

Split-screen recording involves using two cameras which are then combined by a video mixer. Technically, this procedure is fairly easy and inexpensive.

It is important that the camera work should be done by those who are professionally responsible. It is extremely difficult in practice for assistants who are untrained in social or medical sciences to make appropriate recordings. The belief that training in electronics is necessary before operating a camera should be strongly resisted. Recordings made by the therapist may be less technically sophisticated but there are benefits in clinical relevance. Some therapists allow group members to be involved in operating the video equipment. This tends to increase group cohesion and, despite a loss of technical refinements, can lead to considerable additional information about how the participants perceive their interactions.

Using cameras in natural settings poses a considerable set of problems. These recordings are frequently characterised by interruptions, blurring and many changes of camera position as well as the intrusion into the picture of irrelevant objects or people who are not involved in the study. There are some general principles that can be applied to minimise these difficulties. For example, the therapist should be very clear about why he is carrying out the recording in a natural setting, and he should certainly consider the impact he is likely to have on the environment, and to passersby.

Many therapists wish to record an established group in its usual setting, such as a family at home, a class in a school or patients on a hospital ward. It is essential that contact and trust have been established between the therapist and the group in question before video recording commences. It is usually necessary for many visits without video equipment to be made, so that this trust can be established and insight obtained into the normal functioning of the group.

Editing

Editing of recordings is often desirable, especially for demonstration tapes or for self-modelling. Editing during the actual recording by selectively starting and stopping the recorder is often difficult, and so it is normal for tapes to be edited afterwards. Video-editing is more difficult than audio-editing because it cannot be achieved simply with scissors and slicing tape, but has to be carried out electronically via a copying process. Two recorders are the minimum necessary for editing. The original recording has to be of good quality because some quality loss is inevitable in the process of editing.

The "rough editing" technique is characterised by copying the selected scene onto a second recorder without employing special editing facilities. The transition between such rough edits appears on the video monitor as short breakdowns of the picture. Most recorders now provide the user with a facility that allows quality comparable to electronic editing. This is achieved by the fact that the tape is rolled back slightly when the stop button is used; when the machine is switched to "record" the edited scene follows the other one consecutively.

Electronic editing is necessary if very high quality edits are required with exactly defined edits between consecutive scenes. This requires electronic editing devices.

Storage of video tapes

Video tapes should be stored away from extremes of temperature and dampness. The atmosphere should be as dust-free as possible, and the room in which the tapes are stored should be protected from strong magnetic or electrical fields. Video tapes do not last forever even when stored under ideal conditions, and picture deterioration will eventually occur even if the tapes are never played. Noticeable loss of quality will occur after about 100 replays. Precious material which is likely to be extensively used should therefore be copied from the original tape before being used. Tapes for permanent storage can be recorded on celluloid, but this is expensive.

Cataloguing

Many extensive collections of valuable clinical material are practically useless because inadequate cataloguing leads to inadequate retrieval of material. The time to start cataloguing is the day the first video tape is purchased. Each blank video tape acquired should be given an individual tape number which it should keep until it is disposed of (it is important to wipe clinical tapes clean before disposing of them). Each recording should be given an individual number, as should each programme edited from a recording. Each tape should have its own record card stored in a central file indicating what has been recorded on the tape, the recording number and the programme number.

Planning a recording

The therapist should decide the purpose of the recording and the specific aspects of the recording that need preservation. One method of doing this is to use the following components:

1.   Frequency. How often does a component occur, such as making eye contact with another person?

2. Latencies. The length of time it takes an individual to respond to a situation, for example, latency of response in answering a question.
3. Intensity. The degree of magnitude of the response, for example, loudness of voice when expressing an emotion.
4. Duration. The length of time a behaviour continues.
5. Density. The amount of time devoted to a particular class of behaviour, for example, the amount of time spent touching other people.
6. Sequences. The order in which social acts occur, for example, turn-taking in conversations.

A more precise idea of how the recording should be made will be obtained if the therapist evaluates the likely interaction in relation to these categories and where special attention to detail is required.

The problems of recording are compounded when more than two people are involved. It is rarely possible to make individual recordings of each participant as well as the group as a whole. Even if it were feasible, there remains a problem of how to relate the separate records to each other. In general, it is difficult to make tapes which satisfy more than one aim; multi-purpose recordings should be avoided whenever possible.

The planning of a recording differs if it is for applied purposes such as clinical teaching. Here the tapes need to be psychologically appropriate rather than comprehensive. Such recordings benefit from the use of close-ups, fading from one image to another, and other techniques.

Video is not a difficult medium to use if the therapist is aware of the technical basics, the potential problems and the technical and practical possibilities of the tool. However, although video can be a powerful mechanism for research in clinical practice, it is often used without much thought. It is important before purchasing equipment that the use to which it is to be put should be assessed, and that equipment is bought with that purpose in mind.

Ethical issues

Video recording of clients raises several ethical issues that need to be addressed by all practising physicians. The principle area of concern involves protecting the individual rights of people involved in video recording. Unfortunately, this is a developing area and there is no clear consensus between various countries in deciding what the rights of individuals are and the procedures for safeguarding them. The main risks involved are violations of privacy and confidentiality. The following guidelines are criteria developed by the author for use in practical video-recording sessions associated with social skill training.

Consent

A cardinal rule of any video recording of any subject should be that in no circumstances should a video recording be made without the client's prior knowledge and, so far as he can give it, his agreement.

A systematic, formal recording of the client's agreement to video recording should be recorded in writing. The only exception to this procedure is when the tape is going to be shown to the client alone for therapeutic purposes and is then immediately erased: in this case alone, prior verbal consent would probably suffice. Written consent should always be obtained before video recording beings.

Many therapists back up written consent with verbal consent, recorded at the beginning of the first recording. This is included as a recommendation in the Royal College of Psychiatrists' *Guidelines on Ethical Problems of Video Tape and Other Audio-Visual Recordings in Psychiatry*, which is warmly recommended to clinicians as a guide.

A standardised consent form should be used. At present there is no standard formula since the contents may require adaption to local needs, depending on how the tapes are to be used (Figure 8.3).

If at any time either during or after the recording the client withdraws his consent, this *must* be accepted. The tape must be wiped clean and no further recordings should be undertaken.

If, for any reason, the client is unable to consent, it is essential that written consent be obtained from the spouse or nearest relative. Examples would be a child under 16 years of age or someone who is psychiatrically unwell. If the client later recovers or has a sixteenth birthday, he should be given the opportunity to withdraw his consent at this time. Adequate consultation with relevant agencies should be undertaken if there is any doubt about the validity of the client's consent. Recordings should not take place if consent is not available.

Figure 8.3 Example of Consent Form Suitable for Use in Social Skills Training

---

SOCIAL SKILLS TRAINING DEPARTMENT ....HOSPITAL

I .... give permission for the Social Skills Department, ... Hospital, to keep a copy of the video recordings taken of me during social skills training. I understand that the videotape(s) will only be used in my therapy sessions or for the teaching of other staff.

Signed ....

Date ....

Confidentiality

Video-tapes of clients should *never* be shown to non-professional audiences unless it is part of the therapeutic process, for example, other members of a social skills training group. Neither should they be shown to professional audiences outside the domain of the department except by members of that department, and only then provided the client's written consent has been obtained.

It is common practice with psychiatric clients for the responsible consultant psychiatrist to give consent. This concept should be extended to get the agreement of the "key worker" responsible, if that is the style of working prevalent.

Each department using video recording techniques should formulate its own code of practice. Any information about the client's consent should be catalogued. Tapes and information should be kept securely locked and should be handled only by authorised members of staff. All tapes should be erased before being thrown away.

Copyright of video tapes is a difficult area. When the recording has been made by an individual employed to make recordings, for example, a technician, then copyright would belong to the employer. However, if the making of the recording was incidental to a staff member's terms of employment (for example, a psychiatric nurse), then that person could claim copyright on the material recorded, even though the ownership of the tape rested with the employer. However, it has been widely recommended that the copyright should generally be held by the employing authority.

No individual should ever accept payment for the provision of video-tapes or copies of them. In all other circumstances, such as where tapes are to be used outside the department, the client's role should be role-played by an actor (a member of the department).

A difficult problem is whether the client has a right to view the video recording. In the author's opinion, if there is any likelihood of the client not benefitting from seeing the tape then it is wise to include a clause on the standard consent form waiving the participant's right to see the video tape. This is argued on the ground that feedback is part of the therapist's arsenal. Great care is taken with the appropriate timing to give verbal feedback to clients in other therapeutic techniques; and this applies equally to social skills training.

References

Berger M M (Editor) (1978) Video Tape Techniques in Psychiatric Training and Treatment (revised edition), Brunner, Mazel

Kelly G A (1955) The Psychology of Personal Constructs (volumes 1 and 2), Norton

Randall T A (1976) An analysis of observer influence on sex and social class differences in mother-infant interaction, Eric Roberts, edition number 114204, March

Speas C M (1979) Job-seeking interviews skills training: A comparison of four instructional techniques, Journal of Counselling Psychology, 26(5): 405–412

Trower P and Kiely K (1983) Video feedback — Help or hindrance? A review and analysis, in P W Downrick and S J Biggs (Editors), Using Video: Psychological and Social Applications, John Wiley and Sons

CHAPTER 9

EVALUATION

Priestly *et al.* (1978) have suggested that people undertaking therapy with clients should adopt a do-it-yourself attitude to the construction of workable evaluation measures. They see the purpose of evaluation as not being to produce statistically accurate research findings but to help people with problems to check on the progress they are making and to give the therapist feedback on his own performance so that it can be improved. Anything at all that serves these two purposes should be used for evaluation. Techniques should be retained for future use only if they survive the trial of common sense and the ordeal of customer approval. This approach is basically the method that will be outlined in this chapter.

Evaluation techniques are just as important as any of the other components of social skills training. Therapists need to be able to assess objectively the efficacy of their training sessions. The techniques described are practical methods that can provide evaluative feedback on a client's performance even when it may be difficult to be objective. Mahoney (1977) summarised the principal uses of data collection in making decisions about outcomes in therapy: "The most efficient therapist is sensitively tuned to the personal data of the client. He is not collecting data for the sake of scientific appearances, or because that is what is considered proper... The effective therapist uses data to guide his or her own efforts at having an impact, and — regardless of theoretical bias or procedural preference — he adjusts therapeutic strategies in tune with that feedback."

The main purpose of evaluation is to assess therapeutic outcomes. This evaluation helps both therapist and client to determine the type, direction and amount of change in behaviour demonstrated by the client during and after therapy. The data collected during training can be used to monitor whether a strategy is helping a client in the designated way, and whether a client is using the strategy accurately and systematically.

There are a number of practical reasons why it is difficult to use rigorous evaluation techniques in practical settings. The most important of these are: the realities of staff allocation, which usually make it difficult to make sufficient staff available for the procedures needed to carefully evaluate treatment effectiveness; and there may not be sufficient clients available to serve as members of a control group for group treatment evaluation.

For these and other reasons, therapists in applied settings often come to think of any systematic treatment evaluation as research — and they believe that research is something they cannot do. On the other hand, hardly any practitioner will consistently use any form of treatment in the absence of information that at least suggests that the treatment works. Unfortunately, there are a large number of limiting factors associated with casual treatment evaluations. Amongst the most important of these are that the data source is usually limited to the client's subjective reports; these may not be behaviourally accurate and are extremely susceptible to bias. In addition, if improvement has occurred, it may be due to events other than treatment that intercede between early and later client reports.

Non-treatment sources of influence in social skills training

A variety of factors occurring in social skills training can affect treatment outcome, either independently or in conjunction with the application of a particular strategy.

Influence of the therapist

The chemistry of the client—therapist relationship is reciprocal; the client and therapist are mutual sources of influence. It is possible that client changes that occur as a result of social skills training can result from non-specific aspects of the relationship with the therapist. These influences are common to most inter-personal situations and can include suggestion effects from the therapist and faith in the therapist by the client. It is possible that the therapist is actually involved in a great deal of persuasive communication to encourage the client to behave, think or feel differently.

Demand characteristics

Orne (1969) defined demand characteristics as characteristics that included any cues that influence a person's perception of his role in a particular setting. The parameters that a therapist sets at the beginning of training are likely to have influences on the whole of the therapy session, for example, if the client perceives that it is very important to complete therapy assignments systematically, and to turn up every week, and so on, then it is likely to motivate the client to complete assignments regularly and to attend conscientiously. This can easily affect treatment outcomes if these parameters are not clearly laid down.

Instructions

The client's motivation to change and work at the change process is also influenced by instructions. Clients who receive specific and detailed instructions about training strategies are more likely to use the training strategy accurately and to offer unbiased self-reports. Martinez et al. (1977) indicated that a client's behaviour can fluctuate depending on the instructions they receive and on the context or situation in which they are seen or evaluated. As has been frequently observed, part of the success of all forms of treatment can be attributed to the therapist's ability to mobilise the client's expectation of success.

Measurement activity

Reactivity can be defined as the changes in behaviour that occur as a consequence of someone observing and recording behaviour. For example, a client may be instructed to observe and record specific instances of behaviour for two weeks at the beginning of a therapy session before any treatment strategy is employed. At the end of the two weeks, decreases in the client's rate of performing that behaviour may be apparent even though the therapist has not yet implemented specific strategies to help the client reduce these behaviours. In assessing the effectiveness of therapy, the therapist should be aware of these reactive properties.

From a practical perspective, these factors are potentially contaminating sources of influence if the therapist is attempting to infer that the selected treatment strategy was the only cause of therapeutic change. This would have to be borne in mind when conclusions about the effectiveness of a strategy are being assessed.

There are a wide range of objective methods for assessing the impact of social skills training interventions. The choice of treatment evaluation method depends largely on the aims of the therapist, and the questions he wants answering. For example, the therapist may ask whether his client is now better at handling inter-personal situations than he was before treatment started. In other instances, the therapist may wish to elaborate on this question to answer whether both the client is more inter-personally skilled following intervention, and whether this improvement is definitely the result of the training intervention itself.

In addition, treatment assessment procedures are available that can permit a therapist to rigorously evaluate the effectiveness of individual or group social skills training, without the need for untreated control groups. The rest of this chapter will consider sources of information that convey objective information on a client's social functioning, and methods for interpreting the data to answer treatment evaluation questions.

Measures from which the outcome of training intervention can be determined

In any form of treatment effectiveness evaluation, the client's social behaviour must be assessed on several occasions. One of the simplest, though least rigorous, assessment methods is simply to compare the client's pre-training social skills behaviour with their social effectiveness subsequent to training. Another intervention assessment is when social skill measures are taken at different points during the training period. For effective evalutation it is always necessary to obtain measures of the client's social skills performance at various points in time.

A number of data sources can provide the therapist with important information on change in a client's social skills performance as a result of treatment. These include: *objective ratings* of a client's performance during practice social interactions in the treatment setting; *global ratings* of overall social competence obtained during practice social interactions; paper and pencil *self-report* inventories completed by the client, which describe his comfort and behaviour during social interactions; detailed *self-monitoring* information provided by the client on social behaviour outside the therapy setting; *direct observation* of the effectiveness of the client's social behaviour in the natural environment.

Obviously, many of the techniques used in the assessment of the client can be repeated at later stages to evaluate the client's response to the training programme.

Molecular techniques

One of the purposes of the initial assessment is to identify behavioural skill components that a client fails to exhibit or to exhibit appropriately during the practice interactions. The aim is to identify the client's specific skills deficits. One direct way to assess the impact of training intervention is to repeat the same practice interactions at later times and, thereby, to determine whether the client now exhibits those behaviours that had previously been considered deficient. It is important that the assessment situations used in these later evaluation interactions are comparable to those used in the initial assessment. For example, if eight role-play scenes are used during initial pre-training client assessment, the therapist will need to use these same role-play scenes, or comparable scenes, for the later evaluations.

A second requirement for molecular assessment is that the same behavioural components are measured objectively on each occasion. One way of accomplishing this is by rating the client's interactions for the presence or frequency of each behavioural component. If the therapist rates a baseline assessment interaction on, for example, eight component behaviours, and later on in the intervention rates client performance in comparable interactions on the same eight components, it is possible to identify change more objectively in any of them.

A behaviour change analysis can be conducted on virtually any social skill component provided that it can be rated from the client's performance.

One way to incorporate objective evaluation of skills competency into an ongoing intervention is by rating a client's performance during the behavioural rehearsal or practice interactions that are already part of each training session. This is a widely used approach in social skills training.

The only cost to obtaining this objective information on the intervention success is by having an observer rate the client's practice at each session, or by using video techniques to enable later playback of the social interaction.

Molar techniques

By rating a client's practice during simulated role-plays, semi-structured or unstructured interactions, it is possible for the therapist to determine objectively whether a client exhibits specific individual component behaviours that comprise a socially skilled performance of an interaction. For example, at the end of a social skills training-programme focusing on difficulties in communicating, the therapist might rate the behaviour of a client during an eight-minute conversation with a partner and determine that all the trained components are present in the client's interaction. All of these components are being performed at a much more effective level than they were during a comparable eight-minute assessment conversation that had been conducted before training took place. Does this confirm that the client is now a skilled conversationalist, at least in a practice session?

The molecular-molar model of social skills states that to achieve a final, desired goal, each of the molecular behaviours that comprise the skilled performance must be taught. Therefore, one would expect that if a client exhibits all the necessary behavioural components of that skill in his handling of an interaction, the client will also be judged favourably on the global, molar skill. This is an assumption, the validity of which must be checked empirically. One aspect of the validation process is to demonstrate that when an individual engages in a set of learnt behaviours, that person is then more proficient in the global or overall skill that was the original purpose of training.

This aspect of evaluation seeks to relate change in specific behaviours to change in overall social functioning. Without such confirmation there is the potential risk that information might change certain discreet behaviours, but leave the client fundamentally unchanged in the overall skill that was the original target for intervention.

Therapists have often asked an observer to rate not only the occurrence or frequency of specific behavioural skill components during client rehearsal, but also to evaluate how assertive the client behaves, based on a global judgement. Whenever possible, this judgement should be made by someone other than the therapist, since the therapist's global judgement of the client's overall competency in a practice interaction is likely to be biased.

Some social skills therapists have a co-therapist who undertakes role-plays with the client and rates the overall skill shown by the client during the completed interaction. These ratings can be made by asking the co-therapist to complete rating scales, such as an anchored seven-point scale, to describe the client's effectiveness in the interaction. In a conversational training programme, partners could be asked to rate the client's overall performance from extremely poor (score = 1) to extremely good (score = 7) on such dimensions as conversational pleasantness, ease of interaction, the amount of interest shown by the client and partner, and overall conversational ability of the client as assessed by the role-play partner.

Methods of evaluation

There are several methods a therapist and client can use to measure progress towards desired outcomes. Techniques commonly used include: interviews, self-monitoring, self-report inventory, role-playing and observation.

Interviews

The interview is very useful for gathering information about the client's problems and for defining client goals. The interview can also be used to evaluate the degree to which these target behaviours have been achieved. The procedure, as outlined in Chapter 4 on assessment techniques, can be used to structure the evaluation interview.

First, the therapist should use open-ended verbal leads to elicit the client's self-report information about progress towards the desired goals. A second way in which the interview can be used to collect information is to audio-tape randomly selected interview sessions at the beginning, middle and end of the therapeutic process. Segments of these tapes, or entire sessions, can then be rated independently by the therapist or other raters on dimensions of client verbal responses that are representative of treatment goals.

Advantages   The interview is perhaps the easiest and most convenient method of information collection available. It is a relatively "low cost" measurement method, requiring little extra time and effort from either the therapist or client. It is also a good way to elicit the client's perceptions about the value of the therapeutic process that is being undertaken.

Limitations The interview is the least systematic and standardised way to collect information, and the resulting data is usually not very precise or specific. Another disadvantage involves the reliability of client statements. If the interview is to be the only measurement method used, the therapist will have to rely totally on the client's perception of reported progress.

Guidelines for use The interview method may be more effective as an evaluation technique when used in the following way: the therapist should determine in advance some structured open-ended questions to elicit the client's description of progress that has been made. These leads should include client indications of the present extent of the problems, the severity of the problem, and how the problems are different now from those at the beginning of therapy.

These interview questions should be used at several points during the training process, and the therapist should use the leads at each of the "sampling points". Where feasible, the therapist should supplement the use of interview questions with ratings of various audio-taped interview segments on dimensions of client goal-related verbal behaviour.

Self-monitoring

Self-monitoring is a process of observing and recording aspects of one's own covert or overt behaviour. For the purpose of evaluating goal behaviours, a client uses self-monitoring techniques to collect data about the amount, frequency, percentage or duration of the target behaviours.

Advantages Self-monitoring techniques can produce information that more closely approximates the goals of training compared with measures such as inventories. The predictive validity of self-monitoring may be superior to that of other measurement methods, with the exception of direct observation. Self-monitoring can also provide a thorough and representative sample of the ongoing behaviours occurring in a client's environment. It is generally more objective than informal or verbal self-reports, primarily because it encourages people to use a structure for their recording of information. Finally, self-monitoring is flexible.

Limitations Self-monitoring should not be used by clients who cannot engage in observation, because of the intensity of their problems or because of medication difficulties. There is also considerable variability between the standard of self-monitoring, since not all clients can monitor themselves as accurately as others. Neither can all clients agree to engage in self-monitoring. Some clients may resist this as a method of information collection, as it can involve the client in considerable effort and time to make the often frequent records that are required.

As an evaluation tool, self-monitoring data is subjected to two potential problems, namely, reactivity and reliability. With reactivity, simply observing oneself and one's behaviour can produce a change in the behaviour being observed. However, one can argue that other methods of information collection, such as role-play assessments, are subject to as much reactivity as self-report procedures. Another problem associated with self-monitoring is the reliability, consistency and accuracy with which the client collects and reports the information. It has been argued that individuals do not collect and report data about themselves in a reliable manner, especially when they know that no one else will check on them. A particular problem with self-report information occurs if the target behaviours are not easily discriminable.

Both reactivity and reliability can affect the use of self-monitoring as a measurement method. The potential reactivity of self-monitoring should be maximised for therapeutic change, yet minimised for evaluation. Accurate reporting of self-monitored data is essential when used as a measurement method.

Guidelines for use   The behaviours to be observed should be defined clearly so that there is no ambiguity about what is to be observed and reported. This increases the reliability of the self-monitoring. Hawkins and Dobes (1978) have suggested three criteria for adequate response definition: objectivity, clarity and completeness.

Any definition of the target behaviour should be accompanied by examples, so that the client can discriminate between instances of the observed behaviour and instances of other behaviours.

The accuracy of a client's report may be increased by having the client record the target behaviour immediately after performing it, rather than after a delay. A third guideline is that reliability of recording can be increased when clients are trained to make accurate recordings. It is recommended that any client who is going to undertake a self-monitoring programme should practise with the therapist before attempting the procedure alone. A possible training sequence is: to give explicit *definitions and examples* of the behaviour; to give explicit *self-monitoring instructions*; to *explain* clearly to the client how any rating scales or other information collecting forms are to be used; to ask the client to *repeat* the behavioural definitions and instructions; and have the client *practise* self-monitoring on several occasions *under the therapist's supervision*.

Self-monitoring should not be too much of a chore for the client. Sometimes a reluctant client can be encouraged to self-monitor if the demands are minimal. A client can be discouraged from self-monitoring or may record inaccurately if required to record many different behaviours. The client should self-monitor at least one major target behaviour; other behaviours can be added later at the therapist's discretion. It is also advisable that clients should not attempt to self-monitor in situations where they are busy with other tasks and responses.

The therapist may need to "sell" the client on the importance of the self-monitoring process and its accuracy, as it will be necessary to motivate the client to use it. Positive reinforcement of accuracy of reporting can increase the quality of the information.

Differences between self-monitoring techniques and self-report inventories   Self-monitoring techniques differ from self-report inventory measures in several ways. First, the information monitored is more behaviourally specific, because the client is asked to record and briefly describe specific social interactions that occur naturally in the environment. These might be occasions when a client has behaved assertively or initiated a conversation with a member of the opposite sex, and so on. Usually, other specific situational information is obtained, including where the event occurred, who the other people involved were, how the client behaved or felt and what outcome was achieved.

A second difference involves the manner and time frame for which the client provides information. An inventory is completed in one sitting and the respondent retrospectively describes how he usually behaves, usually over an unspecified period of time. On the other hand, self-monitoring techniques are completed in an ongoing or continuous manner. The individual can be asked to make entries concerning each day's social interactions in a self-monitoring diary, or he can even be asked to carry a notebook for recording information about relevant situations immediately after they have been encountered.

For these reasons, self-monitoring techniques provide more specific information than self-report inventories, both in terms of the situation recorded and the time interval over which they occur. An important reason to keep the client's self-monitoring records is to better assess whether the individual's social interactions in the natural environment have occurred over the course of the therapy. In some respects, this may be the single most significant measure of treatment effectiveness that can be obtained since it provides relatively specific behavioural data direct from the natural environment.

Self-monitoring data can be analysed in several ways. When training is intended to increase the frequency with which the client initiates positive social interactions in a natural environment, the number of times that these interactions take place can be examined by the therapist.

Another type of self-monitoring data analysis takes into account the number of occasions when a learnt skill has been used successfully in proportion to the total number of occasions when the client reported wanting to use the skill. The therapist must ensure the client brings the report forms to training sessions for self-monitoring data to be systematically used in treatment evaluation. This, in turn, requires the client to conscientiously record self-monitored information on a daily basis for whatever time intervals the therapist is examining.

Information based on self-monitoring is susceptible to several forms of bias:

1. Some clients may become "fatigued" and devote less attention to recording the occurrence of details of *in vivo* social interactions, than earlier in the self-monitoring procedure. This can result in their "missing" certain interactions that they would have been recorded previously.
2. Clients can also become more proficient in self-monitoring critical *in vivo* events as they acquire more experience in this procedure, thus artificially inflating the number and the nature of these entries in their records as time progresses.
3. The client's perception of social interactions or of his own performance is likely to alter as he progresses in social skills training. This may bias the objective accuracy of the self-monitoring reports of behaviour.

In spite of these limitations, information derived from the client's self-monitoring records represents one of the most valuable ways for the therapist to evaluate the impact and generalisation of the training method.

Self-report inventories

Self-report inventories are used to measure reports of covert or overt behaviours. They should be distinguished from inventories used to measure traits.

Most paper and pencil self-report inventories of social skill yield general information on the individual's behaviour in inter-personal situations. It is difficult to learn from self-report inventory scores exactly which situations are troublesome for a given client, or how the client objectively behaves in those situations. Thus, they are of limited use in planning the exact social skills training that a client will require, or the precise skills behaviour that will need to be covered in the training.

Social skills self-report inventories yield information on how the client feels in social interactions, or how the client reports behaving, not on how the individual objectively acts. However, they can be a useful information source for the overall evaluation of intervention. Self-report inventories are usually used to obtain information about the client's objective evaluations about how he is behaving in various social situations.

Ordinarily, self-report inventories do not require the client to detail behaviour in one particular situation, but instead tap the client's perceptions of how a certain kind of situation is usually handled, or how he usually feels in that kind of situation. It is important to note that while paper and pencil inventories of social skill may be scored or quantified in an objective manner, the data source is actually the client's self-perception or description of his characteristic behaviour. Self-report scores may not always correspond to objective observations of social skills made by either the therapist's observation or even with global judgements of social competency made by an external observer. However, inventories can provide the therapist with useful, although generalised, information about a client's cognitive evaluation or personal perception of his typical behaviour in various situations.

Since social skills training assumes that the client's self-appraisals will become more positive as a result of them developing new behavioural skills, this perceptual change should be reflected by a more positive self-report inventory score.

In general, self-report inventories focus upon the client's description of his current behaviour in certain kinds of situation, and on reported feelings, cognitions or fears in certain kinds of inter-personal interactions.

Advantages The procedure is relatively easy to administer, takes little time to complete, and can help the therapist and client to identify important clinical material.

Limitations   The technique may not measure specific client behaviour or responses. The items in an inventory may not represent specific behaviours of the client in relation to his deficits. Also, the wording of the items on the inventory are sometimes subjected to a variety of interpretations.

Guidelines for use   Inventories should be selected that have been used and validated with more than one subject population, for example, those that have been assessed using psychiatric clients, college students and so on. Second, inventories should be selected in which the wordings of the items or questions is as objective as possible, and related specifically to the client's problems. An inventory may have more meaning when the terms reflected in the items are defined explicitly. Finally, inventories should be selected in which the response choices are in some way quantifiable and not ambiguous. Words such as "always", "seldom" and "hardly" should be clearly defined.

Role-play

The role-play procedure consists of scenes designed by the therapist to evaluate the client's performance of the target behaviours. For instance, role-play scenes can be created to assess the client's performance in stressful or difficult situations, or in specific problem areas. The therapist can organise the client to take part in role-plays before, during or after training. Role-play evaluations of the target behaviour may be especially useful if used in association with other evaluative techniques.

Advantages   Observing the client's behaviour in role-play may be more convenient and practical than using direct observation in the client's natural environment. Role-play assessments can help to avoid ethical problems that might be associated with mishandling of a client's "real life" performance. Role-plays conducted for a social skills training session represent an "ideal context" for making "precise assessments" of client responses to problem situations.

Limitations   Role-plays must be carefully constructed in order to have external validity, for example, to provide accurate information on how the client actually functions in his natural environment. It is possible for role-play assessment to impose "artificial constraints" on a client. The therapist must be aware that the client's performance in even a well constructed role-play test with a variety of different scenes may not correspond to how the client might behave in the actual environment.

The client's performance in a role-play test may be affected by the presence of the therapist, and the client may feel he is being observed.

Guidelines for use   A variety of role-play scenes should be developed as realistically as possible, in order to approximate the number of problem situations that occur in a client's natural environment. These scenes should approximate the real-life situations as closely as possible, to which the target or goal behaviour is directed.

The scenes used for the role-play should be developed on the basis of an individual analysis of the problematic situations being encountered by each client. Role-play assessments should replicate some of the scenes that clients have difficulty with, and have maximum relevance for their everyday life.

There should be some degree of standardisation in the role-play scenes across time, thus ensuring that evaluation of the client's behaviour is not based on changes in the nature of the scene, or in the behaviour of other persons in the scene. A client's performance in the role-play scenes can be assessed by using frequency counts, duration counts, rating scales or checklists.

Observation

A client's social behaviour in the natural environment can be directly observed when: the natural environment is observationally accessible; the social interactions of interest are naturally occurring at either a high rate or on a predictable basis; and the staff trained to conduct such observations are available.

These criteria can usually be met most successfully within residential settings or within schools. When a client's social interactions are observed in a specific setting and on one set of occasions before training occurs, then any later set of observations must also be made under the same situational conditions. The more dissimilar the situational conditions in terms of location, activity, other people present in the observational setting, time of day, and so on, and from one set of observations to the next, the less likely will be any potential for interpreting behaviour change across these different periods.

A second important factor when conducting repeated *in vivo* observations involves the client reacting to the person observing the social interactions. Presumably, the observer here serves as a cue for the client to engage in the trained skills, and it is the observer's presence in the setting that governs whether or not the individual will exhibit the socially skilled behaviour.

Ways to minimise this problem include surreptitious observation so that the client is unaware that he is being watched, or observation conducted by people other than the therapist involved in the training procedure itself, and who is therefore less likely to have this influence.

It has been suggested that information collected from all the methods outlined above should be verified or correlated with direct observation made about the client in his environment.

This observation can be obtained by two methods: the therapist can observe the client's performance in the environment, or the therapist can use significant others in the client's environment who have opportunities to observe the client in various natural situations.

Advantages   In addition to using observations by others to confirm self-report data, there may be times when it is useful to have significant others rate or evaluate subjectively the client's level of functioning, particularly at the end of therapy. This is especially true in cases where clients have altered negative behaviours but may still be mislabelled by others in their environment.

It has been noted frequently that the evaluation of behaviour by others is important independently of the behaviours that the client performs after therapy. The problem with many deviant populations is not merely their behaviour but how they are perceived by others in their environment. Thus it is possible that changing client behaviour may not necessarily alter the evaluations of individuals with whom the clients have interacted.

Limitations   Observations in the natural environment pose ethical problems. The therapist should obtain the client's permission before contacting any significant others; problems of confidentiality may arise in contacting observers. Another major drawback of using observers or of contacting other people is the possibility of raising mistrust with the client.

Because any form of social competence is a complex phenonemon, it is difficult for the therapist to infer from a single evaluation technique that significant behaviour change has occurred. Objectively rating the presence of exhibited skill components during a client's practice interaction is desirable because of its "molecular orientation". The therapist can see whether or not the client exhibits the discreet components taught during training. However, it is limited because it is based on behaviour sampled in the training session, and also because it does not directly evaluate the global adequacy of the client's skill. Obtaining a judgement of overall client social competence during practice interactions can provide subjective global evidence of improvement, but does not relate this to specific client social behaviours. It is still a measure based on performance in the practice setting rather than the natural environment.

Self-report inventories are useful for obtaining a client's self-perception of his social behaviour, but are subject to behavioural inaccuracy and situational non-specificity. Self-monitoring data and direct observation of client skills in the natural environment are excellent *in vivo* measures, but require considerable effort on the part of the client in self-monitoring or other people indirect observation. Additionally, direct *in vivo* observation procedures may be almost impossible to conduct when the client is not in a restricted setting of some kind.

Ideally, the therapist should select different evaluation techniques that are appropriate for each client and should therefore be able to detect changes in the client's social performance.

Measuring behavioural change

There are five commonly used methods for measuring the level of change in achieving target behaviours: verbal self-report; frequency counts; duration counts; rating scales; checklists. Each of these methods should be individualised for any particular client.

Verbal self-report

One measure of effectiveness of clinical outcome is the client's perception of how the therapy is progressing. An extreme form of this approach is that when a patient says there is a problem, then there is a problem; or conversely, when the client says that there is no problem, then there is no problem. Therapeutic interventions are considered to be progressing to the extent that the client reports that things are improving; conversely, therapeutic intervention may be considered to be of no value, or even to be harmful, if the client does not consider any improvement is taking place.

However, this type of information is usually too vague or non-specific to quantify. For example, a client may report that he is feeling less anxious, but he may not know how much the anxious feelings have decreased in amount, number or severity. Because of this, client verbal reports are usually supplemented with other types of measurement that may produce more specific and quantifiable data.

Frequency counts

Frequency counts reflect the number (how many and how often) of overt and covert behaviours. They involve obtaining measures of each occurrence of the target behaviour. Frequency counts are used typically when the goal behaviour is discreet and of short duration. Sometimes it is advantageous for frequency counts to be obtained as a percentage, especially when it is important to determine the number of opportunities to perform the target behaviour, as well as the number of times the behaviour actually occurs. The principle advantage of percentage scores is that they indicate whether the change is because of an increase or a decrease in the number of opportunities to perform the behaviour, or an actual increase or decrease in the number of times the response occurs. However, percentage scores may not be so useful when it is hard to detect the available opportunities, or when it is difficult for the client to collect information.

Duration counts

Duration reflects the amount or length of time a particular response or collection of responses occurs. Duration of measurement is appropriate whenever the goal behaviour is not discreet and lasts for varying periods. The amount of time spent on a task or with another person, the period of time depressive thoughts occur and the amount of time that anxious feelings last are examples of behaviours that could be measured with duration counts.

Another type of duration count involves observing the latency of a particular response, for example, the amount of time that elapses before self-disclosing to another person in a group. These measures can be used in combination.

Frequency counts, percentage scores and duration counts can be obtained in one of two ways: by continuous recording, where the client obtains data each time he engages in the goal behaviour, and time sampling. Sometimes continuous recording is impossible, particularly when the target behaviour occurs frequently or when its onset and termination are hard to detect. In these cases, a time sampling procedure may be more practical. The day is divided into equal time intervals, such as 90 minutes, one hour, two hours, and so on.

The client keeps track of the goal behaviour's frequency and duration only during randomly selected intervals. Information should be collected during at least three time intervals a day, and during different time intervals each day so that representative and unbiased data are recorded.

A variation of time sampling is to divide time into intervals and indicate the presence or absence of the target behaviour for each interval in an "all or none" manner. Time sampling is not so precise as continuous recording, yet it does provide an estimate of the frequency of behaviour.

Rating scales

The intensity or degree of the goal behaviour can be assessed using a rating scale (see Chapter 4). Cronbach (1970) suggested three ways of decreasing sources of error frequently associated with the use of rating scales:

1. The therapist should be certain that what is being rated is well defined and is clearly understood in the client's language;
2. The rating scale should be so designed that there is a description for each point on the scale;
3. Rating scales should be uni-directional, starting with 0 or 1. Negative points or points below 0 should not be included. The therapist should consider the range of points in constructing the scale. Common practice is that the scale should include at least four points and no more than seven; a scale of less than four may limit a person's capacity to discriminate, whereas a scale that includes more than seven points may not be rated reliably by the client because too many discriminations are required.

Checklists

Checklists are similar to rating scales. The basic difference is the type of judgement made. On a rating scale a person can indicate the degree to which a

Figure 9.1 Checklist for Evaluating the Quality of Assessment (Source: Gambrill 1985, in L'Abate and Milan (editors) and reprinted by permission of John Wiley & Sons Ltd)

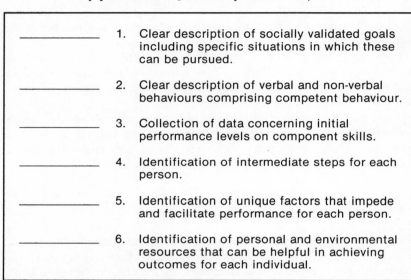

1. Clear description of socially validated goals including specific situations in which these can be pursued.

2. Clear description of verbal and non-verbal behaviours comprising competent behaviour.

3. Collection of data concerning initial performance levels on component skills.

4. Identification of intermediate steps for each person.

5. Identification of unique factors that impede and facilitate performance for each person.

6. Identification of personal and environmental resources that can be helpful in achieving outcomes for each individual.

behaviour is present; a checklist simply measures the presence or absence of a behaviour.

Checklists can describe a cluster or collection of behaviours that a client can demonstrate, and it assesses the client's capability to emit a particular behaviour to a given standard under a given condition. For example, the verbal and non-verbal behaviours associated with a job interview can be listed on a checklist. A checklist can also be used in conjunction with frequency and duration counts, as well as rating scales. As an evaluative tool, checklists can be very useful, particularly when the reference points on the lists clearly define the behaviour to be recorded, and are representative of the particular performance being assessed (Figures 9.1 and 9.2).

Figure 9.2   Checklist for Evaluating the Quality of Social Skills Training Programmes (Source: Gambrill 1985, in L'Abate and Milan (editors) and reprinted by permission of John Wiley & Sons Ltd)

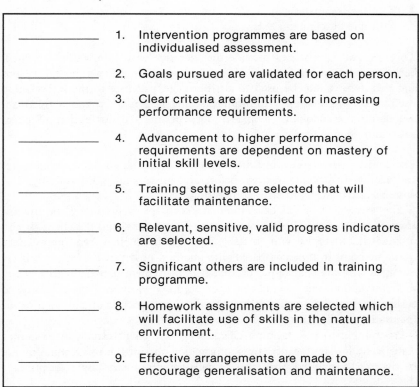

_____	1. Intervention programmes are based on individualised assessment.
_____	2. Goals pursued are validated for each person.
_____	3. Clear criteria are identified for increasing performance requirements.
_____	4. Advancement to higher performance requirements are dependent on mastery of initial skill levels.
_____	5. Training settings are selected that will facilitate maintenance.
_____	6. Relevant, sensitive, valid progress indicators are selected.
_____	7. Significant others are included in training programme.
_____	8. Homework assignments are selected which will facilitate use of skills in the natural environment.
_____	9. Effective arrangements are made to encourage generalisation and maintenance.

Evaluation in applied settings

Evaluation techniques for individual clients

The times when social skills information are collected determine, to a large extent, the rigour of the treatment evaluation design. In addition, the questions that can be answered concerning a client's behaviour also change as a result of social skills interventions. Three procedures can be used to evaluate the effect of social skills training on clients being treated individually in most applied settings. These are:

1. Pre-training and post-training assessment on the same measures;
2. Time series analysis;
3. Multiple baseline analysis.

The first two approaches provide the therapist with information on client behaviour change across time. However, they are not experimental designs and therefore cannot be used to attribute client change to the intervention itself. The single subject multiple baseline is a more rigorous treatment evaluation methodology — and it does permit the attribution of client behaviour change to the intervention.

Pre-training/post-training assessment   Here, all social skills measures are taken at two points in time, before and subsequent to the training. The same measures are used on each occasion.

The advantages of this evaluation approach are its simplicity and the low amount of time and effort it requires by the therapist and the client. It also provides the therapist with objective information on client behaviour change from one point in time compared with another, however, it does not tell the therapist why the change has occurred. Improvement may have been due to the intervention, but it could also have been due to some of the effects noted earlier, such as the practice effect, specific events outside of treatment or the maturation of the client.

Pre-training to post-training changes for one client cannot be examined statistically for significance; thus information obtained in this fashion cannot be rigorously analysed, and must be considered as essentially descriptive.

Time series analysis   This procedure is essentially a modification of the pre-training to post-training assessment method, except that all measures are obtained on a number of differently spaced occasions before, during and after the social skills training. In practice, this approach might be used when a client is assessed on each measure once weekly for four weeks before training starts and again once weekly for four weeks upon conclusion of the intervention. It improves upon the pre-training and post-training assessment method in a number of ways.

Improvement due to practice alone could be detected, because it would be evident if performance improved from one pre-training assessment to another in the absence of training. However, the time series analysis still cannot rule out the possibility that external events have temporarily coincided with treatment and are responsible for any improvements seen in the post-training assessment.

Also, although statistical analysis of time series measurements for individually treated clients have been described, this statistical approach ordinarily requires that measures be taken on a great number of occasions, in excess of what would be practical in most applied settings. However, the therapist who wishes to evaluate skills training intervention with somewhat greater rigour than is possible with a simple pre-training/post-training assessment may wish to consider this approach.

Multiple baseline analysis   This has become an extremely popular method for analysing the effect of client behavioural interventions, including social skills training, with individually treated clients. The reasons for its popularity include its suitability for single client interventions, its ability to clearly establish that client behaviour changes are a consequence of training, and the fact that the methodology does not require any aspect of clinical treatment to be sacrificed for experimental control purposes. The analysis is conducted broadly as follows:

1. Based on interview information, the number of specific inter-personal problem situations are defined;
2. Role-play assessment scenes are constructed to approximate each potentially troublesome situation. Each role-player describes a different situation;
3. Client performance in the assessment role-plays are video-taped and rated to determine deficient component behaviours. The rating procedure consists of having an observer watch each client's role-play using a rating form that lists all the components of the effective skill; thus he can indicate the degree to which each behavioural component is present for each role-play scene. Over the next two sessions, the same assessment procedures are repeated with each client role-playing how he would handle the same set of scenes. These additional assessment role-plays are also rated.

As might be expected, the same components should remain deficient across all three separate assessment sessions, thus demonstrating that: the identified components are consistently deficient; a stable pre-training baseline has been established for each of the component deficits; and the client's role-play performance has not improved over time as a result of repeated practice alone.

The purpose of this initial assessment is to establish a stable baseline. The therapist expects that, when training on one component is introduced, an increase in this targeted component should be evident in the client's practice that day. Since other component behaviours do not receive training attention in the same session, the therapist predicts that they will remain unchanged in that session's role-play. Further, the next component to be trained should increase in the client's practice only at the time it receives specific attention in the intervention.

The multiple baseline method is based on the mechanism that each component should increase when a global skill is broken down into separate independent component behaviours, but only upon the introduction of specific training for it. If all components improved at the same time, when only one of them was being trained, it would suggest that improvement was not due to treatment, since only one aspect of the target skill was receiving attention. Conversely, if a component failed to increase when training was specifically targeted towards it, this would suggest that treatment was ineffective in that session. The procedure necessary to perform a multiple baseline analysis is available if a standard practice interaction is included in each training session. All that is then required is for the therapist or some other observer to rate the client's performance in each session's practice interaction.

Ordinarily, this should occur in training sessions, since the therapist must observe the practice interaction and evaluate the presence of any targeted component behaviours in order to provide feedback to the client. A quantitive or observation procedure is needed to graph the client's performance. This can be accomplished by using rating scales and so on. Multiple baseline analysis, used in this way, only requires the therapist to rate objectively or to count then graph the client's practice performance in each session. Thus it is an evaluation design well suited to applied settings since it does not require outside control groups, removal of any treatment or elaborate costs in time or support.

Multiple baseline analysis, however, does have limitations. Operating in this way, it assumes the component behaviours that are separately trained are independent of one another. If two components are correlated, such as proximity and gaze, it will be assumed that training on one will cause the other to change, even when the second component is not directly treated.

It is desirable to train each behaviour for several sessions when conducting a multiple baseline analysis across social skills components. This should establish more conclusively that the targeted component clearly improves, while the as yet untreated components do not improve. However, the relationships between various molecular components of social skills have not yet been clearly established in many areas.

It is possible to combine multiple baseline analysis of client performance during each session's practice interactions with other measures administered at the beginning and end of the entire intervention. These pre-training/post-training measures might include self-report inventories, global evaluations of overall social competency or self-monitoring records.

Evaluation techniques for group social skills training

The kind of evaluation procedure used to assess the impact of a group's social skills training intervention is determined by both the degree of evaluative rigour desired by the therapist and the availability of a control group. Three of the evaluation procedures are group modifications of individual client techniques: pre-training/post-training assessment; time series analysis; and multiple baseline techniques.

Pre-training/post-training assessment

For individually treated clients, the most rudimentary form of objective assessment is achieved by administering evaluation measures, behavioural and global inventories, and self-monitoring records before and after training. There is no reason why this procedure cannot be used for all members of a social skills training group. Depending on the nature of the sample social interactions used, the performance of all clients in the group might be individually observed in pre-training/post-training interactions, such as in a standard role-play. Alternatively, each client might be asked to repeat the sample interactions that have been constructed specifically for him, both before and after training.

The benefits and limitations of group pre-training assessment are similar to those with single client assessment.

Time series analysis

The time series evaluation approach of conducting a series of assessments both before and subsequent to the training intervention can be used for all group members. Here, each client who will be in the group is individually assessed on a number of occasions, perhaps weekly, and on all measures. After the training intervention, each client is again assessed on the same measures that have been administered before treatment.

The advantages of this strategy are its relatively low requirements for staff and client time and effort.

Its major limitations involve the fact that observed client behaviour change, even if consistently low when sampled across all pre-training occasions and then consistently higher across all post-training occasions, still cannot be conclusively attributed to the intervening training.

Multiple baseline analysis

The same multiple baseline method can be used to evaluate the behaviour change of individual clients when each of those clients is a member of the same social skills training group. This use of the multiple baseline is quite similar to that in individual client applications. Here, treatment is administered to a group of clients rather than to just one.

Each client is individually assessed during his practice interaction, during or immediately after every group session. The therapist must observe the interactions, either directly or by making recordings of them which can be rated later. The ratings are then quantified to give a frequency of occurrence for each component under study, so that this information can be recorded for each client. The effectiveness of the intervention can be established conclusively without the need for external control groups if most clients improve in their individual practice — following training — on the component that received attention.

A wide range of rigorous intervention techniques are available to the therapist, who also has access to control groups against which to evaluate the performance of clients in a social skills training group. Two of these basic methods can be applied practically in applied sessions.

Non-equivalent control group design   This technique requires the presence of two groups of clients, one of which will receive the social skills training and the other serving as the control group. Clients are not randomly assigned to the skills training or control group.

It is desirable for skills training and control group clients to resemble or to be matched with one another as closely as possible on any characteristics that might affect their social functioning. However, because clients are not randomly assigned to the two groups, the design is not as rigorous as when random assignments are used. Its chief virtue is that this is a control group treatment evaluation design that can represent a reasonable compromise between true experimental control and the practical realities that apply in most treatment settings.

All clients in both the skills training and control group are administered the same procedures before the social skills training begins. These measures usually include assessment techniques such as role-play, behavioural rehearsal, self-report inventories, self-monitoring or direct *in vivo* observations.

The clients in the skills training group then receive the social skills training while the clients in the control group receive either no training, or some other form of non-social skills treatment.

At the conclusion of this stage, all the clients are retested using the same assessment test. The therapist is then in a position to evaluate the improvement in skills level of the treatment group relative to the control group.

However, because clients were not randomly assigned to one group or another in this strategy, it remains possible that some outside factors are responsible for the change of one group relative to the other. This is possible even when the clients in the two groups appear to be comparable with one another.

Random assignment control group   Here the strategy used is identical with the non-equivalent control group, except that all the clients are randomly selected to receive either the social skills training intervention or the "no treatment" control.

Selecting techniques

The particular evaluation methods selected will depend on the type of questions the therapist would like to have answered, the degree to which the therapist wishes to rigorously establish that training was responsible for observed social skill improvement, the resources or support available to the therapist, and the therapist's time constraints and interests.

In many cases, simple pre-training and post-training assessment of clients' social skills measures may yield all the information that the therapist seeks on the success of his social skills training. In other cases, more controlled evaluation strategies, such as time series analysis, can be used to provide information.

There are no intrinsically right or wrong intervention assessment strategies, although some approaches do provide more specific and conclusive information than others. A therapist should not take any treatment outcome for granted. Instead, planning a treatment session should also include the planning of objective mechanisms by which the treatment's clinical success can be gauged. By incorporating treatment evaluation measures into social skills training, the therapist will be in a position to gain objective information on whether or not the client(s) have improved. The therapist will be in a position to provide the client with additional training if objective measures indicate that there has been no improvement and the therapist's confidence in the success of his own interventions will be increased if objective measures do demonstrate improvement.

References

Hawkins R P and Dobes R W (1978) Behavioural definition in applied behaviour analysis: Explicit or implicit, in B C Etzel et al (Editors), New Directions in Behavioural Research: Theory, Methods and Applications, Lawrence Erlbaum

L'Abate L and Milan M (Editors) (1985) Handbook of Social Skills Training, John Wiley and Sons

Mahoney M J (1977) Experimental methods and outcome evaluations, Journal of Consulting and Clinical Psychology, 46(4): 660–672

Martinez J A and Edelstein B (1977) The effects of demand characteristics on the assessment of heterosocial competence, paper presented at the Annual Meeting, Association for the Advancement of Behaviour Therapy, Atlanta

Orne M T (1969) Demand characteristics and the concept of quasi controls, in R Rosenthal and R Rownow (Editors), Artifact in Behavioural Research, Academic Press.

Priestley P et al (1978) Social Skills and Personal Problem Solving, Methuen Social Science Publications, Tavistock

Further reading

Cronbach L J (1970) Essentials of Psychological Testing, Harper and Row

Marzillier J (1978) Outcome of social skills training: A review, in P Trower *et al.* (Editors), Social Skills and Mental Health, Harper and Row

Milne D (1984), Skill evaluation of nurse-training in behaviour therapy, Behavioural Psychotherapy, 12: 142–150

Rinn R C and Vernon J C (1975) Process evaluation of out-patient treatment in a community mental health centre, Journal of Behaviour Therapy and Experimental Psychiatry, 6: 5–11

PART 3

SPECIFIC APPLICATIONS

CHAPTER 10

SOCIAL SKILLS AND SOCIAL ANXIETY

The crucial thing to remember about anxiety is that it is perfectly normal for everybody to feel anxious from time to time. Additionally, anxiety can be a useful force. Most people are often slightly anxious in social situations, and this can be helpful as it helps to keep the person alert. It is only when anxiety becomes excessive that it can begin to disrupt someone's social functioning. There has been considerable disagreement about the nature of anxiety, which has been part of a wider debate about the concept of emotion.

Emotion

The concept of emotion is a central one in the study of behaviour. An important distinction is that between emotion and motivation. The most common basis for differentiating between the two assumes that emotions are usually aroused by external stimuli, and that emotional expression is directed toward the stimuli in the environment that arouses it. On the other hand, motives are more often aroused by internal stimuli and are "naturally" directed towards certain objects in the environment (food, water or a mate).

However, there are a number of instances when this distinction does not hold, for example, an external incentive such as the sight or smell of delicious food can arouse hunger in the absence of internal hunger cues. Internal stimuli, such as those caused by severe food deprivation or pain, can arouse emotion.

In the past, psychologists have devoted considerable effort in an attempt to classify emotion, and to find dimensions along which to scale such emotions as sorrow, disgust, surprise, jealousy, envy and ecstasy. Such attempts have not proved worthwhile. However, most emotions can be divided along the following scales: pleasant (joy, love) to unpleasant (anger, fear). Additionally, many emotions can be described by intensity: displeasure to rage, pain to agony, sadness to grief, all of which convey different degrees of intensity.

Physiological responses in emotion

When an intense emotion is experienced, such as fear or anger, a number of bodily changes occur. Most of these result from activation of the sympathetic division of the autonomic nervous system as it prepares the body for emergency action. This sympathetic system causes the following changes: blood pressure and heart rate increase; respiration increases; pupils dilate; perspiration increases; secretion of saliva and mucus decrease; blood sugar level increases; blood clots more easily; the motility of the gastrointestinal tract decreases; blood is diverted from the stomach and intestines to the brain and skeletal muscles; and hairs on the skin become erect.

The notion that different emotions have different autonomic counterparts seems reasonable, especially since emotions are experienced that feel different from one another. Many of these feelings seem to arise from the autonomic nervous system. For example the following colloquial expressions can apply to different vascular responses in the face: "pallor of fear", "purple with rage", and "blush of shame". Similarly, the following experiences can be ascribed to the stomach: "butterflies in the stomach", "it turned my stomach over", and "my stomach was tied in knots".

However, the matter is not so simple during strenuous exercise. Flushing, sweating and increased heart rate occur, and yet emotion is not necessarily experienced.

Theories of emotion

The James-Lange theory James, a Harvard psychologist of the late 1800s believed that the important factor in felt emotion was the feedback from bodily changes that occur in response to a frightening or upsetting emotion (James 1884). His theory implied that people are afraid because they run, or they are angry because they strike. Lange, a Danish physiologist, arrived at a similar position.

There are times when this position makes intuitive sense: if someone is startled by a noise, it seems that autonomic responses (tremor, flushing) occur before there has been time to appraise the stimulus as being threatening or non-threatening. James's theory, in brief, is that certain stimuli evoke visceral responses via the autonomic nervous system and the motor skeletal system. These two classes of response then act as stimuli to bring about emotional feelings in the brain.

Emotional experience is the appreciation of changes occurring in the viscera or motor system. These changes are initiated directly by the perception of an appropriate stimulus. Cannon (1927) outlined the major objections to this theory:

1. Bodily changes do not seem to differ very much from one emotional state to another, despite the fact that people are usually fairly clear about which emotion is being experienced;
2. The internal organs are relatively insensitive structures, not well supplied with nerves, and internal changes occur too slowly to be a source of emotional feeling;
3. Artificially inducing the bodily changes associated with an emotion, for example, injecting a person with adrenaline, does not produce the experience of the true emotion.

The sodium lactate theory of anxiety neurosis   This is a classical extension of the James-Lange theory (1967). The theory proposes that serum lactate, a metabolite of lactic acid formed in the muscles during activity, is causally related to the clinical syndrome of anxiety neurosis. One difficulty with this theory is that normal individuals can exercise strenuously and thereby increase their lactate to "critical" levels and not experience anxiety. The same individual, if given lactate through infusion, will experience some of the symptoms associated with anxiety neurosis. This means that there must be determinants of the psychological state of anxiety other than simply increasing serum lactate. Additional problems with this theory include the fact that not all people suffering from anxiety neurosis have abnormally high blood lactate concentrations, and it is unknown whether patients are susceptible to the effects of lactate because they are anxiety neurotics, or whether they are anxiety neurotics because of their susceptibility to lactate.

The Cannon-Bard theory   Cannon (1927) assigned the central role in emotion to the thalamus. He suggested that the thalamus responded to an emotion-producing stimulus by sending impulses simultaneously to the cerebral cortex and to other parts of the body. Emotional feelings were the result of joint arousal of the cortex and of the sympathetic nervous system. According to this theory, which was extended by Bard (1928), bodily changes and the experience of emotion occur at the same time.

Subsequent investigation has made it clear that it is the hypothalamus and parts of the limbic system that are the brain centres most directly involved in the integration of emotional responses (electrical stimulation of the hypothalamus can elicit fear or anger in many animals). Impulses from these areas go to certain nuclei in the brain stem that control the function of the autonomic nervous system.

Cognitive-label theory of emotion   Most of the emotional states experimentally manipulated using humans have shown a general pattern of excitation of the sympathetic nervous system in emotion. Schachter and Singer (1962) investigated this problem and concluded that it is an open question as to whether or not there are physiological distinctions among the various emotional states.

They described recent work that could be taken to indicate that differences, if any, are at best subtle and that the variety of emotion, mood and feelings are by no means matched by an equal variety of visceral patterns. This rather ambiguous state of affairs led them to suggest that cognitive factors may be the major determinants of emotional states. They proposed that:

1. Given a state of physiological arousal for which an individual has no immediate explanation, that individual will "label" this state and describe his feelings in terms of the cognitions available to him. To the extent that cognitive factors are potent determinants of emotional states, it could be anticipated that precisely the same state of physiological arousal could be called "joy", "fury" or "jealousy" or any of the great diversity of emotional labels, depending on the cognitive aspects of the situation.
2. Given a state of physiological arousal for which an individual has a completely appropriate explanation, no evaluation needs will arise and the individual is unlikely to label his feelings in terms of the alternative cognitions available.
3. Given the same cognitive circumstances, the individual will react emotionally or will describe his feelings as emotions only to the extent that he experiences a state of physiological arousal.

These propositions were tested in a series of famous experiments that have been criticised for several reasons, which are beyond the scope of this book. Although this basic model of emotion may be incorrect, this research has generated exciting interest in the complex interactions that occur between situational variables, cognitions and physiological states.

Models of social anxiety

There is now considerable evidence that anxiety is a much more complex concept than was previously envisaged. It has been found that an individual's response to one type of potential anxiety-inducing threat is relatively independent of the responses to other types of stressors. Furthermore, the specific nature of the anxiety response (sweating palms, pounding head, a feeling of terror) can also vary according to the source of the threat. As a result, there has been a trend towards focusing research on the nature of anxiety within specific situations.

Social situations are one class of situation in which anxiety frequently occurs and is often a significant problem. Four major models have been proposed to explain the development of social anxiety and the processes involved:

1. Conditioned anxiety model;
2. Skill deficit model;
3. Cognitive evaluative model;
4. Three systems model.

Conditioned anxiety model

This model states that the source of social anxiety is repeated exposure to aversive experiences in social situations. This is considered to be a form of classical conditioning in which the neutral cues of interactions become associated with aversive stimuli. These conditioning events can occur in an *in vivo* or vicarious setting, and are judged to occur regardless of the adequacy of an individual's behavioural repertoire. Within this framework, social skills training is viewed as a process of training subjects in responses to inhibit anxiety. For example, it has been argued that assertion and anxiety are mutually incompatible responses and, therefore, that assertion training can inhibit reciprocally social anxiety. This model has been described as incomplete in that it fails to explain why individuals can have a series of aversive experiences in social interactions.

Skill deficit model

In this model, it is proposed that social anxiety results from a deficit in a person's repertoire of socially skilled responses. This may be because an individual may never have learnt the appropriate behaviour, or has learnt inappropriate behaviour, or has forgotten the appropriate behaviour. Because of this inadequate repertoire, the individual is not able to handle the demands of the situation appropriately. He therefore experiences an unpleasant situation that elicits anxiety.

Therapy within this model consists of a range of procedures such as modelling and behavioural rehearsal designed to teach subjects to respond in a socially skilful way to the social situation. An assumption of this approach is that once these new responses are within the person's behavioural repertoire, their use will be maintained by reinforcement from the social environment.

Evidence has suggested that this model is also inadequate, since an adequate social skill repertoire can be described as a basis for effective social functioning. However, many other factors may be involved. Additionally, although social skills training has been found to improve individual social responses, these changes do not always generalise to other situations.

Cognitive evaluative model

This model was evolved to explain the paradox that there may be socially anxious people with socially skilled responses in their behavioural repertoires who are unable to use these responses in social situations. It views the source of social anxiety as being in an individual's cognitive evaluative appraisal of his performance and in the expectation of aversive consequences, not in the performance itself. This faulty appraisal can be the result of unrealistic misperceptions regarding performance, negative self-evaluation or insufficient self-reinforcement. A highly anxious person tends to underestimate his own performance, is greatly concerned with the evaluation of the performance of others, and tends to have a highly generalised need to be liked, and to be motivated to avoid disapproval. Highly socially anxious people have been found to perceive feedback as more negative and as evoking a more negative emotional response than do less socially anxious subjects.

Three systems analysis

This model developed out of the findings that although anxiety reduction methods such as desensitisation, flooding and modelling have been very successful, there has often been bewildering consequences. For instance, a client's behavioural response may be altered but he may continue to complain of excessive fear. Usually, the change in response to anxiety reduction therapy is in the following order: a reduction in the physiological indices of anxiety; improvements in the behavioural components of anxiety; and subjective improvements, although it must be stressed that these factors can be affected by several variables such as the type of therapy used.

These findings led Lang (1970) to conclude that fear was a collection of three components, which he contrasted with the unitory or "lump" theory of fear, as he termed the preceding models. His three components of fear were: avoidance behaviour, physiological reactivity, and verbal report of subjective fear.

The relationship betwen these three factors is by no means clear: Lang himself describes them as "an imperfectly coupled response system". As Rachman (1978a; 1978b) stated: "Self-reports of fear can correlate well with each other: they correlate moderately well with the ratings of fear made by external judges and also with the avoidance behaviour observed in a fear test; self-reports correlate modestly with physiological indices; physiological indices of fear correlate modestly with each other and hardly at all with muscle tension."

The three systems approach is preferable to the so-called "lump" theory of fear, because:

1. It provides a more comprehensive view of a client's responses to fear, and provides a method of analysing them which takes into account cognitive, emotional and behavioural variables;
2. It fits the current research data available more closely than any of the previous models;
3. It has clear clinical applications for practice as it provides an overall view of the client's functioning in relation to fear. Different individuals will present with varying degrees of difficulty on each component. Identification of these differences should become a part of the routine procedure for assessment in order to tailor an appropriate method of treatment to the individual. It is likely that different treatment methods will be used for each of the components: in general terms, systematic

desensitisation could be used for treating clients who have a high physiological arousal as a fear component; cognitive techniques such as stress innoculation should be used to teach the client a set of cognitive coping skills that they can substitute for the negative cognitions; and, for behavioural difficulties, social skills techniques such as modelling can be used to alter the behavioural repertoire.

In conclusion, it has been argued that the three systems analysis model provides a much more comprehensive model for someone suffering from social anxiety. Considerable research is being undertaken to examine the relationship between the three components, and the implications for clinical practice from these developments could be enormous.

Social anxiety and social interaction

Social anxiety has been found to be a common complaint among psychiatric patients reporting social interaction difficulties. A frequent problem relates to the fear of being in any way the focus of attention. This appears to be associated with an expectation of real or perceived failure in social interaction and usually leads to an avoidance of inter-personal contact, despite a desire to mix in a normal manner.

The overt signs of social anxiety are often indistinguishable from unskilled behaviour. Unfortunately, there is also a negative loop that tends to be created: poor social performance tends to evoke negative evaluation in our society, which serves to confirm the individual's anxiety about social interaction.

Hall and Goldberg (1977) found that there were four main categories of complaint from people suffering from social anxiety:

1. Cognitive, behavioural or physical indices of anxiety associated with social situations;
2. An inability to behave in a socially skilled manner in situations requiring assertive behaviour or approach behaviour;
3. Lack of social activity and restricted social outlets;
4. Transient instances where others have been perceived to be staring, laughing or talking about the patient, or knowing what he was thinking, this belief being held with an intensity that exceeds self-consciousness.

The most common pattern was believed to be a combination of complaints from categories 1, 2 and 3, followed by those reporting features of the first category alone.

Treatment options for people experiencing social anxiety

Numerous techniques have been developed in an attempt to reduce social anxiety. These procedures can be divided into three broad target areas that aim to differentiate between: social anxiety principally caused by physiological arousal; social anxiety principally caused by negative cognitions; and social anxiety principally caused by lack of social skill. As previously stated, the relationship between these three dimensions is unclear at present.

Social anxiety principally caused by lack of social skill Many of the techniques previously described in this book can be used in an attempt to improve a client's social skill repertoire, on the assumption that improved social functioning will reduce social avoidance and social anxiety.

Role-play techniques such as role reversal can be used so that the client can experience how he affects other people in social interaction. This technique is especially beneficial if the client's deficit is caused by inaccurate social perception. Alternatively, the client can be taught social skills using modelling if he is deficient. A range of behavioural deficits can be taught in this way, from straightforward exercises such as opening a conversation to complex patterns such as dating behaviour. It can include non-verbal factors such as body language and the art of listening. Other techniques such as coaching and assertion training can also be used to improve the client's behavioural repertoire.

Social anxiety principally caused by cognitive deficits The last 10 years have seen a considerable growth in the awareness of the involvement of cognitive factors related to social anxiety. Many techniques have been used, either alone or as a package of therapies, to restore effective social functioning. Among the most important of these techniques are:

1. Cognitive restructuring. This technique, as with the others described in this section, is more fully discussed in Chapter 11. The client is encouraged to imagine an anxiety-provoking scene in cognitive

restructuring, and to replace negative self-evaluations by positive coping statements. The basis for this approach is the belief that a client's "inner talk" can influence performance, and that negative self-statements can cause emotional distress and thus interfere with performance.

2. Stress innoculation. This procedure attempts to help the client deal more effectively with anxiety-provoking situations, first by educating him about the nature of social anxiety and its possible stages and consequences, and then by teaching various physical and cognitive coping skills to deal with these stages.

3. Cognitive modelling. Here, the therapist shows the client how to "cope" using self-statements while he is in a position that normally elicits social anxiety.

4. Thought-stopping has been found to be particularly useful with clients who tend to ruminate about events that are unlikely to occur or who engage in repetitive anxiety-producing thoughts.

Social anxiety principally caused by physiological arousal The techniques used in this area were among the first developed in an attempt to reduce unwanted anxiety and fear. They have been extensively used over the past 20 to 30 years and have been found to be extremely effective in reducing a client's unwanted anxieties.

Systematic desensitisation has been widely used to reduce anxiety. Based on the concept of reciprocal inhibition, it was developed on the principle that certain behaviours, such as assertion or relaxation, are incompatible with anxiety. Thus, if this new response can be elicited while the client is in the stressful situation, the level of physiological arousal in the social situation will be reduced.

Rapid exposure therapy is also termed flooding or implosive therapy. The aim of this method is to produce a high level of anxiety in a social situation, while preventing escape. This is now thought by many people to be the treatment of choice for social anxiety, although it may not be easy to get the client to comply. It aims, however, to make the client confront his worst fears as quickly as possible after adequate preparation, and to help him to stay there until his anxieties subside.

The remainder of this chapter will cover systematic desensitisation; no procedure will be given for rapid exposure therapy as, in some ways, it is an advanced technique that should be carried out by an experienced therapist.

Systematic desensitisation

Systematic desensitisation is one of a variety of methods that attempts to reduce excessive anxiety. According to social learning theory, anxiety is a persistent, learned, maladaptive response that results from stimuli with the capacity to elicit extremely intense emotional reactions. It is possible for people to experience this anxiety even in situations where there is no apparent danger. Systematic desensitisation attempts to reduce anxiety by inducing in the client a physiological state incompatible with anxiety. This is usually achieved by muscle relaxation. The client is then exposed to a weak, anxiety-evoking stimulus for a few seconds. The stimulus progressively loses its ability to evoke anxiety if exposure is repeated several times.

Systematic desensitisation has been widely used since the early 1960s as an anxiety reduction method. It has been used effectively to treat social anxiety and many other problems, such as stuttering and phobias. Considerable research has been conducted into the efficacy of anxiety reduction techniques. It has frequently concluded that systematic desensitisation is an effective means to reduce anxiety, but that is should not be applied indiscriminately whenever a client displays signs of anxiety. In general terms, systematic desensitisation has been found to be most appropriate when the client has the basic skill to perform in social situations, but either avoids the situation or performs inadequately because of anxiety. Desensitisation is inadequate if the client has a skill deficit. People with many fears or widespread anxiety may benefit more from cognitive strategies or from a combination of therapies in which desensitisation may play a role.

Reciprocal inhibition

This is the mechanism based on classical conditioning that Wolpe (1958) used to explain systematic desensitisation. When reciprocal inhibition occurs, a response such as fear or anxiety is inhibited by another response that is stronger than, and incompatible with, this anxiety response. In other words, if an incompatible response occurs in the presence of anxiety of a social situation, and if that incompatible response is stronger than the anxiety, then desensitisation occurs and the situation loses its capacity to evoke the anxiety. Three processes are required in order for desensitisation to occur according to this theory:

1. A strong counterconditioning response must be present to compete with the anxiety-provoking stimulus. The usual mechanism used is deep muscle relaxation;
2. A graded series of anxiety-provoking situations are presented to the client. These are usually graded in a hierarchy, beginning with low-intensity situations and ending with high-intensity ones.
3. These two factors are paired together, and this is usually accomplished by encouraging the client to achieve a state of deep relaxation and to imagine one situation from the hierarchy while in this state. The client stops imagining the situation whenever anxiety occurs. The anxiety response is extinguished after several successful pairings.

In recent years, some parts of this theory have been challenged as various components of the desensitisation process have been examined. It has also been proposed that extinction processes can account for the results of desensitisation, since anxiety responses diminish as a result of presenting conditioned stimuli without reinforcement. This approach is based on the principle of operant conditioning. However, other studies have indicated that other factors, including habituation and reinforcement, may be partly responsible for the successful results of desensitisation. It is also difficult at this stage to rule out non-specific treatment factors such as client expectancy.

Components of desensitisation

It is important to give the client an overview of the treatment and its purposes before therapy begins. A thorough assessment of each individual's experience of anxiety should be undertaken before therapy starts. In addition, the client should be informed of the principles of desensitisation; and the outcome of desensitisation may be enhanced if the client is given clear instructions and a positive approach from the therapist.

The explanation to the client should emphasise how his fear or other conditioned emotion can be counterconditioned using desensitisation. It should emphasise the stages of therapy and, in particular, the use of an anxiety-free response such as relaxation to replace the conditioned emotion, the construction of a hierarchy consisting of a graduated series of items representing the emotion-provoking situations, and the pairing of the hierarchy items with the anxiety-free response.

The client should also be educated about the nature of "anxiety" and the way in which it can affect people. Examples can be elicited from the client's own experience to illustrate certain points.

There should also be an explanation of the principle of generalisation, and the relationship between the client imagining certain anxiety-inducing scenes in the therapy session and of how this can be applied to his everyday experience.

The therapist can also emphasise that the client can learn coping and self-control skills for tension management by using systematic desensitisation. If this approach is used, the therapist should stress that the client will develop more control over himself in such threatening situations by undertaking therapy sessions.

Assessment techniques

It is crucial that a comprehensive assessment of the client's problem is conducted so that effective therapy can take place. The therapist must isolate each situation in which the client becomes anxious so that a comprehensive profile can be built up and an adequate desensitisation programme developed. This is not always an easy task as first appearances can be deceptive, and it must be remembered that assessment is an ongoing process throughout therapy.

There are at least three ways in which the therapist can attempt to identify past and present anxiety-provoking situations, as follows.

Interview assessment   The interview should be conducted on a structured format. The therapist should aim to establish the specific circumstances and situations in which the client experiences anxiety. For instance, does the client feel anxious in all situations or only those when strangers are present? If so, what types of strangers? Does the client's anxiety vary with the number of people present, or whether the client is accompanied or alone? Does the client experience more anxiety with the same or the opposite sex? What thoughts go through the client's head at the time he is experiencing the anxiety? Is it possible using a structured format for an interview to build up a comprehensive picture of a client's social anxieties?

Client self-monitoring   In addition to the information obtained during the interview, the therapist can obtain other data by encouraging the client to observe and record emotion-provoking situations as they occur. A client can be asked to record each instance in which he experienced anxiety in the period between the initial assessment and the next session with the therapist. In addition, he should be asked to record what was going on, where he was, with whom, and when he detected the emotion for each situation that occurred. He can also be asked to rate the degree of anxiety felt during each situation, on a scale from, say, 1 to 10 (low to high anxiety) or 0 to 100 (no anxiety to panic) (Figure 10.1).

Figure 10.1   Simple Fear Scale

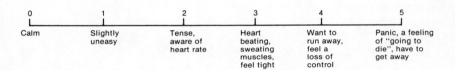

Self-report questionnaires   Another frequently used method to gather additional data about a specific emotion-provoking situations is to encourage a client to complete one of the numerous self-report questionnaires that are available. Among the most common of these questionnaires is the Wolpe-Lang Fear Survey Schedule. An example of a self-report questionnaire is given in Figure 10.2.

The assessment process is not complete until the therapist knows all the factors relating to the onset and maintenance of the client's problems, and until the client believes that he has given the therapist all relevant information concerning his difficulties.

Hierarchy construction

A hierarchy is a list of situations to which the client reacts with varying amounts of anxiety. Hierarchy construction can take a good deal of the therapist's time because of the various factors involved in constructing an adequate one. These factors include: selection of the appropriate type of hierarchy; whether to use a single hierarchy or multiple hierarchies; identification of the situations that will compose the hierarchy; identification of control items; and the ranking and spacing of the various situations composing the hierarchy.

Figure 10.2   Social Avoidance and Distress Scale (Source: Watson and Friend 1969 © 1969 The American Psychological Association)

Name: Date:

Raw score: Percentage of maximum score:

Instructions. Please read the statements carefully. Do not spend too much time thinking about each one. There are no right and wrong answers.

If you feel the statement does apply to you, then put a circle around **True**. If it does not, then put a circle around **False**.

Please answer all the questions without missing out any.

1. I feel relaxed even in unfamiliar social situations — True   False
2. I try to avoid situations which force me to be very sociable — True   False
3. It is easy for me to relax when I am with strangers — True   False
4. I have no particular desire to avoid people — True   False
5. I often find social occasions upsetting — True   False
6. I usually feel calm and comfortable at social occasions — True   False
7. I am usually at ease when talking to someone of the opposite sex — True   False
8. I try to avoid talking to people unless I know them well — True   False
9. If the chance comes to meet new people, I often take it — True   False
10. I often feel nervous or tense in casual get-togethers in which both sexes are present — True   False
11. I am usually nervous with people unless I know them well — True   False
12. I usually feel relaxed when I am with a group of people — True   False
13. I often want to get away from people — True   False
14. I usually feel uncomfortable when I am in a group of people I don't know — True   False
15. I usually feel relaxed when I meet someone for the first time — True   False

(continued)

Figure 10.2   (continued)

16.	Being introduced to people makes me tense and nervous	True	False
17.	Even though a room is full of strangers, I may enter it anyway	True	False
18.	I would avoid walking up and joining a large group of people	True	False
19.	When my superiors want to talk with me, I talk willingly	True	False
20.	I often feel on edge when I am with a group of people	True	False
21.	I tend to withdraw from people	True	False
22.	I don't mind talking to people at parties or social gatherings	True	False
23.	I am seldom at ease in a large group of people	True	False
24.	I often think up excuses in order to avoid social arrangements	True	False
25.	I sometimes take the responsibility for introducing people to each other	True	False
26.	I try to avoid formal social occasions	True	False
27.	I usually go to whatever social engagements I have to	True	False
28.	I find it easy to relax with other people	True	False

RAW SCORE TOTAL:

Types of hierarchies   Based on situations that evoke anxiety, the therapist should select an appropriate type of hierarchy in which to place specific instances of increasing degrees of anxiety. Three types of hierarchies are frequently used: spatio-temporal, thematic and personal hierarchies.

Spatio-temporal hierarchies are developed by using items that represent physical or time dimensions. Examples include the distance from one's house or the time before going to a party. In either case, the degree of anxiety seems to vary with proximity to the feared object or situation. Someone who is afraid to leave the house will get more anxious as the distance from their home increases. It is usual in developing this type of hierarchy to place more items at the high end of the scale rather than at the low end, so that the time differences at the high end of the scale are higher (Figure 10.3).

Figure 10.3   Example of Spatio-Temporal Hierarchy

Fear of giving speeches.

1. Your boss casually mentions that several people need to give speeches at the end of the year.

2. He sends round a memo asking for volunteers. You say that you will do it.

3. You talk about the speech with some of your colleagues. You are not sure what to say.

4. You go to the library to find material for your speech. There isn't much there.

5. You hear one of your colleagues speak. You think that it was really good and wonder how yours will be.

6. It's a week before the speech. You're spending a lot of time working on it.

7. It's the day before the speech. You are going over your notes religiously.

8. It's the night before your speech. You lie awake thinking about it.

9. It's the next morning. You wake up and remember it's the day for your speech. You don't feel hungry.

10. You are walking to work. You meet a colleague who wishes you good luck with your speech.

11. You enter the hall where you're going to speak. There seems to be a lot of people there. You go over the major parts of your speech.

Thematic hierarchies consist of items exposing the client to various components of feared situations. For example, a person who is afraid of criticism or disapproval may find that his anxiety varies depending on who criticises, what is criticised and how the criticism is delivered (Figure 10.4).

Personal hierarchies are especially useful for clients who are persistently bothered by thoughts or memories of a certain individual. They can be used to desensitise anxiety related to the break up of relationships. It is usual to put items at the bottom of the scale that have pleasant scenes or memories, and

Figure 10.4   Example of Thematic Hierarchy

Fear of being rejected.

1.   You speak to a stranger in the street. He doesn't hear you.

2.   You go into a department store and request some information. The shop assistant snaps at you.

3.   You ask a stranger to give you some change and you get a sarcastic reply.

4.   You ask a casual acquaintance to lend you a book. He refuses.

5.   You ask a friend over to dinner. He's too busy.

6.   You apply for a membership to a club and your application is rejected.

7.   You apply for a job and are interviewed. The other person is appointed.

8.   You have an argument with your best friend. You don't hear from her for a while.

9.   You have an argument with your husband. He says that he would rather do things alone than with you.

10.   Your husband asks you for a divorce and says that he does not love you anymore.

progress towards items at the top of the hierarchy that represent painful or extremely anxiety-provoking memories or thoughts (Figure 10.5).

Spatio-temporal and thematic hierarchies are used more commonly than personal ones and it is possible for hierarchies to be constructed that are a combination of any or all of these three types. The particular type used should depend on the client's problems.

Number of hierarchies   Whether one or several hierarchies are used also depends on the client's problems and preferences. Some therapists believe separate hierarchies should be constructed for different problems. However, multiple hierarchies may be less confusing, although they can require more time for construction and presentation. Other therapists suggest constructing a single hierarchy, composed of situations eliciting increasing amounts of anxiety, and regardless of whether the hierarchy items represent any particular theme. It has been suggested that this type of approach may aid generalisation.

Figure 10.5   Example of Personal Hierarchy

Fear of being rejected.

1. You remember a warm, starry night. You ask the woman you love to marry you. She accepts. You are very happy.

2. The two of you are travelling around in a van.

3. The two of you are at the beach, running in the water, generally having a good time.

4. You are eating dinner together.

5. The two of you are disagreeing over how to spend money.

6. You are arguing over your child. She thinks that you should not go out and that you should stay in together. You want to go out and get a babysitter.

7. You start to eat some meals apart. You are working late to avoid coming home for dinner.

8. She is wrapped up in her social activities, you in your work. You go your separate ways at weekends.

9. You have a discussion about your relationship and separate activities. You start sleeping in separate beds.

10. You go to a solicitor to initiate divorce proceedings.

Identification of hierarchy items

The therapist must obtain specific situations from the client in which he experiences anxiety. The client's role in this procedure is extremely important. The therapist can assign homework in an attempt to obtain specific situations if the client has difficulty in responding concretely to the interview questions. One method of self-monitoring is for the client to write down on a separate card each situation that occurs and the factors pertaining to it. The therapist should continue to explore and generate hierarchy situations until a number have been identified that represent a range of situations with varying degrees of emotional arousal.

Typically, a hierarchy contains between 10 and 20 items, based on the following criteria:

1. Control items — several situations should be included that do not elicit anxiety in the client;
2. Each hierarchy item should be concrete and specific. There should be a clear description of the situation and sufficient detail so that the client can clearly visualise the scene. As an example, a situation that reads "I feel bad when I go into crowded places" is far too general. A more specific situation should be developed such as, "When I walk into a crowded room full of strangers, I feel as if I'm going to panic";
3. The situations depicted should be similar to or represent actual situations that the client has faced or is likely to face in the future. Additionally, any commentary on these situations should be in a language relevant to the client;
4. The situations selected should reflect a wide range in which the client's anxiety could or does occur;
5. Items should be included that reflect different levels of anxiety, ranging from low to high intensity.

Identification of control items

A control item is a relaxing or neutral scene to which the client is not expected to have any strong emotional reaction. These scenes are placed at the bottom of the hierarchy and represent 0 or "no anxiety ranking". They have to be constructed individually, of course, but examples of some control items include the following statements:

1. "Imagine that it's spring and that you are sitting beside a river with the lambs in a nearby field."
2. "Imagine a bowl of red roses."

Control items are important because they are used to test the client's ability to imagine the situations that will be presented to him. Some clients can have considerable difficulty in using imagery techniques and it may then be necessary to use alternative techniques. Additionally, control items can be used to enhance the level of relaxation before the therapy session begins.

Ranking and spacing of hierarchy items

After all the hierarchy and control items have been identified, the client can arrange the items in order of increasing emotional arousal using a ranking method. It is normal for the client and the therapist to do this together, but with the client playing the major role in ranking the hierarchy items. The important role for the therapist is to ensure that the spacing between the items is satisfactory. Hierarchy items are usually ranked in order of increased levels of anxiety. The control items are placed at the lowest end of the hierarchy and each progressive item up the scale represents a situation in which more anxiety is experienced. The situations at the top end of the hierarchy represent the situations that are most anxiety-producing and stressful for the client.

The importance of ranking the situations into a hierarchy should be fully explained to the client so that he appreciates that it is necessary to spend some time getting an accurate hierarchy. The educational side of the procedure can be stressed in this situation as it is an opportunity for the therapist to explain once again to the client that desensitisation works by gradually introducing control over more and more stressful situations, and that the client will be able to learn to cope with situations that are relatively easy for him to deal with initially, before progressing to more difficult situations.

There are several methods a client can use to order the hierarchy items, for example, rank-ordering, which is the simplest method. Each item is written on a card and the client rank orders each one, with the least anxiety-provoking situation at the bottom, placing successively more anxiety-provoking situations in an ascending order. The bottom item is a "control" and is usually assigned a number, usually 1, with each successive item being assigned a higher number.

The therapist can go over the order after the client has ranked the cards to determine whether there are too many or too few gaps between the items. Items should be graduated evenly, with a fairly equal amount of difference between them. A few items should be deleted if they are bunched together. New items can be added if there are large spaces between them.

"SUDS" scaling is another way of ordering hierarchy items, devised by Wolpe and Lazarus (1966). Items are arranged according to a point system in which the various points represent levels of emotion or "subjective units of disturbance" ("SUDS"). The most commonly used scale consists of 100 points: 0 (zero) represents complete relaxation and 100 "SUDS" indicates panic or an extremely stressful reaction. The client should be encouraged to place appropriate items at the point between 0 and 100 which he considers to be most appropriate on the scale. After the items are arranged according to the assigned "SUDS", the therapist should make sure that no item is separated from the previous item by more than 10 "SUDS": spacing of no more than 5

"SUDS" between items is necessary at the high end of the scale. Large gaps, greater than 10 "SUDS" should be filled by the therapist and client writing additional intermediate items. Some of the items may be deleted if there are too many at the same level, particularly at the lower end of the hierarchy.

This system may require more explanation to the client and more time for item arrangement but it does have several advantages. For example, the point system makes it easier to determine whether there is too much or too little space between items. The use of the "SUDS" scale at this point in desensitisation introduces the client to a way of discriminating and labelling varying degrees of relaxation and anxiety. In addition, with the high/medium/low ranking method, the client will put low anxiety-producing items in the bottom third, average anxiety-provoking items in the middle of the hierarchy, and high anxiety items will be rated as high. After the items are ordered in this way, the client will then rank order them within each group. The therapist can then go over the items to make sure that the spacing is reasonable.

Whichever ranking method is used, the therapist should emphasise the fact that it is flexible and subject to change. Any type of hierarchy is useful only to the degree that it helps desensitise emotion or enables the client to cope.

Selection of counterconditioning response

According to reciprocal inhibition, for desensitisation to occur the client must respond in a way that inhibits the anxiety. The therapist must select and train the client to use a response that is incompatible with the anxiety. The counterconditioning response that is typically used is deep muscle relaxation.

The procedure has many advantages: it is easily learnt by most people; it is relatively easy to teach; it is also possible for clients to use it easily in their daily life. However, occasionally, a client may have difficulty in engaging in relaxation, and it must be remembered that deep muscle relaxation is not always applicable to *in vivo* situations in which the client may find himself. When deep muscle relaxation cannot be used as the counterconditioning technique, the therapist may decide to substitute an alternative response. In some cases, clients have been desensitised without relaxation. But it may be risky to proceed without any response to counteract anxiety with a client who is very anxious. Many other examples of counterconditioning have been used in desensitisation, including emotive imagery, meditation, assertion responses and music.

Some of these responses have only specific applications, however, one of the above techniques may act as a reasonable substitute if muscle relaxation is not suitable for a client, and they are relatively easy to teach.

The therapist will need to provide training for the client in the particular response to be used. This training may require at least several sessions before the client is proficient. The training in the counterconditioning technique can occur simultaneously with the hierarchy construction. Explanation of relaxation as a coping response should inform clients that they will be made aware of sensations associated with anxiety and will learn to use these emotions as a signal to cope and relax away the tension.

Imagery assessment

The usual administration of desensitisation relies heavily on client imagery. The relearning that is achieved in desensitisation occurs during visualisation of the hierarchy items. This, of course, assumes that the imagination of a situation is equivalent to a real situation, and that the learning in the imagined situation generalises to the real situation. A client's capacity to generate clear and vivid images can be assessed by the use of practice scenes or by questionnaires. Generally, it is a good idea to assess the client's imagery for desensitisation at two different times, namely, when the client is relaxed, and when he is unrelaxed.

A client who is unable to use imagery may not benefit from a hierarchy that is presented via his imagination. Based on the result of the client's imagery assessment, the therapist should determine whether the client's image meets the criteria for effective therapeutic imagery. Four principle criteria have been proposed:

1. The client must be able to imagine a scene correctly, with sufficient detail and with evidence of sensations such as sight, touch, smell and so on;
2. The scene should be imagined in such a way that the client is a participant rather than an observer;
3. The client should be able to switch a scene image on and off upon instructions;
4. The therapist has the following options if these or other difficulties are encountered during imagery assessment: to add a dialogue or script; to provide imagery training; to present the hierarchy in another manner, for example, role-play, *in vivo*, and so on; to terminate desensitisation and use an alternative therapeutic strategy.

Whenever the client is able to report clear and vivid images that meet most of the necessary criteria, the therapist can initiate the systematic desensitisation programme by presenting the hierarchy items. Scenes in the hierarchy are presented after the client has been given training in the counterconditioning response and after the client's imagery capacity has been assessed. There are several possible ways that scenes can be presented to the client, although they usually follow a certain formula and are concluded after 15 to 20 minutes.

The therapist will first need to decide upon the method of scene presentation to be used and explain it in detail to the client. Three methods of scene presentation have been described by Evans (1974):

1. Method R is used primarily when implementing desensitisation according to a traditional model based on the principles of reciprocal inhibition. When the client visualises an item and reports associated anxiety, he is instructed to remove or stop the image, and then to relax. The timing of scene presentation should maximise the amount of time the client imagines the situation without anxiety and minimise the amount of time the client imagines a scene eliciting anxiety. The main reason for the client removing the image is that when his anxiety is escalating to the point where it is becoming stronger than the state of relaxation, it will negate the principles on which reciprocal inhibition works.

2. Method H. When the client indicates anxiety associated with any given scene, the therapist asks the client to hold the image, to continue with the visualisation and to relax away the tension. This method is recommended on the principle that, in real life, the client cannot eliminate a situation upon becoming tense.

3. Method A. When the client indicates anxiety, he is instructed to switch the image to an "adaptive alternative". This might consist of an appropriate response in the feared situation, similar to the coping thoughts taught to clients in cognitive restructuring and stress innoculation.

Signalling systems

During the presentation of hierarchy items there are occasions when the therapist and client need to communicate. In order not to interrupt the client's achievement of a relaxed state, it is necessary to work out a signalling system that he can use in a relatively non-distracting manner. The method selected should be clear to both parties. Some methods include asking the client to: raise a finger while visualising a scene if any anxiety is experienced; slowly raise his hand as anxiety goes up and lower it as it reduces; say "tense" when the anxiety is noticed and "calm" when relaxation is achieved.

Scene presentation

Each scene presentation session should be preceded by a training session involving the designated counterconditioning response. The hierarchy items are presented concurrently with this counterconditioning response. Before the scene presentation begins, the client should engage in a brief period of muscle relaxation or alternative anxiety-competing response. After this period, the client's relaxation rating should be 10 or less on the "SUDS" scale.

At this point, the therapist begins by describing a hierarchy item to the client and instructs him to imagine the scene. The initial session begins with the first or least anxiety-provoking item in the hierarchy. Successive scene presentation always begins with the last item successfully completed at the preceding session. This helps to make a smooth transition from one session to the next and checks on learning retention. Also, starting with the last successfully completed item may prevent spontaneous recovery of the anxiety response. Relapse sometimes occurs between therapy sessions and this procedure is one way of checking for it.

In presenting the item, the therapist should describe it and ask the client to imagine it. Usually, the therapist will present an item for a specified amount of time, say, 20 to 40 seconds, before asking the client to stop the image. The reasons for this are that, inadvertently, some avoidance response may be reinforced if the client signals anxiety before this time and the therapist immediately instructs the client to stop the image. Also, it prevents the recovery of previous desensitised items.

The therapist can instruct the client to stop the scene and to take a little time to relax if he holds the scene for the specified duration and does not record any tension. This relaxation time serves as a "breather" between item presentation. There is no set time for a pause between items. Generally, a pause of between 30 to 60 seconds is sufficient, although some clients may need as much as two to three minutes.

If the client indicates that anxiety *was* experienced during the visualisation, the therapist will instruct him to remove the image and relax (method R), or hold the image and relax away the tension (method H), or switch the image to an adequate or coping alternative (method A). Generally the therapist will pause for 30 to 60 seconds and then present the same item again. Successful coping or anxiety-reduction is required before presenting the next item. When a client successfully completes two successive no-anxiety presentations, this is usually considered adequate to proceed to the next item in the hierarchy. However, it may be necessary to obtain three or four no-anxiety repetitions before proceeding to the next item with very anxiety-arousing items.

If an item continues to elicit anxiety after three presentations, this may indicate some difficulty and a need for adjusting the treatment programme, since there may be a problem in either the hierarchy or the client's visualisation. There are at least three things a therapist can try if this happens:

1. A new, less anxiety-provoking item can be added to the hierarchy;
2. The same item can be presented to the client more briefly;
3. The client's visualisation can be assessed to determine whether he is drifting from or revisiting the scene.

It is important that the therapist gives the client standardised instructions, regardless of whether the client signals anxiety or reports a low or high anxiety rating on any of the scales used. A therapist can inadvertently reinforce a client for not signalling anxiety by saying "good". The client may be eager to please the therapist and can learn to avoid giving reports of anxiety because these are not similarly reinforced.

Each scene presentation session should end with an item that evokes no anxiety, since the last item of a series is well remembered. At times, the therapist may need to return to a lower item on the hierarchy so that presentation of a non-anxiety provoking scene can end the session. Generally, any scene presentation session should be terminated when three to five hierarchy items have been completed successfully, or at the end of 15 to 30 minutes, whichever comes first. A session may be terminated with completion of fewer items or in a shorter time if the client seems restless.

Notation   Most therapists use some form of written recording during scene-presentation sessions. There are several possible ways to make notations of the client's progress; most commonly used is a desensitisation record sheet (Figure 10.6) which is used to record the hierarchy item numbers and the anxiety rating associated with each item presentation.

Figure 10.6 Desensitisation Record

Client's name:

Theme of hierarchy:

	Time needed to relax	Time needed to visualise image
Before commencement of treatment	....	....
After ...... sessions	....	....
After ...... sessions	....	....
At end of treatment	....	....

Date	Session No.	No. in hierarchy	Anxiety rating	Time between items	Comments

Homework Homework is essential to the successful completion of desensitisation. It may include daily practice of the selected relaxation procedure, visualisation of the items completed in the previous session and exposure to *in vivo* situations.

Most therapists instruct clients to practise the relaxation method being used once or twice daily. This is especially important in the early sessions, in which training in counterconditioning occurs. In addition, a therapist can assign the client to practise visualising the items covered in the last session after the relaxation session. Some therapists record three to five items on audio-tape so that clients can administer this assignment themselves. Gradually, *in vivo* homework tasks can be added.

As desensitisation progresses, the client should be encouraged to participate in real-life situations that correspond to the situation covered in the hierarchy item during the session. This is important in order to facilitate generalisation from imagined to real anxiety-producing situations. However, there may be some risk in the client engaging in a real situation corresponding to a hierarchy item that has not yet been covered in the scene presentation sessions. The client should record completion of all homework assignments. The therapist should arrange a follow-up session to assess how the client is progressing after all desensitisation sessions are completed.

Problems encountered during desensitisation

Some of the more common difficulties encountered during desensitisation include: problems in relaxation, ineffective imagery, and inadequate hierarchy arrangement and presentation.

Problems in relaxation can be improved with additional training or with a gradual shaping process. An alternative method of relaxation can be used, or a different type of counterconditioning response can be selected.

A client's inability to generate clear images may be improved by adding a dialogue or script to the item description. If imagery continues to be a problem, *in vivo* desensitisation can be tried. Alternatively, the hierarchy can be presented by other means such as slides, video or role-play.

An inaccurate hierarchy arrangement, the selection of the wrong theme and inadequacies in the method of hierarchy presentation also can be trouble spots. Sometimes these problems can be alleviated by re-analysing the client's problem or by using variations in the method of scene presentation. Occasionally, clients can benefit from a different form of desensitisation.

Variations in systematic desensitisation

The above procedure reflects the traditional model, applied over a series of sessions, to an individual client by a therapist using an individualised hierarchy arranged by the client. However, there are several variations of this procedure.

Massed desensitisation   Desensitisation does not have to be administered over a series of spaced sessions in order to be effective. In order to speed up the treatment procedure, some therapists have explored the effectiveness of desensitisation administered in massed intervals of time. Here, relaxation training may be given for one hour, with hierarchy presentation occurring for two to two-and-a-half hours. In some forms of massed desensitisation, the clients complete only the highest items in the hierarchy. Desensitisation has also been administered in time blocks, varying from 12 hours to five days.

Group administered desensitisation   Administration of desensitisation to a group of clients who share similar concerns or fears also can be effective and is more cost-effective than individualised administration. Usually, a standardised hierarchy and instructions are administered *en masse*.

Self-administered desensitisation   Some studies of desensitisation have indicated that the presence of a therapist is not critical to the effectiveness of the strategy. Using this procedure, the client administers the programme with the assistance of written instructions, audio-tapes or a treatment manual. However, this method is more likely to incur a higher drop-out rate, although this is probably reduced by even minimal therapist contact.

In vivo **desensitisation**   This involves actual client exposure to the situation in the hierarchy. The client performs or engages in the graded series of situations instead of imagining each item. This variation is used when the client has difficulty in using imagery, when he does not experience anxiety during imagery, or when a client's actual exposure to the situation will have more therapeutic effects.

In vivo desensitisation is preferable to imagined exposure if it is actually possible to expose the client to the feared stimuli because it will produce more rapid results and will foster greater generalisation. At times, the therapist can accompany the client to the feared situation. *In vivo* desensitisation resembles participant modelling in which the client performs a graduated series of difficult tasks with the help of induction aids.

The primary procedural problem associated with *in vivo* desensitisation involves adequate and control of the counterconditioning response. Sometimes it is difficult for a client to achieve a state of deep relaxation while simultaneously performing an activity. However, it is not always necessary to use a counterconditioning response to decrease the client's anxiety in threatening situations. Often, exposure alone will result in sufficient anxiety reduction, particularly if the exposure occurs in graduated amounts.

Historically, desensitisation probably has the longest track record of any of the therapeutic strategies in the behavioural field. Its results are well and frequently documented. However, there is far more controversy surrounding its use today than 10 years ago. It has not outlived its usefulness in the repertoire of anxiety reduction techniques, but it is frequently supplemented with, or replaced, by a variety of other methods for reducing and coping with fears and tensions, as previously outlined. The aim of any anxiety reduction strategy should be to teach a client self-control skills so that future stress does not push his anxiety beyond "tolerable limits".

Deep muscle relaxation

In muscle relaxation, a person is taught to relax by becoming aware of the sensations of tensing and relaxing major muscle groups. Relaxation training is not a new technique; it has been used extensively to deal with a variety of different problems, including high blood pressure and insomnia as well as social anxiety. Muscle relaxation should not be applied indiscriminately, since its effects, like those of any other strategy, are related to satisfactory problem identification. The therapist must apply the procedure competently and confidently. There are two areas that the therapist should assess closely before applying these techniques, as follows. It should be ensured that the client is medically cleared to engage in muscle relaxation. For example, a person who suffers from headaches or lower back pain may have an organic base for these complaints. In addition, a client may be taking medication that is incompatible with muscle relaxation. Second, the therapist should aim to discover the causes of the client's reported tension, and assess if muscle relaxation is a reasonable strategy for its alleviation. For example, if the client is experiencing tension in a job situation, the therapist and client may prefer to deal first with the client's external situation. Relaxation training may be more effective on a short-term basis and will probably need to be supplemented with other therapeutic strategies, especially cognitive ones to provide a complete answer.

Steps of muscle relaxation

The therapist should explain to the client the purpose of relaxation before the procedure begins. It should be explained that muscle relaxation is a skill and that it is likely that learning will be gradual and require regular practice. It is also wise to explain that the client may experience some discomfort during the relaxation process and that, if he does, then he should simply move into a more comfortable position. It should also be explained that the client may experience some floating, warming or heavy sensations and that these are normal for some people undergoing muscle relaxation. It should be ensured that the client is willing to try the procedure before starting.

Instructions about dress

The client should be instructed about dressing appropriately before the actual training session. The client should wear comfortable clothes such as a loose-fitting shirt and trousers, or indeed any clothing in which he feels particularly comfortable. It is best to advise clients wearing contact lenses to remove them before the relaxation begins since they may experience some discomfort when they close their eyes.

Creating a comfortable environment

A comfortable environment is necessary for effective muscle relaxation training. It should be quiet and free of distracting noises such as telephones or doorbells. It is common for the clients to lay on their backs, with legs outstretched and arms down by their sides with palms downwards. A mat or blanket to lie on provides additional comfort.

Trainer modelling of the relaxation exercises

Immediately before relaxation training begins, the therapist should model briefly at least a few of the muscle exercises that will be used in training.

Instructions for muscle relaxation

Muscle relaxation training can start after the therapist has given the client an explanation of the procedure and an opportunity to ask any questions about the technique. In delivering instructions for the relaxation training exercises, the therapist's voice should be conversational and not dramatic. It should be remembered that the therapist does not want the client to strain muscles, and so he should not be instructed to tense them as hard as possible. The therapist should also be careful of his vocabulary when giving instructions: it is wise not to use phrases such as "as hard as you can", or "sagging and drooping muscles". Occasionally, it may be useful to supplement instructions to tense and relax with comments about breathing technique or the warm or heavy feelings experienced.

The muscle groups used for client training can be categorised into various groups, as shown in Figure 10.7. Generally, the therapist will instruct the client to go through all 17 muscle groups in initial training sessions. When the client can alternatively tense and relax any one of these muscle groups on command, it is then possible to abbreviate this procedure and train the client in relaxation using just seven muscle groups. Finally, when the client is proficient, relaxation can take place using only the four major muscle groups outlined in Figure 10.7.

Specimen muscle relaxation session

First, the therapist instructs the client to make himself as comfortable as possible. He then instructs the client to close his eyes, although sometimes the client may not wish to do this, or both therapist and client may decide that it is more therapeutic to keep the eyes open during training. In such cases, the client can focus on an object in the room or on the ceiling. The therapist then tells the client to *listen* and to *focus* on his instructions.

Once the client is in a comfortable position, the therapist starts to tell the client to tense and relax alternatively each of the 17 muscle groups. The therapist should proceed slowly and provide ample time for the client to tense and relax each muscle. He should also pause between the presentation of different muscle groups. Usually, each muscle group is presented twice in initial training sessions. The following events should occur for each muscle group: first, the client's attention should be directed to the muscle group; at a verbal cue from the therapist, the muscle group is tensed; the client should hold this tension, usually for between five and seven seconds; upon a verbal cue from the therapist, the muscle group is relaxed; the client's attention is directed towards the feelings of relaxation.

Figure 10.7   Relaxation — Muscle Groups

19 Muscle groups	*7 Muscle groups*	*4 Muscle groups*
1. Dominant hand	1. Dominant arm/ hand	1. Both arms/hands
2. Non-dominant hand	2. Non-dominant arm/hand	2. Face/neck
3. Dominant arm	3. Facial muscles	3. Chest/back/ abdomen
4. Non-dominant arm	4. Neck/shoulders	4. Both legs/feet
5. Both shoulders	5. Chest leg/foot	
6. Forehead	6. Right leg/foot	
7. Eyes	7. Left leg/foot	
8. Mouth		
9. Jaw		
10. Back of the head		
11. Neck		
12. Chest		
13. Back		
14. Stomach		
15. Buttocks		
16. Right leg		
17. Left leg		
18. Right foot		
19. Left foot		

This five-step process is used during initial instruction to help the client to make a clear discrimination between the sensations of tenseness and relaxation. After each muscle group has been tensed and relaxed twice, the therapist usually concludes relaxation with a summary and review.

The therapist can conclude the training session by evaluating the client's level of relaxation on a scale of 0 to 5, or by counting aloud to the client, instructing him to become successively more alert. For example, he might say: "Now I'd like you to think of a scale from 0 to 5, where 0 is complete relaxation and 5 is extreme tension. Tell me where you would place yourself on that scale now," or, "I'm going to count from 5 to 1. When I reach the count of 1, open your eyes. 5...4...2...1...open your eyes now."

Post-training assessment

After the relaxation training session has been completed, the therapist can ask the client about his experiences. The therapist should be encouraging about the client's performance, praise him and build a positive expectancy about the training and practice.

Potential problems during relaxation training

Cramps, spasms or tics   Possibly too much tension is being created in a particular muscle group if the client experiences cramps. If so, the therapist can instruct the client to decrease the amount of tension. In the case of spasms and tics, the therapist can mention that these occur commonly, as in one's sleep, and that the client is aware of them now only because he is awake.

Excessive laughter or talking   This is most likely to occur in group-administered relaxation training. Possibly the best solution is to ignore it or, alternatively, to discuss how such behaviour can be distracting for other members.

Falling asleep   This is the most common problem during relaxation training. The client should be informed that continually falling asleep can impede learning the skills associated with muscle relaxation. The therapist can confirm whether the client is awake or not by observing him throughout training.

Difficulty in relaxing a specific muscle group   Here it may be necessary for the therapist to work out an alternative exercise for that particular muscle group.

Intrusive thoughts   If these become too distracting, the therapist might suggest changing the focus of the thought to something less distracting or to more pleasant and positive thoughts. It might be better for some clients to gaze at a picture of their choosing, placed on the wall or ceiling, throughout the training. Another strategy for dealing with interfering or distracting thoughts is to help the client use task-orientated coping statements or thoughts that facilitate focusing on relaxation training.

Occurrence of unfamiliar sensations such as floating   As previously stated, the therapist should point out that these sensations are common and that the client should not fear them.

Homework and follow-up

The last step in muscle relaxation is assigning homework. The therapist should inform the client that relaxation training, as with learning any skill, requires a great deal of practice. The more the client practises the procedure, the more proficient he will become in gaining control over tension, anxiety and stress. The client should be instructed to select a quiet place in which to practise, away from distracting noise. The client should be encouraged to practise muscle relaxation exercises for about 15 to 20 minutes, twice a day. Relaxation exercises should be carried out when there is no time pressure. After the exercises are completed, the client should be encouraged to compile a record of his practice. He can rate his anxiety on a scale of 1 (little or no tension) to 5 (extremely anxious), before and after each practice session. Alternatively, he can use a video or audio-tape of relaxation exercises (Figure 10.8).

A follow-up session should be arranged after the muscle relaxation procedure is completed to ensure that the technique is generalised.

Variations of muscle relaxation techniques

Recall   The therapist first instructs the client about the rationale for using this variation of relaxation training. Recall proceeds according to the relaxation exercises for muscle groups without muscular tension, and can be used after the basic muscle relaxation procedure has been learnt. The therapist instructs the client to focus on each muscle group, then to focus on one of the four muscle groups (arms; face and neck; chest, shoulders, back and stomach; legs and feet), and to then relax and recall what it was like when the tension was released for that particular muscle group. The therapist might suggest that if there is tension in a particular muscle group, the client should just relax or send a message for the muscle to relax and allow what tension there is to "flow out". The therapist gives similar instructions for all four muscle groups. Again, the client recalls what the relaxation felt like for each muscle group.

Generally, recall can be used after first using the tension—relaxation

Figure 10.8 Videotaped Vicarious Desensitisation

Combining the use of videotape with systematic desensitisation procedures has become one of the most widely used applications. Standard systematic desensitisation requires the client to imagine a series of anxiety-provoking scenes, graded according to the intensity of anxiety the imagined scene arouses. Each scene is then exposed to an imcompatible stimulus, such as relaxation. One of the common reasons why systematic desensitisation fails is the inability of the client to imagine the scene effectively.

Videotaped vicarious desensitisation is a procedure in which the client *sees* the hierarchy of anxiety-provoking scenes on video. This is a relatively cheap technique in terms of the therapist's time as it can, to a large extent, be automated.

A programme should include the following components:

1. An explanation of systematic desensitisation;

2. Instruction on relaxation;

3. The therapist, on videotape, gives instructions on how to use the tape, after which the hierarchy of anxiety-provoking scenes is presented.

4. Clear instructions to the client about what to do if they feel uncomfortable.

The client should be provided with typed instructions to support the video.

The tape is usually produced using the subjective camera technique, with the actor looking directly into the camera.

An alternative technique is to show the client a video of a model undergoing "live" desensitisation.

contrast procedure for the four muscle groups. Gradually, the client can use recall to induce relaxation in self-directed practices. Recall can also be used in combination with counting.

Counting The purpose of counting is that it helps the client to become very deeply relaxed. Again, the therapist explains the procedure: the client will count from 1 to 10 and after each number the client will feel more relaxed. The therapist can use this technique with recall.

The client can also be instructed to use counting in real-life situations that create tension. Counting is one type of direct-action coping skill used in techniques such as stress innoculation. Counting can increase relaxation and decrease tension and clients should be encouraged to practise it outside the session.

Differential relaxation This variation may help to generalise the relaxation training from the treatment session to the client's world. The idea of differential relaxation is to help the client recognise what muscles are needed in various situations, body positions and activities in order to differentiate which muscle groups are used and which are not. As an example of differential relaxation, the therapist might help a new client sit down in a normal chair and then ask the client to identify which muscles are used and which are not when sitting. The client is instructed to induce relaxation in any muscles not required for sitting, but in which tension is felt.

After several practice sessions, the client can be assigned homework to engage in various levels of these activities. Examples might be sitting in a quiet cafeteria, sitting in a noisy cafeteria while eating, standing in a queue or walking in a busy shopping centre. In practising differential relaxation, the client tries to recognise whether any tension exists in the non-essential muscle groups. The client concentrates on dispelling any tension in the non-engaged muscles.

References

Bard P A (1928) A diencephalic mechanism for the expression of rage, with special reference to the sympathetic nervous system, American Journal of Physiology, 84: 490–513

Cannon W B (1927) The James Lange theory of emotions: A critical examination and alternative theory, American Journal of Psychiatry, 39: 106–124

Evans I M (1974) A handy record card for systematic desensitisation hierarchy items, Journal of Behaviour Therapy and Experimental Psychiatry, 5: 43–46

Hall R and Goldberg D (1977) The role of social anxiety in social interaction difficulties, British Journal of Psychiatry, 131: 610–615

James W (1884) What is an emotion? Reprinted in M Arnold (Editor) The Nature of Emotion (1968), Penguin

Lang P (1970) Stimulus control, response control and desensitisation of fear, in D Levis (Editor) Learning Approaches to Therapeutic Behaviour Change, Aldine Press

Rachman S (1978a) Fear and courage, Freeman

Rachman S (1978b) Human fears: A three system analysis, Scandinavian Journal of Behaviour Therapy, 7: 237–245

Schacter S and Singer J C (1962) Cognitive social and physiological determinants of emotional states, Psychological review, 69: 379–399

Watson D and Friend R (1969) Measurement of social evaluative anxiety, Journal of Consulting and Clinical Psychology, 33: 448–457

Wolpe J (1958) Psychotherapy by Reciprocal Inhibition, Stanford University Press

Wolpe J and Lazarus A A (1966) Behaviour Therapy Techniques, Pergamon

Further reading

Halford K and Foddy M (1982) Cognitive and social skills correlates of social anxiety, British Journal of Clinical Psychology, 21: 17–28

Jupp H and Dudley M (1984) Group cognitive/anxiety management, Journal of Advanced Nursing, 9: 573–580

Lang P J (1978) Anxiety: Toward a psychophysiological definition, in H S Akisal and W H Webb (Editors) Psychiatric Diagnosis: Exploration of Biological Predictors, Spectrum Publication

Marks I M (1969) Fears and Phobias, Heinneman

Marzillier J S, Lambert C and Kellet J (1976) A controlled evaluation of systematic desensitisation and social skills training for socially inadequate psychiatric patients, Behavioural Research and Therapy, 14: 225–238

Stearn R S (1978) Behavioural Techniques, Academic Press

Trower P, Yardley K, Bryant B and Shaw P (1978) The treatment of social failure, Behaviour Modification, 2(1), January

Wolpe J and Lang P J (1964) A fear survey schedule for use in behaviour therapy, Behaviour Research and Therapy, 2: 27–30

CHAPTER 11

SOCIAL SKILLS AND COGNITIVE THERAPY

Traditionally, social skill training has focused principally on overt behavioural components that are clearly visible, such as inter-personal distance and starting up a conversation. Over the past few years there has been an increasing awareness that cognitive processes can have considerable influence on behaviour. This chapter will briefly review cognitive behaviour modification techniques before describing four methods of cognitive therapy in detail.

The strictly behavioural approaches to social skill training have been criticised as being overly simplistic. However, it is equally short-sighted to assume that social skills are not "skills" at all, but rather "cognitions". The aim of cognitive behaviour and modification techniques is to alter the client's "cognitions". The underlying assumption is that maladapted "cognition" can influence social behaviour and that it is possible to improve social behaviour by altering a client's cognitive processes.

The cognitive learning model

This model, developed from the work of Bandura (1977), Mischel (1973), and others, takes into account the clinical work of Ellis (1962) and Kanfer and Phillips (1970). It is based on the view that a person is a complex organism capable of adaptation with his environment and that he relates to this environment by a continuous feedback relationship. Behaviour changes are influenced by the current physiological state of the person, his past learning history, the existing environmental situation, and a variety of interdependent cognitive processes, (such as selective attention, anticipated consequences, and so on).

The most significant feature of the cognitive learning model is its role in human learning. It is apparent that human beings utilise memory and thought processes to attempt to deal with interactions with the environment. Thus, using this model, one possible cause for an individual not functioning receptively in the community could be that the intermediary cognitive processes are not functioning effectively.

Several different types of cognitive distortion have been commonly found. They include: *over-generalisation*, where the client gives a single negative event a much broader interpretation than it deserves; *black and white thinking*, where the client perceives himself as a total failure if his performance falls short of "perfect"; identification, where the client *associates* himself with a *negative external event* for which he was not primarily responsible; *jumping to conclusions* where, for example, the client presumes that someone is reacting negatively to him, even though there may be no evidence to support this; *rejecting the positive* — the client rejects positive experiences by "not counting" them and accepts only negative feedback; *"should" statements* — the client tries to motivate himself using "shoulds" and "should nots" as if he had to be whipped and punished before he will do anything. The frequent consequence of this type of approach is that the client feels guilty.

"Cognition" in depression and anxiety

Beck (1976) has presented extensive anecdotal evidence that depressed and anxious clients exhibit negative thoughts. He found that the thought content of depressed clients was characterised by low self-regard, self-criticism and self-blame, overwhelming problems, frequent self-command, and the desire to get away, often including suicidal desires.

Similarly, Lewinsohn (1976) has found that depressed individuals report more negative thoughts and fewer positive thoughts than non-depressed psychiatric controls or normal subjects.

Different types of cognitions have been implicated in different types of social inadequacy, and these include: negative thoughts; negative and/or irrational beliefs; social perception; self-perception; social problem-solving; attributional style; and memory distortion.

Negative thoughts   Negative thoughts have been found to be involved in some clients experiencing social inadequacy. There appears to be at least four ways in which negative thought patterns are related to social inadequacy:

1. Evidence from mood induction studies shows that negative thoughts may contribute towards depressed mood and less active speech;
2. Thoughts of negative consequences might lead some individuals to avoid social situations;
3. Negative thoughts could interfere subtly with active communication processes. Singer (1975) has reviewed research suggesting that negative thoughts during social situations can be detected by reduced eye movements, less eye contact and by the eyes being slightly out of focus;
4. It is possible that negative thoughts could produce more obvious performance deficits during communication, although, to date, research in this field has been only moderately successful in isolating differences in the behaviour of socially adequate and inadequate individuals.

Negative and/or irrational beliefs   It is possible that negative beliefs could be antecedent to clinical problems, or they could simply be factors that reflect previous learning. There has been considerable research into the role of negative beliefs in depression but, to date, there is still a great deal of ambiguity in this area and it is difficult to draw conclusions.

Social perception   Social perception refers to the process of monitoring events in social interaction, which it is assumed will improve social effectiveness. A similar, related concept is that of self-monitoring, which has been described as an overlapping process; self-deception is concerned with the conception of others, and self-monitoring with the perception of oneself. The way in which a person perceives himself and the social environment is seen to be an important factor in social functioning.

Self-perception   The paradox in attempting to relate self-deception and the problems of social inadequacy is that behavioural self-monitoring is seen to be facilitating in its self-regulatory role, and interfering in the case of social anxiety. It has been found among depressed subjects that instructions to self-monitor mood or activity can improve mood and rate of activity. Hence, increased self-observation appears to be therapeutically beneficial for depressed subjects. However, little research has been conducted on self perception to date.

Social problem-solving   D'Zurilla and Goldfried (1971) defined problem-solving as "a behavioural process, whether overt or covert in nature, which: (a) makes available a variety of potentially effective response alternatives for dealing with the problematic situation, and (b) increases the probability of selecting the most effective response from amongst the various alternatives."

As such, problem-solving seems to be a mixture of what can be considered cognitive and behavioural processes. Five steps are outlined by D'Zurilla and Goldfried to describe effective problem-solving: the adoption of a problem-solving orientation; problem definition and formulation; generation of alternatives; decision making; and verification.

Spivack presented a similar process to this and maintained that the following steps were involved in successful inter-problem solving: an awareness of potential problems when human beings interact; the generation of alternative solutions to problems; specifying the necessary means to carry out the steps to resolve the problem; understanding the consequences of a specific solution for oneself and others; cause—effect thinking, understanding that social interactions can be a two-way process and that it is affected by the behaviour of other people (Spivack *et al.* 1976).

Little research has been conducted so far on social problem-solving. However, it appears to be essential that a therapist should distinguish social problem-solving ability from non-social problem-solving or general intellectual impairment.

Attributional style   This refers to the particular manner of ascribing responsibility or making causal inferences from a behaviour or event. Attributional processes have been used to explain the development and aetiology of depression. The learned *helplessness model* proposes that a style in which depressed individuals attribute negative outcomes to internal factors can contribute to depression. To date, no specific attributional style has been postulated for other types of psycho-pathology.

Current research largely supports the notion of a strong relationship between an attributive style for negative events and mild to moderate depression. However, whether this depressive attributional style is specific to depression and whether it is a characteristic of clinically depressed and more mildly depressed subjects remains to be demonstrated. The depressive attributional style is associated with, or plays a causal role in, the development of social inadequacy among depressed clients.

Memory distortion   Beck's (1976) cognitive model for psycho-pathology and therapy proposes that depressed individuals have and maintain a negative view of the world, themselves and the future, by engaging in a number of cognitive distortions such as magnification and over-generalisation. Data on memory distortion generally indicate that depressed subjects show a negative bias when recalling positive feedback. However, they are accurate in their recall of negative feedback and it is "normal" for them to distort recall of negative feedback in a positive direction.

These findings suggest that cognitive components of social skills training should be geared towards teaching clients a slight positive bias in their interpretation and memory of social experiences. The depressed client's memory distortions may weaken the effects of therapeutic approaches that focus only on increasing the skill and frequency of social interaction.

In general terms, it has been found that each of the cognitive deficits outlined here have been associated, to some extent, with social inadequacy.

Cognitive behaviour therapy

In recent years more attention and effort have been directed towards developing and evaluating procedures than at modifying thoughts, attitudes and beliefs. These procedures come under the broad umbrella of cognitive therapy or cognitive behaviour modification. Several basic assumptions are made about cognitive change procedures, one of which is that a person's thoughts and beliefs can contribute to maladaptive behaviour. Another is that maladaptive behaviour can be altered by dealing directly with present beliefs, attitudes or thoughts. It has been pointed out by many clinicians that a client's unreasonable self-standards and negative self-thoughts can diminish the power of most treatment programmes. Attention to these beliefs and expectations may be essential for other therapeutic strategies to be successful.

Many ways have been found to conceptualise cognitive problems: Lazarus (1971) found that clients who think in extremes, over-generalise, attempt to please everyone, and who regard cultural values as absolute are prone to cognitive disorders. Beck (1976) proposed that people who distort or misperceive reality and who engage in illogical thinking are more likely to have social interactional problems. Mahoney (1974) categorised cognitive problems into five areas:

1. Selective inattentiveness, in which the client attends to irrelevant cues and ignores relevant ones;

2. Misperception, in which external or internal cues are mislabelled;
3. Maladaptive focusing, in which external, irrelevant stimuli or events are focused upon;
4. Maladaptive self-arousal, in which internal, relevant stimuli or cues are focused upon;
5. Skills deficit, in which limited or inadequate behaviour is due to a deficit in either cognitive or behavioural skills.

In the clinical world, it is more common to see a client who has difficulties in several of these areas, all of which may interact. For example, a client may feel anxious in social situations with strangers partly because of deficits in skills such as initiating conversations. At the same time, he may feel anxious because he thinks the person he is talking to is non-receptive. Exploration of the client's problems might reveal that he also mis-perceives or ignores cues in other types of situations. It is likely that at any cognitive change procedure will need to be directed towards altering multiple rather than singular cognitive problems.

Cognitive behaviour therapy has been the subject of much debate in recent years. The treatment involves a combination of behavioural (such as task assignment) and cognitive techniques (for example cognitive modelling). Typically, between 15 and 20 sessions are necessary to explore various aspects of the client's current functioning. The sessions concentrate on discovering a connection between the client's thoughts and the other components of his performance, such as emotional and behavioural factors. The aim is to encourage "distancing" of the client from his negative thoughts and to loosen the connection between these thought patterns and the client's performance difficulties. Some of the treatment components commonly used in cognitive behaviour therapy include: featuring of self-monitoring thoughts; teaching how to set appropriate goals; teaching self-reinforcements or achievements; teaching how to find alternative responses for negative thoughts; cognitive modelling; stress inoculation; and thought stopping.

Rational emotive therapy

One theoretical framework for altering self-statements stems from the rational emotive therapy (RET) model developed by Ellis (1962). The basic premise of RET is that maladaptive behaviour results largely from irrational belief systems that influence what people say to themselves and thereby control their behaviour. Ellis takes the position that inappropriate behaviour is less the function of a particular event than it is of what one says to oneself about that event. A client who receives bad news may exhibit more maladaptive behaviour if he tells himself that he is worthless or that the news is terrible or catastrophic, than someone who does not respond in this way. The objective model helps the individual to identify events leading up to specific behaviours, to analyse the irrational belief systems considered to be controlling these reactions, and to replace them with rational ones that are more likely to lead to adaptive behaviour.

The RET therapist helps the client to identify which of these irrational ideas are caused by their belief systems and emotional reactions. According to RET, it is possible to resolve a client's problems by "cognitive control of illogical emotions or responses". Such control is achieved in RET primarily by re-educating the client through the use of what Ellis refers to as the ABCDE model. This model involves showing the client how irrational beliefs (B) about an activity or action (A) result in irrational and inappropriate consequences (C). The client is taught to dispute (D) irrational beliefs (B) that are not facts and have no supporting evidence, and to recognise the effects (E).

One of the major assumptions that RET cognitive restructuring and stress inoculation share is that a person's beliefs and thoughts can create emotional distress and maladaptive responding. Another shared assumption is that someone's cognitive system can be changed directly, and that such changes result in different and, presumably, more appropriate consequences.

There are some differences between RET and cognitive behaviour modification procedures. For example, cognitive behavioural procedures do not assume that certain irrational ideas are generally held by all. In cognitive restructuring and stress inoculation, each client's particular irrational thoughts are identified and assumed to be idiosyncratic, although some elements may be shared by others. A second difference involves the method of change. In RET the therapist attempts to help the client alter irrational beliefs by verbal persuasion and teaching. Emphasis is placed on helping the client to discriminate between irrational beliefs that have no evidence, and rational beliefs that can be supported by evidence. In cognitive restructuring and stress inoculation a client is taught the skill of using coping cognitions in stressful situations.

Rational emotive therapy holds that certain poor, irrational ideas that are frequently observed clinically are at the root of much inadequate performance. Among these ideas are:

1. That it is essential for a person to be loved by everyone for everything he does, instead of concentrating on his own self-respect, on receiving approval for practical purposes and on loving rather than being loved;
2. That certain acts are wicked, and that people who perform such acts should be severely punished, rather than that certain acts are inappropriate or anti-social, and that people who perform such acts are behaving stupidly and ignorantly, and would be better helped to change;
3. That it is horrible when things are not the way one would like them to be, instead of the idea that it is too bad, that one would better try to change or control conditions so that they become more satisfactory and, if that is not possible, that one had had better temporarily accept their existence;
4. That human misery is caused externally and is forced on one by outside people and events, instead of the idea that emotional disturbance is caused by the view one takes of conditions;
5. That one should be terribly upset if something is or may be dangerous or fearsome, instead of the idea that one had better face the situation frankly and try to render it non-dangerous or, if that is not possible, accept the inevitable;
6. That it is easier to avoid than to face life's difficulties and self-responsibilities, instead of the idea that the so-called "easy way" is invariably the much harder in the long run;
7. That one needs something other or stronger or greater than oneself on which to rely, instead of the idea that it is better to take the risks of thinking and acting independently;
8. That one should be thoroughly competent, intelligent and achieving in all possible respects, instead of accepting oneself as an imperfect creature with general human limitations and specific fallibility;
9. That because something once strongly affected one's life, it should affect it indefinitely, instead of the idea that one can learn from one's past experiences but not be overly attached to or prejudiced by them;
10. That one must have certain and perfect control over things, instead of the idea that the world is full of probability and doubt and that one can still enjoy life despite this.
11. That human happiness can be achieved by inertia and inaction, instead of the idea that people tend to be happiest when they are vitally absorbed in creative pursuits, or when they are devoting themselves to people and projects besides themselves.

12. That one has virtually no control over one's emotions and that one cannot help feeling certain things, instead of the idea that one has enormous control over one's emotions if one chooses to work at changing the basis on which they have developed.

In using cognitive methods with social skills training, certain tentative conclusions have been reached. For example, that training should be presented in a relaxed rather than a rigid manner, establishing rapport and individualising according to a client's development and skill level. Due to the heavy reliance on language in cognitive skills, the client with language, cognitive and attentional deficits may require extensive systematic instruction before cognitive techniques can be used. After acquiring these basic skills, the client should be involved in determining the training procedures to be used. Through questioning, the therapist should get the client to identify for himself an effective self-training strategy, rather than imposing one on him. The client's own language should be used wherever possible.

One major problem encountered in training clients in cognitive techniques is that "self taught" clients may become mechanical, in which case they are unlikely to be effective in controlling maladaptive behaviour. To prevent this happening it is suggested that training should be conducted so that the client knows that he should say only what he genuinely means and not just things to please the therapist.

A final consideration is the quantity of instruction. The procedures outlined are designed to be presented over an extended period of time, ideally on a daily basis. The therapist using cognitive approaches should be committed to regular instruction over a period of weeks. During and following training, monitoring should make certain that the client's cognitions are appropriate and that the client is using the appropriate cognitive mechanisms to direct and control his behaviour.

Technique 1: Cognitive modelling with self-instructional training

Some of the most impressive work using self-instructional training techniques has been undertaken by Meichenbaum (1977) in the United States. He first became interested in the effects of "self-statements" during research into the modification of schizophrenic "crazy talk". He observed that many of these people, who had been trained to think more "normally" maintained their improved social performance by using overt self-instruction such as "be more relevant", "be more coherent".

Cognitive modelling is a procedure in which the therapist shows a person what to say to himself while performing a task. A person models a set of verbalisations and behaviours that characterise a strategy that could be used in performing a task. This cognitive modelling and self-instructional training has been used effectively to reach hospitalised schizophrenics to alter their thinking and language while performing tasks (Meichenbaum and Cameron, 1973). According to these authors, cognitive modelling with self-instructional training consists of five steps:

1. The therapist serves as a model and first performs the tasks while talking aloud to himself;
2. The client performs the same tasks (as modelled by the therapist), while the therapist instructs the client aloud;
3. The client is instructed to perform the same task again while instructing himself aloud;
4. The client whispers the instructions before performing the task;
5. The client performs the task while instructing himself covertly.

The method described in this book consists of seven stages: explanation of the procedure to client; cognitive modelling; overt external guidance; overt self-guidance; faded overt self-guidance; covert self-guidance; and homework.

Introduction

The therapist should explain to the client how the therapy sessions will be structured and the purpose of the procedures by saying, for example: "It has been found that some people have difficulty in performing certain kinds of tasks. Often, this difficulty is not because they do not have the ability to perform the task, but because of what they say or think of themselves while performing the task. In other words, a person's 'self-talk' can get in the way or interfere with his performance. For instance, if you get up to give a speech and you think, 'I can't do this — look at all those people looking at me,' then this type of thinking is likely to affect how you deliver your speech. The procedures we are going to use will help you to have more control over your thoughts in these types of situations."

Cognitive modelling

First, the therapist should instruct the client to listen to the therapist's "self-talk" while the therapist is performing a specified task.

The therapist then models performing the task while talking aloud to himself. The first part of the therapist's "self-talk" should ask a question about the nature and demands of the task to be performed. The purpose of these questions are to compensate for a possible deficiency in the client's comprehension of what he has to do, and to provide a general orientation to the therapy approach.

The second part of the therapist's modelled "self-talk" answers the question of what to do, or how to perform the task. The answer is designed to model cognitive rehearsal and planning in order to focus the client's attention on relevant task requirements.

Self-instruction in the form of self-guidance while performing the task is the third part of the modelled "self-talk". The purpose of this self-guidance is to improve the client's attention to the task and to inhibit any possible overt or covert distractions.

Modelled self-reinforcement is the fourth part of this stage and is designed to maintain the client's involvement in the task and to reinforce success. The last part of the therapist's modelled self-talk contains coping self-statements to handle errors and frustrations, with an option for correcting errors.

Overt external guidance

After the therapist has modelled the cognitive strategy, the client is instructed to perform the task as modelled by the therapist. The therapist coaches the client through the task or activity. The therapist should make sure that the coaching contains the same five elements of self-guidance that were outlined in the therapist's model, namely, question, planning, focused attention, coping self-evaluation, and self-reinforcement.

Sometimes in the client's real life situation, other people may be watching when the client performs the task. If the presence of other people appears to interfere with the client's performance, the therapist should decide on role plays that incorporate this element, perhaps by including coping statements that can be used in this type of situation. The therapist should attempt to make this type of procedure resemble closely what the client will actually encounter in his real-life environment.

Overt self-guidance

The therapist next instructs the client to perform the task while instructing or guiding himself aloud. The purpose of this step is for the client to practise the kind of "self-talk" that will strengthen attention to the demands of the task and minimise outside distractions. The therapist should look carefully at the content of the client's self-verbalisation. Again, as in the two preceding stages, the verbalisation should include the five component parts, and the client should be encouraged to use his own words. The therapist should intervene and coach if the client's self-guidance is incomplete or if the client gets stuck. The therapist can return to the previous steps, if necessary, either modelling again or coaching the client while he performs a task (overt external guidance). When the client has completed this step, the therapist should provide feedback about those parts that the client completed adequately and about any errors or omissions. Additional practice may be necessary before moving on to the next step, which is faded overt self-guidance.

Faded overt self-guidance

The client next performs the task while whispering the "self-talk". This part of cognitive modelling serves as an intermediate step between the client verbalising aloud, as in overt self-guidance, and the client verbalising silently, as in covert self-guidance. Whispering the self-guidance is a way for the client to approximate successfully the end result of the procedure, which is thinking to oneself while performing.

It has often been found necessary to explain this procedure to a client, who may seem hesitant or concerned about the approach. It may be more beneficial to repeat overt self-guidance several times if the client finds the whispering approach alien or difficult and then move directly to covert self-guidance. An additional practice might be required before moving on if the client has difficulty in performing this step or leaves out any of the other five parts.

Covert self-guidance

Finally, the client should perform the task while guiding himself (instructing covertly) "in his head". It is very important that the client should instruct himself covertly after practising the self-guidance overtly. Afterwards the therapist could ask him for a description of the covert self-instruction he used. If distracting or inhibiting self-talk has occurred, the therapist can offer suggestions for more appropriate verbalisation or "self-talk", and can initiate additional practice.

Homework

Assigning the client homework is essential for generalisation to occur from the therapy session to the client's own environment. The therapist should instruct the client to use overt verbalisation while performing the appropriate behaviours alone, outside the therapy session. The homework assignment should specify what the client would do, and how much and how often. The therapist should also provide a way for the client to monitor and reward himself for completion of homework.

Technique 2: Thought-stopping

Thought control techniques were introduced as early as 1928 by Bain. The thought control procedure of thought-stopping was developed by Taylor (1963) and has been described by both Wolpe (1973) and Lazarus (1971). Thought-stopping is used to help the client control unproductive or self-defeating thoughts and images by suppressing or eliminating these negative cognitions. Thought-stopping is particularly appropriate with clients who ruminate about past events that cannot be eliminated or changed ("crying over spilt milk"), those who ruminate about events that are unlikely to occur, or those who engage in repetitive, unproductive and negative thinking, or repetitive anxiety-producing or self-defeating images. These cognitions may take the form of thoughts or visual images. For example, a person who is always bothered with the idea of a spouse having an affair may engage in repetitive thoughts such as, "What if this happens to me?" or "It would be just my luck to have her/him cheat on me". Another client concerned over the same event might report repetitive images, visualising the spouse with another person. Olin (1976) has suggested that thought-stopping may not be appropriate for all clients who have such intensely troubling thoughts that they cannot control them. It has also been suggested that thought-stopping works better with clients who are troubled with intermittent rather than continuous self-defeatist thoughts.

Of course, thought-stopping should be used only with clients whose thoughts are clearly counterproductive. Wolpe has distinguished between problem-solving thoughts that lead to actions, that is, desirable thoughts, and those that lead to a dead end, that is, negative thoughts. Thought-stopping has been used for a variety of clinical problems, including the reduction of hallucinatory images, the reduction of fantasies of dressing in clothes of the opposite sex, to reduce obsessive and self-critical thoughts, to reduce anxiety attacks about epileptic seizures, and to eliminate constant thoughts and images of a spouse's extramarital affairs.

Although the clinical case reports of thought-stopping indicate encouraging results, there is very little evidence available from controlled investigations to lend empirical support to the procedure. Thought-stopping has been effective in reducing smoking and helpful in reducing outpatients' obsessive thinking. However, because of limited data, a number of questions about the mechanism of thought-stopping remain unanswered.

Nevertheless, thought-stopping is frequently used, often in conjunction with other strategies, and there are several distinct advantages to the procedure. It is easily administered, usually understood by the client and is readily employed by the client in a self-regulatory manner. There are six major components of the thought-stopping strategy: introduction; therapist-directed thought-stopping (overt interruption); client-directed thought-stopping (overt interruption); client-directed thought-stopping (covert interruption); a shift to assertive, positive or neutral thoughts; and homework and follow-up.

Introduction

First, the therapist should explain the purpose of thought-stopping. Clients should be aware of the nature of their self-defeating thoughts or images before using the strategy. Wolpe suggests that the therapist should point out how the client's thoughts are futile and the ways in which he would be better off without being bothered by such thoughts or images. If the client agrees to try out thought-stopping, the therapist should describe the procedure without displaying too graphically the way in which thoughts are stopped, since the initial surprise is most effective.

Therapist-directed thought-stopping

In this first phase of thought-stopping, the therapist assumes responsibility for interrupting the thoughts. The interruption is overt, for example a loud "Stop!" accompanied by a noise such as a hand clap, a ruler hitting a desk or a whistle. In the first therapist-directed sequence, the client is instructed to verbalise aloud all sorts of images. The verbalisation enables the therapist to determine the precise point that the client shifts from positive to negative thinking.

The sequence is as follows: the therapist instructs the client to sit back and let any thoughts come into his mind; the therapist instructs the client to verbalise aloud his thoughts or images as they occur; the therapist interrupts with a loud "Stop!" at the point where the client verbalises a self-defeating thought or image (sometimes a loud noise stimulus can also be used); the therapist points out whether the unexpected interruption was effective in terminating the client's negative thoughts or images.

After this sequence, the therapist directs another thought-stopping sequence in which the client does not verbalise his thoughts aloud but uses a hand signal to inform the therapist of the onset of a self-defeating thought or image. This sequence is similar to the first one with the exception of the hand signal: the therapist asks the client to sit back and let thoughts come naturally to his mind; the therapist instructs the client to signal with a raised hand or finger when he notices himself thinking negative or self-defeating ideas; when the client signals, the therapist interrupts with "Stop!" These three steps are repeated in the session as often as necessary: generally, this is until a pattern is established that inhibits the client's self-defeating thoughts by using the therapist's command.

Client-directed thought-stopping (overt interruption)

After the client has learned to control negative thoughts in response to the therapist's interruption, the client himself assumes responsibility for the interruption. At first, the client directs himself in the thought-stopping sequence with the same overt interruption techniques used by the therapist, that is, a loud "Stop!" The method is as follows: the client deliberately invokes thinking about something and lets all kinds of thoughts come into his mind; the therapist instructs the client to say a loud "Stop!" whenever he notices a self-defeating thought or image.

These two steps are repeated until the client is able to suppress self-defeating thoughts by overt self-interruption. Sometimes a client may report that even the word "Stop!" or a clap is not a strong enough stimulus to actually terminate the undesired thought. In these cases, a smack of a rubber band on the hand or wrist, at least for a short time, may add to the potential of these stimuli to stop negative thoughts.

Client-directed thought-stopping

In many cases, it would be impractical and unwise for clients to interrupt themselves overtly. One can imagine the scene if a client in a bus, taxi or shop suddenly yelled "Stop!". Therefore in the next sequence of thought-stopping, the client substitutes covert for overt interruption. The same two-step sequence occurs: the client lets any thoughts or images come to mind; when he notices a self-defeating thought, the client stops by covertly saying "Stop!"

These two steps are repeated until the client is able to terminate self-defeating thoughts using only covert instructions.

A shift to positive or neutral thoughts

In some instances, a client's negative thoughts may contribute to a greater level of anxiety. In others, the client's thought patterns may be cued by some preceding anxiety or tension. In both cases, some degree of anxiety or arousal may be present in addition to the ruminative thinking pattern. It has been suggested that the client learns to think assertive thoughts after self-defeating thoughts are interrupted in order to reduce individual anxiety.

Since assertiveness inhibits anxiety, it is assumed that assertive thoughts will also inhibit any anxiety or arousal that may occur, even after the client has learned to suppress undesired thoughts. Essentially, the client is taught to shift thoughts to assertive responses following the interruption. These responses may either contradict the content of the negative thoughts or be unrelated. For example, a client who is constantly worrying about having a nervous breakdown learns to replace these negative thoughts with more positive thoughts. Such assertive thoughts contradict the client's self-defeating thoughts. An example of an unrelated and yet still assertive thought that this same client could use might be "Here are some of the new things I am going to start in my job..." or "I have got some important ideas for the next time I..."

These assertive thoughts should be realistic and geared towards any actual danger in a situation. There is a great deal of similarity between these thoughts and the coping thoughts that the client is taught in cognitive re-structuring. Not all therapists who use thought-stopping will direct the client to shift from self-defeating thoughts to assertive ones. Instead of using assertive thoughts, the client can be asked to focus on a pleasurable, reinforcing or a neutral theme, such as an object in the environment. In one report on thought-stopping, clients who were constantly engaged in self-degrading thoughts were taught to stop the chain of thoughts and replace them with a variety of self-reinforcing thoughts. For example, someone who finds himself thinking "I will never be any good at anything because I haven't got any abilities", can stop these thoughts and shift to neutral or positive ones, such as "I am really not that bad..." or "I am quite good at..." It is important for the client to shift to other kinds of thoughts after the self-defeating ones have stopped. However, the substituted thoughts should be adapted for the client and the nature of the self-defeating thoughts.

The steps involved in teaching the client to shift from self-defeating thoughts to assertive, positive or neutral thoughts are as follows: the therapist explains the purpose of substituting different thoughts for the negative or unproductive ones by saying, for example, "In addition to stopping yourself from ruminating over all the possible horrible ways that you might die, it is helpful to substitute different kinds of thoughts that are unrelated to death. This part of the procedure will help you learn to shift to different thoughts after you stop yourself from self-defeating thinking." Then the therapist models the type of thoughts the client can substitute after terminating the self-defeating ones, and gives some examples. The client is asked to identify others and to practise using these aloud. The therapist might say, "After using 'Stop!' to yourself, shift your thoughts to something positive, like a beautiful sunset or something interesting that you have done during the day, or an interesting object in the room, like a picture on the wall. If you can think of several things like this, then you should think about them from time to time, and just practise these things aloud." Next the client is asked to practise this change after another sequence of self-directed thought-stopping with overt interruptions. As soon as the client says "Stop!", the shift to another kind of thought should be made. The client should verbalise aloud the specific thoughts used: "This time repeat the thought-stopping where you stop your negative thoughts by saying 'Stop!' aloud. Then practise substituting one of these thoughts that you have picked, like thinking about what a good film you saw last night.

After this practice, the client will engage in covert practice. He will stop his thoughts covertly and substitute different thoughts without verbalising them aloud: "When you notice any thoughts popping into your mind, relating to a horrible death, think 'Stop!' and then think about lying on the beach on a warm day."

The client should be encouraged to practise substituting assertive positive or neutral thoughts. Each time the client should use a different thought so that association and constant repetition from only one thought does not occur. A cuing device might help if a client has difficulty in making a shift from negative thoughts to the others. For example, the client can write positive or assertive responsive notes on small notepads and carry these around, or he could put a rubber band on his wrist and use it as a cue for making the shifting thoughts.

Homework

When the client has learned the thought-stopping procedure, he should practise it outside the clinical setting. At first, he should be instructed to practise the thought-stopping sequence several times each day. This homework practice then strengthens the client's control over stopping a chain of self-defeating thoughts as they occur. Some therapists have used a technique where a client uses a tape recording of his "Stop!" messages in the initial phase of homework practice to strengthen thought control. Gradually, the client's use of the tape-recorded messages with daily practice is eliminated.

In addition to daily practice, clients can initiate thought-stopping whenever they notice they are engaging in negative or self-defeating thinking. The client can keep a record of his daily practice and record the number of times thought-stopping is used *in vivo*. As with the application of any strategy, a later follow-up session should be arranged (Figure 11.1).

Both cognitive modelling and thought-stopping involve helping a client to stop distracting or self-defeating ruminations. The next two methods are

Figure 11.1   How Does Thought Stopping Work?

There is no single accepted explanation of what the client learns while using the thought-stopping technique. It is assumed that the method produces some sort of control over obsessive or repetitive thinking.

There are at least four ways in which thought-stopping may help a person learn to control and reduce unwanted thoughts and images:

1. The word "Stop!" may be *an aversive stimulus* that punishes the client's self-defeating thoughts;

2. The word "Stop!" may be *a distraction* that breaks the chain of maladaptive thoughts;

3. The word "Stop!" has *an assertive quality*. If this is the case, the sub-vocalised stop will inhibit anxiety that may trigger the negative thoughts;

4. The instruction "Stop!" may be *incompatible* with the maladaptive thoughts and images the client is trying to eliminate.

designed to help clients to stop self-defeating thoughts and to replace them with incompatible coping thoughts and skills. These techniques are supposed to be a replacement for, and not merely an elimination of, self-defeating cognitions.

Cognitive restructuring and stress inoculation both assume that maladaptive emotions and overt responses are influenced or mediated by one's beliefs, attitudes and expectations, the relationship between cognition and the resulting emotion and behaviour. Both of these procedures help a client to determine the relationship between cognitions and the resulting emotions and behaviour, to identify faulty or self-defeating cognitions, and to replace these cognitions with self-enhancing or positive thoughts. Clients learn how to cope in both strategies. Indirect benefits include an increased feeling of forcefulness, the ability to handle a problem an enhancement of the self-concept.

Technique 3: Cognitive restructuring

Although cognitive restructuring was described by Lazarus (1971) and has its roots in rational emotive therapy, more recently it has been developed by

Meichenbaum (1977), under the name of cognitive behaviour modification, and by Goldfried and Davidson (1976), under the name of systematic rational restructuring. Cognitive restructuring has been used to help anxious clients to cope with social inter-personal anxiety. In related areas, cognitive restructuring has been used to treat depression and pain-related stress. Goldfried and Davidson have recommended cognitive restructuring for problems related to unrealistic self-standards, and this technique is often a major component of assertion training. The procedure is often used in conjunction with other therapeutic strategies and the client's beliefs becomes part of the target for change. There are six principal components to the procedure of cognitive restructuring: an explanation to the client of the procedure; identification of the client's thoughts during difficult situations; the introduction and practise of "coping thoughts"; shifting from "self-defeating" to "coping thoughts"; introduction and practise of positive or reinforcing self-statements; and homework.

Introduction

The introduction of cognitive restructuring attempts to strengthen the client's belief that "self-talk" can influence performance and, particularly, that self-defeating thoughts or negative self-statements can cause emotional distress and interfere with performance. The therapist might say: "We are going to learn how to control our thought processes. The control of our thinking, or what we say to ourselves, comes about by first becoming aware of when we are producing negative self-statements." Examples can be given to the client.

In addition to providing a standard introduction, the cognitive restructuring procedure should be prefaced by some contrast of rational and self-defeating or irrational thoughts. This explanation may help clients to discriminate between their own rational and self-defeating thoughts during treatment. The aim of cognitive restructuring is to show clients how negative thoughts are unproductive, and how they prevent goals being achieved, rather than that the client's ideas are irrational and wrong.

One way to contrast these two types of thinking is to model some examples of positive and enhancing self-thoughts, and negative, defeating self-talk. These examples can come out of personal experiences or relate to the client's problem situation.

This technique should be an explicit attempt to point out how self-defeating or negative thoughts and statements are unproductive and can influence emotions and behaviour. The therapist is attempting to convey to the client that whatever someone tells himself, he is likely to believe and to act on that belief. The importance of providing an adequate explanation for the technique cannot be over-emphasised. Research indicates that people may be more resistant to changing beliefs if they are pushed or coerced to abandon them and to adopt those of someone else. The procedure should be implemented slowly by gradually encouraging clients to agree to the underlying process. The therapist should not proceed until the client's commitment to work with the technique is obtained.

Identifying client's thoughts in problem situations

This next step involves an analysis of the client's thoughts in anxious or distressing situations. First, the range of situations and the contents of the client's thoughts in these situations should be explored. The therapist should question the client about any specific distressing situations he has encountered, and the things the client thinks about before, during and after the situation.

In identifying these negative or self-defeating thoughts, the client might be helped by a description of possible cues that compose the self-defeating thoughts. The therapist can point out that the negative thoughts may have a "worry quality" such as "I am afraid" or a "self-orientating quality" such as "I won't be well." Many of these thoughts may also include elements of catastrophising ("If I fail it will be awful") or exaggerating ("I never do well" or "I always blow it"). It should be proposed that clients can identify the extent to which unrealistic thinking contributes to situational anxiety by asking three questions about his anxiety-provoking situations:

1. Do I make unreasonable demands of myself?
2. Do I feel that others are approving or disapproving of my actions?
3. Do I often forget that this situation is only one part of my life?

The therapist can ask the client to recall the situation, as if running a film through his head, if he has trouble identifying negative thoughts. The therapist may need to point out that the thoughts are the connection between the situation and the resulting emotions, and ask the client to notice explicitly what this link seems to be. The therapist can model this connection if the client is unable to identify thoughts, using either the client's situation or a situation from the therapist's life. The therapist can also get the client to identify a situation by monitoring and recording events and thoughts outside the interview, in the form of homework. An initial homework assignment might be to have the client observe and record for a week, at least three negative self-statement situations in a particular stressful situation.

Using the client's data, the therapist and client can determine which of the thoughts were productive and which were self-defeating and unproductive. The therapist should encourage the client to discriminate between the two types of statements and identify why the negative ones are unproductive. This identification suits several purposes. It is a way to determine whether the client's present repertoire consists of both positive and negative self-statements, or whether the client is generating or recalling a negative thought. This data may also provide information about the degree of distress in a particular situation. If self-enhancing thoughts are identified, the client becomes aware that alternatives are already present in his thinking style.

Introduction and practice of coping thoughts

At this point in the procedure there is a shifting focus: the client's negative self-statements or self-defeating thoughts are moving on to other kinds of thoughts that are incompatible with the self-defeating ones. These incompatible thoughts are usually called coping thoughts, coping statements or coping self-instruction, and they are developed for each client.

The introduction and practice of coping statements is crucial to the overall success of the cognitive restructuring procedure. The purpose of coping thoughts should be explained clearly. The client should understand that it is difficult to think of failing as an experience (a self-defeating thought) while at the same time concentrate only on doing one's best, regardless of the outcome (a coping thought). The therapist should also model an example of coping thoughts so that the client can differentiate clearly between a self-defeating and a coping thought.

Types of coping statements   There are four types of coping statements.

1. Situation-orientated: some coping statements should refer to the nature of the situation itself, such as "It won't be too bad", "This is a challenge", "Only a few people will be watching me". These coping statements help

the client to reduce the potential level of stress of the anticipated situation.

2. Task-orientated: other coping statements refer more to the plans, steps or behaviour the client will need to demonstrate during the stressful situation, such as "Concentrate on what I want to say", "Think about the task" or "What am I trying to achieve?"

3. Anxiety-orientated: another set of coping thoughts can be used to help the client stay calm and relaxed at tense moments. These statements include self-instruction such as "Stay calm or relaxed and take a deep breath".

4. Positive self-statements: these coping statements are used to reinforce or encourage clients when they have coped. They can be used during, and especially after, a stressful situation.

A variety of potentially useful coping statements are available for each client, and particular types of coping response may be more useful for some clients. To date, very little is known of the specific effects of each of these kinds of coping thoughts.

Client examples of coping thoughts   After providing some examples, the therapist should ask the client to think of additional coping statements. The client can select some of the therapeutic examples or make them up with positive statements that he has used in other situations. The client should be encouraged to select coping statements that are most natural to him. He should be able to identify coping thoughts by discovering convincing counter-arguments about unrealistic thoughts.

Client practice   Using client-selected coping statements, the therapist should ask the client to practise verbalising coping statements aloud. This is very important because most clients are not accustomed to using coping statements.

Such practice may well reduce some of the client's usual discomfort and strengthen confidence in being able to produce different "self-talk". Also, clients who are trained formally to practise coping statements systematically may use a greater variety and more specific coping thoughts, and they may report more consistent use of coping thoughts *in vivo*.

At first, the client can practise verbalising the individual coping statements he selected before entering the situation. Gradually, as the client gets accustomed to using coping statements, the coping thoughts should be practised in the natural sequence in which they will be used. For example, the client would anticipate the situation and practise coping statements before the situation, and he should practise coping thoughts during the situation, by focusing on the task and coping with any overwhelming feelings.

It is important for the client to become actively involved in these practice sessions. The therapist should try to ensure that the client does not simply rehearse the coping statements by rote. Instead, the client should use these practices in an attempt to internalise the meaning of the coping statement.

Shifting from self-defeating to coping thoughts

After the client has identified his negative thoughts and practised self-coping thoughts, the therapist should teach him how to switch from self-defeating to coping thoughts during stressful situations. Practise of this shift helps the client to use a self-defeating thought as a cue for an immediate switch to coping thoughts.

Therapist demonstration of shift   The therapist should model this process before asking the client to try it.

Client practise of the shift   After the therapist's demonstration, the client should practise identifying and stopping self-defeating thoughts, and replacing them with coping thoughts. The therapist can monitor the client's progress and coach if necessary. The rehearsal of this shifting involves four steps: the client imagines the stressful situation or carries out his part in the situation via a role play and the therapist can gradually decrease the amount of assistance. Before homework is assigned, the client should be able to practise and carry out this shift in the interview session in a self-directed manner.

Introduction and practise of positive or reinforcing self-statements

The last part of cognitive restructuring involves teaching clients how to reinforce themselves for having coped. This is accomplished by therapist modelling and client practise of positive or reinforcing self-statements. Many clients who could benefit from cognitive restructuring report not only frequent self-defeating thoughts, but also few or no positive or rewarding self-statements. Some clients may learn to replace self-defeating thoughts with coping thoughts and feel better but not satisfied with their progress. The purpose of including positive or reinforcing self-statements in cognitive restructuring is to help the client to learn to praise or congratulate themselves for signs of progress. Although the therapist can provide certain reinforcement in the interview, the client cannot always be dependent upon encouragement from someone else when confronted with a stressful situation.

After providing examples, the therapist should ask the client for additional positive self-statements. The therapist should demonstrate to the client how he can use a positive statement after having coped with the situation. The client should then be instructed to practise using positive self-statements during and after the stressful situation. The practice occurs first within the interview and gradually outside the interview with *in vivo* assignments.

Homework and follow-up

Although homework is an integral part of every cognitive restructuring procedure, ultimately the client should be able to use cognitive restructuring whenever it is needed in the problem situation. The client should be instructed to use cognitive restructuring *in vivo*, but should be warned not to expect immediate success. A client can monitor and record the instances in which he has used cognitive restructuring over several weeks.

The therapist can use the follow-up sessions to encourage the client to apply the procedures in stressful situations that could arise in the future, and to check progress. He should encourage the client to generalise the use of cognitive restructuring in situations other than those that are presently considered problematic.

Occasionally, a client's level of distress may not diminish, even after repeated practise of restructuring self-defeatist thoughts. In some cases, negative self-statements do not contribute to a person's strong feelings. Some emotions may be classically conditioned and, therefore, treated more appropriately by a counter-conditioning procedure such as systematic desensitisation. However, it is possible even in classically conditioned fears that cognitive processes can play a role in maintaining or reducing the fear.

When cognitive restructuring does not reduce a client's level of distress, depression or anxiety, then the therapist and client may need to re-define the problem. The therapist should consider the possibility that his assessment has been inaccurate and that there are, in fact, no internal sentences that are functionally tied to this particular client's problems. Problem definition is similar to hypothesis testing, and a therapist's first analysis may not always turn out to be accurate. Assuming that the original problem assessment *is* accurate, a change in parts of the cognitive restructuring procedure is necessary. Some possible revisions include:

1. Increasing the amount of time that the client uses to shift from self-defeating to coping thoughts, and to imagine coping thoughts;
2. The nature of the particular coping statements selected by the client may not be that helpful; a change in the type of coping statements may be beneficial;
3. Cognitive restructuring may need to be supplemented with either additional coping skills, such as relaxation, or with other components of social skills training.

Stress inoculation

Stress inoculation is an approach to teaching both physical and cognitive coping skills. It has been described as a type of psychological protection that functions in the same way as a medical inoculation that provides protection from disease. Stress inoculation gives the person a set of skills to deal with the distressful situations. As in medical inoculation, a person's resistance is enhanced by exposure to a stimulus strong enough to arouse responses without being so powerful that it overcomes them. Stress inoculation involves three major components:

1. Educating the client about the nature of stressful reactions;
2. Encouraging the client to rehearse various physical and cognitive coping skills;
3. Helping the client apply these skills during exposure to stressful situations.

Of these three components, the second, which provides coping skills training, seems to be the most important. Stress inoculation has been used to help people to monitor a variety of reactions, to control anger, and to help people learn how to tolerate and cope with physiological pain and tension headaches.

Meichenbaum and Cameron (1973) found that stress inoculation was superior to systematic desensitisation and to other anxiety-relief treatments in reducing avoidance behaviour and in promoting treatment generalisation in multi-phobic clients. One of the major advantages of stress inoculation compared to other cognitive restructuring and relaxation techniques, is that relaxation and cognitive coping skills are learned and applied as part of the stress inoculation procedure. Stress inoculation consists of seven major components:

1. Explanation of technique;
2. Information-giving;
3. Acquisition and practise of direct action coping skills;
4. Acquisition and practise of cognitive coping skills;
5. Application of all coping skills to problem-related situations;
6. Application of all coping skills to potential problem situations;
7. Homework and follow-up.

Explanation

The therapist should explain the purpose of stress inoculation and the mechanisms that will be used to help the client. First, he should help the client to try to understand the nature of his feelings and how certain situations provoke these feelings. Second, the client will learn some ways to manage these feelings and to cope with the situations in which they occur. After learning these coping skills, the situations will be set up for a client to practise using these skills and to help him control his feelings. Again, the client's co-operation is essential for effective use of this technique.

Information giving

In this procedure, before learning and applying various coping strategies, it is important that the client is given some information concerning the nature of the stressful reaction and the possible coping strategies that can be used. Most clients see stress as something that is automatic and difficult to overcome. It is helpful for the client to understand the nature of the stressful reaction and how various coping strategies can help control the stress. Three specific elements should be explained to the client: a framework for the client's emotional reaction; information about the phases of reacting to stress; and examples of possible types of coping skills.

Framework for client's reaction   The therapist should explain the nature of the client's reaction to a stressful situation. Although understanding one's reaction to a stressful situation may not be sufficient for changing it, the framework lays some basis for beginning the change process. Usually, the explanation of a type of stress (anxiety, anger, pain) involves describing the stress as having two components; physiological arousal and covert self-statements or thoughts that provoke anxiety and/or pain. This explanation may help the client to realise that coping strategies should be directed towards the arousal behaviours and cognitive processes.

Phases of stress reaction   After explaining a framework for emotional arousal, it is helpful to describe the probable times when the client's arousal level may be heightened. Meichenbaum (1977) has pointed out that anxious or phobic patients tend to see their anxiety as one massive panic reaction. Similarly, clients who are angry, depressed or experiencing pain may interpret their feelings as one large continuous reaction that has a certain beginning and end. Clients who interpret their reaction in this way perceive the reaction as being too difficult to change because it is so massive and overwhelming. One way to help the client see the potential for coping with feelings is to describe the feelings as specific stages or phases of reacting to a situation. For example, the therapist may use four stages to help the client to conceptualise the various critical points of a reaction, namely, *preparing* for a stressful, painful or provoking situation; *confronting* or handling the situation or the provocation; *coping* with critical moments or with feelings of being overwhelmed or agitated during the situation, and *rewarding* oneself after the stress for using coping skills in the first three phases. An explanation of these stages in the preliminary part of stress inoculation helps the client to understand the sequence of coping strategies to be learned.

Information about coping strategies   Finally, the therapist should provide some information about the kind of coping strategies that can be used at these critical points. The therapist should emphasise that there are a variety of potentially useful coping skills. Research has indicated that coping strategies are more effective when clients choose those that reflect their own preferences. Both "direct action" and "cognitive" coping skills are taught in using stress inoculation. Direct action coping strategy is designed to help the client use coping behaviours to handle the stress; cognitive skills are used to give the client coping thoughts (self-statements) to handle the stress. The client should understand that both kinds of coping skills are important and have different functions.

Acquisition and practice of coping skills

In this phase of stress inoculation, the client acquires and practises direct action coping skills. First, the therapist discovers and models possible methods of coping; the client should select several methods to use and practise them with the therapist's encouragement and assistance. These coping skills are designed to help the client to acquire and apply certain behaviours in stressful situations. The most commonly used direct action coping strategies include: collecting objectives or factual information about stressful situations; identifying short-circuit or escape routes, or ways to decrease the stress; mental relaxation methods; and physical relaxation methods.

Information collection   Collecting objective or factual information about a stressful situation may help the client to evaluate the situation more realistically. Also, information about a situation may reduce the ambiguity for the client and indirectly reduce the level of the perceived threat. This coping method has been widely used in childbirth classes. In using stress inoculation to help clients control anger, collecting information about the people who typically provoke them may help. Also, clients can collect information that can help them review provocation as a task or a problem to be solved, rather than as a threat or a personal attack.

Identification of escape routes   Identifying escape routes is a way to help a client to cope with the stress before it gets out of hand. The idea of an escape route is to short-circuit the explosive or stressful situation. This coping strategy can help abusive clients learn to identify cues that elicit a physical or verbal abuse, and thus take preventative action before striking out. These escape or prevention routes can be very simple things that the client can do to prevent losing control or losing face in the situation, for example, counting to 60, leaving the room or talking about something humorous.

Mental relaxation   Mental relaxation can also help clients to cope with stress. Mental relaxation may involve a tension diversion tactic: angry clients can control their anger by concentrating on solving a problem, by counting the floor tiles below them, by thinking about a joke or by thinking about something positive about themselves. Attention diversion tactics are commonly used to help people control pain: instead of focusing on the pain, the person concentrates very hard on an object in a room or on the repetition of a word or number. Some people find that mental relaxation is more successful if they use imagery or fantasy. Generally, imagery as a coping method helps the client to focus or go on a fantasy trip instead of focusing on the stress, the provocation or the pain.

Physical relaxation Physical relaxation methods are particularly useful for clients who report physiological components to anxiety and anger, such as sweaty palms, rapid breathing or heart beat, or nausea. Physical relaxation is also a very helpful strategy for pain control, because body tension heightens the sensation of pain. Physical relaxation may consist of muscle relaxation or breathing techniques.

Each strategy should first be explained to the client, and include a discussion of its purpose and procedure. Several sessions may be required to discuss and model all the direct action coping methods. After the strategies have been described and modelled, the client should select the particular method to be used. The number of coping strategies used by the client will depend on the intensity of the reaction, the nature of the stress and the client's preferences. With the therapist's assistance, the client should practise using this skill in order to be able to apply it in simulated *in vivo* situations.

Acquisition and practice of cognitive coping skills

This part of stress inoculation is similar to the cognitive restructuring strategy described earlier. The therapist models examples of coping thoughts that the client can use during stressful phases of problem situations, and the client then practises substituting these coping thoughts with negative or self-defeating thoughts. The therapist helps the client to understand the nature of the emotional reaction by conceptualising the reaction in phases.

In helping the client to acquire cognitive coping skills, the therapist may first wish to review the importance of learning to cope at crucial times. The therapist can point out that the client should learn a set of cognitive coping skills for each important phase: preparing for the situation; handling the situation; coping with critical moments in a situation; and rewarding oneself after the situation. The first phase refers to coping skills before the situation; the second and third phases involve coping with a situation; and the fourth phase refers to coping after the situation.

Modelling coping thoughts   After explaining to the client the four phases of cognitive coping skills, the therapist will model possible examples of coping statements that are essentially useful for each of the phases.

Client's selection of coping thoughts   After the therapist models possible coping thoughts for each phase, the client should add some or select those that he feels most comfortable with. The therapist should encourage the client to try and adapt his thoughts in whatever way he feels most natural. The therapist should help to tailor a coping programme at this stage specifically for the client. If the client's self-statements are too general they may lead only to "rote repetition" and will not function as effective self-instruction.

Client practice of coping thoughts   After the client has selected coping thoughts to use in each phase, the therapist should instruct him to practise these self-statements by saying them aloud. This verbal practice is designed to help the client become familiar with the coping thoughts. Afterwards, the client should practise the selective coping thoughts in the sequence of the four phases. This helps the client to learn the timing of the coping thoughts and the application phase of stress inoculation.

Application of all coping skills to problem-related situations

The next part of stress inoculation involves the client applying the coping skills in the face of the stressful, provoking or painful situations. Before the client is instructed to apply the coping skills *in vivo*, he practises applying coping skills under simulated conditions with the therapist's assistance. The application phase of stress inoculation appears to be important for the overall efficacy of the procedure. This application phase involves providing the client with exposure to simulations of problem-related situations. For example, the client who wants to control anger would have an opportunity to practise coping in a variety of anger-provoking situations. During this application, it is important that the client is faced with a stressful situation and also that he practises the skill in a coping manner. In other words, the application should be arranged and conducted as realistically as possible. The angry client can be encouraged to practise feeling very agitated, and perhaps to rehearse the feeling of starting to lose control; he should apply the coping skills to regain control. By imagining losing control, experiencing anxiety and then coping with it, the client is able to practise the thoughts and feelings that are likely to occur in a real-life situation.

Modelling applications of coping skills   The therapist should first model how the client could apply the newly acquired skills in a coping manner when faced with a stressful situation.

Client application of coping skills in imagery and role-play practice   After the therapist modelling sequence, the client should practise a similar sequence of coping skill. This can occur in two ways, namely, imagination and role-play. Some therapists have found it useful to have the client first practise the coping skills while imagining problem-related situations. This practice can be repeated until the client feels comfortable in applying the coping strategies to imagined situations.

The client can then practise the coping skills with the therapist's aid in a role-play of a problem situation. The role-play practice should be similar to *in vivo* situations that the client is likely to encounter. For instance, the angry client can identify specific situations and people with whom he is most likely to become angry or lose control. The client can imagine each situation (using a hierarchy of situations) and the effective use of coping skills. The client can then practise these skills in a role-play situation.

Application of all coping skills to potential problem situations

An adequate therapeutic strategy should prevent future problems as well as resolve current ones. The prevention aspect of stress inoculation is achieved by encouraging the client to apply the newly learned coping strategies to situations that may not be problematic now but could be stressful in the future. The effects of the inoculation may be very temporary if this phase of stress inoculation is ignored.

Application of coping skills to other potentially stressful situations is accomplished in the same way as application to the specific problem area. First, after explaining the usefulness of coping skills in other areas of the client's life, the therapist demonstrates the application of coping strategies to a potential, hypothetical stressor, or the therapist might select a situation that the client has not yet encountered, but that might require active coping. Such situations could include not getting a desired job promotion, facing a family crisis, moving to a new place, retirement, or becoming ill, and so on. After the therapist has modelled the application of coping skills to these types of situations, the client would practise applying these skills in these or similar situations that he himself identifies.

References

Bandura A (1977) Social Learning Theory, Prentice Hall

Beck A T (1976) Cognitive Therapy and the Emotional Disorders, International Universities Press

D'Zurilla T J and Goldfried M R (1971) Problem-solving and behaviour modification, Journal of Abnormal Psychology, 78: 107–126

Ellis A (1962) Reason and Emotion in Psychotherapy, Stuart

Goldfried M R, and Davidson J C (1976) Clinical Behaviour Therapy, Holt, Rinehart and Winston

Kanfer F H and Phillips J S (1970) Learning Foundations of Behaviour Therapy, Wiley

Lazarus A A (1971) Behaviour Therapy and Beyond, McGraw Hill

Lewinsohn A T (1976) Cognitive Therapy and the Emotional Disorders, International Universities Press

Mahoney M J (1974) Cognition and Behaviour Modification, Ballinger Press

Meichenbaum D (1977) Cognitive Behaviour Modification: An Integrative Approach, Plenum Press

Meichenbaum D and Cameron R (1973) Training schizophrenics to talk to themselves: A means of developing attentional controls, Behaviour Therapy, 4: 515–534

Mischel W (1973) Towards a cognitive social learning reconceptualization of personality, Psychological Review, 80: 252–283

Olin R J (1976) Thought-stopping: Some cautionary observations, Behaviour Therapy, 7: 706–707

Singer J L (1975) Navigating the stream of consciousness: Research in day dreaming and related inner experience, American Psychologist, 30: 727–738

Spirack G, Platt J J and Shure M D (1976) The Problem-solving Approach to Adjustment, Jossey-Bass

Taylor J G (1963) A behavioural interpretation of obsessive-compulsive neurosis, Behaviour, Research and Therapy, 1: 237–244

Wolpe J (1973) The Practice of Behaviour Therapy, 2nd edition, Pergamon Press

CHAPTER 12

ASSERTION TRAINING

Assertion training is the one form of social skills training that has received the greatest attention in both the research literature and in clinical practice. Indeed, until recently, the terms "assertion training" and "social skills training" were often used interchangeably, and it was not clearly recognised that assertiveness represented one specific type of inter-personal skill. Assertion training is based upon the premise that every individual possesses basic human rights and that the goal of assertiveness should be to stand up for these rights without violating the rights of others. These rights include: the right to refuse requests without feeling guilty, to set one's own priorities, to make mistakes, and to feel that one's own needs are as important as the needs of others.

The Oxford English Dictionary defines assertiveness as "the action of stating positively, declaring or claiming". Additionally, assertive behaviour is honest and non-manipulative and involves the direct expression of one's feelings, preferences, needs or opinions in a manner that is neither threatening nor punishing towards the other people involved.

Considerable confusion has been caused by the different concepts of assertion and aggression. Alberti and Emmons (1978) proposed a three-category distinction between assertive, non-assertive and aggressive behaviour, which is commonly used by therapists.

Assertiveness involves directly telling someone what is wanted or preferred in such a way as to appear neither threatening nor punishing and not to put down the other person. It is not aimed simply at getting what is wanted, if achieving these aims means affecting the needs of others. It also involves being open about one's feelings and being able to express what is wanted without experiencing undue anxiety while doing so. This does not necessarily involve being totally honest about one's feelings in every situation. *Aggressiveness* also involves an expression of feelings and opinions but in a way which threatens, punishes or puts down the other people involved. The aim is to get what is wanted, no matter what effect it has on the other people involved. On the other hand, *non-assertiveness* or passive behaviour involves the hope that one will get what is wanted, but that one will leave it to chance or to another person.

Differences between assertive, aggressive and non-assertive behaviour

Assertiveness

The client can: express feelings directly but without accompanying threats; politely refuse unreasonable requests; make reasonable requests; express opinions while not automatically agreeing with those of others; stand up for his own rights or needs and make clear what he wants, while making no attempts to infringe upon the rights of others; perform these behaviours without undue fear or anxiety; express anger and affection appropriately; maintain the appropriate non-verbal behaviour.

Aggressiveness

The client: is capable of expressing strong feelings, but for his own benefit; tends to dominate conversation with threats and demands, adopting a behavioural style that is dominating and demeaning to other people; gives no consideration to other people's rights, needs or feelings; may resort to verbal abuse and often make an attempt to humiliate other people; does not take into account other people's points of view; sometimes adopts non-verbal behaviour that is interpreted as a precursor to physical attack, such as overlong eye contact and threatening gestures.

Non-assertiveness

The client: tends to comply with unreasonable requests; often agrees with opinions that he does not share; often avoids people because they may ask him to do things and he finds it difficult to say no; sometimes fails to express his own opinions; may fail to make requests or ask favours of other people; usually avoids forthright statements, and often gives confusing messages.

Non-verbal aspects of assertive behaviour

Generally, an assertive person establishes good eye contact, stands or sits comfortably without fidgeting, and talks in a strong steady voice, neither shouting nor mumbling.

Assertive statements generally include: "I think", "I feel", "I want", "let's", "we could" (examples of co-operative statements), or "what do you think?" "how do you feel?" (empathic statements).

A non-assertive response is usually accompanied by: a shifting of body weight; aversion of eye contact; and a slumped body posture.

Non-assertive statements include: "maybe", "I wonder if you could", "would you mind?" (examples of qualifiers); "you know", "well, well", "uh huh" (these and various other kinds of "fillers" are often used to indicate unsure behaviour); "it's not really important", "don't bother" (negative statements).

An aggressive response is typically expressed by inappropriate anger or hostility which is loudly and explosively expressed. It is characterised by: glaring eyes, leaning forward excessively, exaggerated gestures such as pointing and pushing, and an angry or loud tone of voice.

Aggressive statements usually include threats such as "you'd better do that or else", "if you don't watch out I'll ...", or putting the other person down, for example, "you don't know what you're talking about", and so on.

Occasionally, an example of indirect aggressive behaviour is seen, in which a person will use the verbal language of the non-assertive response with the body language of the aggressive response.

Assertiveness training programmes

Assertiveness training programmes usually concentrate on developing a number of specific skill areas. These include: the ability to cope with manipulation and criticism without responding with counter-criticism; the ability to make requests and state points of view, and to refuse unreasonable requests; and the ability to express feelings in social situations.

Today, most therapists use a variation of the following treatment programme, which can be used either with groups or with individual clients.

1. Assessment: an initial assessment of the client's skill deficits relating to assertiveness can be undertaken by the use of self-report questionnaires, setting up behavioural role-play situations or by using behavioural rating scales.
2. Education: an introduction to the theory of assertive behaviour and the distinction between assertive, aggressive and non-aggressive behaviour should be given to each client. Examples and instruction in how to behave more assertively can also be given. The client should be taught how to set assertive goals that can be achieved realistically during the training sessions. These objectives can be achieved by using lectures, demonstrations and discussions. They can also include written and oral material, which can be developed using a standardised format if clients are presenting with similar problems.
3. Assertive skills training: this component attempts to teach the client the behavioural skills that are judged to be lacking or inadequately developed. The components used are: modelling, role-playing, behavioural rehearsal, feedback, and homework.
4. Anxiety reduction: if the client has the social skills necessary for assertive behaviour but cannot use them effectively because of anxiety, then some variant of systematic desensitisation or relaxation therapy should be used to reduce the level of anxiety that is interfering with effective social performance.
5. Cognitive restructuring: if the client's cognitive processes are inhibiting his assertive skills, it will be necessary to modify these deficits using one of the techniques outlined in Chapter 11. Standard procedures that have been used effectively include discovering and challenging irrational beliefs, paying attention to societal sex roles, and seeing how the client's assertive behaviour can affect his personal situation.
6. Homework, follow-up and generalisation: the client should practise the newly learnt behaviours and integrate them into his everyday life. Self-monitoring techniques can be taught to help the client gain some control over his behaviour.

Types of client problems suitable for assertiveness training

It has been proposed that a person can be unassertive for at least three separate reasons: a genuine skill deficit (the person does not know how to be assertive); inadequate stimulus discrimination (the person does not know the appropriate circumstances in which assertiveness techniques should be used); and the client fears the rational or irrational consequences of being assertive.

The following types of clients are among the most frequent presenters:

1. Skills deficit — unassertive people:
   (a) Psychotics. People who have real difficulties in relating to other people and whose bizarre behaviours, aloofness, withdrawal, unusual affect or paranoia interferes with inter-personal communication.
   (b) Excessively shy people. Avoidance of social situations has resulted in a real skills deficit. These people usually consist of excessively shy young men and women, the men tending to seek help for situations relating to dating, initiating relationships and similar types of problems.
   (c) Women wishing to break out of the stereotypic feminine role.
   (d) People who are beginning to develop assertive skills, but who need further help to develop.
2. Skills deficit — aggressive people:
   (a) These clients tend to have problems with loss of control of aggressive feelings, and have occasional outbursts caused by impatience. Generally, they are in control of their behaviour, and may be unassertive people who hold things in and then are overcome by their feelings.
   (b) Impatient, irritable people who are always "blowing off steam".
   (c) Severely impulsive people whose angry outbursts lead to trouble or violence.
3. Fear of loss of control or feelings:
   (a) Fear of loss of control of intense feelings such as anxiety, fear, anger or love, can inhibit the assertive response. The person is anxious about showing these feelings, especially anger or love, or is anxious about not being able to control the intensity of his feelings or the response. Usually, this is not caused by a skills deficit, but the anxiety over the loss of control inhibits the response.
   (b) Related to the fear of loss of control is the fear of the consequences of an assertive response, either rationally or irrationally. These fears are usually situationally specific. An example of these difficulties can be seen in some women who consider that men do not like assertive women and

can have cognitive ideas such as "If I'm assertive, I won't be liked".
(c)   A third inhibition is that other people cannot control their feelings. It should often be tested to see whether there is some basis in reality, since it can be dangerous to be assertive with people who are overly aggressive and prone to violence.

Assessment

Since there are so many different assertiveness procedures and treatments, and clients have such a variety of different presenting problems, assessment needs tend to vary. As always, it is essential to bear in mind that assessment is an ongoing process and needs to continue throughout therapy.

Generally, the therapist must keep the following questions in mind when conducting an assessment of clients who are suspected of having difficulty with assertion:

1. Is this a non-assertive person or is the problem one of being too aggressive?
2. Which category is the most problematic? Does the problem involve several categories or just a few? Does the client respond to other people's assertive and aggressive responses, or does this person primarily need help in initiating assertive responses? Examples of some of the categories to be used are: initiating interactions; refusing unreasonable requests; expressing disagreement, displeasure or criticism; speaking up in groups; expressing opinions and making suggestions; being able to receive criticism; and asking for help.
3. Does this person know what he is currently feeling, what he wants to achieve at present and what his rights are in difficult situations? Is he clearly able to state these components?
4. Is this a general skills deficit? If so, is it the verbal or non-verbal component which is deficient, or both? Which aspects are the most deficient — facial expression, voice or tone?
5. Does the person know when to be and when not to be assertive?
6. What are the social and cultural factors operating in the person's background in the present situation?
7. What are the consequences for this person of being more assertive? Is the person aware of these consequences and willing to take risks if necessary? (For example, is he likely to get the sack if he is assertive with his boss?)

8. Does anxiety or other similar feelings inhibit this person from responding assertively? How well does this person handle these intense feelings?
9. What is this person's opinion of himself? Is this person's lack of assertive skills related in any way to a poor self-appraisal?

Assessment scales

There are a considerable number of assessment scales that are suitable for measuring assertiveness. Most of these are self-report inventories that provide information on the frequency with which a client believes that he asserts himself in situations that require such behaviour. Among the most frequently used are the Wolpe-Lazarus assertiveness questionnaire, the Rathus scale and the assertiveness inventory.

Wolpe-Lazarus assertiveness questionnaire (1966) This consists of 30 social situation questions, such as "Do you protest aloud when someone pushes in front of you in a queue", and "Do you generally express what you feel, or do you usually keep quiet for the sake of keeping the peace?"

The Rathus scale This consists of a 30-item questionnaire derived from the Wolpe-Lazarus scale.

The assertiveness inventory This was developed by Gambrill and Richey (1975). It collects three types of information, each consisting of 40 items attempting to measure how uncomfortable a person feels in specific social situations, how likely it is that the person is to react assertively in those situations and in what situation the person is likely to act more assertively (Figure 12.1).

Many therapists prefer to use behavioural assessments rather than paper-and-pencil measures. It is usually helpful to conduct a behavioural assessment in additional to using self-report measures, in order to assess the extent of the social skills deficit, and whether or not anxiety and cognitive factors are having any influence. Several rating scales have been developed that assess verbal, non-verbal, cognitive and social anxiety variables of assertive behaviour.

Figure 12.1   Assertion Inventory (Source: Gambrill and Richey 1975)

Many people experience difficulty in handling interpersonal situations requiring them to assert themselves in some way, for example, turning down a request, asking a favour, giving someone a compliment, or expressing disapproval or approval. Please indicate your degree of discomfort or anxiety in the space provided before each situation listed below. Use the following scale to indicate the degree of discomfort.

1 = None;
2 = A little;
3 = A fair amount;
4 = Much;
5 = Very much.

Then go over the list a second time and indicate after each item the probability or likelihood of you displaying the behaviour if you were actually presented with the situation.* For example, if you rarely apologise when you are at fault, you would mark a 4 after that item. Use the following scale to indicate response probability:

1 = Always do it;
2 = Usually do it;
3 = Do it about half the time;
4 = Rarely do it;
5 = Never do it.

* Note: It is important to cover your discomfort ratings (located in front of the items) while indicating response probability. Otherwise, one rating may contaminate the other and a realistic assessment of your behaviour is unlikely. To correct for this, place a piece of paper over your discomfort ratings while responding to the situations a second time for response probability.

(continued)

Figure 12.1 (continued)

Degree of discomfort	Situation	Response probability
	1. Turn down a request to buy your car	
	2. Compliment a friend	
	3. Ask a favour of someone	
	4. Resist sales pressure	
	5. Apologise when you are at fault	
	6. Turn down a request for a meeting or date	
	7. Admit to fear and request consideration	
	8. Tell a person you are intimately involved with when he/she says or does something that bothers you	
	9. Ask for a rise	
	10. Admit ignorance in some area	
	11. Turn down a request to borrow money	
	12. Ask a personal question	
	13. Turn off a talkative friend	
	14. Ask for constructive criticism	
	15. Initiate a conversation with a stranger	
	16. Compliment a person you are romantically involved with or interested in	
	17. Request a meeting or a date with a person	
	18. Your initial request for a meeting is turned down and you ask the person again at a later time	
	19. Admit confusion about a point under discussion and ask for clarification	
	20. Apply for a job	
	21. Ask whether you have offended someone	

(continued)

Figure 12.1   (continued)

Degree of discomfort	Situation	Response probability
	22. Tell someone that you like them	
	23. Request expected service when such is not forthcoming, eg, in a restaurant	
	24. Discuss openly with a person his/her criticism of your behaviour	
	25. Return defective items, eg, to a store	
	26. Express an opinion that differs from that of the person you are talking to	
	27. Resist sexual overtures when you are not interested	
	28. Tell the person when you fee he/she has done something that is unfair to you	
	29. Accept a date	
	30. Tell someone good news about yourself	
	31. Resist pressure to drink	
	32. Resist a significant person's unfair demand	
	33. Quit a job	
	34. Discuss openly with a person his/her criticism of your work	
	35. Request the return of borrowed items	
	36. Receive compliments	
	37. Continue to converse with someone who disagrees with you	
	38. Tell a friend or someone with whom you work when he/she says or does something that bothers you	
	39. Ask a person who is annoying you in a public situation to stop	

Assertiveness training

Assertiveness training can be conducted effectively with individuals, with small closely related groups or with large groups. It can also be seen as covering a continuum from a one-day workshop to long-term individual treatment. However, group training has certain distinct advantages over individual therapy in most cases. For example, a one-day workshop can be used to introduce standardised procedures to large numbers of people. A one-day workshop can provide an effective introduction for many people unable to commit themselves to any other form of treatment. In addition, group training provides opportunities to share common difficulties with people who have similar problem areas, such as distinguishing between aggressive and assertive responses in difficult situations. Group training also provides an effective mechanism to assess problems of assertiveness. Participants do not need to describe their own unassertive behaviour as they are clearly observable in the group setting. For example, someone who has difficulty in initiating interactions because of shyness may be confronted by someone who monopolises conversations; thus, ample opportunity for role-play is provided

Figure 12.2   Summary of Assertion Training Programme

AN ASSERTION TRAINING PROGRAMME SHOULD INCLUDE:

— the basic theory and philosophy

— recognition of the difference between

   (a) assertion
   (b) non-assertion
   (c) aggression

— identification of personal assertiveness training needs

— rehearsal and role-play of appropriate skills

— practise of learnt behaviour in everyday situations

— evaluation of effectiveness of training programme

to explore the issues raised. Another advantage of group training over individual therapy is that the group can take a more self-directed route after initial directions from the therapist, thus enabling a greater diversity of experience to be brought to the therapy. A group will also often include people of various ages, occupations and social positions that individual clients may be unlikely to meet in everyday situations, thus increasing the likelihood that generalisation will occur. Group support and feedback can be a major element in encouraging individuals to try out new behaviours (Figure 12.2).

Individual workshops

Typically, such groups run for four to eight hours, often with a follow-up session in one week's time. The usual number of participants is between 12 and 20. A workshop can be used as an initial assessment technique after which individuals are then directed to other forms of therapy, as appropriate. Additionally, there can be a follow-up workshop if homework is set as a result of the first workshop; the results of the homework are used to explore issues raised in the second workshop. One-day workshops usually attempt to convey the basic ideas behind assertion training by using discussion, teaching, structured exercises and role-play. Workshops of this type have been held for a wide variety of people, including professional groups.

Group training

These groups usually meet for one-and-a-half to two hours per week over a period of six to eight weeks. The purpose of each group varies and can be designed to deal with specific problem areas, such as women's groups or couple therapy, or to deal with particular social problems, such as shyness or aggression. Alternatively, the group can contain people with mixed difficulties.

The therapist is usually highly active in structuring the initial stages of the group. He will be involved in providing information, devising exercises, controlling role-plays, and ensuring that each member of the group is involved, and that group cohesiveness develops. Gradually, as the group gels, the clients themselves can take over some of these roles from the therapist. The group is often ready to work without the leader at the end of the six to eight weeks; he can then remain available to give advice when required.

The following are examples of exercises that can be used in assertiveness training groups. Many other methods and ideas are equally as suitable, and the reader is referred to the references at the end of the chapter for a number of manuals that offer alternative approaches.

Starting a group   In the opening session, group members are seated in a circle and the therapist asks individuals in turn to give their first names and to state briefly why they have come to the group. Each client can also be asked to describe a recent situation in which they felt that they had some difficulty because lack of assertion was a problem. Approximately three to five minutes can be spent with each person.

What is assertiveness?   Using material from the first exercise above, the therapist can introduce the three concepts of assertiveness, non-assertiveness and aggressiveness, emphasising (by using relevant teaching techniques) the problems people can have in social situations as a result of difficulties in this area. It is usually helpful to give reading material in the form of handouts, emphasising the differences so that the client can refer to this material between sessions.

The therapist can demonstrate the differences between the three types of behaviour, either by using video-tape recordings or by role-play using a co-therapist. It is useful to demonstrate at this stage the techniques the clients will be using later on in the course, such as role-play and video, and to give them an opportunity to discuss their feelings about using these techniques.

Initial role-playing   The therapist next selects a client who is willing to present and work on his problem. It is better to start with a more general problem (such as learning to be more comfortable in a social situation with your boss) than more personal problems. The volunteer is asked to describe briefly a situation in which he has difficulties. The therapist then constructs a role-play using this as a scenario. Other members of the group can be involved in the role-play or as the therapist feels appropriate, or a co-therapist can be used. After the role-play has been conducted, the therapist should encourage the group to engage in feedback on the performance, and a discussion should be encouraged to explore some of the pertinent issues raised.

In assessing the role-play, both participants can be asked how they felt during it. The presenting client can be asked to self-rate his assertiveness, focusing first on what he liked about it and then what he was unhappy with. Possible questions to help the subject clarify the issues are: what were you trying to achieve in this situation? What were your rights in this situation? Were they being violated? What did you really want to say to the other person involved? How do you think the other person experienced what you were trying to say?

Video feedback can be used at this stage if it is a technique being used with the group.

Next, the other members of the group are asked for positive feedback on the client's performance. Emphasis should be given to the differences between verbal and non-verbal components, which can then be broken down into other factors such voice tone and body posture. Rating scales and structured exercises can be used if the therapist feels that they are appropriate. Then the group can be asked to comment on areas where changed behaviours could improve the client's social performance. Initially, care should be taken to ensure that this is not too threatening for the client, and that this feedback is positive and does not criticise the client.

Feedback should also be given on the performance of the role-play partner. This can be a valuable source of feedback to the client and, if this partner is a co-therapist, situational variables can be manipulated to accentuate particularly relevant aspects of the interaction.

When the client has been given sufficient feedback, goals must be set by asking him to decide in which areas he feels he should work to improve his social performance. The agreed target areas should be specific and clearly understood by all the people concerned.

Role-play 2   The client can now attempt to role-play the situation again, following the same procedures as in the first exercise. The therapist must keep all group members as involved as possible and be on the alert for signs of the group giving negative feedback and advice to the client. Additionally, the therapist should judge whether or not the client is becoming overloaded with information, or starting to suffer from anxiety or exhaustion.

An alternative is to ask another member of the group with a similar problem to attempt the role-play. This has the advantage of widening the group involvement and preventing the group from seeing itself as being monopolised by one person's problems. Another alternative is for a competent group member to model how he would handle the situation. This has to be carefully controlled as it is essential that this should be portrayed as someone "coping" with the situation rather than being super-confident; this will avoid alienating the original group member and prevent the setting of unreasonable goals that he is unable to achieve. Another alternative is that the therapist and co-therapist should model the "coping" behaviour. The therapist should judge at this stage which is the most appropriate of the above routes to follow.

It is usual for similar subject areas to be used throughout each session. Towards the end of the role-play, the therapist should attempt to bring together the main established points and to set homework for each client related to these points. Finally, a subject area for the next session should be agreed.

Homework assignments   When the group is a one-day workshop or an ongoing group, appropriate assignments should be given to each member that are specific to their problematic behaviour. The group as a whole should be instructed to self-monitor and observe their particular assertiveness problems, and to set small goals for changes. These can be agreed either on an individual or a group basis.

Homework follow-up   The next session should begin with a review of the homework assignment. In particular, each client should be asked to recount: if they achieved their target behaviour; any particular situations where difficulty occurred; and the results of their self-monitoring. The information gained from this exercise can be used as material for the following session.

Additional exercises   During discussions of role-plays and while giving feedback, a particular area of concern may be expressed by a number of group members. These can be used as a lead into other exercises. Commonly encountered problems are: appearing foolish in certain social situations — role-play or other exercises such as anxiety reduction or cognitive restructuring can then be used to explore these difficulties along the principles outlined above; or the fear of being bullied — additional to the above exercises, experimential exercises can be used to help clients to explore their own reactions to the bullying.

One possible exercise is as follows: the clients form two lines facing each other. Initially, one line non-verbally bullies their partner on the other line (by pointing a finger, grimacing, and so on), while the other partner is instructed to stand up to the person while noting what they are experiencing. The roles are then reversed. During the next round, verbal components of bullying, such as yelling, can be added. Finally, in a group discussion, individual's feelings concerning bullying can be explored and individual problems can be used as a focus for role-play to further explore in detail individual problems.

There is a need for continuous feedback as clients try out these assertive skills in therapy. Each session in an ongoing group should begin with the client providing feedback about what has happened to him since the previous session, and how he has developed his assertive skills. Common issues that need to be addressed include the timing of social interactions, the difficulty in acquiring the different relevant responses to different social situations, and the fact that perseverance is necessary to achieve change in behaviour.

Themes in succeeding weeks

A new theme can be introduced weekly in an ongoing group. Generally, groups begin with work problems and social inhibitions. As the group continues, more personal issues are introduced. A great deal of time may need to be spent working on the cognitive aspects of assertiveness. It is always important to emphasise that as one learns to respond assertively the probability of others responding differently in turn may be increased, although there is no guarantee that other people will change. An important related issue is that of the cause and effect of one's feelings, and the fact that this may need to be explored.

Special problems in running assertiveness groups

Refusal to participate in role-play

In most groups there is at least one person who has probably just come to watch or to say very little, and who generally refuses to participate, even if pressed to do so. Sometimes such people can be encouraged to join in by gentle introduction such as identifying one group member with whom they can practise talking. If they still remain silent after encouragement, it is best not to force the issue. A thorough assessment on an individual basis should be undertaken if this is possible.

In almost every group, and occasionally in individual work, someone refuses to role-play, declaring that it is silly and unreal. They often want instead to talk about their problems. Since role-play is a potent vehicle for changing unassertive responses, discussions about problematic behaviour is often relatively unproductive. Watching others in the group role-play is often the needed incentive for reluctant participants, but there are some who will leave in disgust, stating that the workshop or group was not the lecture or class they had expected. Again, gradual and gentle suggestions to show how aspects of a problem may help them to get in touch with their own inhibitions may encourage the individual into the group. Many unassertive people are initially self-conscious about role-playing, and slow entry is necessary for some people.

Very disturbed people

In assessment workshops there are occasionally one or two people with a multitude of problems who need much more therapy than a one-day workshop can provide, or whose problems are so general that assertiveness training is not really a suitable starting point. Occasionally, extremely paranoid clients come in as members of assertiveness training groups. Extreme caution should be taken here and it is usual to make a thorough individual assessment process to identify clear therapy goals before including this person in an ongoing group. Considerable individual therapy may be necessary before group work can be attempted.

Client variables

In the process of changing from being non-assertive to assertive, some clients may become too aggressive as an intermediary step. Some clients, as they change from keeping their feelings buried to becoming more aware of themselves, become irritable, grumpy and disagreeable. The therapist must observe these changes and perhaps provide individual therapy for a short period to help the client accept and deal with this stage of change.

Other people become aware of their rights in particular situations as they change from being non-assertive to assertive. They may become self-righteous and rigid, and insist that other people listen to or understand their points of view, or they may press for an acknowledgement that their view of the situation is correct. Again, since new behaviours are emerging, the client may need help to adjust through this period.

Change is too slow for some people and they will become impatient to try out their newly acquired assertive skills on everyone. It is important to train clients to tackle situations using small steps and to use appropriate behaviour in social situations.

Some clients may need help in learning when not to use their newly acquired skills. Since being assertive is new to them, they feel that it is important to assert themselves in any situation in which they feel that their rights are being violated. Helping to select appropriate situations and appraise the consequences is therefore important.

Therapeutic problems

There are few failures in working with people on assertiveness training. Most people who continue to work in assertiveness training programmes do change. Most of the problems develop as the client begins to try out his not-quite-developed assertiveness skills.

The largest group of problems involve clients who are too impulsive in trying out assertiveness skills. They may try to tackle difficult life situations after just one role-play and without adequate preparation. People often come for assertiveness training with unrealistic goals or else they are not suitable because they have so many other problems. Additionally, as the therapy sessions develop, it may become obvious that the presenting assertiveness problems are not the main issue.

Therapist variables

As with all therapy, the attitude of the therapist is important. It is as important that therapists know themselves and have an understanding of how effective they are personally in dealing with issues relating to assertiveness. It is particularly important for therapists to be able to communicate feelings and to receive feedback. Several problems may occur that can interfere with the therapist's effectiveness. These can include the wish to be liked, problems in giving negative feedback, and a tendency to take responsibility for and to nurture clients, and therefore to interfere with the client's struggle for self-help. It is highly recommended that therapists begin work in assertiveness training by participating in a training group as a participant. The following problematic areas commonly occur:

1. Problems in exercising authority. One problem that frequently occurs among therapists is the concern that they do not know all the answers to the clients' questions.

2. Many therapists struggle to exercise power and provide direction when it conflicts with the protection of clients. In assertive training, the wish to protect may interfere with the therapist's ability to give honest feedback.
3. Many therapists are not able to say no to clients, students and supervisers who want more of their time. Therapists commonly complain that they have no time for themselves. It is important for therapists to reconcile self-interest and availability to others, as this is often a problem with which clients are faced.
4. Some therapists prefer to sit out therapist groups and avoid directing role-play or taking charge of the group. Often, these therapists are after intellectual knowledge or are themselves rather inhibited and/or intellectually orientated. While an inhibited therapist might be effective in helping a client be more assertive, awareness of how difficult it is to role-play and direct a group may help such a therapist be an even more effective role model.

Ford and Hogan (1978) conducted clinical research into assertion training to assess the importance of the therapist's specific actions and the client's perception of the therapist's empathy, warmth and genuiness. The results indicated that, regardless of the treatment type, clients who perceived a non-supportive therapeutic relationship in the early stages of therapy quickly dropped out, whereas those who viewed the therapist as most supportive in middle sessions tended to gain the most from assertion therapy. At different points in therapy, different actions by the therapist produce this favourable client reaction: for example, communicating concern and involvement appeared essential early on in therapy; later, talking less and encouraging the client to review his successes were regarded as being more important.

Non-verbal aspects of assertive behaviour

The following aspects of non-verbal behaviour frequently need attention in assertion training.

Stance and posture

It is difficult for the client to begin to make an assertive response unless he faces the person he is to address. If seated, leaning forward slightly denotes interest, concern and a lack of fear.

Eye contact

If a client finds prolonged eye contact difficult, he should be persuaded to practise at a distance and gradually move closer to the person for increasingly longer periods of time. Another way of beginning is to get the client to focus on some other part of the face and progress gradually towards eye-to-eye contact. Eye contact tends to convey sincerity and lack of fear and is an important component of assertive behaviour.

Facial expression

The client can practise this alone in front of a mirror. Using either this method or video will teach clients the differences between what they feel like inside and think they are conveying, and what it actually looks like when viewed by another person.

Use of gestures

Confident but not exaggerated hand gestures do much to enhance social performance. These must not be too aggressive, such as striking the palm of the hand, since the main point is, as with all other non-verbal behaviour, that gestures should be congruous with other behaviour.

Voice level and tone

It is not uncommon to meet clients with loud voices who think that it is unlikely that they can be heard. Similarly, clients with squeaky, quiet voices may think that they are perfectly audible to the person who is listening to them. Tape recorders are a useful way of dealing with this problem as the client can hear themselves and try to improve their voice levels. In addition to an appropriate voice level, appropriate inflection adds conviction to a performance.

Desensitisation as part of assertion training

Many people feel unable to assert themselves because they fear the emotional

336 Social Skills Training for Psychiatric Nurses

and behavioural consequences of so doing. To a limited extent, it might be useful to try to analyse with the client exactly what he expects to happen as a result of self-assertion and to point out any inconsistencies or exaggerations in his beliefs.

Clients often believe that their condition of shyness is inborn. Fear and anxiety will be partly conditioned through previous bad experiences, and any escape or avoidance responses that reduce this fear will have been reinforced negatively. Alternative ways of reducing anxiety must therefore be employed.

This reduction of anxiety can be handled partly through the therapist's arrangement of a gradual progression from simple to demanding tasks. Such a procedure not only aids the acquisition of new responses, but also acts as a kind of desensitisation therapy, with the client feeling relaxed as his performance improves, and as a new, benign association gradually builds up. However, care must be taken to ensure that the client does not get out of his depth too quickly, with the result that the old vicious circle is re-established.

Once the new assertive responses have been learnt, they may be regularly enforced in place of avoidance behaviour, since their deployment will reduce anxiety. These assignments are best pre-planned with the client and the likely sequence of events can be sorted out beforehand, together with possible variations.

Discrimination training

These types of exercises can be used to teach the client to discriminate accurately between assertive, non-assertive and aggressive behaviour. In these cases, discrimination training is used partly to clarify the different types of behaviour and partly to provide opportunities for helpful feedback (Figure 12.3).

Additional exercises

Other commonly used exercises in assertion training include the following:

Toss the ball — toss your name

This is a commonly used and simple introductory exercise to warm up many

Figure 12.3 Simple Assertiveness Discrimination Exercise

Exercise

Your spouse or friend arrives late and the meal you have prepared is ruined. You feel annoyed. You say:

1. Hello, have you been busy? You must be hungry; what can I get you to eat?
   (a) Assertive
   (b) Non-Assertive
   (c) Aggressive

2. I hope you have a good explanation! I've been waiting for an hour and the meal I've made is now ruined.
   (a) Assertive
   (b) Non-Assertive
   (c) Aggressive

3. I wonder you bother to come home at all. Where the hell have you been? This is the last time I ever cook for you. You're just too inconsiderate to bother with.
   (a) Assertive
   (b) Non-Assertive
   (c) Aggressive

With a little practice it is relatively easy to think up situations where an assertive response is required and then to identify its aggressive and non-aggressive alternatives.

Answers

1. (b) Non-assertive. Feelings are being disguised and there is a pretence that nothing of importance has happened.

2. (a) Assertive. Feelings are expressed and the consequences spelled out, but an opportunity to explain is left.

3. (c) Aggressive threats and sarcasm are used and the incident is generalised.

types of groups. The clients are arranged in a circle, facing inwards. The therapist begins the exercise by looking at one client and saying, as he tosses the ball to him, "Hello, I'm John Smith"; the client should then throw the ball to a fellow client saying, "Hello, I'm Bill Bloggs". This continues until all the clients have tossed the ball and participated. If the therapist wants the exercise to continue, he can expand it by throwing the ball and saying "Hello Fred", and the recipient of the ball says back to the therapist, "Hello John". This continues until all the clients have tossed the ball. Near the end of this exercise, the clients often get confused about people's names. This is an opportunity for the therapist to make the point that it is often necessary to ask for clarification. The therapist can also point out that it is essential for individuals to retain control of the situation they find themselves in, and that he makes the decision about where the ball should be thrown. An additional point can be made that if the client is feeling anxious, it can tend to direct attention inwards rather than outwards.

Past success stories

The group breaks into smaller groups of three to four people. Each client is asked to recall one successful experience from any time in their life and to write a brief description of it. In each group the first person then explains or reads his successful experience to the others, saying why he felt it was successful. The remaining clients listen and identify one attribute in the client. The other members of the group then recount their experiences in turn, their main strength being identified by the other members. When all the members have finished speaking, their strengths are fed back and discussion should ensue around people's strong points. Initially, this can be a threatening experience for some clients and it should be introduced carefully by the therapist. The following points should be stressed: it is important to project to others strengths rather than weaknesses or failures. The more this is done, the more the client will feel successful, act successful and become successful. In addition, the client must be aware of his strengths in order to do this. Thus, it should be pointed out to the clients that this exercise can help them to identify their strengths.

Other exercises can be based on the differences between assertive, aggressive and non-assertive behaviour, for example, by asking the clients what the differences are and using various situations and role-plays to explore these differences. Possible homework sessions based on the above would be for the therapist to instruct the clients that the next time somebody asks them to do something that they do not want to do, but to which they would normally say "yes", they should say "no" instead. Afterwards, the client should write down what he felt, what the other person did and how things ended up at the end of the interaction. It is often practical to role-play potentially difficult situations such as this in therapy before assigning homework.

How assertive am I?

The therapist can use any assertion checklist (Figure 12.4) that clients are instructed to complete. When going through the completed checklist, the therapist can explore some of the issues that are raised and use this as an example to identify individual problem areas to work on.

What happens if I'm assertive?

This is a standard role-play that can be applied to many different situations.

Role-play — standing up for your rights!   Two main participants are required for the role-play: each is given a role description of which the other participant is unaware. The scene is a clothes shop. The first role-player bought a shirt two weeks ago from the shop. He washed it yesterday for the first time and it shrunk and is now unwearable. He is instructed that he wants his money back or, as a last resort, a new shirt. The second role-player plays the part of the shop assistant. He is briefed that the shops policy is to try to convince the customer that it is not the company's fault and, if this fails, that the customer can replace the shirt with another of identical price, or he can pay the difference and buy a dearer shirt, but under no condition can he have a cheaper shirt. As a last resort, the customer can have his money back.

This type of role-play can be applied effectively to many situations. The number of participants can be increased to make the scene more realistic and to involve other group members. The reader is referred to Chapter 5 for other factors involved in role-play and for possible variations to this type of role-play.

Figure 12.4   Self-Assessment Scale — Assertion

	Wife/husband girlfriend/ boyfriend	Parents/ other family members	Friends of the same sex	Friends of the opposite sex	Children	People in authority	Shop assistants/ waitresses
Expressing positive feelings							
1. Start conversation							
2. Give compliment							
3. Receive compliment							
4. Make requests							
5. Express appreciation							
Express negative feelings							
6. Show justified anger							
7. Show you feel hurt							
Standing up for your rights							
8. Making a complaint							
9. Making a request							
10. Expressing your opinion							

Assessment. To assess your level of assertiveness in each activity, ask yourself on the scale provided how comfortable you feel in carrying out the activity with the person named.

1	2	3	4	5
Very easy	Easy	Not bad	Difficult	Impossible

References

Alberti R E and Emmons M L (1978) Your Perfect Right: A Guide to Assertive Behaviour, 3rd edition, Impact, San Luis Obispo

Ford J D and Hogan D R (1978) Assertiveness and Social Competence in the Eye of the Beholder, a paper presented at the annual meeting of the Association of Behaviour Therapy, Chicago, December

Gambrill E D and Richey C A (1975) An assertion inventory for use in assessment and research, Behaviour Therapy, 6: 550–561

Wolpe J and Lazarus A A (1966) Behaviour Therapy Techniques: A Guide to The Treatment of Neuroses, Pergamon Press

Further reading

Liberman R P, King L W, DeRisi W J and McCann M (1975) Personal Effectiveness: Guilding People to Assert Themselves and Improve their Social Skills, Research Press

Rathus S A (1973) A 30-item schedule for assessing assertive behaviour, Behaviour Therapy, 4: 398–406

APPENDIX I

ACCESS TO RESOURCES

Social skills training manuals

These are practical books which, while not replacing teaching by skilled practitioners, offer considerable advice and expertise on the problems and pitfalls of social skills training.

1. Trower P *et al.* (1978) Social Skills and Mental Health, Methuen

   An excellent and comprehensive book in two parts based on research undertaken at Littlemore Hospital, Oxford. Part One is a thorough review of social skills training; Part Two is a detailed training manual suitable for devising and running social skills training. The method used is detached and includes comprehensive assessment procedures. Highly recommended.

2. Goldstein A P *et al.* (1976) Skills Training For Community Living: Applying Structured Learning Therapy, Pergamon Press

   Well developed American system backed by considerable research. Very comprehensive, backed by audiovisual material.

3. Wilkinson J and Canter S (1983) Social Skills Training Manual: Assessment Programme Design and Management of Training, John Wiley

    Good basic introductory manual. Sound approach to basic social skills problems. Makes little use of micro-techniques.

4. Priestley P *et al.* (1978) Social Skills and Personal Problem-Solving: A Handbook of Methods, Tavistock Publications

    An interesting book, drawing from many different fields including social work, education and management training. Broadly based on principles similar to the nursing process. Excellent source book for use in practical sessions.

Practical work books

There are numerous books available which describe "how-to-do-it" approaches and they usually contain numerous exercises/approaches for application in the therapy situation.

1. Priestley P and McGuire M (1983) Learning to Help: Basic Skills Exercises, Social Series Paperback, Tavistock

    A superb book, full of helpful techniques. Based on the social skills approach it contains exercises for: analysing behaviour into simpler skills and devising ways of measuring their effective performance; assessing strengths and weaknesses; improving and developing skill; monitoring and evaluating progress toward more skilled behaviour. Highly recommended.

2. Hopson B and Scally M (1981), Lifeskills Teaching Programmes. Available from: Lifeskills Associates, Ashling, Back Church Lane, Leeds LS16 8DN.

    A useful system devised for teachers that can be applied easily and includes practical exercises on skills such as: how to communicate effectively; how to be assertive; how to find a job; how to manage negative emotions.

3. Liberman R P *et al.* (1975) Personal Effectiveness, Research Press
   Describes a wide range of exercises.

4. Remocker and Storch (1982) Action Speaks Louder: A Handbook of Non-
   verbal Group Techniques, Churchill Livingstone

   Provides over 50 exercises, particularly for psychiatric clients to improve
   communication with emphasis on non-verbal techniques.

5. Preiffer J W and Jones J E (1974) Structured Experiences of Human
   Relations Training; A reference guide, University Associates (numerous
   volumes)

   Provides a vast range of exercises; seems slightly outdated and
   "American" now.

6. Saskatchewan Newstart (1972) Life Skills Coaching Manual, Department
   of Manpower and Immigration, Prince Albert, Saskatchewan

   One of the formative books on social skills training. Usually available on
   loan from the British Library.

7. Kanfer and Goldstein (1975) Helping People Change: A Textbook of
   Methods, Pergamon Press

Social skills training and psychiatric nursing

The following are intended to indicate the increasing number of articles
applying social skills training to psychiatric nursing. It is not intended to be a
comprehensive list.

1. LeLievre J, Gilbert M T and Reauley W (1983) Social Skills Training
   Mental Health Nursing, 12–14, May 18

   A report by psychologists on the development of a social skills training
   course for psychiatric nurses. They conclude that a brief introductory
   course can increase the knowledge of therapeutic skills of psychiatric
   nurses. They also remark on the high level of interest shown.

2. Alues E A (1981) The nursing contribution to SST for psychiatric inpatients, Nursing Times, 77: 1026–1029

    Describes a joint project with psychologists at Broadmoor. Confronts some practical issues such as therapist roles, generalisations. Good outline of practical difficulties encountered in setting up inpatient groups.

3. Brunning H (1981) Social Skills and personal effectiveness training for student nurses, Nursing Times, 77: 919–920

    Describes a two-day workshop at Epsom, Surrey, covering a vast amount of material.

4. Briggs K (1983) Counselling skills for students, Mental Health Nursing, 4–6, March 16

5. Briggs K (1982) Inter-personal skills training for student nurses during introductory course, Nurse Education Today, 2: 22–24

6. Mental health forum 9 (1983) Nursing Mirror, September 21

    Pull-out supplement on social skills training, containing article by Robert Ravat, Paul Fisher and Martin Vousden, Frank Hardiman and Jackie Knibbs.

Background material

Theory

Learning

1. Bandura A (1977) Social Learning Theory, Prentice Hall

    Pulls Bandura's ideas together into one book. A difficult book, but worth reading.

2. Borger R and Seaborne A (1982) The Psychology of Learning, Penguin Education

    Sound introduction to the concept of learning, including skill.

Social skill   Michael Argyle's books provide the soundest introduction to the vast area of social skill.

1. The Psychology of Inter-personal Behaviour (1984)

2. Social interaction (1969) Methuen (with Furnham A and Graham J A)

3. Social Situations (1981) Cambridge University Press

4. Morris D (1977) Manwatching: A Field Guide to Human Behaviour, Jonathan Cape

    This book provides a useful "laymans" introduction to the field of human behaviour.

Non-verbal communication   A vast literature has developed about this subject, some of it extremely complex. A good introduction is provided by the following:

1. Argyle M (1975) Bodily Communication, Methuen

2. Hinde R A (Editor) (1972) Non-verbal Communications, Cambridge University Press

    Not an easy book, but one of the best.

3. Mehrabian A (1972) Non-verbal Communication, Aldine Atherton

    The following are very stimulating books on particular aspects of non-verbal communication. Particularly useful are:

4. Morris D *et al.* (1979) Gestures: Their Origins and Distributions, Jonathan Cape

5. Ekman P and Friesen L ·V (1975) Unmasking the Face: A Guide to Recognising Emotions From Facial Cues, Prentice Hall

    This is an excellent American book describing research into facial expressions, and is of considerable practical relevance to social skills training.

6. Bull P (1983) Body Movement and Inter-personal Communication, John Wiley and Son

   Describes the current research into bodily communications with particular reference to psychiatric populations; well worth reading.

Social skills training   There have been several major evaluations of social skills training published recently. These are often difficult books to read and contain considerable technical jargon, but they provide considerable insight into the practice and problems of social skills training.

1. Curran J and Monti P (Editors) (1982) Social Skills Training: A Practical Handbook for Assessment and Treatment, Guildford Press

2. Bellack A S and Hersen M (Editors) (1979) Research and Practice in Social Skills Training, Plenum Press

3. Ellis R and Whittington D (Editors) (1983) New Directions in Social Skill Training, Croom Helm

4. Trower P (Editor) (1984) Radical Approaches to Social Skills Training Croom Helm

   This latter book is an important contribution to the social skills training literature as it questions the very foundations on which it has developed. Provides many interesting ideas about possible areas for development. Difficult, but highly recommended.

Practice

There are many fields of current practice that have relevance for social skills training. Some introductory books are outlined below.

Behaviour therapy

1. Barker P (1982) Behaviour Therapy Nursing, Croom Helm

   An excellent introduction to behaviour therapy as applied to psychiatric nursing. Includes useful chapters on designing treatment programmes and the psychiatric nurse as a therapist.

2. Sheldon B (1982) Behaviour Modifications, Social Science Paperbacks Tavistock Publications

Social psychology

1. Breakwell, Foot and Gilmour (Editors) (1982) Social Psychology: A Practical Manual, The British Psychological Society and Macmillan

    A useful practical manual dealing with areas such as: questionnaire design; attitude measurement; person perception.

Therapies

1. *Assertion training*

    Galassi M D and Galassi J P (1971) Assert Yourself! Human Sciences Press

2. *Cognitive therapy*

    Meichenbaum D (1977) Cognitive Behaviour Modification: An Integrative Approach, Plenum Press

3. *Groupwork*

    A useful and sound introduction can be obtained from the books by Tom Douglas, in particular. For example, Groupwork Practice (1976), Basic Groupwork (1978), Groups (1983). All are obtainable from: Social Science Paperback, Tavistock Publications.

4. *Rational emotive therapy*

    Dryden W (1984) Rational Emotive Therapy: Fundamentals and Innovations, Croom Helm

5. *Role play*

    Morry van Ments (1983) The Effective Use of Role-play, Kogan Page

    A superb practical book on role-play, full of useful information from the field of education. Widely applicable to psychiatry. Deserves to be widely read.

Lewis and Mee (1981) Using Role-play: An Introductory Guide, National Extension College

6. *Stress reduction*

Bond and Kilty (1983) Practical Methods of Dealing with Stress, Human Potential Research Project, Department of Educational Studies, University of Surrey, Guildford, Surrey GU2 5XH

Full of practical exercises for use in workshops. Useful section on assertiveness. The work of Heron can be obtained from the same address, and has relevance to social skills training.

7. *Video*

Heilviel I (1984) Video in Mental Health Practice, Social Science Paperbacks, Tavistock

American, rather psychoanalytically orientated book, full of useful methods.

Dowrick P W and Biggs S J (Editors) (1983) Using Video: Psychological and Social Applications, John Wiley and Sons

Excellent book, very relevant to social skills training, includes chapters on self modelling, social skills training and training professional skills.

APPENDIX II

SOCIAL SKILLS THERAPISTS

The author will be pleased to advise individuals or health authorities about workshops and so on. He can be contacted at:

29 Dorchester Road
Upholland
Lancs WN8 0AD
(Tel. 0695 622994)

In addition, the following people have agreed to act as local contacts for those requiring further information about social skills:

England

Bedfordshire

Jacques Michel, RMN, SRN, ND(Cert)
Nurse Therapist
C/O Weller Wing
Bedford General Hospital
Kempston Road
Bedford

Cheshire

Ken Allen
Behaviour Nurse Therapist
CPN Services
Parkside Hospital
Macclesfield

Cheshire (cont)

Andy Farrington
Behavioural Nurse Therapist
CPN Services
Parkside Hospital
Macclesfield

Derbyshire

Ian Heath
Nurse Therapist
Dept of Psychotherapy
Mill Hill Lane
Derby

Devon

Cathy Peacham
Clinical Teacher
Nursing Studies Centre
Moorhaven Hospital
Bittaford
Ivybridge

Gordon Deakin
Course Tutor
Behaviour Therapy Nursing Service
Moorhaven Hospital
Bittaford
Ivybridge

Essex

Noel Sawyer
Nurse/Behaviour Therapist
Baddow Road Psychiatric Day Unit
Baddow Road
Chelmsford

Hampshire

Adrian Clarke
Nurse Therapist
Psychotherapy Dept
Dept of Psychiatry
Royal South Hants Hospital
Graham Road
Southampton

Peter Coles
Psychology Dept
St James Hospital
Locksway Rd
Portsmouth

Claire Tweedie, SEN(M)
Havant Day Hospital
Park Way
Havant

Hertfordshire

Kevin Gournay
Behaviour Therapist
Behaviour Therapy Unit
Barnet General Hospital
Wellhouse Lane
Barnet

Lancashire

Michael Dudley
Nurse Behaviour Therapist
Charles Day Hospital
Psychiatric Unit
Leigh Infirmary
The Avenue
Leigh

Sue Greenwood
Clinical Nurse Manager
Psychiatric Community Services
Ridge Lee Hospital
Quenmore Road
Lancaster

London

Valerie Ardimento
Nurse Therapist
Psychiatric Day Hospital
Greenwhich District Hospital
Vanburgh Hill
London

Peter Lindley
Education and Training Officer
Regional Conference and
Training Centre
David Salomans House
Broomhill Road
Southborough
Tunbridge Wells

Mary McArdle
Senior Tutor
School of Nursing
The Maudsley Hospital
Denmark Hill
London

Robert McDonald
Course Supervisor ENBCC 650
Clinical Teacher
Psychological Treatment Unit
The Maudsley Hospital
Denmark Hill
London

Erville Miller
Course Supervisor ENBCC 650
Psychological Treatment Unit
The Maudsley Hospital
Denmark Hill
London

Ian Rickard
Senior Nurse Therapist
6 Casselman Gardens
Arundel Terrace
Barnes
London

Northamptonshire

Victor Hole
Behaviour Nurse Therapist
Psychology Dept
Beechwood House
St Crispin Hospital
Duston
Northampton

Northumberland

Brian Scott
Nurse Therapist
CPN Dept
St Nicholas Hospital
Gosforth
Newcastle-Upon-Tyne

Surrey

Chavanjit Singh
C/N Behaviour Therapist
Psychology Dept
Netherne Hospital
PO Box 150
Coulsden
Surrey

Sussex

Colin Blowers
Behaviour Therapist
Dept of Clinical Psychology
New Sussex Hospital
Windlesham Road
Brighton

Marie Gilbert
Nurse Tutor
Nurse Education Centre
Spitalfield Lane
Chichester

Mary Golden
Clinical Tutor Behaviour Psychotherapy
Dept of Clinical Psychology
Graylingwell Hospital
Chichester

James Manchester
Senior Nurse
Behaviour Therapist
Community and Day Care
CPN Service
Graylingwell Hospital
Chichester

Brian Pate
Nurse Therapist
CPN Dept
St Francis Hospital
Haywards Heath
West Sussex

Scotland

Stephen Tilley
Nurse Therapist
C/O Ettrick
Crichton Royal Hospital
Dumfries

Southern Ireland

Gerard Butcher
Behaviour Nurse Therapist
St Patricks Hospital
PO Box 136
James Street
Dublin 8

Charles McHugh
Nurse Therapist
Letterkenny General Hospital
Dept of Psychological Therapy
Letterkenny
Co. Donegal

In addition, people throughout the country can contact:

Behaviour Therapy Forum, B.C.N.
Martin Brown
Flat 2
Nicholson Road
Addiscombe
Croyden
Surrey

INDEX

FLY-DRESSING II

By the same author
Fly-Dressing

FLY-DRESSING II

DAVID J. COLLYER
Line drawings by Susan and Sharon Collyer

DAVID & CHARLES
NEWTON ABBOT   LONDON   NORTH POMFRET (VT)

To Susan, Sharon, Patsy and Stephen

British Library Cataloguing in Publication Data

Collyer, David Jerome
    Fly-dressing II.
    1. Fly tying
    I. Title
    688.7'9   SH451

    ISBN 0-7153-8145-8

© David J. Collyer 1981

First published 1981
Second impression 1983

Typeset by Typesetters (Birmingham) Limited
and printed in Great Britain
by Redwood Burn Limited Trowbridge Wilts
for David & Charles (Publishers) Limited
Brunel House   Newton Abbot   Devon

Published in the United States of America
by David & Charles Inc
North Pomfret   Vermont 05053   USA

CONTENTS

LIST OF COLOUR PLATES

ACKNOWLEDGEMENTS

My thanks to John Wilshaw of *Trout Fisherman* magazine for which I currently write. To Brian Harris, although he is no longer editor of either *Angling* or of *International Flyfisher*, in both of which periodicals he was kind enough to give me a column. My thanks are also due to Alistair Dumbell for his excellent photography. Finally my appreciation to my daughters, my twins Susan and Sharon, who are at present going through the traumas of A levels and who devoted their entire summer holidays to producing the first-rate drawings in this book.

INTRODUCTION

I said in the introduction to my first book, *Fly-dressing*, that it was an unknown angler who had finally sparked me off to actually get down to work and write that book. Since then I have heard from this 'unknown angler'; his name it turns out is Vic Whiting of Shurdington near Cheltenham. I am certain he will not mind my quoting from his letter; it helps to show what a kindly and friendly group of people anglers are – at least, that has generally been my experience.

> Dear Dave,
>
>   I know you are very pleased to hear of any success with your flies or lures so I am sending you a cutting from the Western Daily Press, September 5th, 1975 edition. The fish was caught on an Ace of Spades tied small (a number 8 trout hook) so thanks for the dressing.
>
>   You will probably remember me, I met you at Chew Valley Lake about two years ago. We had a chat about writing a book on fly tying. Your friend had split his waders [that was Tony Claydon, what a careless fellow] so I loaned him a pair for the couple of days you were stopping, we were by Wick Green car park.
>
> Cheers,
> Vic Whiting

So it was that we finally learned who our benefactor was on that summer's day – and now you know who to blame for these two books!

  The cutting tells the story of a Cheltenham teenager who caught the biggest fish of the season at any of the Bristol Waterworks' fisheries. It weighed just 6lb 15oz and it took an

11

Ace of Spades at Blagdon – just about my favourite of all the English reservoirs – and it was a splendid achievement for a young man of only fourteen. Vic Whiting is his grandfather and Ian McKie is going to be a name to be reckoned with. What do I mean 'is *going* to be', he is already there.

I have tried to make this book a natural continuation of *Fly-dressing*. When I was asked to write an updated version of that book by David and Charles, to bring in some new patterns, techniques, tackle and attitudes that have come about during the last ten years or so, I thought that it would be fairly simple to do so. That was until I began to re-read some of my later articles. I then realized that there was not only enough material for another book but that it was essential that I write it. There was too much that was both new and (I hope) interesting to be condensed into just one book.

Once again every single fly that I have written about here has proved its worth through its ability to catch fish. Perhaps you will now find some of your favourite flies in these pages that lack of space forced me to omit from *Fly-dressing*; certainly you will find new patterns here that I or my clients and friends have tested and which have been good fish-takers.

I have avoided one pitfall that seems to beset many writers on fly-tying matters, and that is the duplication of previously used patterns. This has always seemed to me to be a form of plagiarism and to cheat the reader, rather like re-titling previously published work. You will not find one fly in this book that was written about in the previous one, although there are often references to flies that appeared there – but, that is just me being sneaky and trying to get you to spend your money on both books. You've got to watch me you know.

I have tried here, as in *Fly-dressing*, to make the introduction to each fly as readable as my limited ability allows so that if the casual or non-fly-dressing reader should pick it up, he or she can at least read and, I hope, enjoy some of my experiences that have filled my fishing days with such pleasure over the years.

D.J.C.
Reigate, Surrey   September 1980

SECTION ONE

DRY FLIES

CHAPTER ONE

WINGED DRY FLIES

HOUGHTON RUBY

In this life of constant change and 'progress' it is pleasant to find a thread of continuity running through anything with which we are connected. At Stockbridge on the lovely river Test in Hampshire the Houghton Club has its headquarters. This most famous and exclusive of angling clubs has had the same family – the Lunns – as its head keepers for three generations. It all started back in 1886 when William James Lunn was engaged to care for this beautiful stretch of river. He was not only an excellent keeper but also a keen observer of the fly life on the river, which led him to creating his series of flies, all of which are excellent patterns. The real beauty of these flies lies in their simplicity, no fancy foreign bird plumage being involved. All have one thing in common; they are created from materials which are easily gathered from the average farm-yard or from a friendly gamekeeper.

All the Lunn patterns are well worth dressing and they will all warrant a place in your fly box. We start here with a pattern that incorporates the name of the club that the Lunn family have served so well for almost a century, the Houghton Ruby.

Method of tying
Run your tying silk from the eye to the bend of an up-eyed hook and there catch in three fibres from a white cock's hackle to form the whisks or tail. Choose the stiffest strands taken from the tip of one of the largest hackles on the cape. As soon as these are tied in, fix in the tip of a white hackle stalk which has been dyed crimson or scarlet – I prefer the scarlet, but I am told the crimson does very well at times. This is where waterproof marker pens come in very handy because you can dye just the

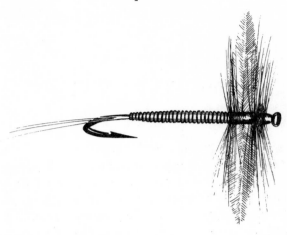

Houghton Ruby

number of stalks you need, as you need them. All you have to do is to press the marker pen on to the stalk on a hard surface and then draw the stalk through. Do this on each side and you have a lovely rich colour which will not run in water and which dries very quickly. I am certain the late Mr Lunn would have approved of these pens as they simplify things no end.

Wind the hackle stalk in close, touching turns up the shank for about three-quarters of the length of the hook, tie in and trim off the surplus. You will notice that because the stalk tapers you get an automatic and most pleasing taper to the body. The wings are of the very rare blue dun hackle tips, taken from the hen's breast, although blue dun dye on a white hen's neck hackle is a reasonable substitute. If you have the correct feathers then so much the better, of course, but blue dun is *extremely* rare, although with the new photo-dyeing techniques now being used there are very good capes coming on to the market, even if they are somewhat expensive.

The wings are set in the spent or flat position. This is achieved by winding figure-of-eight turns of tying silk over the roots until they are in the correct position. A single hackle of Rhode Island Red cock is tied in, in front of the wings, and a couple of turns are wound there and then three or more are wound behind the wings, where the hackle tip is caught in and trimmed off. The silk is then taken carefully through the hackle to the eye where a whip finish is made and the head varnished. You should end up with a most attractive fly that you could almost fancy a nibble at yourself!

The Dressing:	Houghton Ruby
Hooks:	16 up eye, Old Numbers
Silk:	Crimson
Whisks:	Three white cock hackle fibres
Body:	White hackle stalk dyed crimson or scarlet
Wings:	Blue dun hackle tips from hen's breast
Hackle:	Rhode Island Red cock

SHERRY SPINNER
The Sherry Spinner has been a very useful pattern to me during evening rises, not so much on the chalk-streams for which William Lunn invented it but on the reservoirs and the small stillwater fisheries which seem to spring up almost overnight these days.

Method of tying
This fly is tied using exactly the same techniques as those described for the Houghton Ruby except that it has a body of floss silk and a gold wire rib. I have tried a version using an orange dyed hackle stalk and this works possibly even better than Mr Lunn's floss silk version − I hope he will forgive me! This is probably because I did not use any gold wire for a rib and in consequence it tends to float rather better. Also the hackle stalk does not sop up water like the floss silk, which has to be very well treated with a floatant such as Dick Walker's Permaflote to stop this absorption.

The floss silk you should use is the artificial type of a brand called Salome number 403, but I have not been able to obtain any of this particular material and a good substitute seems to be a really bright (not hot) orange floss from your normal suppliers. Remember that both this pattern and the Ruby are spent patterns to simulate the spinner stage of the fly's life cycle and in

Sherry Spinner

consequence the hackle should be fairly sparse because it needs to sit low in the surface film as does the natural after laying her eggs. So no big bushy hackles, please.

The Dressing:	*Sherry Spinner*
Hook:	14 up eye, Old Numbers
Silk:	Pale orange
Whisks:	Light ginger cock hackle fibres
Rib:	Gold wire
Body:	Deep orange floss or orange dyed hackle stalk, unribbed
Wings:	Pale blue dun hackle points set spent
Hackle:	Rhode Island Red cock

WICKHAM'S FANCY

The true origins of the Wickham's Fancy are a mystery; at least two people (both named Wickham of course) in the last century laid claim to being its inventor. I do not intend to delve too deeply into its history, but suffice it to say that it is an excellent pattern that has taken some really good bags of fish – and it can get the big ones as well. It is one of the old favourites, like the

18

Greenwell's Glory, that never goes out of fashion, either with the trout or the angler.

No matter who was responsible for the invention of this fly we should be very grateful that it *was* invented, for without it fly-fishing would be much poorer. It is an excellent fly on the chalk-streams, the rocky rain-fed rivers and of late it seems to be gaining favour on the stillwater fisheries. It takes fish right through the season and can be used either wet or dry. Its one drawback is that it can be a bit of a so-and-so to dress! It is very difficult at first to get the palmered body hackle to take evenly spaced turns down the smooth tinsel body because it constantly tends to slip. It is definitely worth persevering with though.

I think that probably my most interesting experience with the Wickham was down at Blagdon Lake in Somerset a few years ago. I had a boat anchored just in front of the lodge and I was taking trout (rainbows) of 3lb plus using one of Cliff Constable's Wallop Brook mini-rods, all six-feet-odd of it. There was a lovely hatch of Lake Olives but the trout still kept coming up for the floating Wickham's Fancy – funny that, anything less like a lake olive is hard to imagine. What made it so memorable was not so much the fly or the trout's unusual behaviour but the rod. If you have not tried taking big trout on light gear, really light gear I mean, then you still have something rather special to experience in this angling world of ours. It will shake you rigid, the difference in the fight they put up. Even relatively small trout of a pound or so will make your wrist ache when there is only about two thirds of the normal rod length to apply leverage with. I really urge you to try it; if you have got a small, light-actioned rod and you have got the trout feeding fairly close to you, then put a fly over them and wait for the sparks to fly. The normal nine-foot-plus reservoir rods are fine if you want to throw a really long line, but for real fun give me the little 'uns any day. It was taking me a quarter of an hour plus to land each of those three pounders at Blagdon, and that is perhaps five or six times as long as it would have taken on the normal tackle. The fish is going to be killed anyway so you might just as well let it give of its best rather than hammering it on over-powerful tackle.

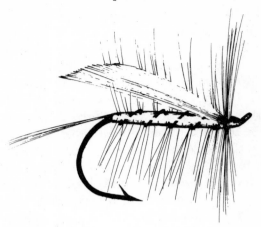

Wickham's Fancy

Method of tying

I am only going to give the modern dressing methods here but I shall give the original version in the dressing at the end so that you can try that if you wish.

Wind the tying silk from the eye to the bend of the hook and there tie in three or four fibres of cock hackle. As on all my dry flies I like to slope the tail slightly *downwards* to provide a further point of balance and support to the floating fly. It is not all that important on this type of fly, which has a palmered hackle, but certainly it helps on the normally hackled dry flies. But I will not hold it against you if you decide to point the whisks upwards slightly in the traditional way! After the tail is secured, catch in a piece of fine gold wire and leave this hanging. Wind the silk back up the shank over the stub of the tail fibres and the end of the ribbing tinsel to fix them securely. When you are about three-quarters of the way up the length of the hook fix in a length of flat gold Lurex or tinsel and take this down the body to meet the tail and then come back up again over the first layer and trim off at the point where it was first secured.

After stripping off the fluff at the base of a good quality ginger cock hackle, tie this in by the stalk end and catching the tip in your hackle pliers wind nice evenly-spaced turns down the body to the tail. It is tricky to stop it slipping about, but just keep at it. When the hackle is wound to your satisfaction take the ribbing wire up the fly, going in the opposite direction to that taken by the hackle. This has the effect of securing the hackle stem firmly at several points. Trim off the wire and the hackle tip after securing the wire with the tying silk.

The standard practice now is to tie in a split wing of starling slips, but I much prefer to tie in my Wickham's with wings sloping back over the body as you would for either a wet fly or a sedge pattern. This has two advantages; the first is that I am pretty certain the fish prefer it this way, and the second is that the fly can then be used either wet or dry. And that, as they say, can't be bad, can it?

When the wing is in place I wind a second hackle in front of the wing, but this is not normal practice; usually there is only one hackle on this pattern. The front hackle may detract somewhat from the light appearance of the fly and make it slightly more bulky but it certainly aids its floatability.

The Dressings

Wickham's Fancy – *the modern dressing*

Hooks:	12 – 16 up or down eye, Old Numbers
Silk:	Brown (Sherry Spinner)
Whisks:	Ginger cock hackle fibres
Rib:	Gold wire
Body:	Flat gold tinsel or Lurex
Hackle(s):	Ginger cock
Wing:	Starling primary feathers

Original Wickham's Fancy

Hooks:	14 – 16 Old Numbers
Silk:	Brown (Sherry Spinner)
Whisks:	Gallena (guinea fowl) dyed reddish brown
Rib:	Gold wire
Body:	Flat gold tinsel
Body hackle:	Ginger/red cock
Wing:	Medium starling dressed split
Front hackle:	Two ginger/red cock hackles

21

Dry Flies

PINK WICKHAM
(See drawing of Wickham's Fancy)

The Pink Wickham was invented by Francis Francis and while this is a good fly I do not find, in my own experience, that it is as effective as the normal version. But for them as wants to try it. . . . Both this pattern and the original Wickham's Fancy have suffered at the hands of the professional fly-dresser so that I am forced to give both the new, modern dressing and the original version. Over the years the professional fly-dressers have tended to use whatever material came to hand to dress a fly and then this gradually came to be accepted as the original dressing by the non-fly-dressing public. The consequence of this is that many excellent patterns have been so changed that they are virtually lost to us. These days I am inclined to believe that most professionals are more caring and do make a real effort to stick to the original dressings, even when some of the materials are, to say the least, unusual!

Method of tying

The method of dressing is exactly the same as on the Wickham's Fancy except that the body is usually pink floss silk. I find, however, that my clients seem to prefer the body to be of pink wool. That rather nauseous shade of 'ladies underwear' pink sold as Tup's wool for dressing the Tup's Indispensable is ideal. Incidentally that wool is totally wrong for the Tup, but more of that later.

Having a wool or floss silk body will certainly make this pattern a lot easier for you to dress, and it occurs to me that maybe that is why Francis Francis invented it in the first place — perhaps he was having trouble getting a decent hackle on that tinsel body as well.

The Dressings

Modern Pink Wickham

Hooks:	12 – 16, Old Numbers
Silk:	Brown (Sherry Spinner)
Whisks:	Ginger cock
Rib:	Gold wire

22

Dry Flies

Body:	Pink floss silk or wool
Hackle:	Ginger cock
Wings:	Starling

Original Pink Wickham

Hooks:	14 – 16, Old Numbers
Silk:	Brown
Whisks:	Dyed red/brown guinea fowl
Rib:	Gold wire
Body:	Pink floss or flat gold tinsel
Wing:	Landrail
Front Hackle:	Two ginger/red cock

QUILL GORDON

Some flies such as the Coachman, Greenwell and the Beacon Beige are as at home catching trout on a reservoir as on the rivers for which they were invented. Such is not the case with this pattern – at least that has been my experience (says he, hastily!). I have yet to take my first stillwater trout on this fly and it is not for the want of trying. This pattern is a favourite dry fly of mine on almost any river or stream so the inclination is there to try it on the reservoirs, always with a remarkable lack of success. (Mind you, next time I try it the trout will take it as if it were their last meal on this earth. I know trout, and if I go into print and make a statement like this they will be delighted to prove me wrong . . . again.)

While Theodore Gordon invented many excellent fly patterns for use on such beautiful American rivers (past tense should be inferred as some of his favourite rivers are now little better than open sewers) as the Beaverkill, Neversink and the Willowemoc in the past century and the early part of this, without doubt this fly is the most famous and certainly the most effective on our rivers.

I have taken many trout on it over the years; true the bulk of these have come from the Southern chalk-streams but a few have also been enveigled to have a go on the mountain and moorland waters. I think of it primarily as a chalk-stream fly and it is one of those patterns on which I have found it absolutely essential to

23

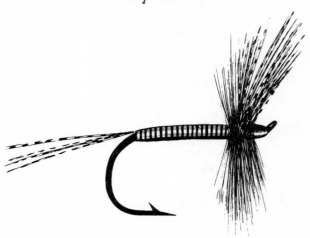

Quill Gordon

perform my usual winged-dry-fly-butchery. I take a straight slice across the bottom of the hackle with sharp scissors so that the preferred surface is the flat one directly under the wing.. I find it essential on the Quill Gordon because the rolled wing is slightly heavier than the usual slips or hackle points and the fly always flops over on its side unless that flat area is there. At least then I know that for approximately fifty per cent of the time the fly will be fishing the right way up, whereas without it I know equally well that I will have a fly that has fallen over on its side floating over trout every single time: I figure it is better to be right fifty per cent of the time than not at all.

Method of tying
The tying silk is wound down the shank of the hook from the eye to a point about a third of the way down the hook's length. There I tie in a thin bunch of the brown mandarin duck feather fibres (you will find it almost impossible to get the summer duck feathers that Theodore Gordon used; the mandarin is however an excellent substitute) taken from just under the forward part of the wing on the breast of the bird. Tie this in just as you would a wet-fly wing, sloping back over the body. Trim off the stumps of the feather leaving a short space at the eye of the hook to take

the hackle. Lift the wing into an upright position and take several (you *will* need several) turns of silk behind it just round the shank of the hook to hold it perfectly upright. When the wing is satisfactory take the silk down the hook to the bend – mind that wing now!

At the bend tie in three strands of the same feather as the wing for whisks. Now, at the same point, tie in a piece of stripped peacock quill. This is one of the few flies where I have found that it does not seem to make any difference whether the quill is shaded dark and light or not; this barred effect does not seem to affect its performance in the slightest. Wind the peacock quill up the shank almost to the wing, secure it and trim off the surplus. Carry the silk to the eye going carefully *under* the hook where the wing is or you will pull it out of true. Tie in your hackle by the stalk and wind two or three turns in front of the wing and the same number behind, secure the hackle tip and cut off the surplus. Take the silk carefully through the hackle to the eye, make a small neat whip finish head and varnish.

The Dressing:	*Quill Gordon*
Hooks:	12 – 14 up eye, Old Numbers
Silk:	Brown (Sherry Spinner)
Wings:	Brown mandarin duck breast
Whisks:	As for wing
Body:	Stripped peacock herl
Hackle:	Honey or blue dun

BLACK AND RED ANTS

The ants, both black and red, are only occasionally needed but when those occasions do arise you will find life most frustrating if you have not got the correct pattern in your box. I think in all the time I have fished for trout only on about five or six occasions have I been on the water when the ants have fallen. As I remember it, it seems that each time the weather was sultry, still and with a very high humidity – sweating weather, in fact. Once at Blagdon the water was covered in corpses all afternoon and the trout had a field day. I took a limit bag on that occasion but I had to be quick. The trout started rising to the ants as soon as they appeared on the scene and I had my eight fish in the first half hour; other anglers who were not quite so fast off the mark or had not the correct pattern lost out because after the first few were taken the vast clouds of ants came down and the water was covered with them. The competition was then too great from the naturals to allow much success from one artificial. I think only two or three anglers had limits that day out of about thirty who were on the water. The moral of the story is to get tying my friend!

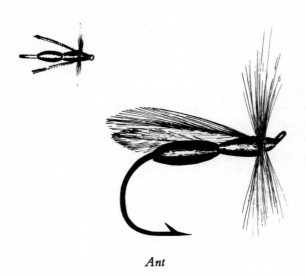

Ant

Method of tying
The ants are very similar to each other and the method of dressing one applies equally to the other; only the colour of some of the materials change. The next time you see a flying ant have a close look at it remembering that that is the body shape we are trying to imitate.

Start the tying silk just short of the bend of the hook, not at the eye which is the normal position with most dry flies. I always tie in in this position because the middle of the body of the fly needs no more than one layer of silk otherwise it is difficult to get that nice wasp-waisted effect. Wind a neat abdomen for

26

about one-third of the hook's length, and build up the silk to give a tapered but rounded effect. Look at the illustration for the correct proportions and shape.

Leave a slight gap after the abdomen is formed (one layer of silk) then wind the same shape but shorter and smaller for the thorax. Whip finish. Varnish the whole body several times until it is perfectly smooth and shiny. When the varnish has dried completely tie in two hackle point wings so that they slope back over the body but are slightly spread to each side of it.

Take the silk to the eye and wind on a hackle for four or five turns. Secure and trim off as normal.

You will not need either of these flies very often, but when you do you will need them badly. Half a dozen, three of each colour is enough and I promise you that the space taken up in your fly box will not be wasted.

The Dressing:	Black and Red Ants
Hooks:	12 – 14 up eye, Old Numbers
Silks:	Black or brown (Sherry Spinner)
Body:	Tying silk varnished until smooth
Wings:	Pale natural blue hackle points
Hackles:	Black or red cock

HAWTHORN

The Hawthorn is generally considered to be a river pattern, but if anybody has seen the prolific hatches and fish rising to the fly at Chew Valley Lake in early May they will know that this is also a fly to have by you on still waters.

It is a rather large, bumbling fly not unlike a midge (or buzzer) in appearance but the really distinctive feature about it is its long trailing legs. I once took a limit on what would have otherwise been a very difficult day indeed at Chew by fishing this pattern in the surface film. The rises were firm and the fly disappeared in a large swirl each time with the leader and fly-line being dragged along the surface. Each of the eight trout was hooked firmly in the scissors and that bag was taken in just three-quarters of an hour. Dress a few – you will find that you won't regret it.

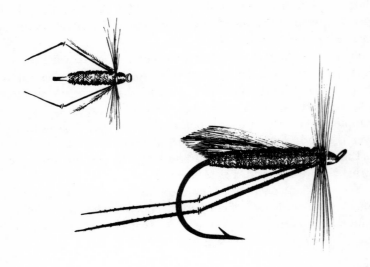

Hawthorn

Method of tying

I have experimented with several different dressings of the Hawthorn (or Hawthorne) over the years and I think this one is about the best I have come across; at least that is how it has turned out for me.

Fix your hook in the vice and you can either do what I used to do and test each hook by gently twanging it up and down with the finger nail of your forefinger or you can follow my current practice which is to test about five per cent of each batch of hooks to destruction. This tends to be rather more accurate because normally there is little deviation within a batch of hooks and once you have found out whether they are satisfactory (or not) you can stick with that brand or switch to another. I must say that my flies are at present all being dressed on the VMC fly hooks marketed by Geoffrey Bucknall: they seem fine and they have yet to let me down. Mind you, when they do. . . .

Assuming that your hook is allright, fix in the tying silk a shade back from the eye and run it down to the bend of the hook, but not round it – the body on this fly is straight, not hooked like the midges. At the bend catch in about three strands

28

of peacock herl. Run a layer of varnish up the hook shank and, after twirling the strands together to form a rope, wind the herl up the body for about two-thirds of its length, tie in and trim.

Now take two strands of swan feather dyed black and tie a simple overhand knot in them; do the same with another two strands but these should be taken from the opposing side of the feather. Try to keep the knots the same distance from the tips of the fibres. Have a look at the illustration as this should give you an idea of the right proportions. Tie the strands in on each side of the body so that they trail back and below the fly. The wings consist of two blue dun hackle-points – they can be dyed if you do not have the natural. Set them flat but separate so that they lie low over the back in a narrow, slightly open V.

In front of the wings tie in a pair of black cock hackles, back to back, and wind on two or three turns of the two hackles. In effect this gives you four to six turns because they are doubled. This is a very good practice when tying relatively heavily-hackled dry flies because it gives the fly-dresser two advantages; one is that the two feathers curve and because of this when they are placed back to back these two curves work against each other and the hackle fibres support each other, with the result that the hackle is set straighter on the fly. The other advantage is that when using natural hackles one side is almost invariably chalky in appearance and the two hackles combined give good colour to both sides of the fly. Anyway, on this particular fly I do not think this last aspect matters a lot because I normally use dyed black hackles because the colour is much more intense than the natural black. I reckon you get a much more killing fly with the dyed hackles, and I have tried both. In fact I shall go further than this and say that nearly all the black materials I use are dyed; for instance for the hairwing on the Sweeney Todd the natural black squirrel tail fibres are not in fact black but a dark grey tinged with brown. I think that deep black is a really effective shade for taking trout and no material in nature is in fact black.

After the hackles are secured at the back, the tips are trimmed off and the silk is taken carefully through the fibres back to the eye. When winding the silk through the hackle it is best if it is kept really taut and slowly see-sawed through the fibres. If you only take one turn through the hackle from back to front the minimum number of fibres should be displaced. Make a neat small head, whip finish and apply a coat of cellulose varnish.

The Dressing:	*Hawthorn*
Hooks:	10 up eye, Old Numbers
Silk:	Black
Body:	Peacock herl
Legs:	Dyed black swan, knotted
Wings:	Pale blue dun hackle tips
Hackle:	Black cock

WHITCHURCH DUN

This is a fly not merely of the chalk-streams but of *the* chalk-stream; the Hampshire Test, without doubt the finest and the most sought-after river in the world. This is the river that first springs to mind when anglers talk about the dry fly. This river is the ultimate. The Whitchurch Dun was tied for use on the Test, and the fact that it is also an excellent fly on other waters is merely incidental. The Test is its true home.

The Whitchurch Dun is also known as the Little Marryat (according to A. Courtney Williams) after G. S. Marryat. This fly is again one that has suffered at the hands of various writers and professional fly-dressers over the years, perhaps with more reason than most, the materials listed for Marryat's original fly (given with the other two dressings at the end) being difficult to obtain, to say the least.

Method of tying

The Whitchurch Dun is dressed in the normal dry fly manner and should present no real problems if you have got over the winging snag that gets to just about everybody at some stage of their fly-tying career. The only real way to learn how to wing flies, wet or dry, is by practice. You can watch someone do it and it looks very easy which it is, believe it not, but you still won't get the hang of it without wasting a lot of feathers and spending a lot of time.

Start winding the silk at the eye and carry it down to the bend

Whitchurch Dun

where you secure the whisks. As always with my dry flies I slope
the tails or whisks down slightly to provide another point of
balance on the water surface and to help lift the hook point clear
of the water. When the hook penetrates the surface film it drags
the rest of the fly down after it, and if you can help prevent it
sinking the fly by pointing the tail downwards it will make the
fly float for longer and possibly make it more attractive to the
trout. Try it – you will find it really does work. The body that
I normally use for this fly is white undyed seal's fur (Australian
opossums are a little thin on the ground in Surrey!). This I dub
on to the silk and wind up the hook for about two-thirds of its
length, trying to get a slight taper to it.

The wings are of palest starling primary feathers and are now
tied in, in front of the body. For years I tied these wings in by
the normal wet fly method so that they lay low over the body
and were then lifted into the upright position ready for splitting
and spreading. This was because I always thought that when
they were lifted upright the lower section of the web would be
pulled back to bring the tips into line with the front, if you see
what I mean. It never really worked and I was never completely
happy with the results I got. One day I tied the wings in upside

down and drew the slips into the upright position; what do you know, the tips lined up beautifully. I seem now to be able to tie a decent dry fly wing with a shape to it that I really like. The only problem is that I cannot understand *why*. When something happens that seems a little weird there is usually an easy explanation for it, but I cannot think what it might be in this case. I am sure, though, that someone out there can tell me.

Back to the wing. . . . Lift it into that upright position I just mentioned and carry the silk on a diagonal line from the front and bottom of the hook to behind the wing, just round the shank. This silk winding should hold the wing upright . . . well, it will once you have got it right. Take your dubbing needle and very carefully separate the two wing slips which have probably stuck together during the lifting stage, separate them at the tips and slide the needle down until it is pressing right on the base of the slips where they are tied in. Give it a fair amount of pressure and the slips should stay apart for long enough to wind a figure-of-eight through them with the silk. To get the normal split-wing angle a couple of figure-of-eight turns are enough, but I tend to prefer to use the semi-spent position on my own dry flies and this requires more turns.

When the wings are secured to your satisfaction, tie in a cock hackle just behind the eye, wind two or three turns in front of the wings and the same number behind them. Carry the silk forward to the eye going *under* the hook as you pass the wings otherwise you will push them out of shape. The silk has to be kept very taut of course. Make a small, neat head, whip finish and varnish. All the dry flies should have heads as neatly tied and as small as you can make them.

The Dressings

Whitchurch Dun

Hooks:	12 – 16 up eye, Old Numbers
Silk:	White
Whisks:	Pale creamy white cock hackle
Body:	White seal's fur
Wings:	Pale starling primary slips
Hackle:	As for whisks

Dry Flies

The 'Normal' Whitchurch Dun

Hooks:	12 – 14 up eye, Old Numbers
Silk:	White or cream
Tail:	Light ginger hackle fibres
Body:	White wool
Wings:	Natural blue hackle fibres tied upright as a bunch
Hackle:	As for tail

Original Little Marryat

Hooks:	00 or 000, New Numbers (16 – 17, Old Numbers)
Body:	Spun fur from the flank of the Australian opossum
Hackle:	Pale buff cochin cock
Wings:	Palest starling

JOHN STOREY

The John Storey is a Yorkshire pattern that does not mind a bit being used by we sharp Southerners. When I wrote about this fly first I was taken to task because I gave the wrong dressing. I have in fact found about five different dressings all calling themselves the John Storey and about the only thing they have in common with each other is that they all float. I wonder perhaps if there is right now someone, lurking somewhere, dressing a John Storey nymph, wet fly or salmon fly. You never know, do you.

The first pattern I give in the dressings is my favourite and certainly it is the version that I like most for taking grayling. Strangely, although it was invented mainly as a trout fly I have not found it to be very good in that capacity.

Method of tying

Run the silk from eye to bend and there catch in a few strands of cock hackle. Immediately after the tail is tied in catch in a strand of scarlet silk – tying silk seems to be the normal thing but I have found that scarlet DFM (daylight fluorescent material) floss is even better. After the silk fix in three or four strands of

John Storey

peacock tail herl, twist these together to form a rope and then wind them about two-thirds of the way up the hook over a light coating of wet varnish, tie in and trim off the ends. Come up the body with the ribbing silk going on the opposite spiral to that taken when winding the body material, which, along with the drying varnish, will lock the body firmly in position. The wing is composed of grey mallard feather and this I usually tie in as a 'shaving brush' wing, upright, although I am inclined to believe that the original pattern used the wings sloping forward over the eye and split in the manner of the Mole fly or Lee Wulff's American patterns. I also sometimes use grey mallard primary feather slips tied in by the normal split wing techniques. That fly works very nicely for grayling.

The hackle is again red game-cock hackles as are the tail fibres and I normally wind this fairly sparsely behind the wing.

The Dressings

John Storey

Hook:	14 up eye, Old Numbers
Silk:	Brown (Sherry Spinner)
Tail:	Red game-cock hackle
Rib:	Red tying silk or DFM floss

Body:	Peacock herl
Wing:	Grey mallard (bunched and split over the eye of the hook)
Hackle:	As for tail

Possible original John Storey

Hooks:	10 – 14, Old Numbers
Silk:	Brown (Sherry Spinner)
Body:	Peacock herl
Wing:	Speckled mallard breast feather pointed forward over the eye
Hackle:	Dark red cock

IRON BLUE

When fishing the chalk-streams and other rivers, it is often seen that, while there is an extremely good hatch of flies – say olives – and the trout are obviously feeding freely, they will not take what appears to the angler to be a perfectly good representation of the fly on the water. Why? Often the theory has been advanced that the imitation is simply not good enough and this

Iron Blue

seems fair comment because nobody's fingers can produce anything remotely approaching the real thing. Why then, during other rises to other types of fly, do the trout take avidly flies that are far worse representations of the natural than the fly you are putting over them during this particular rise to the olives? We know that the olive, when seen from below, exhibits a reddish colour and we have faithfully introduced this into the artificial; the wings are set correctly; the fly looks all right to us as it sails down the river towards us. There he comes again; another sipping rise and another olive disappears – or was it? Certainly a fly vanished, but was it in fact one of the olives that are sailing so obviously down the current? What was that little dark fly that nearly got lost in the crowd! There it is again; it's an iron blue. There comes the trout once more; a gentle rise and from amongst all the big burly olives he selects that tiny insignificant, dark fly. There is the reason for our frustration; that is what the blighter has been at – he was not on the olives at all!

How many times I wonder has this happened? I know full well that it has caught me more than once and I really ought to know better. I have known for many years that trout have this perverse habit and still I wonder what it is I am doing wrong. The pattern looks right, etc. etc., but I am just not getting the fish to rise to my fly. For some reason – perhaps they just prefer the taste of the iron blues to the olives, and I cannot think of any better reason for preferring one food to another – the trout are picking out those iron blues each time. When it finally sinks into my thick skull what is going on then I can do something about it, assuming I have a suitable imitation in my fly box of course. This fly is an excellent imitation and during a hatch of olives it is as well to have the odd little Iron Blue along.

Unless you are fishing this fly very close to you, say within ten or twelve yards, they are very difficult to see on the water, particularly if it is a bright day. You will find that if you cover a fish that is a fair distance away you have to judge the exact moment when the fly is drifting over him. I find these days that I can pretty well judge the drift and I tighten at the sight of a rising fish; it is not my favourite way of fishing a dry fly but it is necessary when the fish is at a distance.

Method of tying

In the past I have always avoided using wax on my tying silk because it is thoroughly nasty messy stuff and I often found that when the whip finish was pulled tight at the end of the dressing a small blob of wax was pulled into the eye. Then, when the head was varnished, the varnish ran over the wax blob and neatly sealed the eye of the hook. It meant unpicking the eye of each fly dressed and in professional fly-dressing time is money and this was time consuming. However, if I left out the wax, then on a very shiny hook the dressing could slip, so wax could often be an advantage. I have now found a very simple way round this problem. All I do is wax the first three or four inches of the silk and by doing this I get the best of both worlds – the silk bed does not slip and at the same time when you make the whip finish with the silk all the wax is in the dressing and you are pulling clean silk through the whip, with no blob.

Run your (waxed!) tying silk from the eye to a shade round the bend of the hook. Catch in three or four strands of cock hackle fibres (these can be any lightish colour, although I usually use pale fawn). They should point slightly downwards and be fairly long – around twice the body length seems about right. Strip the flue (the fluffy bits) from a piece of peacock herl. The best way of doing this is by laying it on a hard, smooth surface and rubbing the flue off with an ordinary pencil eraser. The quill should be as dark as possible and it does not matter whether or not it has the light and dark stripe that is so desirable on most flies incorporating this material. If you have not got a dark one, then you will not go too deeply into my bad books if you run a marker pen over it to darken it slightly. The tip of the quill is tied in at the tail and wound up the shank in close, even, touching turns to a point about two-thirds of the way along. Tie in and trim.

I have been very fortunate in getting hold of some rather handsome natural black cock capes and it is the tips of two of these feathers that I tie in, in the semi-spent position – this is midway between being fully cocked and being tied in flat or spent. It seems to be a very effective angle at which to set wings, especially as the trout like it. If you have not got any natural black hackles, and they are *very* rare, then you can use dyed black, but they are not as good. This is one of the few occasions that you will hear me say that — normally I prefer the dyed black material over the natural, but not here though. Sometimes on the very bottom of a furnace (Greenwell) cape, or even more likely on a Coch-y-bondhu, there are some black hackles; have a look, you might be in luck.

The hackle is a very dark coloured, slate shaded cock hackle tied in before and behind the wings in the normal manner and the head finished off as usual.

The Dressing:	Iron Blue
Hooks:	14 – 16 up eye, Old Numbers
Silk:	Black
Whisks:	Light coloured cock hackle
Body:	Dark peacock quill (stripped)
Wings:	Natural black cock hackle points
Hackle:	Dark slate coloured cock hackle

ORANGE QUILL

Strange as it may seem, the Orange Quill seems to be particularly effective during hatches of olives. Skues was a champion of this fly. Contrary to popular belief G. E. M. Skues was primarily a dry-fly angler who, only during his later years, began working on the idea of nymphs being an effective and sporting method of catching trout. I always get the feeling that he was as deeply indoctrinated with the dry fly cult as anybody. When speaking of nymphs he seemed to be on the defensive, even faintly apologetic. Nobody can deny that Skues had a vast influence on fly-fishing thinking and writing during the last sixty or seventy years. Perhaps rather strangely (at least I am sure he would have found it so) that influence has been much greater on the stillwater fly-angler, than on the chalk-stream fly-fisher.

There is no doubt that the easiest and most practical method of catching chalk-stream trout is on the dry fly. It is not merely that nymphing is a *different* method, it is also a technique that is far more difficult at which to become proficient. You see you are then working in three dimensions rather than the two which apply with a floating fly. Let's face it, the slower your reflexes when using a dry fly, the better. With nymphing it is different. If you do not strike the moment you see that white mouth opening, the leader drawing across the surface or that golden wink deep in the water as a trout turns, he has gone. Nymphing in my opinion is considerably more difficult than the dry fly and is therefore indeed (as Skues entitled one of his books) a 'Minor Tactic of the Chalk-stream'. The dry fly is by far the major tactic.

Orange Quill

On stillwater fisheries nymphing really does come into its own. There it is as useful and effective a tactic as the fly-angler has at his disposal and the methods of dressing nymphs, and indeed the fishing, are largely the result of work by such anglers as Skues, Frank Sawyer and, to a lesser degree, Oliver Kite. For a day on the chalk-stream, though take along a few Orange Quills as there may well be a hatch of olives.

Method of tying
After waxing the first few inches of the silk, fix it in just behind the eye of the hook and wind it down to the bend. There tie in a

few strands of orange dyed red cock hackles as whisks. Do not forget to slope the tail down slightly. Carry the tying silk back up the body and wind it up and down the shank to slightly taper the body. The body material is tied in at the tail end and wound up the shank in close, touching turns. You can use stripped condor, peacock quill or the one which I prefer, white, orange dyed hackle stalk. Fix in and trim off the surplus when it is wound about two-thirds of the length of the shank.

The wings are now tied in and the normal dry fly, split wing method is used. The hackle is tied in and wound an even number of turns in front and behind the wings, thus providing support both fore and aft and helping to keep the wings nicely in position. Tie off with a good four or five turn whip finish at the eye, and then run on a coat of thin cellulose varnish.

The Dressing:	*Orange Quill*
Hooks:	14 up eye, Old Numbers
Silk:	Orange
Whisks:	Red cock tinted with orange marker pen
Body:	Orange dyed, condor, peacock quill or hackle stalk
Wings:	Rather heavily tied medium coloured starling primary slips
Hackle:	As for whisks

CHAPTER TWO

HACKLED DRY FLIES

BEACON BEIGE

Peter Deane designed this pattern primarily for use on the Devon rivers but it has proved to be very useful just about everwhere. I use it with great confidence on chalk-streams like the Test and the Itchen, and it has also taken many fish for me on the reservoirs. It is an excellent representation of the Olive Dun. I know it is one of Peter's favourite patterns, and that chap knows what he is talking about.

The major problem you may find with this pattern is getting hold of the Plymouth Rock cock hackles − they are a little on the rare side. There was an imported batch that came in a few years ago and I bought all that I could afford. I am afraid that grizzle really is not the same and the only reasonable substitute that I have found is to mark up a plain white hackle with black bars across it using a marker pen; the best way to mark hackles using these pens is to dab them on rather than drawing the pen across the hackle as the latter method just makes a mess of the feather.

Method of tying
Wind tying silk down the shank from eye to bend in close, touching turns, and at the bend tie in four strands of hackle from a Plymouth Rock hackle − the straighter the barring of black on white the better the hackle, along with the normal requirements of any dry fly hackle, of course; long stalks and short, even length fibres.

Make the whisks longer than normal and use fibres as stiff as you can find. Peter usually points his tails upwards in the traditional method but again I employ that slight downward slope; it is more a matter of style than firm conviction, I am sure.

41

I am also sure that he will forgive me for my little idiosyncrasies.

Strip a strand of peacock herl taken from the eye part of the tail feather; it should be as well marked as possible. Run a layer of varnish up the body and wind the stalk over it in close, touching but not over-lapping turns. Tie off and trim when you have reached about three-quarters of the way up the shank.

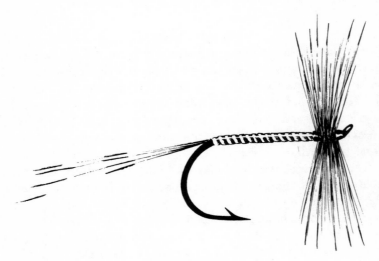

Beacon Beige

Get two hackles of the same length of fibre, one from a well marked Plymouth Rock cape and the other from a really dark-red game neck and place them back to back; as I explained in the previous chapter this has the effect that the opposing curves push against each other and you end up with a lovely vertical hackle and a really splendid mix of the black and white barred feathers and the deep red game hackle fibres. This double hackle is normally wound on for three or so turns. All hackles, even the very best quality, have an in-built curve to them. If, as with so many people these days, you are reduced to using B grade capes for your fly-dressing you will find that this simple technique has a further advantage of the two hackles supporting each other, and consequently the fly becomes a much better floater. Whip-finish the fly and varnish the head.

The Dressing:	*Beacon Beige*
Hooks:	12 – 16 up eye, Old Numbers
Silk:	Brown (Sherry Spinner) or black
Whisks:	Four long fibres from a Plymouth Rock neck
Body:	Well marked stripped peacock quill
Hackles:	Plymouth Rock and dark red game

TERRY'S TERROR

This fly always sounds to me as though it ought to be one of those three hook-lure jobs that were so popular a few years back, but it is not. In fact it is a relatively inoffensive dry fly and another of Peter Deane's favourites. The trout on the big reservoirs seem to like this one fished on the edge of a slight ripple. The best method I have found is to just cast it out and let it drift round with the breeze until it is suddenly engulfed.

Peter says that it also fishes well as a wet pattern but I have not as yet tried it in that capacity. In the dry version it seems to be useful when the sedges are about – there are of course many other better imitations of sedges – but it wants to be in the larger sizes at these times. While it seems to be primarily a fly for

Terry's Terror

stillwater use, it will also take fish on rivers and can be used successfully right through the season.

Method of tying
Wind silk from the eye to the bend and tie in a small bunch of mixed goat hair in about equal quantities of orange and yellow. Trim off to make a short stiff tag. Tie in a length of fine flat copper tinsel or Lurex and one strand of bronze peacock herl. Wind the herl up the shank and tie off and trim off the surplus when you are about a quarter of the shank's length away from the eye. With the copper tinsel wind a neat rib going in the opposite direction to that taken when winding the herl. Tie in and trim. Tie in, back to back, two medium-red, good quality cock hackles and wind a fairly substantial hackle, say four or five double turns; come through the hackle to the eye with the silk, wind a neat head, whip and varnish.

The Dressing:	*Terry's Terror*
Hooks:	8 – 14, Old Numbers
Silk:	Brown (Sherry Spinner)
Tail:	Orange and yellow goat's hair, clipped short
Rib:	Fine flat copper tinsel or Lurex
Body:	One strand of peacock tail herl
Hackle:	Medium-red game cock

KITE'S IMPERIAL

The late, and much lamented, Oliver Kite invented several fly patterns but there is no doubt as to which achieved the greatest popularity – his Imperial. Primarily Oliver Kite was an angler/ naturalist before he was a fly-dresser. He was one of those all too rare people with a real feel for fish and fishing. While most of us search in vain for his expertise, we are fortunate in having this fly pattern bequeathed to us, for the Imperial is an excellent fly. I find this is particularly so on the rivers in the early season. It has not done very much for me on stillwaters but it can prove to be very useful indeed on some of the small moorland streams and mountain becks in the early spring, especially when used in the smaller size. It will bring a rise when nothing else will.

Kite's Imperial

Method of tying

You start the silk just back from the eye and wind down the shank to the bend, tie in the tail using my slight downward slope to the fibres. Immediately in front of the tail tie in a length of fine gold wire and then the body material, which consists of a few strands of heron's primary feather. You will find that you can to a certain extent stop that ugly lump forming at the tail where the body material is tied in by allowing a greater length of fibre, fixing it in and then, with the tying silk, binding up the shank over its tag end for about half the shank's length. This should stop the lump forming as it has the effect of spreading out the turns of silk, making the fixing more secure and also taking the silk up the shank to where it will next be needed.

Wind the heron herl up the shank for half its length and secure with the tying silk. Rib the body carefully and evenly with the gold wire, tie in and trim off where the body finished.

Now for the part Major Kite said was most important. The heron herl must be doubled and redoubled over the back of the thorax to get a pronounced hump on the fly's back. The thing to do is this. The silk is wound forward in even touching turns, but leave more room at the head end than you normally would just to take a hackle – say twice as much space. Take the heron herl

45

over the bed of silk and tie it down just back from the eye. Wind the silk evenly back over the previous layer of silk and heron herl to where the abdomen finished, carry the herl back over the silk and bind it down with the tying silk. Wind the silk back to the eye once more, then take the herl back over the top again and secure it with two or three good tight turns of silk. Again the silk is wound forward, the heron herl is again taken over the top of the hook and this time it is secured and the tag end trimmed off.

You will find that the doubling takes up a lot more space than you would think on the hook and it takes practice to get the proportions correct. The hackle that Major Kite preferred was the honey dun but these capes are like gold dust these days and your only chance of getting one is to send off for one of the photo-dyed capes: make no mistake about it, these new-style capes tend to be excellent and the best are certainly as good if not *better* than the naturals. The dyeing process seems to increase the sparkle and stiffness of the original hackles and even second-grade capes can be made into first quality by this process. If you cannot afford to buy a cape of this lovely colour, then it would be acceptable to use a pale ginger hackle. Wind two hackles back to back and make a firm whip finish at the head. Run the varnish on using the tip of an old dubbing needle. Do not use a brush; they are useless for this purpose. The dubbing needle is stiff and the point is fine enough to allow you to direct a small drop of varnish to exactly the spot you need it. When the varnish begins to build up on the point just scrape it off with a penknife. Whatever you do though, *do not* use the same dubbing needle that you use for picking out dubbings to put on varnish.

The Dressing:	*Kite's Imperial*
Hooks:	14 – 16 up eye, Old Numbers
Silk:	Purple
Whisks:	Honey dun cock or pale ginger
Rib:	Fine gold wire
Body:	Heron primary feather fibres
Thorax:	End of body material doubled and redoubled
Hackle:	As for whisks

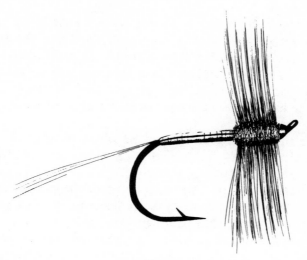

Half Stone

HALF STONE

Some years ago I was down in Eastbourne to visit Peter Deane, the famous professional fly-dresser; we began discussing dry flies and I mentioned one that had a few days before caught me a lot of trout on the river Blythe on the Packington estate at Meriden. It was my Dark Tup (described in the author's previous work, *Fly-dressing*). The first thing that Peter said when he saw it was that it reminded him of the Half Stone; indeed it is very similar, except for the colour of the hackle and whisks. Up to that time I had not tried the Half Stone but as Peter had recommended it I decided to dress a few, and I have never regretted doing so.

This fly was invented for the West Country streams and rivers and it is often dressed as a wet fly, but I have found it to be far more effective as a dry pattern, although I do tie a wet version for use as a nymph on the reservoirs. The tail is very short and the hackle is tied in as two bunches either side of the thorax, the two bunches of hackle fibres being tied in as beard or false hackles. This is the same technique that I use for my Water Tiger (again described in *Fly-dressing*) and is a method of hackling that has grown in popularity since I first thought of it – it makes extremely effective nymphs.

Method of tying

Fix your hook in the vice – I think perhaps I had better explain here the correct method of mounting a fly-hook for dressing as it is very important that it is done correctly. If you pick up a hook in your finger and thumb and look at it you will see the point, then the barb and then a longer straight piece of metal. That is called the bite of the hook *and that is all that is gripped in the vice jaws.*

If you insert more than this and go past the bend of the hook, you stand a good chance of ruining the hook, particularly if the point is offset – you can properly muck up the metal on that type of hook if you put too much of it into the vice and tighten down on it. What is more, you are liable to find out about it when you are attached to your first three pounder of the season! So just put the bite of the hook in the vice and none of the bend, and make sure that the point is masked by the jaws otherwise you will be constantly clipping off the silk as you wind it.

I have said previously that I no longer test hooks by twanging each one as I used to. The reason I have changed my mind about testing hooks by this method is that I am inclined to believe that the simple act of testing the hooks can induce weakness into the metal, particularly so on the fine wire dry fly hooks. As I said, I now test about three to five per cent of each batch to *destruction*; that I think tells me far more about a hook's shortcomings than pussyfooting around with each hook I dress. This way I know that each fly has had as little stress applied to it as possible. If I get a bad batch then back they go to my suppliers and that percentage rate of testing nearly always shows it up. If you are dressing only in small quantities for your own use, discarding the odd hundred or so is unlikely to bust the bank; but when like me, you are ordering in the tens of thousands, then the bad ones *have* to go back.

Right, now I have got that little lot off my chest let us get on with tying that Half Stone, shall we? Run the tying silk down the shank to the bend and there catch in three strands of blue dun cock hackle. Did you like the way I said that? All calm and easy, just as if you actually had a blue dun cape. All right, I'll let you off, dyed will do, but natural is better . . . I think. Wind the silk

Houghton Ruby   Sherry Spinner

Wickham's Fancy   Pink Wickham

Quill Gordon   Black Ant

Red Ant   Hawthorn

Whitchurch Dun   John Storey

Iron Blue   Orange Quill

Beacon Beige

Terry's Terror

Kite's Imperial

Half Stone

Tup's Indispensable

Leckford Professor

Red Tag

Grayling Witch

Brown Palmer

Black Bivisible

Brown Bivisible

Iron Blue (hackled)

back up the shank, covering the butts of the whisks as you go and stop about two-thirds of the way up. Tie in a length of yellow floss silk and wind this thinly down the shank to the tail and then come back up the body over the first layer to where it was first tied in and trim off the remainder. This double layer, starting other than at the tail end, avoids the dreaded lump which spoils the back end of so many flies. I use it on all my floss and tinsel bodies unless they require to be made really thin. Tie in immediately after the body a blue dun cock's hackle by the tip and leave it hanging. To the right of the hackle dub on a fair amount of mole's fur and wind it almost to the eye of the hook. Catch the butt of the hackle in your hackle pliers and wind the hackle palmer-fashion over the mole thorax, make the turns evenly spaced and tie in at the eye and finish in the normal manner.

The Dressing:	*Half Stone*
Hooks:	12 – 14 up eye, Old Numbers
Silk:	Black
Whisks:	Three fibres of blue dun cock hackle
Body:	Back half yellow floss silk, front half mole's fur
Hackle:	As for whisks, wound over mole's fur, palmer-fashion

TUP'S INDISPENSABLE

Tup's Indescribable, as it is often referred to by the less respectful amongst us, is an absolutely first-class fly that has been messed about by the professional fly-dressers until its designer, Mr R. S. Austin of Tiverton, must be positively thrashing about in his grave. We will now rectify matters; we will dress ours properly. I warn you though there is one fairly vital ingredient – from whence comes the name – that may present some difficulty, not to say danger to the perfectionists amongst us.

The first thing we have to do is a little harmless thieving. Sneak into the kitchen when your wife has her back turned and make off with her grater/blender attachment of the food mixer. This is far and away the best method of mixing dubbings that I

51

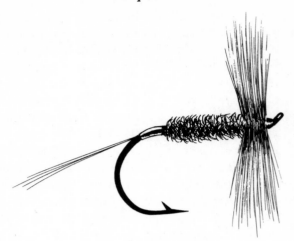

Tup's Indispensable

have ever found and I am indebted to John Darling for telling me about it, even if the cakes in our house have tended to be rather peculiar in texture lately . . . I need to lose weight anyway.

The ingredients you will need for this particular witches' brew do not include eye of newt and toe of bat, although it is pretty near that sort of thing. We have got Austin's mixture for the dubbing, all right, but as far as I know nobody knows the correct incantation. However the fly seems to do pretty well without it, so, let us proceed. First, as Mrs Beeton says, catch your ram (or Tup). Oh boy!

Take a fair bunch of wool (white) from the ram's scrotum and . . . Oh well, if you feel like that we'll forget the whole thing here and now! I must confess that I have not actually tried it but I have a distinct feeling that the ram might well object, so what I do is gather the wool which is always hanging in tufts on any barbed wire or hedge where sheep are kept – I am sure there cannot by *that* much difference, can there? Now we are going to assault another of our dumb friends, this time a dog. To be specific, a spaniel. We want a matching quantity of goldish coloured hair from him. I think that a substitute that does as good a job is that sandy coloured fur in the patch along the side of a hare – that is what I use anyway. I have not got a choice really, as nobody I know has a spaniel, gold coloured or otherwise, but if they had. . . . Now take a smallish amount of the dark fur from a hare's ear and a little scarlet mohair; actually, seal's fur seems equally as good.

What we do now is put all the ingredients on a sheet of paper and cut them through and through with scissors until all the hair and wool fibres are about the same length. Then we stick the whole mess into the blender and turn it on for about ten seconds, take the top off and there you are, a splendidly mixed dubbing. Wasn't that worth ruining your marriage for? Of course it was. You vary this mix until you arrive at a very vague shade of pink, nothing definite you understand. I have also found that a few strands of chopped-up fluorescent scarlet floss seem to help the mix; at least it does not seem to put the fish off.

Method of tying
Start the tying silk in the usual way just behind the eye of the hook, wind to the bend and tie in a few strands of either blue dun or honey dun hackle fibres, or pale ginger as a substitute. Take the silk up the shank again, but only for a very short distance. On Austin's original fly the tip at the tail end was of tying silk but I am inclined to think that floss silk does a better job. Make that tip very short indeed. Most people dress this fly with half the body of yellow floss; it is wrong. Now dub on your lovely mix and wind this almost to the eye.

The hackle is now wound on using the usual techniques and the fly finished off in the normal way. It does not look much like your 'normal' Tup, does it? It will catch a lot more fish though.

The Dressing:	Tup's Indispensable
Hooks:	12 – 16 up eye, Old Numbers
Silk:	Grey or brown (Sherry Spinner)
Whisks:	Fibres of blue or honey dun cock hackle
Tip:	Yellow tying silk or floss
Thorax:	Mixed dubbing
Hackle:	As for whisks

LECKFORD PROFESSOR

Some years ago I was visiting Birmingham on business and I was staying at what is euphemistically known as a commercial hotel. I was fed up to the back teeth; business had been bad, the hotel food was awful, the bed was lumpy, the television was terrible and on top of all that I had not been fishing in a week. I was decidedly not in a good humour! Suddenly someone tapped me on the shoulder and asked 'Haven't I met you somewhere before?' The stranger was a commercial traveller and it seemed he had seen my photograph in one of the weekly angling papers the week before. We were quickly discussing what turned out to be our mutually favourite subject. Even the bottled fizz that passed for beer seemed to taste better as we roved through barbel, tench and salmon until eventually we arrived at trout. Trout it seemed were his first love and he had access to this stretch of river in Shropshire where the fish just adored this fly that was tied the wrong way round. Do you think either of us could think of the name of it? We could not! It was of course the Leckford Professor. Since that chance meeting I have found out just how useful this fly can be. I have even fished it on the stretch of the Test after which it is named. It is a fiddly fly to dress but well worth the effort.

Leckford Professor

Method of tying

Wind on the silk as usual from eye to bend. There you catch in a good quality white cock hackle. Wind this *within* the bend of the hook: make sure the turns of stalk are close and touching: three or four turns should be enough. You will probably find that after the hackle is wound you need to pick out the fibres with a dubbing needle because they tend to get caught up on one side of the bite of the hook. After winding the white hackle the next thing to do is to tie in another hackle, this time a deep-red game cock. Wind this so that the glossy side faces towards the eye. The glossy side of the white one should of course be facing the bend, and the two natural curves of the hackle fibres then work against each other, keep each other vertical and provide support, one for the other. Tie in the ribbing tinsel next, tight up to where the hackle ends.

Hare's fur is now dubbed on to the silk and wound up the shank to the eye. The secret in applying dubbing is to take the amount you think you are going to need, halve it, then halve it again and maybe you will then have about the right amount, although the odds are that it will still be a bit on the heavy side! Remember it is easy with dubbing to add more but it is rather more difficult to take it off the silk once it is rolled on. I like to get a taper to it to get the fly-body shape. Run a nice evenly spaced rib down the body and tie off at the eye of the hook. This fly tends to float rather better than most conventionally tied dry flies because the main weight of the hook – the bend – is fully supported by the hackle and the eye comes directly on to the leader. With this pattern it will certainly pay to grease the end of the leader as this will then be the support for what would normally be the hackle end of the fly. Tails or whisks on a reversed dressed fly are completely superfluous.

The Dressing: *Leckford Professor*
Hooks: 12 – 14 up eye, Old Numbers
Silk: Brown (Sherry Spinner)
Hackles: White and red cock
Rib: Fine flat gold tinsel or Lurex
Body: Hare's fur

RED TAG

This pattern is without doubt a grayling fly, perhaps one of my top three or four favourite flies for one of my favourite fish. It is very pleasant to spend a few weeks after the trout season finishes still wielding a fly-rod. You have to speed up your reflexes a bit though, as grayling tend to rise much more sharply than trout. If the water is clear I often strike at the flash of a rising fish before he even breaks the surface, they are that quick at times. Any later than this on many occasions and I find I have missed altogether; forget the 'God-save-our-Queen' pause that worked for trout. I reckon that any angler after a season of trouting who can connect with more than one grayling out of every two offers on a chalk-stream is good.

Red Tag

I remember going down to my favourite reach of the Test on a glorious October day a few years ago. The sky was freckled with those puff-ball clouds of summer that are normally only a memory at this time of year; the leaves were turning amber and gold and the daylight hours getting shorter. This particular day might well have been three months earlier, for I fished in shirt-sleeves and never missed my jacket until the evening.

This was one of those days when the grayling only wanted a

fly with red in it. I tried other favourites such as the Greenwell's Glory and the Beacon Beige and they would not look at them, but as soon as a Red Tag drifted over them they shot up through five feet of crystalline water and the fly was taken.

During the summer you are restricted to one beat on this river for the trout: in October I was free to wander where I pleased; the whole of the estate's river was mine for the day. So long as I stuck with the basic rule of having some red in the fly, and the Red Tag in particular, I could not miss. I covered a shoal and almost every time one would come up and have a go at me. That is not to say that I connected every time by any means; far from it, but I did have a superb day's sport.

Method of tying
The Red Tag is a fly that is very easy to dress, as are most of the hackled patterns. Run the tying silk from eye to bend and catch in a tuft of red (scarlet) wool. This is tied in very short – a fifth of the hook length is plenty. Next, catch in three or four strands of green peacock herl, wind the tying silk up the shank over the tag-ends of the herl and the wool, binding them down firmly. Apply a thin coat of cellulose varnish to the shank and twist the strands of herl into a rope and wind it up the hook over the wet varnish. Trim off at a point slightly short of the eye. If the fly is to be fished dry – and this is the way I much prefer to fish it – then tie in a nice stiff red game cock hackle and wind it from the eye back to the body, secure the hackle tip and wind the silk through the hackle to the eye. Take just one turn through the hackle for this and keep the silk taut. You gently work the silk backwards and forwards in your fingers so that it eases past the hackle fibres without crushing them out of place. Tie a neat, strong whip finish, trim off and varnish the head.

The Dressing:	*Red Tag*
Hooks:	12 – 14 up eye, Old Numbers
Silk:	Brown (Sherry Spinner)
Tail:	Red wool, short
Body:	Peacock herl
Hackle:	Red game cock

GRAYLING WITCH

Continuing with the grayling theme, I well remember a day, again on the Test – I do love that river – when there was this particular fish that I was having great difficulty in covering properly. He was in mid-stream with a dense bed of *Ranunculus* between us, and the channel that lay between that weed-bed and the bank carried the fastest push of water in that stretch of the river. As soon as the fly landed, the current dragged it immediately into the weed-bed. He was a good fish and he was also very free-rising, so I got my stubborn streak going and became more and more determined that I would have him, even if I spent all day at it! I was not going to be defeated by any damned fish and a bit of fastish water.

Grayling Witch

I then remembered reading in an American magazine about using an extremely long, fine leader to cover fish in these circumstances. The idea is that the leader (say 2lb b.s. straight monofil and at least twenty feet long) is cast upstream of the fish and it all lands in a heap – Oh brother, does it ever land in a heap! The current then draws out the fly from this mess of nylon and it floats down over the fish without drag. It actually works

. . . on about one occasion in three or four. The other times you have a lovely heap of knitting to unravel. Anyway, it worked on this fish over the weed-bed; he came up for it like a good 'un and somehow I managed to connect. There is, you see, another slight problem about this very long, light leader business: when you strike you have got to lift enough line and leader to connect with the fish. I was fortunate; my leader tangled so that just the right amount floated out of the bird's nest for the fish to take it but when I tightened it caused a tangle and I came directly to the fish. I have tried this technique since then and the only time it seems to work at all is with trout. It is absolutely hopeless with grayling because they require a much faster strike. However it did work this time and I caught a beauty that failed to make the 2lb mark by 1oz. The fly by the way on this occasion was the Grayling Witch. I am sure you wanted to know that.

Method of tying
This fly is almost identical to the Red Tag except that it has a rib of flat silver tinsel. The pale blue dun hackle is normally wound at the front, but I prefer a palmered hackle secured with that ribbing tinsel.

The Dressing:	*Grayling Witch*
Hooks:	12 – 16 up eye, Old Numbers
Silk:	Brown (Sherry Spinner)
Tail:	Red floss silk or wool
Rib:	Fine flat silver tinsel or Lurex
Body:	Peacock herl
Hackle:	Blue dun cock

BROWN PALMER

This fly is dead easy to dress and it is always handy to have a few of them in your fly-box in assorted sizes. This is because when you run out of sedges, Invicta's or whatever, you will often find that the trout will take one of these in their place. This is not to say that the Brown Palmer is not a good pattern in its own right: it is. But I find that I usually use it as a last resort, which is rather sad really. Poor old Palmer, all out in the cold. Ahhhh . . . .

Brown Palmer

Another facet of the variety of uses to which the palmer patterns can be put came to light when I was fishing a particularly rough bottomed lake in Wales. It was full of enormous rocks and the trout were right down deep but every time I used a sinking line I snagged and it was beginning to cost me a fortune in flies and leader material. Finally I tied on a really stiff-hackled Brown Palmer and figure-of-eighted it slowly back. The line draped itself all over those sunken rocks and the fly was being inched along on its stiff hackle-tips. Not once did I get snagged up again but I did manage to catch a brace and a half of nice trout that I am certain I should not have caught by fishing a fly two or three feet off the bottom. As you can see from that little story, this type of fly can be useful fished to sink as well as being a handy dry fly.

Method of tying
Fix your tying silk in at the eye and run it down the hook to the bend, where you catch in a length of fine, flat gold tinsel or Lurex. I much prefer Lurex because it does not tarnish like the metallic tinsels. True, it is not as strong but I rarely find that it fails on me; if it does it is almost invariably because a trout's teeth have cut it. If a fly has caught a trout then I reckon I have

60

had good value from it; the flies that I cannot stomach are the ones which disintegrate while you are casting, and some flies I have seen do that on the *first* cast.

The next thing is to dub some brown wool on the silk and wind this up the shank almost to the eye. Leave a short space between the body and the eye. Tie in a nice bright hackle by the stalk at the eye and wind a couple of turns in that space you left, then wind the remainder down the shank to the bend in nice even turns. Leave the tip of the hackle hanging and wind back up the body with the ribbing tinsel in the opposite direction to that taken by the hackle so that each turn goes over a turn of the hackle stalk, locking it into place and holding it very firmly indeed. Tie in the tinsel at the eye, trim off and varnish the head.

The Dressing:	*Brown Palmer*
Hooks:	10 – 14 up eye, Old Numbers
Silk:	Brown (Sherry Spinner)
Rib:	Flat fine gold tinsel or Lurex
Body:	Brown wool
Hackle:	Red/brown game cock

BLACK AND BROWN BIVISIBLES

In my previous book *Fly-dressing* I wrote about Peter Deane's Shadow Mayfly. I said that it was an excellent floater because there was no ribbing tinsel or body material to weigh it down. The same thing can be said of these two American patterns. They float better than almost any other flies, and this without being treated with floatant. I use Dick Walker's Permaflote to get my dry flies to stay on the surface and very good it is too – just about the best I have found, anyway. But I would still prefer not to have to treat my dry flies with anything and with these two flies it is completely unnecessary: they float like little haystacks, all unassisted! The main purpose of this style of dressing – and there are several other colour variations on the Bivisible principle – is to render them easier to see, particularly in rough or broken water. You will find that they do work very well in this way.

I remember I had some great sport at Blagdon when the sedges were hatching some years ago. The light had nearly gone and there were fish moving everywhere. The water was in almost constant movement and because of this and the lack of light it was very difficult indeed to see when a fish had come to my fly and when it had merely risen close to it. It was most surprising the difference it made when I put on the Bivisible. It enabled me to fish for a further ten minutes and to catch another brace of trout. I suppose I might have got them by feel on the other fly but I somehow doubt it because none of the fish I had caught previously had taken hard enough for me to feel them.

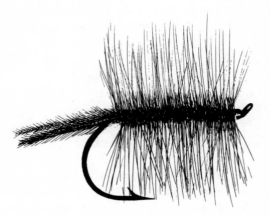

Brown Bivisible

Method of tying

These Bivisible patterns have no ribs so the hackles are always tied in by the tips. The way I do it is like this. I start the tying silk as usual at the eye and wind it down to the bend. I now select two hackles and tie these in back to back, the tips being left sticking out to the rear of the fly to form the tail. The hackle fibres must be stroked forward to allow the tips to be tied in like this, otherwise you will get problems trying to wind the remainder of the hackles because a lot of the fibres you want to stick out will be trapped; so stroke all the fibres forward except those you are tying in to form the tails. The two hackles are now wound together up the shank to a point just short of the eye where they are then secured by a couple of turns of silk, and the ends trimmed off. In front of this double hackle is wound a single white hackle. This one is tied in by the stalk, after tearing off the fluffy, useless fibres at the base. The tying silk is taken back to where the other two hackles ended and left hanging for a moment. The white hackle is then wound down the shank to meet the body hackles, secured by two or three tight turns of silk, and the end trimmed off. The tying silk is then held very tautly and wound through the white hackle to the eye. I like to use one turn but others use more; I feel that the more turns used the more there is a chance of crushing the hackle fibres out of position. Try my way; if you do not like it you can always go back to the other method and tell everybody that Old Collyer's talking through the top of his hat!

The Dressings

Black Bivisible

Hooks:	10 – 12 up eye, Old Numbers
Silk:	Black or white
Tail:	Tips of hackles
Body:	None; hackles wound palmer form a sort of body
Hackles:	Two black cock hackles with a white cock hackle in front

Brown Bivisible

Hooks:	10 – 12 up eye, Old Numbers
Silk:	Brown (Sherry Spinner) or white
Tail:	Tips of hackles
Body:	Hackles
Hackles:	Two brown cock hackles, white in front

IRON BLUE (HACKLED)

This fly is a good switch pattern for the winged version that I wrote about in Chapter One. Sometimes the trout will go for the lighter effect of the hackled version in preference to the winged fly. It might be as well to dress a few of these – for that day on the river when the fish turn 'picky'.

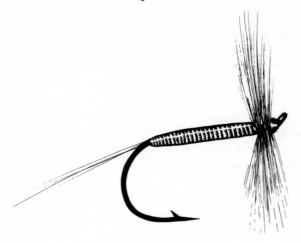

Iron Blue (Hackled)

Method of tying

This pattern is altogether lighter in tone than the other version. The tail and the body material is tied in in the normal way but this time use a lighter and more clearly marked peacock quill for the body. The hackle is – and why is Collyer everybody's favourite? – honey dun. I will forgive you if you decide that £10 or £12 for a honey dun cape (if you can even find one at that price) is rather over the odds! So, all right, you have got to use a light ginger. I like honey dun and I am sure that everybody else does too, but whether the trout give a darn I rather doubt.

Wind the hackle neatly and try to keep the fibres as close to vertical as you can. Finish off the head in the normal way. Now, with these two patterns you are all set to go and do a sneaky on the trout when they think they have got you going on the olives; we will show the blighters!

The Dressing: Iron Blue (Hackled)
Hooks: 16 up eye, Old Numbers
Silk: Brown (Sherry Spinner) or black
Whisks: Light ginger cock hackle
Body: Light, well-marked peacock quill
Hackle: Honey dun cock or pale ginger

FURNACE

In 1886 when F. M. Halford first had his book *Floating Flies and How to Dress Them* published, the Pennell or so-called New Numbers were commonly used for hooks. This system has never really been accepted by the trade and great confusion has arisen over the New and the Old Numbers we use almost exclusively today.

It is only in fly-fishing circles that anglers seem loath to give up the anachronistic New Numbers. I constantly get orders to supply flies dressed on size 00, 000 or even (Heaven help us!) 0000 hooks. Now this is not too bad because it is easy enough to do the conversion if you are in the know. (Just remember that size 0 equals size 15 New Numbers, 16 is 00, etc. etc.) The problems arise when the client gets confused and mixes up the two systems. Oh brother! You see, in the middle of the two ranges the sizes almost coincide; a size 8 Old Number equals a size 7 New Number, so if the customer gets confused he can easily order size 10s on the Old Numbers and actually get size 5s on the New Numbers. Have I managed to confuse you? Good! Maybe if enough people become confused and annoyed with this daft arrangement they will stop using the New Numbers and forget about them altogether.

Furnace

The book from which I took this dressing is Halford's (along with the able assistance and help of his friend G. S. Marryat) most interesting work; he uses the New Number system, as I said, and so indeed did virtually all his contemporaries. There is no need to worry however; I shall do the conversions for you at the dressings' stage. Nowadays of course it is very rare to get hooks in other than even numbers because the odd and even sizes are so close together that most people, and certainly most fish, could not tell the difference anyway.

We get rather a similar area of confusion with leaders and the X sizes. O/X is normally reckoned to equal about 9lb test at the point. I feel it would save much confusion to merely put the breaking strain at the point on the knotless tapered leader packets (plus, if you insist, the point diameter). This everybody would then understand.

One final word on angling anachronisms. The word *cast*. This is what the fly-angler does to propel his fly across the water; it is not the word to use for the leader on which that fly is tied. Leader is a much more sensible word and I am glad to see that more and more fly-anglers are coming round to this point of view.

Finally, we now get around to the fly. The Furnace is not a particularly common fly these days but it is nonetheless effective for all that. Halford used it and liked it and, although many of the older patterns become obscured over the years by the more modern inventions, they caught fish once and if you try them nowadays you will find they will still be effective and the trout willing to have a go at them.

Mr Halford says that this fly is 'a very favourite hot-weather pattern'. I, strangely enough perhaps, have found it also to be an excellent winter grayling fly.

Method of tying
Start the tying silk at the eye and run it down the shank in touching turns to the bend. At this point catch in a piece of peacock sword feather. The flue on this strand should not be too long otherwise when it is used as a rib it tends to obscure too much of the body. Tie in the sword feather strand by its tip, not

Furnace

Caperer

Silverhorn Sedge

Montana Nymph

*Sawyer's
Pheasant Tail Nymph*

Sawyer-type Olive Nymph

Ivens's Brown & Green Nymph

Cooper's Marabou Nymph

*Walker's
Pheasant Tail Nymph*

Walker's Mayfly Nymph

Stick Fly

Sawyer's Grayling Bug

Ivens's
Green & Yellow Nymph

Cove's
Pheasant Tail Nymph

Invicta Sedge Pupa

Amber Nymph

Teasy Weasy

Collyer's
Hatching Green Midge

Collyer's
Hatching Black Midge

Collyer's
Hatching Red Midge

Rube Wood

Wood Ibis

the butt end – the bright outside curve of the flue should be facing the eye of the hook. Carry the silk up the shank to a point just behind the eye and there catch in a length of orange floss silk – a single strand of marabou is ideal. Wind this down the shank to the bend, making the turns as smooth and even as you can, and when the bend is reached and you have made sure that you have covered any turns of tying silk at the bend with the body material, come back up the shank to the eye again, tie in and trim off the surplus.

There are several things that show whether or not a fly has been well-dressed; turns of tying silk showing at the bend is a sign of untidy and uncaring fly-dressing, as are sloppy, uneven ribbing, trimmed off tails and badly set wings. All of these are give-aways to the discerning eye. Have a look at your own flies and study these points – how would you feel about my looking them over? As I constantly say to my adult education class, 'It's just as easy to tie them correctly as it is to make a mess of them – and a lot more satisfying'.

It is the hackle on this fly that gives it its name, Furnace. The other common name for this colour of hackle is Greenwell because the late Canon Greenwell used it for his dressing of the Glory. It can be a fairly expensive cape to buy as they are not all that common, although most red and ginger capes have Greenwell hackles in the bigger sizes of feather. Red hackle capes on the other hand are relatively plentiful and comparatively cheap to buy, and a perfectly acceptable furnace hackle can be produced by dyeing the centre of a Rhode Island red hackle with a black waterproof marker pen. You just apply the colour by dabbing the felt-tip on to the centre portion, up the stalk section, leaving the outer parts of the fibres their natural red colour. Badger hackles are dyed using exactly the same procedure on a white hackle. Remember to do the marking on several sheets of old newspaper because anything underneath the feather will also get dyed.

Take the hackle, strip off the soft fibres and tie in the stalk end at the eye of the hook, right tight up to it. Make certain that the hackle sits vertically on the hook-shank which should ensure that the hackle fibres when wound will stand out at right angles from

Dry Flies

the hook. Wind the hackle, fix, trim off and make the head in the normal way.

The Dressing:	Furnace
Hooks:	0 long or 00 long; 14s and 16s on normal length hooks seem to fish rather better for me
Silk:	Black or light brown
Rib:	A strand of peacock sword feather
Body:	Orange floss silk
Hackle:	Furnace cock (Greenwell)

Before I leave this chapter I must mention a new (I think) system of dressing dry flies invented by a writer named Neil Patterson. His system is called the 'Funnel-duns' and I have found them to be very successful indeed. The flies fish upside down, with the hook points facing skyward, and this method of tying allows the larger sizes of hackles to be used even on the smaller sizes of fly.

At the eye of the hook a blob of dubbing is wound on and behind this the hackle is wound. The hackle is then pulled forward over the eye of the hook and turns of silk bound tightly round the portions of fibre situated between the wound stalk and the blob of dubbing. This has the effect of spreading the fibres out into a funnel-shaped hackle surrounding the hook's eye. If a small section of these fibres are then snipped away tight to the blob on the top of the hook it gives a preferred surface and the fly has the tendency to lie on this side thus keeping the hook point upwards and stopping it piercing the surface film and dragging the fly underwater. This is the most normal cause of dry flies sinking. The hackle fibres also lie flat on the water surface and then the length of the fibre supports the fly rather than the tip.

The wound hackle stalk and the blob of dubbing provide an in-built thorax for the fly, and a wing can be tied inside the bite of the hook if you wish, although it is rather more difficult to do this than to tie on a wing in the normal position. Neil points his tails upwards and I can see his reasoning behind this as it does make the fly look more natural. It sits at the same angle as any of the duns but I think that the Funnel-duns that I have used float

70

longer and better if the tails are tied in so that they lie perfectly straight and in line with the length of the shank. It seems to me that there is a large area of experimentation possible with these dressings. Certainly almost any of the standard dressings, Tups Indispensable, Greenwell's Glory, Blue Dun and many others, will happily convert to this system of dressing and I am inclined to believe that they are by far the better for it.

Neil has designed a series of dun patterns especially for this style of fly, but I cannot as yet see that there is any real advantage to using new patterns over and above the proven favourites which convert to this system so easily.

I may be wrong but I think that this Funnel-dun method of tying dry flies could well be the biggest single advance in dry-fly design and improvement since the advent of the eyed hook.

CHAPTER THREE

SEDGES

CAPERER

The Winged Caperer or Welshman's Button, as it is often called, is another of the W. J. Lunn patterns from the Test, but do not let that put you off if you do not happen to fish on the chalk waters. When I have used this fly on the clear, fast rivers of the South-East it has never been very successful, but it has proved to be excellent on the reservoirs and small still waters, and I have also taken several fish on it from small mountain streams in Wales and the West Country. Any water which gives a decent hatch of sedges (and there are few that do not) will give you a chance to extract a fish on this pattern.

It should not be moved at all. I have found that if it is cast out on to stillwater in the evening and allowed to sit among the rings of rising fish it will not be long before a trout finds it irresistible. Most dry sedges produce better results for me if they are retrieved to form a striking wake, the trout then follow this along, sometimes for many yards and the take can often be very savage indeed. This is perhaps the most exciting single style of fishing a fly to trout that I have ever used – certainly not a technique that I would suggest anyone with heart trouble should employ! The Caperer though is a different matter altogether: the fish like him stationary – not capering.

Method of tying
Wind the silk from the eye to bend and catch in three strands from a light buff or cinnamon turkey tail. Wind these for about a quarter of the body length and then tie them in. Do not trim off. Now tie in two strands from a yellow dyed swan or goose feather, wind a couple of turns immediately behind where the turkey fibres were tied off, fix and trim the surplus. Wind the

72

Caperer

turkey up the shank again for about a quarter of its length, tie in and trim. This should give you a body of cinnamon with a ring of yellow in the middle. Bleach a pair of coot primary feathers to as light a colour as possible. Take out two slips and dye them a deep chocolate colour. Take the slips and tie them in as a normal split wing. Most sedges are dressed using the rolled wing technique so that the wings lie along the back of the fly in the rest position, giving a realistic impression of the normal attitude in which a fly is usually seen. Though the wings on a sedge are mostly seen by the trout out to the side of the fly, you just have to look at the smaller sedges fluttering around the reeds in the evening and you will see what I mean.

There are two hackles on this pattern, a Rhode Island red and a natural black cock. The red one is wound behind the wing and the black one in front. Whip finish the fly at the eye and then varnish the head.

The Dressing:	Caperer
Hooks:	12 – 14 up eye, Old Numbers
Silk:	Crimson
Body:	Three or four strands of cinnamon turkey tail with two strands of dyed yellow goose or swan wound in the centre to make a ring

Wings:	Coot dyed chocolate brown
Hackles:	Rhode Island red behind a natural black cock

SILVERHORN SEDGE

It has been said — I may even have said it myself — that any idiot can invent a complicated fly pattern and call it 'new', but that it takes a touch of genius to invent a fly that is both new and simple. I have now to tell you that we have here a nice complicated fly pattern that I invented! It does have some merit however . . . it catches trout.

Silverhorns are a very common sedge on our stillwater fisheries and the trout seem to like them. Some people seem to be doubtful as to their value to the angler but I have many times seen them taken by fish. When examining stomach contents I have often found them, albeit a little knocked about but still recognizable. I think this is where this misconception arises — the 'horns' always seem to be the first things to vanish so that it appears that all you are left with is just another ordinary sedge. Perhaps the strong stomach acids of the trout attack the fine antennae first. Rest assured, however, silverhorns *are* eaten by trout, and so is this pattern, complicated or not!

Silverhorn Sedge

When you fish this fly it seems to need a much slower retrieve than is often the case with other sedge patterns. Dick Walker's famous patterns derive most of their attractiveness from the large wake they create when being pulled quite fast. The same thing can be said of the Great Red sedge, these flies needing speed of retrieve to make them give of their best. I find that a slowish figure-of-eight gather is the most successful speed for me with this fly; this has the added advantage that the fly is being pulled across the surface of the lake at a steady, continuous rate, something that the trout often find irresistable.

Method of tying

Take the tying silk from eye to bend and leave about three or four inches hanging surplus at the bend; this will become your rib. Tie in several strands of turkey-tail and wind it up the shank to within about one-eighth of an inch from the eye. Secure the tag-end so that it sticks up vertically; you are going to need this shortly so do not trim it off. The body hackles are two red cock hackles tied in back to back and wound together palmer-fashion down the body to the bend. The tying silk rib is now wound up the hook going in the opposite direction to that taken by the hackles, thus locking the stems on to the body in several places. Secure the rib and trim off the surplus.

Now take the fly out of the vice – you can always make a whip-finish at this point if you are nervous that it might all come undone. Trim off the body hackles as close to the body as you can, both on top and below the body, leaving just the side fibres. The fly will float low on the water but it will float very well and with great stability when you mutilate the hackle in this way. Replace the fly in the vice.

Bend the stub ends of the body material back over the body and tie them down with a couple of turns of silk so that they lie low over the back of the fly. Trim off the butts with your scissors so that they are square and level with the end of the hook.

The antennae can be made of one of two different materials and I am hard put to say which I consider best. Teal breast feather is certainly softer and the trout can certainly take the fly more easily because it is so soft, but this is also a drawback because it tends to get soggy and to stick to the body of the fly or to twist underneath and get caught on the hook during casting. Generally speaking, I think that perhaps a fine hackle stalk taken from a well marked Plymouth Rock cape with the fibres stripped off has the edge over the teal. If you do not have any Plymouth Rock hackles it is perfectly easy to mark up a white hackle stalk using the waterproof marker pens.

The two antennae are tied in so that they slope back over the body and I like them to point outwards. In front of the wings come the front hackles, which again are two red cock hackles back to back and wound together, but this time just the bottom portion of the hackle is trimmed off flat. Make your head, use a good five-turn whip-finish and run a couple of coats of thin, clear cellulose varnish over the head.

The Dressing:	Silverhorn Sedge
Hooks:	12 – 14 long shank, Old Numbers
Silk:	Brown (Sherry Spinner)
Rib:	End of tying silk
Body:	Dark speckled turkey tail
Body tackle:	Two red cock hackles palmered and clipped top and bottom
Wings:	End of body material
Horns:	Two strands of teal breast or two hackle stalks from a Plymouth Rock cape
Front hackles:	Two ginger or red cock hackles clipped bottom only

NYMPHS, LARVAE AND PUPAE

CHAPTER FOUR

NYMPHS

MONTANA NYMPH

This fly is rather a peculiar looking creation to British eyes and just what it is supposed to represent I have not the faintest idea. I rather doubt that anything that looks even remotely like this lives in the lakes or rivers of Western America, or anywhere else for that matter. It does however have one saving grace – it catches fish. Perhaps our trout are either more widely travelled than I am or they have better imaginations and therefore think they know a good thing when they see it.

I first used this fly at Weirwood reservoir and I did not catch a lot of fish on it but it was one of those nearly impossible days of brassy sun and brilliant blue skies, so to catch anything at all was doing rather well. The way I fished was to figure-of-eight it fast back just under the surface on a floating line. I put a small split shot about four feet up the leader to make certain that there was no line-wake and the leader was close to twenty feet long. The trout took it surprisingly gently; I was expecting it to be taken with smash takes if anything, but no, the leader merely checked and I tightened and the fish was there. They were hooked in the point of the jaw, not the scissors. I reckon that scissor-hooked fish are generally confident feeders whereas the jaw-hooked fish are merely trying the fly out to see what it tastes like. It must be a bit disconcerting when it bites back.

Method of tying
Take a long-shanked hook and fix it in the vice. If you are going to test hooks individually rather than using the batch testing method I now favour, do not forget to test the hook by twanging it both upwards and downwards; the upward twang will tell you whether the barb has been cut too deeply. If there is

79

Montana Nymph

any doubt at all over the hook discard it — it is far better to find out about a hook's shortcomings before hooking a big fish.

Wind the silk from eye to bend in open turns and there catch in a bunch of dyed hen hackle fibres for a tail. Do not make them too long, a quarter of the hook's length is fine. Tie in three or four strands of dyed black ostrich herl, twist them together to form a rope and then wind them up the shank over a layer of wet varnish. Tie off and leave the ends hanging when you have reached about half-way up the shank. Tie in by the tip a black cock's hackle where the rear half of the body ends and leave this hanging also. Strip off a quarter of an inch of the fluffy fibres from a piece of yellow chenille and wind this almost to the eye, then tie in and trim. Wind the hackle, palmer-fashion to the eye, fix and trim. Take the ends of the ostrich herl over the thorax to the eye and again, tie and trim off. Two sections of fibre from a dyed black turkey tail feather (opposing sides) are now tied in so that they slope back over the body; they should only reach roughly halfway along the abdomen, two strands being enough for each side. Trim off the surplus at the head, make a neat whip finish and run on a coat or two of varnish.

I am sure that you will be surprised at the results this fly can bring. It is somewhat similar in size and shape to my Water Tiger, and that too is a good fly.

The Dressing: Montana Nymph
Hooks: 6 – 8 long shank, Old Numbers
Silk: Black

Tail:	Short, dyed black hen hackle
Hackle:	Black cock over front half of body only
Body:	In two halves, black ostrich herl at rear, yellow chenille at front
Wing cases:	Ends of black ostrich body material
Horns:	Two sections from dyed black turkey tail

SAWYER'S PHEASANT TAIL AND OLIVE NYMPHS

Frank Sawyer's nymphs are world famous; if someone says that they have taken a fish on a PT nymph you can pretty well bet that it is one of Frank's. They are nothing much to look at from a human point of view, but *do* they catch fish! When I say 'fish' I do not just mean trout – they are also one of my top patterns for grayling in the autumn and winter. They can also involve a method of fishing which is different to most techniques used when fishing the upstream nymph. This technique, evolved by Frank Sawyer and publicised by the late Oliver Kite, is known as the induced take, and it really does work. It is also very difficult indeed to learn to its best effect as it takes a lot of practice and you must develop water vision – you have to learn to spot fish without getting so close that you scare them. As I said it is not easy, but it is very worthwhile. The thing to remember is that this technique *only* works with fish that you can see, which often means doing the hands-and-knees thing – you have *got to* stalk your fish and Polaroid glasses are a great help for the seeing.

Assuming that you have got within easy casting range of your fish you then make your cast sufficiently above him to allow the nymph to sink below his level or at the very least to his depth in the water. This is where the tricky bit comes in. When the

Sawyer's Pheasant Tail Nymph

81

nymph is about a foot or six inches from his nose you raise the rod-tip so that the nymph rises through the water towards the surface, giving the impression that it is just leaving the silt or gravel and is ascending to hatch. The fish should take immediately. I have found that if it does not work after three or four tries it is best to leave the fish and try for him again later, otherwise he will bolt and you will not see him again. The main problem with this technique is in judging just how far from the fish that tiny nymph is. Believe me you have got to have really exceptional eye-sight to actually see a tiny size 12 or 14 nymph through three or four feet of running water. You can (maybe that ought to read 'I can') have enough trouble seeing a relatively enormous trout let alone something less than half-an-inch long. The induced take does not seem to work very well on lakes, perhaps because trout rarely take up station as they do on rivers and therefore it is difficult to pull nymphs past fish that are constantly on the move.

There is a somewhat similar scheme that does seem to work on the smaller fisheries these days, though – at least it does on those with very clear water. The idea there is to spot a big trout and to note where his patrol takes him and then to station yourself very inconspicuously somewhere along it. You cast out a large, easily seen nymph and let it sink to the bottom. When our large friend swims past, the offering is pulled past his nose. This method is very similar to that described above and has accounted for some of the really enormous trout we have seen caught over the last few years. It really is exactly the same idea that Sawyer taught us many years ago. On the big lakes and reservoirs, though, it is an entirely different matter; there I have had no success trying to 'induce' fish. These nymphs are therefore really only for use on the clear limestone and chalk rivers, there being better designs for use on lakes and the coloured rivers.

Method of tying
The Sawyer Nymphs are tied entirely without the aid of tying silk, the tying medium being copper wire. I once used silk but my fears that the half-hitches used to secure the wire at the head

would be liable to come undone proved groundless. The wire
gives a much firmer fixing with half-hitches than does silk and it
is almost impossible to do a whip finish with wire, I know –
I've tried!

The first thing to do is to obtain the very finest grade of
copper wire and that is not easy. The best way I have found is to
beg or steal (you will not be able to borrow, they want it back in
the condition in which it was lent) an old electrically powered
toy from your children, and then do a ruthless destruction job on
it and extract the coil. With any luck this should have the correct
grade of copper on it. I find the lighter, brighter shade is best but
beggars cannot – as they say – be choosers.

Wind the wire down the shank from the eye for about a
quarter of its length then form a roundish lump for the thorax.
Now take the wire down to the bend where you catch in three or
four strands of cock pheasant tail fibres, twist the wire and the
fibres together to form a mixed rope, then wind the rope up the
hook in the same direction you wound the copper wire underbody, otherwise it will all come undone – yes, I have been there
too! When you reach the thorax hump stop winding and
separate the wire from the pheasant tail fibres; wind this, again
in the same direction, to secure the feather behind the thorax.
Wind the wire neatly over the thorax to the eye, carry the fibres
over the thorax, secure with two or three turns of wire, take the
wire back again behind the thorax and repeat. This should give
you a neat and relatively heavy nymph that will ensure that it
will sink quickly to the correct depth. The final operation is to
finish the fly behind the eye with two or three half-hitches. I
then soak the whole of the head with several coats of varnish.

I do not know whether Frank has used an olive version of his
PT nymph or not but I have found that one tied using precisely
the same construction as above but dressed with pale, olive dyed
swan feather fibres is very useful indeed.

The Dressings
Sawyer's Pheasant Tail Nymph
Hooks: 12 – 16, Old Numbers
Silk: None, replaced by finest copper wire

Tail:	Tips of body material
Body:	Cock pheasant centre tail fibres and copper wire twisted together
Thorax:	Copper wire base with several thicknesses of pheasant tail over

Sawyer-type Olive Nymph

Hooks:	10 – 16, Old Numbers
Silk:	None, replaced by finest copper wire
Tail:	Tips of body material
Body:	Olive dyed swan herls, twisted together with copper wire
Thorax:	Wire base with swan doubled and redoubled over the top

IVENS'S BROWN AND GREEN NYMPH

Tom Ivens – I hope he will forgive my saying this – is the father of modern reservoir fishing for trout as we know it nowadays. His book *Stillwater Fly-fishing* is a classic and any angler who fishes the stillwaters of the United Kingdom should have a copy on his bookshelves. That is not to say that I agree with all that Tom has to say, far from it, but we agree to differ over some points and there is never any animosity. So it is with his flies – some I find excellent fish-takers and others just never catch a fish for me, but then the same can be said for many other flies designed by many other anglers.

For the first time a few weeks ago I used a Black and Peacock Spider and actually caught a trout on it at Ardingly reservoir; she was a lovely brownie with a deep gold belly and very thick at the shoulders, and she weighed just a shade under 2lb. That is the first trout I have *ever* caught on a B and P. Everyone else catches fish on this fly of course but up until that Sunday morning at about five thirty I had never so much as had a fish cast a glance at it. There is an old maxim that says you cannot catch a fish on a fly that is in your box, and of course it is true. If you do not use a certain pattern then you surely will not catch on it. We all develop preferences and we tend to select the flies for our leaders that will give us results and if a strange fly does not produce the goods within a few casts it tends to get removed from the leader and another, probably an old favourite, is tried in its place. This is how our prejudices develop: 'Peter Ross? Never catch anything on that. I don't think anybody else does either . . .'. If I had a pound note for every time I have caught trout on the Peter Ross and another for every time I have heard those words or very similar I could retire a wealthy man!

There are a couple of Tom's nymphs that have always proved to be good fish-takers for me and one is his Brown and Green nymph. This I have found to be a superb pattern that fishes best for me if it is tied up with some lead incorporated into the dressing. I like to fish this fly just as fast as I can immediately under the surface using a figure-of-eight gather. It has produced its best results when used in conjunction with a very long leader – say twenty feet – and either a small split shot squeezed on the leader up towards its butt to just keep the wake of the leader away from the fly, or with a layer of lead wrapped round the hook shank and the dressing made over the top.

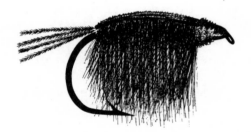

Ivens's Brown and Green Nymph

Tom reckons that trout often mistake this nymph for a small fish and that is the reason it seems to be so effective when fished fast. I doubt that. I am inclined to believe that it is taken as a hatching sedge pupa – they can come through the water at a rate of knots too! The reason I do not think they are taken as a small fish is because when I have taken trout on this pattern I have tried, immediately afterwards, with fish-imitating patterns such as the Polystickle or the Sinfoil's fry – nothing. Both these patterns will usually take trout if they are on the fry, one to

imitate the fingerling stage of growth and the other the pinhead
stage. No, I think those fish reckon that the Green and Brown
nymph is a sedge. Of course, on the *odd* occasion I have been
known to be wrong. . . .

Method of tying
This fly is fairly simple to dress and I am sure you will get good
results with it. Carry tying silk from the eye to the bend and
catch in four strands of peacock herl, leaving the tips sticking out
behind to form a tail. Next, tie in a length of oval gold tinsel for
the rib and a strand of green and a strand of brown ostrich herl.
Wind these together up the body without twisting them so that
you get alternating colours that blend into each other. Take the
herls up to about three-quarters of the body length and tie in and
trim off the surplus. Rib the body with the gold tinsel going in
the opposite direction to that taken when winding the herls, and
tie off where the body ended. Carry the peacock herl over the
back of the fly and tie in just in front of the body. Now wind a
bold head by twisting the fibres together and taking this round
the hook a couple of times just behind the eye. It is best to wind
the head over wet varnish. Finish the head as normal.

The Dressing:	Ivens's Brown and Green Nymph
Hooks:	6 – 10, Old Numbers
Silk:	Olive or brown (Sherry Spinner)
Tail:	Four strands of green peacock herl
Rib:	Oval gold tinsel
Body:	Two strands of ostrich herl, brown and green
Back:	As for tail
Head:	Peacock herl

COOPER'S MARABOU NYMPHS
Doug Cooper is an excellent angler and among his main fishing
interests he enjoys trout-fishing on the reservoirs, for which
purpose he invented these patterns.

They are not particularly difficult to dress but care should be
taken with the marabou body, for without doubt that is the
trickiest bit. There are two basic colours that Doug uses but

being what I am I had to have a finger in the pie and experiment a little myself. Actually all I did was to combine the two colours and arrived at the good old British compromise that our politicians tell us we are so good at. It did turn out a nymph that had that certain attractiveness that is essential, not perhaps from the trout's point of view but from the angler's – in fly-fishing, confidence is, if not all, at least a very large percentage. My mixture caught fish, not in enormous numbers but in sufficient quantity to prove the trout liked the look of it too.

Doug usually fishes his nymphs to trout that he can see feeding on the surface or just beneath it. He uses a quick-sink leader and recovers the line at sufficient speed to keep the fly about two or three inches under the surface, although sometimes the nymph is allowed to bulge the surface. These flies are always fished by Doug near to weed-beds and he says they are no use in the open water, nor more than two feet below the surface. (I reckon he is being a bit pedantic there because I tried these patterns deep down with lead under the dressing and I certainly caught several fish in ten to twelve feet of water, scratching the bottom.)

In the larger sizes this fly will make a good pattern to imitate such underwater mini-monsters as dragon fly larvae or the damsel fly larvae.

Cooper's Marabou Nymph

Method of tying
Mount your hook in the vice and carry your tying silk down the shank to the bend and tie in the tail, which consists of three strands of cock pheasant centre tail fibres; these are tied in long, about two-thirds of the body length. Immediately in front of them fix in the ribbing tinsels and the marabou herls for the

body. Take the silk up the shank for about two-thirds of its length, tying down the ends of these three materials as you go. This will hold them really firmly in position.

Wind the marabou up the shank to where the tying silk was left hanging in the bobbin holder. I am assuming that you *do* realise the benefits of using a bobbin holder? A member of my fly-dressing class amazed me by saying that he did not think there was any advantage to be gained by using one of these tools. I then explained that he was wasting a lot of silk by cutting off eighteen-inch lengths each time; far better to have it on a continuous spool. Finally, I bullied him into agreeing that it was better, not just for the saving in silk but also to have that weight to keep the silk taut when you have to leave it hanging during the tying operation; so much better than fiddling around trying to get the silk to stay put under the rubber button on the vice. I have since wondered how many other people have struggled on without realising the advantages of using bobbin holders. I use one for each colour of silk, and I am particularly fond of the long-nosed plastic type which has now come on the market – they seem perfect for weight and they also take the spool and hold it at just the right tension.

The rib is wound up the body on the opposite spiral so that each turn of marabou is locked into place by the corresponding turn of ribbing tinsel. Trim off the surplus.

Tie in the tips of a bunch of cock or hen pheasant centre tail fibres – the tips should be pointing to the right. Trim off the points so that they do not stick out over the eye of the hook. Wind a fairly thick thorax of ostrich herls twisted together and then bring the pheasant tail fibres over the top, secure and trim off at the eye. Turn the fly over in the vice to receive a false or beard hackle of soft honey dun cock or hen hackle if you have it, although I think Doug would forgive you if you decide that a pale ginger hackle would do instead.

The Dressing:	*Cooper's Marabou Nymphs*
Hooks:	8, 10 or 12 long shank, Old Numbers
Silk:	Brown (Sherry Spinner)
Tail:	Three strands from a cock pheasant centre tail

Rib: Oval gold tinsel
Body: Olive, russet gold (light brown) or mixed
              marabou fibres
Wing Cases: Pheasant tail strands
Thorax: Light brown ostrich herl
Hackle: Soft honey dun

WALKER'S PHEASANT TAIL NYMPH

Dick Walker's version of the PT nymph is somewhat similar to my own nymph dressing using this material, Collyer's Brown Nymph. I think however that in some ways it is slightly better designed. I have not used it all that much but I have taken several trout on it and it seemed to me that they were hooked further back in the mouth than fish that I have taken on my own nymph. That may not sound anything to worry about but if you think about it, what happens is this: the trout comes along and sees the nymph moving through the water; he decides that it looks tasty and eats it. If the fly is a good imitation of some underwater denizen and the fish is not made suspicious in any way, then he will be hooked far back in the mouth. So if you are hooking fish at the front of the jaw then you have not found the answer to what they want; either that or they are not very hungry and are only playing with the food. This is particularly so with lures fished mid-season; most fish taken are hooked at the tip of the jaw and quite often they are foul-hooked on the outside of the mouth. So, the farther down the trout's throat your nymph is, the better the imitation. I have taken a lot of trout on my Brown Nymph (see my book *Fly-dressing*) over the years and

Walker's Pheasant Tail Nymph

I have noticed that the hook-hold is generally in the front portion of the mouth. It is nonetheless a very good fly but perhaps Dick's pattern just has the edge on it on the stillwater fisheries; however, I cannot detect any difference at all when I use them on rivers.

Method of tying

Dick's fly is certainly more complicated to dress than my version but I think you will find that the finished product justifies the extra effort involved. Start the silk in the normal way and carry it down to the bend of the hook; do not go round the corner this time, though. Catch in several strands of cock pheasant centre tail fibres, plus a length of copper wire – why is it I wonder that whenever anybody designs a pheasant tail nymph they specify that the rib should be of copper wire? The only exception I can think of is me; my Brown Nymph has an oval gold tinsel rib, but then I always tend to be a bit awkward. However, the consensus favours copper. The tips of the feather fibres are left sticking out as a tail, the rest of the feathers being wound forward to form a tapering abdomen. Stop it about two-thirds of the way up the shank and rib with the wire, again going against the grain.

Tie in about a dozen strands of pheasant tail fibres so that the tips stick out over the *eye* of the hook; these should reach about as far as the hook point when they are bent backwards. Bind the silk over the fibres and carry it back to where the abdomen finished. Tie in another bunch of fibres and this time twist them into a rope and wind a thorax with them. Tie in and trim off the surplus. In practice you will find that two, or at most three, turns of the rope are sufficient. The tips of the fibres sticking out at the front should now be carried back and under the hook to form legs or a kind of false hackle. When the legs are in place carry the butt end over the thorax and tie in at the head. Whip and varnish. (If that little lot sounds complicated from where you are reading it, brother, you should try writing it!) I find that on the version I tie of Dick's PT nymph the fly fishes on a much more even keel if the legs are divided into two bunches and tied down either side of the thorax in the same manner I use for my Water Tiger. I reckon it also improves the look of the fly.

The Dressing:	*Walker's Pheasant Tail Nymph*
Hooks:	10 – 12, Old Numbers
Silk:	Brown (Sherry Spinner)
Tail:	Cock pheasant centre tail fibres
Rib:	Copper wire
Body:	As for tail
Thorax:	As for tail
Wing Cases:	As for tail
Legs:	As for tail

WALKER'S MAYFLY NYMPH

Dick Walker invented this nymph some years ago for use on the small stillwater fisheries and rivers. It is a most unlikely looking creation – at least it is in the colour that it is most commonly tied in, which is white. This is the wrong colour, the correct shade being lemon-yellow angora wool. This material is very soft and when the fibres are picked out from the sides of the body they give an extremely lifelike and effective imitation of the natural nymph. Dick has altered the dressing of this nymph several times over the years, which can be a little disconcerting for the professional fly-dresser because his clients write to him asking for Walker's Mayfly Nymph and expect to receive the very pattern that they saw written about in the article that appeared in 'last month's fishing magazine', which is fine just so long as they specify which magazine, which month or even better if they cut out the article in question and send it with the order. If they just assume that the fly-dresser is clairvoyant they are most likely to be disappointed because they will get the dressing with which the pro is most familiar. I often have people who write to me asking for some March Browns, which is the same thing carried to extremes, there being at least twenty different dressings of this fly, coming as winged dry flies, hackled dry flies, salmon flies, wet flies, and I even saw a March Brown lure! So, if a non-fly-dresser reads this and is thinking of ordering flies by post, please bear in mind that it pays to be specific.

When I said earlier that white is the wrong colour that was not strictly true; there is a version which uses white wool or ostrich herl but the best shades to aim for are pale yellow or cream. The main use of the white version is on stillwater fisheries which stock with the really huge trout; here the white nymph has a big advantage, which I will explain. The system is this: the angler who wants to catch the big trout and not to fiddle about with mere six or seven pounders spends several hours creeeping round the fishery on his hands and knees until he spots a trout which he deems worthy of his attention; usually this will be estimated to weigh at least 10lb. He then studies this fish and works out its route round its particular part of the lake; he notes where it passes certain underwater vegetation or distinctive shapes of mud or rock; he then lays in wait. This is where his nicely visible Mayfly Nymph comes in; not only is it white, so that it sticks out like the proverbial sore thumb, but when it is lying on the bottom it is also much larger than the normal nymphs, so when the poor unsuspecting trout comes by he can hardly miss seeing this apparition rising from the bottom (neither can the angler). The fish is overcome by the sight and is seduced into having a taste (hopefully) of this obviously live and interesting mouthful and with any good fortune the nymph disappears, the line tightens and all hell breaks loose!

The point of all that being that although the lemon-yellow angora is a splendid imitation of the natural fly, for sheer see-ability you cannot beat white – and for this type of fishing being able to see the nymph on the bottom in ten feet of water, even if it is crystal clear, is no easy matter.

I have not, as yet, used the Mayfly Nymph on rivers during a hatch – or perhaps I should say in the late evening after the hatch, which is apparently the time when this pattern is at its best. On the rare occasions I am invited down to our Southern chalk-streams during the mayfly fortnight I tend to want to use a dry fly. On the stretch of the Kennet which I fished this year at that time no nymphing is allowed until July anyway.

Method of tying

This is possibly the most complex of all the nymph patterns to dress. It is also one of the most difficult to dress correctly but it is well worth it when you see the finished article.

Run tying silk from the eye to the bend on a long-shank hook

then take the silk back to the eye and catch in a strip of lead
about a sixteenth of an inch wide. (If my metric calculations are
correct that should be approximately one millimetre.) Wind the
lead in close, touching turns down the shank to the bend. If you
then tweek the lead to break it off rather than cutting it you get
three rather useful effects: one is that it pulls everything tight;
the second is that it breaks off cleanly; and the third is that it
tends to stretch the lead so that it tapers slightly and smooths off
the dressing. An additional point is that it does not blunt your
scissors. It is always worth keeping a separate pair of scissors for
trimming tinsel or hard items rather than clipping off silk,
though I must say that generally I do not bother – I just buy a
new pair when they become ruined, but then I am a spendthrift!
Take the silk down to the bend again but this time going over
the lead. This will lock it into place, but if you have any doubts
you can always run a layer of varnish or, better still, an instant
adhesive such as the Loc-tite Super Glue 3 over the lead – that
really will fix it permanently. At the bend tie in half-a-dozen
strands of cock pheasant centre tail fibres as a tail; these want to
be about a quarter of the hook length long. At the same point
catch in a length of mid-brown nylon thread – sewing thread is
fine – for the rib.

Walker's Mayfly Nymph

Dub or wind on a turn or so of the wool, then take a turn of the cock pheasant centre tail fibres after twisting them into a rope. Now comes another turn of the wool and a further turn of the tail fibres follows it. Keep the turns of feather fibres fairly close together; if you look at the drawing it will show you the correct gap. Wind the wool up the shank to create the body until it is about a third of the way from the eye. Now wind the ribbing thread in nice even turns to where the abdomen finished, tie in and trim. Take a hefty bunch of cock pheasant centre tail fibres and measure them along the hook so that the tips (which will be used to make the hackle) reach just past the point where the abdomen finished. Now tie in the butts in front of the finished part of the body, wind a slightly thickened thorax of angora wool, carry the pheasant tail fibres over the top of the thorax, tie in at the eye, bend the points backwards and at the same time separate them off into two evenly sized bunches and tie them in so that they lay along each side of the thorax. Carefully coat the top and the bottom of the abdomen with a PVC varnish such as Vycoat and when this has dried pick out the strands of soft angora wool each side to simulate the filaments on the sides of the natural. You should end up with a super-looking fly that will impress the trout. If you want to catch a big one, though, dress the same fly but use white wool instead; in this case you do not have to worry too much about what the trout sees because generally speaking the fish will have a go at any nymph which is lifting in the water past its head. The main thing is that *you* can see it and then are able to judge the exact moment to lift your rod to induce the take.

The Dressing:	*Walker's Mayfly Nymph*
Hook:	8 – 10 long shank (leaded) Old Numbers
Silk:	Brown (Sherry Spinner)
Tail:	Cock pheasant centre tail fibres
Rib:	Mid-brown nylon thread
Body:	Lemon yellow angora wool
Wing Case:	As for tail
Legs or Hackles:	As for tail

CHAPTER FIVE

LARVAE

STICK FLIES

The walk from the fishing hut was of necessity a long one, for this was the first day of the season and the crowds were to be avoided. All the frantic rod-waving was at the dam end of the reservoir, where anglers were jammed together along the concrete. True, fish were being caught, but it looked so very alien to what fishing should be all about. The mile-long walk had certainly thinned the crowds; the only ones who had walked this distance had to be keen. That did not stop them wading to the tops of their thigh boots and hurling lures as far as possible though; this, after all, was *the* method for early season, was it not?

When you are fishing in the midst of a lot of other anglers you have very little choice about the methods you can employ; really it is lures or nothing. It is virtually impossible to fish an imitative pattern to good effect when all about you are hurling fly-lines as far as they will go and bringing them back through the water at a fair rate of knots – let alone all the disturbance caused by all those size ten waders marching back and forth to the shore. No, what you need to fish small imitative patterns effectively is essentially solitude, or as close as you can get to it, and on our crowded waters that involves walking.

The nearest angler was just around the corner of the cove – the tip of his rod could just be seen over a patch of scrubby weeds. The area either side was clear of anglers for at least seventy yards; solitude indeed on opening day! First thing to decide was on what were the fish likely to be feeding? If they were feeding at all! The two rods were made up now and the only things to be added were the flies. Far out in the reservoir a fish rose, a oncer, nothing to go by. The weed-bed stirs slightly just off to the right, nothing much; an inch one way and then

95

back again as though a fish's body had brushed it or a puff of wind had moved the tops of the weeds. But there was no wind.

Again it came, that slight tell-tale movement. A trout taking olive nymphs perhaps, knocking them out of the tangle of weed-stems and taking them as they dropped. Now the entire front of the patch of plants was gently shaking, a ten yard area of weed-bed was moving very slightly. Was it perhaps the effect of an undertow? No, now there was more violent movement farther into the bed. A patch of mud rose through the weed-stems and spread lazily on the surface. Bottom grubbing; for what?

Of course, there they lay, millions of them, all along the shoreline: caddis cases, sedge larvae.

Cold, hasty fingers tie on a Stick-fly to the point of the leader, make certain the five-turn, tucked half blood is snugged down tight. Trim off the end of the 5lb nylon so that it lies neatly. The leader 12ft long, is attached to a number 6 fluorescent double taper line.

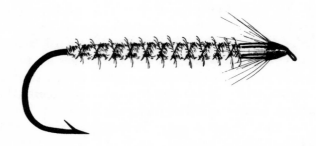

Stick Fly

The carefully degreased leader sank, the equally carefully greased end of the fly-line floated and remained highly visible so that the least twitch could be detected in the flat calm. The fly is allowed to sink for a timed two minutes. Although the water is only about seven or eight feet deep here it is as well to let the fly get right down. The fly-line is not so much retrieved as inched back into the waiting line-tray. Now the leader appears to be climbing vertically up the outer weed-stems. It is not of course because it describes an arc that keeps the fly crawling slowly across the sandy bottom.

When the fly has almost reached the foot of the stems the trout sees it; its body stiffens very slightly, the head dips, white lips part and it delicately sucks in the fur and feather that pretends to life.

On the surface the gaudy tip of the fly-line dips just a shade, an inch perhaps. The right hand turns over and gently the rod-tip flicks in response, the hook drives home and the line hauls up hard to the bending rod.

Suddenly the rod-top is wrenched over as the line pours out through the rings; now the reel is shrieking, the handle a faint blur. The trout surfaces in spray twenty yards from the bank and then he jumps. The rod-hand dips a shade so that no extra, sudden pressure will come onto the leader point when the fish drops back.

Another jump and then a third. Now the fight turns into a slugging match. The fish takes line, which in turn is recovered, and gradually the skilled hands and gentle rod action win and the trout is sliding over the net rim: safe.

While the little story I have just told can and indeed does happen many times during a season, more often it does not. Many anglers give up on nymphs and opt for the much simpler method of pulling a lure through the water as fast as it will go. Right, it catches fish, but you will feel so much more satisfaction after taking a fish with delicacy and skill. The thing we should aim for (and of this I am as certain as I can be of anything to do with angling) is to be versatile and to use the methods which will not only put fish on the bank, although this is the main object of the exercise of course, but which will also provide us with lasting memories of having done everything just *right*; of having used a technique which suited the fish, the water conditions and our own attitude towards the sport.

Sedge larvae (as opposed to sedge pupae) are not all that easy to imitate. The stick-flies are about the best attempt to come to grips with the problem that I have found to date. The caddis, or sedge larva, lives in a case made up of debris picked up from the bottom of the lake or river in which the larva lives. This it forms into an open ended cocoon. This gives protection from most predators of a relatively small size but trout will happily chomp up the whole thing. What we have to do is try to dress a fly that imitates this case with the larva's head protruding as it drags the case along the bottom. (Although, just to confuse matters the fish will very often take stick-like flies as they drop through the water.) The larva itself is relatively easy to imitate in feather and silk. All you need is a whitish-yellow body just showing in front of the case, a few strands of soft hackle to represent legs and a large, darkish head at the eye of the hook. It is the case that presents the problem; fly-dressers have tried all sorts of things, some of which are so far removed from fly-dressing as to be out of sight! For instance, there is the effort which involves coating the hook shank in fast drying adhesive such as fifteen-minute Araldite and sticking bits of twig and sand to it − it does work, but please, dear client, do not ask me to dress them like that! For the 'exact imitation' purists there is the school of thought that says you should break up the actual caddis cases found on the shore of your local lake and stick these to the hook − this method does not work because all the bits break up and fly off during casting. Then we come to the practical fly, dressed using normal materials.

There are a couple of dressings that have worked well for me over the years. You should remember that with these dressings the particular water you are going to be fishing is very important in your choice of artificial. The caddis grub uses the materials which are most readily available in the construction of its home and these, of course, vary greatly from lake to lake or indeed river to river. In fact they can also vary very considerably from one end of the lake to the other. The idea of the case is not just as protection from the predators jaws but also to provide excellent camouflage, to hide the animal and allow it to approach its own prey unseen, these sedge larvae being as fierce creatures as you could wish to find underwater.

I have found that with a mixture of different body materials, either as wound materials or as dubbing, and with a mixture of different coloured ribbing you can achieve a great variety of effects and shades. One of my favourites involves using cock pheasant centre tail fibres (these are available in many shades, ranging from nearly black melanistic through to the very light coloured, almost unmarked feathers) mixed with olive dyed swan herl, then ribbed with gold, copper or silver wire or a mixture of any or all of them. The rib not only gives additional colour and a little flash to the patterns, it also greatly increases their strength and resistance to the abrasive qualities of a trout's teeth.

Method of tying

What I should like to do now is to take you through a couple of dressings of a typical pair of Stick-flies as I might dress them for use at my local reservoir, Ardingly.

The tying silk is taken down the shank from the eye to the bend, where you tie in two lengths of wire, copper and silver. Leave them hanging off the tail-end of the fly. Tie in by the tips several strands of cock pheasant centre tail fibres (dark) along with a few, say four, strands of olive dyed swan herl. Coat the shank with varnish for about three-quarters of its length, twist the herls together to form a loose rope effect, and wind this up the shank. Tie in where the varnish finished and trim off the ends. Wind one of the ribbing tinsels up the shank going in the opposite direction to that taken when winding the body. This locks the herls firmly down on to the hook-shank. Tie in a strand of bronze or green peacock herl at the front of the body and wind this down to the bend and then come up the body again with the other rib locking the peacock on to the other materials as you go. Wind in the opposite direction to that taken with the first rib. I call this a double-locked rib and it is as secure a method of tying a fly as you could wish for, especially when used with Dick Walker's idea of underbody varnishing.

In front of the case a short length of lemon or off-white floss silk is wound on to form the thorax of the larva. This should be very short — about an eighth of an inch on a size 10 long-shank hook. In front of the thorax is wound a very short-fibred cock or hen hackle, for about two turns at most. Ginger is fine but I generally prefer the dun shades. The hackle is made to slope back slightly along the body. The head should be fairly bold and also be well varnished. The most popular of the stick-flies that I dress for my clients is tied just like this but the body is merely plain-wound peacock herl with no rib. I have been experimenting and I think that if you want a dark pattern then by all means use the plain bodied version but I do think there is a definite advantage to ribbing it, particularly using copper wire. The trout seem to prefer this. Perhaps it just breaks up the rather harsh, dark outline slightly. Again, though, wind your body over wet varnish for strength's sake.

The Dressing:	*Stick Flies*
Hooks:	8 – 10, long shank, Old Numbers
Silk:	Black or dark olive
Ribs:	Copper, silver or gold wire or any combination of these
Body:	Cock pheasant centre tail fibres, dyed swan herl, peacock herl, various dubbings mixed to give the correct colours for the water to be fished
Thorax:	Yellow or grubby off-white floss silk
Hackle:	Pale ginger or dun cock or hen hackle, sparse
Head:	Bold in tying silk, varnished until glossy

SAWYER'S GRAYLING BUG (GRAYLING LURE)

This is possibly the best imitation of a maggot that you will ever come across! I am certain that Frank did not intend it as such . . . I think. Nonetheless, if you feed in maggots upstream of a shoal of grayling by puncturing a tin from the inside to the outside, so that the maggots can crawl out rather than be trapped by the sharp edges, and suspend this tin of creepy crawlies over the water, those old fish get worked up to a frenzy! Then if you cast your Grayling Bug up into the shoal . . . watch out – the leader will slide across the water as fish after fish take your fly.

On most of our chalk-streams the grayling are looked on as being a pest; I really do not know why, because they fight as well as a trout, pound for pound. They eat better when fresh. (Never, ever try and freeze grayling. My brother Pete still hasn't forgiven me for the packet of frozen grayling I gave him a few years ago. He stored them for a couple of months and then, when he opened the packet up and thawed them out, the stink was dreadful – he reckons it took him about a week to rid himself of the last, lingering traces. So, I would advise you to eat your grayling fresh or give them away to someone who will.) I also think that in a lot of ways they are a more handsome fish than trout – with their tall dorsal fin and lilac striped bodies, they really are lovely. They are also available to us when virtually no other fish will feed because it is too cold for them, and most of all they are obliging. You can botch a cast and have it land in a heap, you can strike and miss, not once but several times and they will still come back for another go. Oh yes, I like grayling very much indeed. Trout tend to be a lot less forgiving, and I need all the help from the fish that I can get!

Sawyer's Grayling Bug

Method of tying
This fly is one of the simplest to dress, and at the same time it can be said to be one of the most frustrating. The reason is that the body material, Chadwick's darning wool in shade 477, seems to be almost impossible to get hold of. For some strange reason the shops that I visit carry just about every colour except this one – it is most annoying.

After writing the paragraph you have just read I decided to go out and find the reason for people not carrying this particular shade of wool, and I found out in no uncertain manner. I toured round all our local haberdashers and they all said that since Chadwick's have changed hands and now belong to the Coat's group you cannot order individual colours of wool; you have to take a full box and that box can contain whatever colours the manufacturers feel like supplying! Finally I got around to asking to see the latest colour charts and, guess what, the shade we are after, good old 477 is no longer listed. That, I can tell you, is the story of my life.

Although this particular shade is no longer available there are several very similar colours in the same range and the one I have taken to using is number 454 which hopefully will remain in existence for a few more years – or at least until someone decides that it is no longer a 'viable' colour.

Fix your silk in the normal way and wind down to the bend, bring the silk up the body again, tie in a length of fuse wire slightly back from the eye (I normally use lead strip and it does not seem to make any difference to the fly's effectiveness), wind a double layer down the shank for about three-quarters of its length, and then finish and trim off the surplus at the eye. Wind a double layer of the darning wool down to the bend and up again to the eye, trim and whip finish – and that's it!

I often dub the wool on rather than winding the strands. This is because I find that the wool tends to slip if wound as a strand; it certainly does after the fish have had a go at it. However, with dubbed bodies I rarely if ever find this happening, and it is also easier to build up a nice maggot shape with dubbed wool. Try both methods and see which you prefer. Whatever else you do, though, tie up a few of these flies because you will find they are not only good for grayling on the rivers but also an excellent pattern for lake trout – now where do they get a taste for maggots?

The Dressing:	*Sawyer's Grayling Bug (Grayling Lure)*
Hooks:	14 – 18, Old Numbers
Silk:	Olive or brown (Sherry Spinner)
Underbody:	Fuse wire or lead strip
Body:	Chadwick's darning wool number 477 if possible, otherwise 454

CHAPTER SIX

PUPAE

IVENS'S GREEN AND YELLOW NYMPH

This is another of Tom Ivens's flies with which I have experienced a fair amount of success over the years but it is a total contrast to his previous fly; this one needs to be fished as slowly as possible. I know Tom likes to use just the wind to drift the fly round without any retrieve being used at all. Watch the junction of leader and fly-line for that drawing away that signifies a take, lift gently on a soft rod and nine times out of ten the hook will snick into the scissors at the corner of his mouth. As my good friend Brian Harris has been known to say, 'If the fly's in the back of the throat you know you *really* deceived him!' I must say though that with this particular fly the odds seem to be that you will end up hooking your fish in that firmest of hook-holds, the scissors.

Method of tying

This must surely be one of the simplest of flies to dress, but, as is usually the case, simplicity generally produces the best results and so it is in this instance – you should find this fly very effective indeed. Take your silk down to the bend as usual, tie in two strands of green dyed swan or goose feather, and carry the silk back up the hook for about half its length. Apply a layer of varnish up the shank over the layer of silk, wind the swan herl up the hook to the silk in close-butted turns, tie in and trim. Take two strands of yellow swan or goose and repeat the procedure, except that you do not use the other half of the hook up completely. You now have to wind the peacock head of which Tom is so fond and, after the head is wound, whip finish and varnish. Dead easy, wasn't it?

Ivens's Green and Yellow Nymph

The Dressing:	*Ivens's Green and Yellow Nymph*
Hooks:	10 – 12, Old Numbers
Silk:	Olive
Body:	In two sections, swan herl dyed green and yellow
Head:	Peacock herl

COVE'S PHEASANT TAIL NYMPH

One of the toughest and most useful feathers used in fly-dressing is the cock pheasant centre tail; it is strong in the fibre and when wound on the hook shows a pleasing amount of flue. You can find it in most shades of brown ranging from a very pale ginger through to a deep chestnut, almost a black. In fact the melanistic strain of pheasant are as near to black as you can get without dyeing the feathers. In fact this is the one drawback I have found with these feathers – they do not take dye at all well. I have tried many times to get a decent colour, say an olive, but without any great success. The method I have tried is to first bleach the feathers and then apply the dye in the normal way. Brown is the worst of all colours to remove from anything, and the same thing applies to grey squirrel tails. You can get the black out beautifully but you just cannot shift the brown – at least you can, but I just do not happen to know the technique and people who I have approached in the fur trade just tell me that it is a trade secret. I also have a feeling that it is not at all simple; I think it will be rather a costly and difficult process once the secret does come out because I have had some excellent chemists giving it their attention, without any favourable results as yet. But we do know it *can* be done because there are some lovely deep-coloured dyed grey squirrel tails available on the market – at a price. I am sure that if this material can be bleached and then dyed without distorting the shades of even the very light colours, such as primrose and light orange, then the same thing can be done with pheasant tails, to the advantage of all fly-dressers.

However, even left in its original state the cock pheasant centre tail fibres make an excellent fly and are the basis of many popular and effective flies, particularly nymphs. My own brown nymph is basically a pheasant tail pattern and perhaps the most famous of all the PT nymphs is that which Frank Sawyer invented for use on the chalk streams. In that environment there are few nymphs to touch it, but Frank's fly does not work too well on stillwaters – at least that has been my experience (I had better qualify that because someone, somewhere has surely made a killing with it on a stillwater).

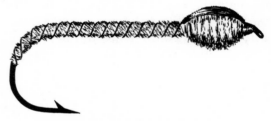

Cove's Pheasant Tail Nymph

Arthur Cove's nymph on the other hand has been specifically designed for stillwater use. It looks at first sight to be a brute of a thing! I always think it looks as though it cannot make up its mind whether it wants to be a nymph or a lure. Arthur prefers to use this nymph dressed on a size 8 long-shank hook and it really does look *enormous* in this size; the idea is that this big, heavy hook should sink as deeply and quickly as possible and still be an effective fish-catcher. He uses very long leaders with this pattern on the point and usually one or two other flies, normally nymphs or pupae imitations, further up the leader. Sometimes that leader is twenty five feet long in level 6lb b.s. nylon. The only problem with this set-up is that if the other flies are set on droppers to fish close to the surface then you have to forget all about landing nets

– the beaten fish has to be beached because the top fly will jam in the top ring and you will then need either a very long landing net handle or extremely long arms! This long-leader technique works very well from the bank but obviously cannot be used with more than one fly (unless the droppers are set close to the point fly) from a boat; believe me, you can be in all sorts of trouble if you try it, I know. If you do decide to try Arthur's technique of nymphing remember that the essence of it is in seeing the take and striking into the trout rather than waiting to feel the pull of a taking fish. The newish fluorescent orange and yellow fly-lines now available in the UK are a real boon for this type of fishing – they stand out extremely well at a range of up to twenty five yards and providing you grease the tip of the line so that it floats it really will multiply your chances of catching nymphing trout by several times. I realise that if you use most of the proprietory brands of line grease you will ruin your fly-line within a season but the way I look at it is this; the whole purpose of buying the fly-line in the first place is to catch trout and if this technique helps and you ruin the line in the process, so what? That line is not worth a damn if it does not catch fish for you. I can be extremely ruthless when it comes to tackle; as far as I am concerned if an item of tackle can be improved in performance at the risk of ruining it over a period of time, then its days are numbered!

Method of tying
Take your silk down the hook to a point halfway round the bend and tie in a length of copper wire and at least fifteen strands of the longest fibred cock pheasant centre tail fibres you can find. I know that fifteen sounds a lot but they have to wind most of the way up the shank of a rather large hook. What you *do not* do now is to twist the strands together to make the usual rope. You keep them flat and wind them up the shank for about three-quarters of its length and secure with the silk. If you had wound on a rope of fibres they would have made the body too thick and bulky; the body should be very slim. Rib the abdomen with the copper wire going in the opposite direction to that taken when you wound the pheasant fibres; this makes the body very much

stronger than if you wound the wire with the grain.

The thorax is made from dubbed-on rabbit underfur, the soft fur with the bluish tinge to it; you will find that you can pull out the brown guard hairs and just be left with the blue. For anybody who has experienced problems with dubbing this is the fur for you – it is beautiful to apply. Would that seal's fur were as easy! The thorax should end up as ball-shaped and the tag-ends of the body material are now carried over the top of the thorax and tied in at the eye. Make a good four- or five-turn whip finish and run on a couple of coats of varnish with the point of a dubbing needle.

The Dressing:	Cove's Pheasant Tail Nymph
Hooks:	8 – 12 long shank, Old Numbers
Silk:	Brown (Sherry Spinner)
Rib:	Copper wire
Body:	Cock pheasant centre tail fibres
Thorax:	Blue rabbit underfur

INVICTA SEDGE PUPA

I invented this fly back in 1974 and since then I have made a couple of improvements (I think!) to it. It has taken quite a few fish during hatches of sedge and I find it fishes best for me either really deep or just humping the water surface. As with the Amber Nymph pattern the takes can be quite vicious so keep the leader strength to a reasonable level. I do dislike people who boast that they 'got busted' four or five times and actually seem to feel that this is something to be proud of – it isn't. I hate leaving hooks and nylon in fish; when I hook one I want him landed and dispatched cleanly or released, if the rules of the fishery allow it, but not with any lasting memory of the fight still attached to him.

The reason I invented this pattern was because of its parent fly, the Invicta. I took a long hard look at this dressing which is, after all, one of the most effective flies you can use on our stillwater fisheries. Everybody seems to agree that 'it resembles a sedge'. Indeed it does, and if fished dry I can understand why the trout hit it with such unbounding enthusiasm. However, it is

not fished dry, it is used as a wet fly and it never seems reasonable
to me that a trout should expect to find a fully-winged sedge fly
swimming about underwater! I do think that the trout take it as
a sedge and not as a little perch, which has been suggested, and I
feel that it is this sedge-like quality that accounts for its
effectiveness. I also think that by cutting out the basic mistake of
having the wings and making it look more like the sedge pupa it
is supposed to imitate we may – dare I even breathe it? –
improve on the standard pattern. This then is what I have done:
made the wings into wing cases and generally 'cleaned up' the fly.

Invicta Sedge Pupa

Method of tying

Fix a number 10 hook in your vice and as usual wind your tying
silk from the eye to the bend. There you tie in a strip of oak
turkey wing about an eighth of an inch wide. At the same point
fasten in a length of oval gold tinsel. Dub a fairly fat abdomen of
yellow wool up the shank for about two-thirds of the hook's
length. Rib with the tinsel in fairly wide open turns (four turns
are enough on a size 10 hook), tie in and trim off the end of the
rib. Carry the turkey strip over the back of the abdomen and tie
down where the rib finished, hold the feather back over the tied-
down wing case and take a turn or two of silk over the feather so
that no silk is left showing when the thorax is wound. Now dub
on the thorax of mixed dark green and brown wool. This is
where my latest version differs somewhat from the original; I
now usually continue the thorax colour with the yellow wool
but I pick out both with the dubbing needle to give a fuzzy
effect rather than the harder outline I used to get with the
unpicked wool.

Reverse the fly in the vice and apply a beard hackle of blue jay wing fibres. The correct length should be just to the hook point. Whip finish and varnish the head.

The Dressing:	*Invicta Sedge Pupa*
Hook:	10, Old Numbers
Silk:	Olive
Wing Cases:	Oak turkey wing strip
Rib:	Oval gold tinsel
Abdomen:	Yellow wool
Thorax:	Mixed dark green/brown wool or yellow wool
Hackle:	Blue jay

AMBER NYMPH

This pattern, invented by Dr H. A. Bell primarily for use on Blagdon and Chew Valley Lake, has since shown itself to be a very effective imitation of the sedge pupae on many lakes throughout the United Kingdom. It is one of the few dressings of the immature sedges available to the trout angler, and I always think it is rather a pity that Doctor Bell called it the Amber Nymph rather than the Amber Sedge pupa – I feel that it could tend to confuse people who are new to the terminology of our sport. There are two sizes of this fly, but over the years I have found that the big one is far more effective for me than the small version. There is only one difference between them, aside from the hook sizes; the smaller one has a thorax of hot orange rather than brown seal's fur used on the larger version.

I often find that the addition of lead helps with this pattern. Wind the lead on in the normal way and then dress over the lead if the fish are thought to be lying deeply or you want to fish the imitation quickly without causing a heavy wake close to the fly from the leader. Using lead I find that a two foot pull with about a four or five second pause is a useful method of fishing this fly, but watch out for smash takes as the fly drops back at the pause stage and do not use too light a leader – four or five pounds breaking strain is reasonable, but even at these I have been smashed a couple of times on the take.

Method of tying

Fix your hook in the vice and wind your silk down to the bend;
tie in a strip of feather fibre so that it sticks out behind the hook
with the shiny side (the bad side) facing upwards. There is no rib
to tie in so the next stage is to apply the dubbing, which is an
amber shade. Some people prefer to use floss silk but I much
prefer the seal's fur; the floss is too smooth and I like all those
'sticky-outy' bits that you get with the fur. I reckon they add to
the attraction of the fly. The feather fibre is carried over the
abdomen and tied in in front and the end trimmed off. A thorax
of dark brown seal's fur is now dubbed on to the front third of
the hook and the fly is then reversed in the vice to receive the
false hackle. The hackle consists of a few strands of pale ginger or
honey cock hackle tied in beard fashion. Finish the fly in the
usual way.

Amber Nymph

This pattern is fairly simple to dress but it is no less effective
for that. Sometimes it is difficult to get the correct shade for the
body and the only real way this can be achieved is to dye your
own seal's fur. It is quite easy to dye your own materials
provided your wife will let you mess up her kitchen for an hour
or so. Perhaps you could suggest she pays a visit to her mother —
it has got to be better than the other way round!

The Dressing: Amber Nymph
Hooks: 10 – 12, Old Numbers
Silk: Brown (Sherry Spinner)
Wing Cases: Strip of grey brown feather

Body: Amber (dark yellow/gold) seal's fur
Thorax: Brown seal's fur or hot orange on the small
               version
Hackle: Sparse honey or pale ginger cock

TEASY WEASY

Some years ago I was fishing at Blagdon when I got talking to
some other anglers who told me about a pattern that had
apparently been getting very good results for them. It had a
rather peculiar name; apparently it was named after a certain
ladies hair dresser – do not ask me why, I did not invent it. I
reckon the chap who did was a bit stuck for something to call it.
Anyway, it is a sort of adulterated version of the Mallard and
Claret, that most popular of trout wet flies. It does have a rather
nice beetle-like appearance and I would feel happier tying this
pattern on the leader than I would the wet fly. I know that the
Mallard and Claret catches fish, but not for me, but I cannot for
the life of me think why – it does not look like anything I have
ever seen swimming around underwater. I suppose that this
could also be said for most attractor-type flies but the trout love
them. Strange animals trout – almost as weird as human beings.
The Teasy Weasy has not caught anything for me as yet, perhaps
because I am afraid of being asked, 'What'd he take then?' Can
you imagine all the heads turning when I answered? Therefore it
has not had the proper testing it should have been submitted to,
but I have sent out a few samples to clients and friends and the
several reports I have had back have been quite favourable.
Anyway, the dressing is there if you fancy giving it a try.

Method of tying
Wind on the tying silk in open turns to the bend of the hook,
then come back up the hook to the eye and tie in a strip of lead
– this can be either wire or the flat lead such as you find round
decent-quality wine bottle tops. Maybe it is my imagination but
it strikes me that this wine-bottle-type-lead is not all that heavy;
maybe the bottlers mix it with something else, but I reckon that
if I take a length of heavy lead wire and tap it with a hammer
until it is the same thickness as the wine bottle lead it feels

111

Teasy Weasy

heavier – probably imagination, but I still prefer to use my flattened wire for weighting nymphs. Cut a strip off about a sixteenth of an inch wide, tie it in at the eye, wind it down the shank to the bend, and trim off. Come down over the lead layer with tight turns of tying silk. At the bend tie in a strip of bronze mallard feather so that it lies flat with the bad (shiny) side facing upwards. Leave this strip hanging off the back of the fly. Now tie in a rib of gold wire and dub a fairly thick body of claret seal's fur up towards the eye; run the rib up the body in even turns – four turns would be about right on a size 12 hook. Carry the mallard feather over the top of the body, tie in at the eye and trim off the surplus. Now, if you have them tie in a pair of tiny jungle cock eye feathers either side of the head so that they just lie behind the head. If you have no real jungle cock – and there are not too many who have got any these days – then you will have to use one of the substitutes. Pick out the body with your dubbing needle so that it fuzzes out nicely and gives a nice buzzy feel to the fly.

The Dressing:	*Teasy Weasy*
Hooks:	10 – 12, Old Numbers
Silk:	Brown (Sherry Spinner) black or olive if leaded
Back:	Bronze mallard feather
Rib:	Gold wire
Body:	Claret seal's fur
Eyes:	Jungle cock (small)

112

COLLYER'S HATCHING MIDGES

I first produced these flies in about 1965, and, while there are now plenty of midge pupae imitations available to the fly-dresser, this was not the case then. At that time you were more or less restricted to the Black Buzzer, unless you had an inventive turn of mind. It was about that time that everybody was messing about with deer body hair and trying to find patterns other than Muddlers to use it on; sedges, dry flies, nymphs and even a couple of wet fly patterns were invented that incorporated this material. Today, we still see the occasional fly hailed as a break-through because it uses deer hair.

When I started dressing these flies I had but one thought in mind – to make the thorax of the midge pupae as buoyant as I possibly could. This material was not ideal but it did have several advantages over the various other things I could have used, such as cork or expanded polyethelene. For a start it was easier and faster to work with and it had that texture that is so important. Deer body hair is an easily worked and shaped material and was nearly ideal for my purpose. When a chironomid (or midge) is in the process of hatching at the water surface it hangs tail down, so what was needed was a pattern that let the bend of the hook sink while the eye was supported at the surface. Since those days John Goddard has tried to solve the same problem with his pupa imitations that involve tying a lump of polyethelene up in a piece of nylon stocking and tying this in above the eye. Maybe it is just me, but I do not like them. Not only does the polyethelene look like an enormous lump growing out of the head of the fly but the times I have tried it the fly sinks unless you use a very large piece

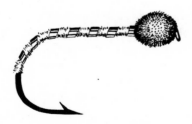

Collyer's Hatching Midge

113

of foam-plastic indeed. With my patterns I find that if the leader is greased up to the fly and a little grease worked into just the deer hair then they seem to float perfectly adequately – and they look reasonable to both myself and the trout. Please do not think that I am decrying John's invention; far from it, I am assured that these patterns work very well at times. It is just that they do not inspire *me* with any degree of confidence. I find that my own hatching midges do the same job perfectly adequately and I think they look more like the real thing.

These three flies are very simple and are only really colour variations of the same patterns, as with my series of nymphs.

Method of tying

Fix your hook in the vice and start the tying silk about a quarter of the way down the shank in order to leave a space for spinning on the deer hair thorax. (This must be done over a bare hook shank; it is impossible to do it satisfactorily over a bed of silk.) The silk is wound in open turns to a point half-way round the bend and there a length of ribbing tinsel is caught in. Carry the silk back up the shank to where it was first secured and catch in a piece of floss silk. Wind this down the shank to the ribbing tinsel and then come back up over the first layer, making certain the body lies smoothly. Tie and trim off the surplus floss. I sometimes use feather fibre for the bodies and in this case it is only necessary to wind it up the shank as one layer, tying the strip in at the bend where the rib is secured.

In your left hand take a fair-sized bunch of deer body hair and lay it along the shank, parallel to it. Wind two *loose* turns of silk over the hair and then gently tighten by pulling straight downwards on the tying silk. This, on the bare hook shank has the effect (with any luck at all) of spinning the hair round the shank and flaring it out – you end up with a right old hedgehog, but be not put off my friend! Take your trusty scissors and make four clean cuts all round the hair so that it is well pruned. You need very little hair left for the pattern to be effective and the cuts are repeated until the shape is achieved. You should then find, if you got your proportions correct, that the fly looks like the illustration. If you have to spin on another bunch of hair one of two things has happened; either you allowed too much space on the shank for the thorax or, and this is more likely, you did not use enough hair. It never fails to amaze me how frightened some fly-dressers are of using a fair sized bunch of deer hair; it is cheap enough, isn't it?

These three hatching midge pupae are really very good (says he modestly) and if you fish them virtually stationary in the surface film during a hatch of buzzers you should get decent results. The body colours can be varied, of course, to match whatever colour midge happens to be hatching. I reckon these three colours are generally the most useful.

The Dressing:	*Collyer's Hatching Midges*
Hooks:	6 – 12, Old Numbers
Silk:	Black, olive or brown (Sherry Spinner)
Rib:	Flat gold, silver or copper Lurex
Body:	Olive, scarlet or black floss silk or feather fibre
Thorax:	Deer body hair

SECTION THREE
WET FLIES

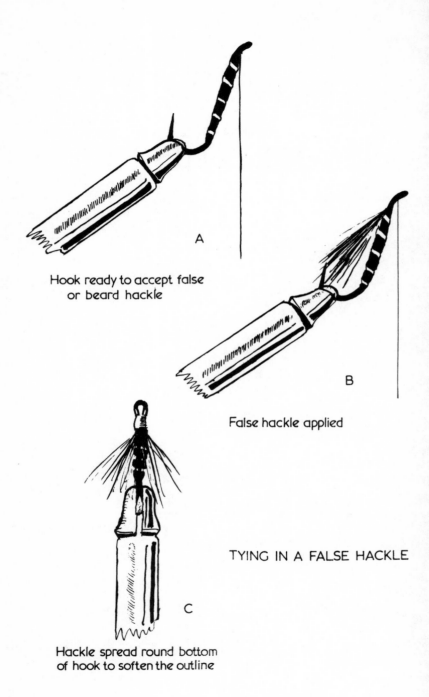

A

Hook ready to accept false
or beard hackle

B

False hackle applied

C

Hackle spread round bottom
of hook to soften the outline

TYING IN A FALSE HACKLE

CHAPTER SEVEN

WET FLIES

RUBE WOOD

I am as vain as the next chap. Actually, Marjorie, my wife reckons that I am a darned sight more so when it comes to fishing! So, I do not like seeing my name against nil returns in the fishing logs at the lodges on reservoirs – who does? I have therefore worked out this system that operates fairly smoothly as far as I am concerned. What I do is this; I commence fishing at the start of the day with flies in which I have great confidence, flies that I am pretty certain will prove acceptable to the trout. Certain nymphs for instance, or a Muddler, my Ace of Spades perhaps.

Depending on the mood of the fish I shall take perhaps a brace or a brace and a half in the morning. Now, that number of fish looks quite respectable in the fishing book, even if it is all I get. The afternoon I devote to experimenting for the writing side of my fishing. I switch flies, lines and methods of fishing until I arrive at some sort of result that will allow me to write with confidence about a particular fly or flies. It is not by any means always successful; sometimes I am certain that I should do a lot better if I stuck to the patterns that I was certain would take fish. Fairly often I shall take the brace or so and then blank the rest of the day. Sometimes, let us face it, I shall blank the *whole* day! Mind you, I do try really hard to avoid that situation.

By and large though, this system of mine works fairly well and it then allows me to write with confidence that certain flies *will* take our English trout, flies perhaps that many anglers have never heard of but which can, on occasion, be real killers. This is what happened with this pattern which is an American fly dressed in the traditional wet fly style.

Where my columns and books have been concerned I have

always tried to be completely honest; I do not just pick up a book on fly-dressing and filch a dressing or two from it and say 'Oh yes, old so-and-so says this pattern catches fish, so let's stick it into the column'. I like, where possible, to give the flies I write about as thorough a testing as I can and if the results are good, *then* I write about them. This cannot always be the case because there are several instances where I just plain cannot catch a trout on a certain fly and other anglers are knocking them out like there was no tomorrow! One thing you can rest easy about though, if that is the case I will tell you so; after all if that did not happen we would all use just the same few flies and nobody would have any favourites.

Rube Wood

The Rube Wood filled out my limit bag on at least four separate occasions. I found that it fished best when I was using a sink tip line and retrieving fairly fast, about a foot or eighteen inches under the surface. I am particularly fond of sink-tip lines for traditional boat fishing on the drift on our reservoirs; this is because they ensure that any line-wake is well away from the flies. You can always use very long leaders to achieve the same results but this tends to mean that many more fish will be lost on the take because of the elasticity and stretch of the nylon. For fishing just sub-surface I reckon it is hard to beat a weight-forward or shooting head sink-tip, especially one which you have constructed yourself; I have done very well with them. They are especially useful where trout are surface cruising and you want to

whip a wet fly or lure across their nose without scaring them –
line-wake scares trout almost as much as dropping the line on
their head if you botch the cast.

Method of tying
I have slightly altered the dressing given by Ray Bergman in his
book *Trout* by using fluorescent floss silk as the tag on my
dressings – it seems to improve it. Anyway, wind your silk in
the usual manner from eye to bend and there tie in a short length
of either scarlet floss silk or fluorescent scarlet floss as a short tag.
Next tie in a tail of teal breast feathers – barred teal. Strip the
fluff off about a quarter of an inch of white chenille and tie in the
core of cotton just forward of the tail and the tag. Wind the silk
back up the shank over the ends of the tail fibres to fix them
really securely. Wind the chenille up the body in even turns and
tie off and trim just short of the eye.

Now reverse the fly in the vice and tie in a false hackle of
brown hackle fibres – hen hackle is best if you have got it. Make
sure it spreads round the bottom of the shank to soften the
hackling and does not hang like a lump under the throat of the
fly. The best way to do this is to lay the fibres of the hackle
against the near-side of the hook after they have been trimmed to
length; take a loose turn of silk round them and then release
them while at the same time tightening the silk. This should
have the effect of spinning the hackle halfway round the shank.
It works in a similar way to the method used to apply deer hair
to a Muddler Minnow's head, but not to such a marked degree.

Turn the fly the right way up again and tie in a wing of grey
mallard feather. (I generally use lightly marked teal for the wing;
it is rather easier to obtain than the mallard feather and does not
seem to affect the fly to any degree.)

Whip finish at the eye and make a neat head and then run on
two or three coats of varnish to make it nice and glossy. It might
not affect the fly's effectiveness as far as the trout are concerned
but a beautifully glossy head does look great, doesn't it?

This fly is somewhat similar to the Missionary, which is a
favourite of Dick Shrive, and he seems to catch the odd fish or
two! May you do the same.

The Dressing:	*Rube Wood*
Hooks:	6 – 12, Old Numbers
Silk:	Black
Tag:	Scarlet floss silk or fluorescent scarlet floss
Tail:	Teal breast fibres
Body:	White chenille
Hackle:	Brown hen or cock
Wing:	Grey mallard or lightly marked teal

WOOD IBIS

The Wood Ibis is another from Ray Bergman's book *Trout*, another all-American pattern that is nonetheless effective in the United Kingdom. There are many different flies in his book that seem to be completely useless on this side of the Atlantic – I cannot speak for t'other side, having not fished there . . . one day maybe. The Wood Ibis is a useful pattern to have in your box though; just a couple, nothing extravagant.

I remember fishing this pattern from a boat at Weirwood some years ago and I found the takes were coming really close to the boat just as I was lifting off to go into a roll-cast preparatory to extending the line again. I have had the same thing happen quite often when using the Invicta and the Connemara Black, so maybe it is something to do with the palmered-hackle style of dressing which is common to all three patterns. I can tell you this: it is very easy to lose fish when this happens. Either the roll-cast is starting and the powerful turnover of the line breaks the leader, or the fish takes and you cannot quite get your right hand back far enough to set the hook. But on the occasion in question I found that the fish were getting hooked very nicely in the scissors and all was well.

Method of tying
Fix your hook in the vice and run tying silk down the shank from eye to bend. There you catch in the tail fibres which should be rather shorter than usual. (Mr. Bergman says that this tail should be of 'orange-brown mallard'. Well, that is a very funny coloured mallard feather. The more usual version of this fly is tied using ordinary brown mallard underneath with ibis

Wood Ibis

substitute over the top; it probably does not matter too much to the trout. I have never tried it but it must be the devil's own job to dye up brown mallard to any colour, let alone orange-brown. However if you want to try it. . . .) Over the top of the undertail tie in two slim matched strips of ibis substitute, and at the same point the tip of an orange hackle. Wind on a dubbed body of claret wool for three-quarters of the length of the hook, tying down the tag ends of the tail as you wind up the shank. You can, if you wish, wind the wool as a strand but generally you get much better results if you dub it on to the silk.

Grip the butt of the hackle in the hackle pliers and wind this up the body going in the opposite direction to that taken when winding the wool. Tie in and trim just past where the body ended. The wing that Ray Bergman used he describes as 'iridescent black': the feathers that I find come closest to this description are either magpie centre tail, crow or blue mallard and that is what I normally use. Two slips are tied in to lay as low as possible over the body; if you opt for the blue mallard you will find that it helps the tying in if you moisten the slips between your lips just before you tie them in. It makes this rather intractable feather somewhat more pliable.

The Dressing:	Wood Ibis
Hooks:	6 – 12, Old Numbers
Silk:	Black
Tail:	Dyed orange cock, tied palmer fashion

Body: Dark claret wool
Wing: Blue mallard, crow primary feather or magpie
             tail

MISSIONARY

The old dressing of this pattern has been around for some considerable time – at least fifty years as far as I can make out. According to Courtney Williams in *A Dictionary of Trout Flies* it was invented by Captain J. J. Dunn for use at Blagdon. It has had great success all over the world but its recent fame has sprung from its effectiveness in the hands of such men as Bob Church and Dick Shrive on the Midlands reservoirs (albeit a slightly different version from the original).

I spoke to Dick Shrive a few years ago at Draycote after he had taken a very respectable limit bag by lunchtime on this fly while the rest of us were struggling . . . well, *I* was struggling! He said that the secret was in the way it was fished. Apparently most, if not all, of his takes came while the fly was sinking after the cast was made. This was why he uses a different winging method to that on the older pattern. The wing was a whole grey mallard feather or very lightly marked teal feather. The wing was set low over the body of the fly so that it sank with a slow fluttering movement. This slow sinking style of fishing the trout seem to find irresistible – at least when Dick uses it.

Using the old dressing of this fly has never done very much for me in the past so I resolved to dress some of Dick's pattern and see how I did with them. While I never achieved anything like his results, it has proved a useful pattern to have on hand, and it has saved several blanks on what otherwise could have been deadly days. The interesting thing is that, again, most of the takes appear to come on the drop, with no retrieve at all. Perhaps there is scope for designing other patterns with similar fishing actions – I shall have to give it some further thought.

Method of tying
Let us take the old pattern first and see what can be made of that. Wind your silk from eye to bend and catch in a bunch of white cock hackle fibres as a tail. Take your silk up the shank over the

124

Missionary (Original)

tail ends to hold them securely and take the silk back again to the
bend. Dub on some white wool and wind a slightly carrot-
shaped body. Reverse the fly in the vice and tie in a false hackle
of white cock, remembering to spread it around the shank. Turn
the fly the right way up again, tie in a slim underwing of natural
black turkey tail that extends well back past the hook bend, and
on the outside of the turkey tie in strips of dark, barred teal as an
overwing. An alternative is to fold a single wide strip of the teal
and make a roof wing over the turkey. That, I think, gives a
better result. Finish the head in the normal way.

For Dick Shrive's version we start in the same way by carrying
the silk from the eye to the bend and tying in a bunch of cock
hackle fibres; this time they are not white though but ginger or
light red. Next tie in a length of flat silver tinsel or Lurex – the
wider strip is better than the narrow. Take a length of white
chenille, strip off a quarter of an inch or so of the fluff from the
central cotton core and tie the cotton in directly in front of the
tinsel. Tying in just the central core ensures that we do not bulk
up the fly's backside! (We do not want it looking like one of
those Spanish flamenco dancers, do we?) The chenille is now
wound up the body almost to the eye, tied in and the surplus
trimmed off. The body is ribbed with the tinsel and then that is
tied in and trimmed at the same point.

Turn the fly over in the vice and tie in a false hackle of the
same material as the tail. Turn the fly the right way up again and
we are now ready for the winging. It seems to be rather difficult
at present to get decent mallard feathers, be they bronze or grey,

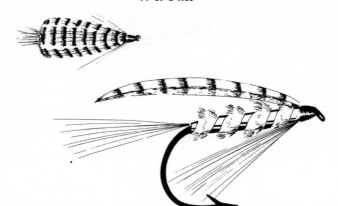

Shrive's Missionary

so I normally use lightly marked teal breast, the sort of feather that will not be used for dressing Peter Ross's or Teal, Blue and Silver – I like those feathers to be well marked with a distinct black and white barring, while the feathers for the Missionary are the ones that would normally hang around for years and never get used up. Strip off all the fluffy fibres at the base of the feather so that you are left with two even sections of fibres on the central stalk. being certain to choose a feather which will give nicely balanced sides and not have longer fibres on one side than the other. Now run the feather through your lips to moisten it and to make the fibres cling together – if you are fastidious (I am not!) you can always use wet finger tips. Secure the stalk flat over the body with two or thee turns of silk and then, by pulling gently on the stalk, ease it through until it is the correct length, at the same time making sure with your left hand that it remains flat along the body. This will ensure that it will as sink as slowly as it should. Whip finish and varnish the head. I was told just the other day that this pattern is improved if you add eyes to the head by painting on a white dab of varnish with a black centre.

The Dressings

               The original Missionary
Hooks: 8 – 10, Old Numbers
Silk: Black

Tail:	White cock hackle fibres
Body:	White wool
Hackle:	As for tail
Wing:	Black turkey tail with teal over

Dick Shrive's Missionary

Hooks:	6 – 8 long shank, Old Numbers
Silk:	Black
Tail:	Dark ginger or red cock hackle fibres
Rib:	Flat silver tinsel or Lurex
Body:	White chenille
Hackle:	As for tail
Wing:	Whole grey mallard or teal breast feather, set flat

CAHILL

Over the last few years the use of hair as a winging material on lures and wet flies has become quite common and I think that we can largely thank one man and one fly for this – Dick Walker and his friend Sweeny Todd. What a marvellous name for a fly with a slash of red across the throat – it could hardly fail, could it? The undoubted success of the Sweeney Todd and other patterns like the Stoat's Tail has led to further experimentation with hairwings and we have now got several other useful flies. We British, being our usual insular selves, seldom realise that the Americans have made use of this material for many years and we still have a lot to learn from them.

This pattern and the Hairwing Montreal are possibly the most effective hairwing American patterns that I have used in the UK (I do not include the Muddlers of course – they are in a class of their own).

This fly is a darkish pattern and I have found that is is at its best in coloured water. The sort of situation that I am thinking of is where on stillwaters you get a strong crosswind over a length of shallows; on the lee-side of those shallows you will often find trout working up from the deeper water to pick up the various creatures washed down with the clouds of silt. There is a lot of water of this type at Chew Valley Lake and I have found that this fly works very well indeed if it is pulled through slowly and steadily, with as few pauses as possible, about a foot or eighteen inches under the surface. One of the best ways of getting a fly to work at that depth is the use of a floating line; a shooting head generally works best because you often have to retrieve the flies a long way before a confident take comes, and a shot squeezed on to the leader a foot or two above the fly will sink the leader. Generally the largest split-shot I would use is a BB. This is because anything larger makes the leader 'hinge' at the point where the weight is and it tends to make everything land in a heap, with all the subsequent tangle problems. By using a shot on the leader you get a quite interesting effect, not so much on this pattern, which is best retrieved as smoothly as possible, but with the stop-start retrieve used with so many nymphs; by using the weight you get a vertical movement in the fly as well as a forward movement. When you pause the lead takes over and the fly starts to dive: trout often find this totally irresistable. You get a similar effect with leaded nymphs, of course, but the advantage of using lead on the leader is that the fly is more versatile because it can then be used either way – you have a choice – and it also sinks the leader so that you do not get that line wake close to the fly, which can be very off-putting indeed to the trout.

Method of tying
The Cahill is very simple to dress, as indeed are most of the hairwing flies. Start the tying silk in the usual way and run it down the shank almost to the bend. There you catch in a bunch of light-red cock hackle fibres for the tail. Bind the ends of these firmly to the shank and then bring the silk down the hook to the bend again. Dub on to the silk a fair quantity of grey fur – I generally use a mixture of mole and rabbit underfur that makes both a really attractive body and dubs on very easily – and wind the dubbing up the hook to make a carrot-shaped body. Leave about a quarter of the shank free of dubbing at the eye.

The fly is now reversed in the vice and a false hackle is tied in under the shank. Do not forget to spread this round the bottom of the shank to soften it; you do not want it to hang as a lump.

Cahill

The fly is now turned over in the vice to receive the wing. Select a bunch of fibres from a barred brown squirrel tail; do not make it too big a bunch because this material is fairly thick in the fibre and it is very easy to bulk-up the head too much. Secure the fibres with several turns of silk. (Make certain right through your fly-dressing that all turns of silk − or any other material for that matter − are tight. If they are not tight then they might just as well not be there.) Lift up the front of the fibres and with the butts held in your left hand run the scissors in one straight cut across them. The cut should be at an upward angle so that the hair slopes down the eye. This means that when the silk is wound it will follow the shape of the cut hair and, with any luck, you should end up with a nice, neat head. Never try to trim off the butts of the hair *before* it is tied in. If you do, they will look a mess, which is all rather strange because I make it a rule to always trim off the butts of false hackles *before* they are tied in. The reason for this seeming anomaly is that the hair is hard and springy and you would lose control of it whereas the hackle fibres are largely soft and tie in much more easily. There is also the fact that on down-eyed hooks the eye gets in the way when you are trying to trim off under the 'chin' of the fly . . . well, that is the most plausible excuse that I can think of at the moment!

129

When the wing is securely fixed lift it into a vertical position and apply two locking turns, which consist of two or more turns of silk taken just around the base of the hair fibres. The wing is then lowered down into the normal wet-fly position and the silk is bound over the locking turns and the normal neat head made. The whip finish and varnishing are done in the usual way.

This is the normal method of fixing hairwings and I have used it very successfully for years now, but since the advent of the instant super-glues – the Cyanoacrylate adhesives – I find it much easier and better to just apply a dab of adhesive to the cut ends of the fibres and then wind the silk over the wet glue. Nothing will budge them if you use this method, whereas with locking turns there is always the possibility that if a fish manages to pull out just one or two fibres the rest may become loosened and the whole lot then comes adrift and there is no way you can make the locking turns tight enough to prevent this happening.

The Dressing:	*Cahill*
Hooks:	8 – 12, Old Numbers
Silk:	Black or brown (Sherry Spinner)
Tail:	Light natural red cock hackle
Body:	Dubbed grey fur
Hackle:	As for tail
Wing:	Brown barred squirrel tail

HAIRWING MONTREAL

This fly is very similar to the Cahill and seems to work quite well in the same circumstances where that pattern is successful, but it is also very useful as a dropper fly on a three-fly leader. In contrast, the Cahill does not seem to work very well like this – it is better fished as a single fly. I first tried the Hairwing Montreal like this when I was drift fishing on Grafham Water in the Midlands – foreign parts – and the trout were following the flies along. However they would only take the Hairwing Montreal when it was positioned on the middle dropper; the point or the bob would not do, it was the middle dropper or nothing. The strange thing was that when I went through the box and tried other flies in that position, including such favourites as the Invicta and the Zulu, they just ignored the whole lot, but when I went back to the Montreal there was promptly a fish hanging on the end. Pretty funny animals are trout.

Method of tying
Run silk down the shank from eye to bend and catch in a bunch of scarlet dyed cock hackle fibres for the tail. At the same time tie in a length of fine flat gold tinsel or Lurex. I think Lurex is better because it never tarnishes but is rather more 'tender', so you must not be surprised if it breaks after a fish has cut it with his teeth. I am inclined to think that if you have caught a fish on a fly then you have had good value from it and any subsequent fish on that fly should be looked on as a bonus. As I said previously, the thing that I cannot stand is when a fly is being cast and has not even touched the water, much less the fish, and it then begins to break up; that is a badly dressed fly and no excuses. If this happens to your flies then I suggest that you spend a lot more time at the bench and also learn to pull your silk tighter; that is usually at least half of the trouble.

Hairwing Montreal

Take the tying silk back up the shank towards the eye and, allowing the usual space for wing and hackle, tie in a length of claret floss silk. Wind the floss down the body over the ends of the tail fibres and the rib and form a slightly carrot-shaped body.

Run the ribbing up the body in even, open turns. Always make your ribs as evenly spaced and angled as you can – nothing spoils a fly more than sloppy ribbing. Tie in the tinsel in front of the body and trim off the surplus. Apply a false or beard hackle under the throat of the fly and then tie on a wing using the same technique as that used for the Cahill.

You know, if you look at one of these flies through squinty eyes you would swear it was a Mallard and Claret. Why is it, do you suppose, that I can catch trout on this pattern and not on the Mallard and Claret? Strange, isn't it?

The Dressing:	*Hairwing Montreal*
Hooks:	8 – 12, Old Numbers
Silk:	Black
Tail:	Scarlet dyed cock's hackle
Rib:	Flat gold tinsel or Lurex
Body:	Claret floss silk
Hackle:	Claret cock hackle
Wing:	Brown squirrel tail

GOLDEN OLIVE

This is a nice traditional fly; it is a good fly, a kindly fly, in much the same way that a Connemara Black is a good fly. It is generally considered to be an Irish pattern – certainly it is much more commonly seen there than in other parts of the British Isles. Spend a little time in getting it exactly right and it will repay you handsomely, not just in fish caught (though it is an excellent fish-taking pattern) but in the satisfaction of seeing it in your fly-box and knowing that some day it is going to do great things for you.

I like to fish the Golden Olive as the point fly in a three-fly leader; that, it seems to me, is where it fishes at its best. For some strange reason I do not usually use it as a single fly; this is probably due to the fact that although I normally much prefer to use a single fly rather than fish a team, this particular fly does not raise any confidence in me except as part of a team of flies.

Golden Olive

Method of tying

Run your tying down the shank to a point just before the bend and there catch in a strand of orange floss silk. When using the Marabou flosses I always pull off one strand along its neighbouring strand. When this is trimmed off it means that one strand is longer than the other; using this method you can go right through the spool without ever having to separate the strands more than once. The floss is wound as a tag and then a tail of golden pheasant crest is tied in. Make sure that the crest is completely straight and in line with the shank, otherwise it will spoil the appearance and the way the finished fly fishes; it will make it keel over on one side slightly and I promise you that it will catch less fish because of it.

Next, fix in the ribbing material, which in this case is oval gold tinsel or, in the case of the smaller sizes, gold wire. Dub a quantity of golden olive seal's fur on to the silk and wind this up the shank to make the body. When applying dubbing it is always as well to take about half the amount of dubbing material you think you are going to need, halve that again and you should have just about the right amount. You can always add more but it can be most frustrating to try and remove it from the silk – except when you do not want it to come off of course. Take the dubbing up the hook to a point about a quarter of the hook's length from the eye. Reverse the hook in the vice and tie in a false hackle. Try to match the shade of your hackle as closely to

133

the body material as you can; if you dye your own materials (and really you should) use the same dye batch for the hackle and the seal's fur.

Turn the fly right side up again and tie in a wing of bronze mallard feather. For this feather I rarely use matching slips taken from opposing feathers; I merely take one wide slip and, after clipping off any of the stalk left adhering to the butts of the fibres, I fold the slip in half, even up the tips of the fibres and tie it in the normal way. I also use this technique for barred teal feathers or any of the few other feathers which allow themselves to be used in this way – there are not many of them.

There are a couple of variations on this pattern. Roger Woolley used one that had no tail, just the tag and an underwing of golden pheasant tippet fibres laid below the wing. There was also one I saw catching a lot of trout in Ireland which had a tail which was the same colour as the body in dyed cock hackle. All three patterns seem to me to be effective but I prefer the standard dressing.

The Dressing:	*Golden Olive*
Hooks:	8 – 12, Old Numbers
Silk:	Olive
Tag:	Orange floss silk
Tail:	Optional: golden pheasant crest or golden olive cock hackle
Rib:	Oval gold tinsel or gold wire
Body:	Golden olive seal's fur
Hackle:	Golden olive cock
Wing:	Bronze mallard with optional underwing of golden pheasant tippet fibres

FIERY BROWN

I remember one day fishing from a boat on one of the big Midland reservoirs. The wind was howling across the open water and it was getting very cold. I still wanted to fish (my latent masochistic tendencies coming out perhaps?) but my hands were going numb; nothing takes away heat from the body faster than a wind – scientists call it the wind-chill factor. Although this was well into June it felt more like November. The water running off the constantly retrieved line was making my life a misery, so I decided to dap. Now, I do not know just how legal that was because for some strange reason some of our reservoir authorities ban dapping, but I thought 'to hell with the regulations, at least I can get one hand warm at a time and still be in with a chance of taking a fish or two'. Normally when dapping I would reckon to use at least a twelve foot rod and this would be coupled with either a floss-silk blowline or better still a swan breast feather hitched to the leader to act as a sail and carry the fly away from the boat. On this raw day none of this was necessary; casting was made virtually impossible anyway because the back-cast was being driven down on to the water by the wind.

Fiery Brown

The wind carried the line (an ordinary size 6 floater) well out from the boat and I then contrived to do the famous 'tripping-the-bob-fly-across-wavetops' thing, which is more than I can do when fishing conventionally. If you can dap it is a method that works very well indeed – at least it did on this occasion and a couple of others that I can think of. I had a Golden Olive on as the point fly and the Fiery Brown on the dropper, the bob fly. Six of my eight-fish limit came to the Fiery Brown and they took with a vicious, slashing rise through the sides and crests of two foot high waves – and I was fishing in relatively sheltered water! It was really exciting fishing, with most of the action on the surface. Soon my frozen hands were forgotten and what had started out as a miserable day ended as one to remember, savour and linger over by the fireside with a stiff Scotch in one hand and the fly-box in the other.

Method of tying
This fly is dressed using almost identical techniques to that of the Golden Olive so I do not propose to repeat it. There are a couple of points to remember, however. You are going to have trouble dyeing the fiery brown seal's fur to the correct shade so I would suggest that you buy some ready dyed and use that as a reference point. The wings on both these flies are better tied in fairly heavily and what I often do to get a little more bulk into the bronze mallard slip wing is to use my folded slip method, laying another slip over the first and then folding the two together. That makes the wing much more substantial – it also costs twice as much.

The Dressing:	Fiery Brown
Hooks:	8 – 12, Old Numbers
Silk:	Brown (Sherry Spinner)
Tag:	Optional, orange floss silk
Tail:	Golden pheasant tippet fibres
Rib:	Oval gold tinsel or gold wire for the smaller sizes
Body:	Fiery brown seal's fur
Hackle:	Natural red cock
Wing:	Bronze mallard

TEAL, BLUE AND SILVER

The Teal, Blue and Silver is a fly that I like very much for the West Country sea trout. It seems to produce most takes after a really scorching day. If it is drifted down the pool after dark a sudden pull can come as an electrifying shock. This is a good fly for the rivers but I have never done very much with it on the stillwaters. It must be pretty effective, though, because a lot of the entries in the return books list it as the successful pattern. I shall have to try it more often. Friends tell me that it does well if it is brought back just under the surface, which is the way I often fish another of my all-time favourites, the Peter Ross. The Peter Ross, by the way, was developed from another of the teal series, the Teal and Red, and is now regarded by many to be the premier fly of the traditional stillwater patterns.

Method of tying
Secure your hook in the vice and run the tying silk down the shank to the bend in open turns. There you fix in the tail which is composed of a few strands of golden pheasant tippet fibres. Take the silk back up the shank, binding down the butts of the tippet fibres as you go. This has the double effect of not merely filling in the interstices of the first open layer of silk, but also of locking the tail fibres into position. I promise you they will never slip using this method and you will arrive at an underbody of silk that is not only nice and slim but also smooth.

Teal, Blue and Silver

Leave a small gap at the eye to take the wings and hackle and tie in a length of silver tinsel or Lurex. As I have said previously I much prefer the Lurex because being non-metallic, it cannot tarnish; it is also much more pleasant to work with. It is easier to tie in; for instance you do not have to taper the end of the strip with a cut from your scissors, you can just tie it straight in. It lies on the shank better and certainly makes a much neater, prettier fly than flat tinsel. The fact that it is softer and therefore more easily cut by a trout's teeth can be easily overcome by the simple expedient of winding on a rib of silver wire.

Take the tinsel down the shank in close, touching turns to the tail, make certain that no black silk is left uncovered where you secured the tail as it looks most untidy. Come back up the fly over the first layer and tie in and trim off the surplus where the tinsel was first fixed.

Turn the fly over in the vice and tie in a false or beard hackle. The fly is now turned back up the right way and the wing is tied in using the method I advocated for the bronze mallard used in the Golden Olive, a single wide slip being folded and tied down in the normal way. This has three main advantages: it is a much quicker technique than the normal pair of matched slips; the two sides of the wing will match each other perfectly; and, finally, it allows you to use single feathers and not have to bother finding two matching feathers with sides of equal length and colour. It really is a much improved method for those feathers that will allow you to use them in this way.

When applying wings and false hackles to wet flies it is most important that they are level. They should both spring from the same point on the hook shank. It looks all wrong when the wing is tied in forward of the hackle and this is invariably what happens when the dresser is afraid of disturbing the hackle by taking turns of silk too close to it. Go on, chance it! You will find that with practice it will all come right.

The Dressing:	Teal, Blue and Silver
Hooks:	6 – 12, Old Numbers
Silk:	Black
Tail:	Strands of golden pheasant tippet fibres
Rib:	Optional, silver wire
Body:	Silver tinsel or flat Lurex
Hackle:	Blue dyed cock
Wing:	Teal breast feather

TEAL AND BLACK

This is another fly in the Teal series of patterns. There are several flies in this series, just as there are the same groups of flies in the grouse, mallard and woodcock series. The only thing that really alters between these series of flies is the winging material. The body colours are many and various – colours like red, black, green, yellow; there is also, usually, a mixed colour body, so you can get a Teal and Mixed, Woodcock and Mixed or a Mallard and Mixed. I suppose they have all caught fish in their day but it is seldom these days that you will find an angler who has more than a couple of different colours in his fly-box. Of the Teal series there is no doubt in my mind as to which I find most effective in the solid colours; it is the Teal and Black.

Teal and Black

It must have been seven or eight years ago when I went down to Weirwood on opening day, along with the rest of the lads from *Angling* magazine. I took a rare old pasting that day. No matter what I tried I could not catch trout; everybody else caught the blighters but not me. It really was frustrating. After a while it became a matter of honour to succeed. I could imagine all the others talking behind my back (this angling business can make you paranoid you know!) . . . 'That Collyer, what an angler he turned out to be . . .', you know, little pleasantries like that. Oh boy, do you *ever* need to catch trout! The fact that in reality they are all being quite sympathetic because on other occasions they have been there themselves has no bearing on the matter whatever. We all of us get blanks, and do not let anybody tell you otherwise. I suppose I have fished with some of the best known anglers in this country and believe me, they are all ordinary mortals. The only difference between the top man and the average angler is that the man with the reputation to protect has to try harder. Because he tries harder he catches more fish, which in turn increases his experience. But nobody can *make* a trout feed if it is disinclined to do so.

That day at Weirwood wore on and I became more and more despondent. There was a certain gentleman with a shop in Edmonton who kept complaining that taking fish were interrupting his casting rhythm. As I recall I suggested gently that if he just wanted to cast, why did he not take the b . . . . . fly off and stop complaining − I was getting a little frayed around the edges. (Actually, I think he may possibly have been kidding.) Evening came and I knew I had to get home soon for a business appointment. Visions of a first day blank loomed closer.

At the eleventh hour we all agreed on a move round to the south bank and I elected to fish by the boat bay. In front of me, 20 yards out, a fish moved. I cast to it, and what do you think happened? He totally ignored it! I had already been right through the fly-box with no result at all. Everyone else was taking fish on black flies so, as my final fling, I tried on a Teal and Black. Now there were two or three fish moving in front of me. I cast out and with the first pull the line went tight and I heaved a sigh of relief; fish on. I *very carefully* played out that twelve inch rainbow; I treated him like a four pounder. He looked marvellous to me lying in the bottom of the net. Two or three casts more and I made it a brace and then it was time to be off, honour and reputation salvaged.

Method of tying

Start your tying silk as normal and at the bend tie in a bunch of black cock hackle fibres as a tail. Directly in front of these fix a length of oval silver tinsel. Dub on to the silk some black wool or seal's fur − I think the seal's fur is better − and wind a carrot-shaped body up the shank to just in front of the eye. An alternative body material is black floss silk but I do not like the fly tied using floss; it is too smooth. Most of my flies I like to see sleek and slender but this particular pattern seems to take more fish for me if it is dressed rough. Wind the rib evenly up the body and tie off and trim where the body finishes.

Turn the fly over in the vice and tie in a false hackle of black cock. Now a wing of folded teal is fixed in to lay sleekly over the back of the fly. This is where the real advantage lies of using the false or beard hackle system for wet flies. If the hackle is wound in front of the body there is no way you can avoid the wing being pushed into a high attitude over the body except by building up the turns of silk to make a bed which will be level with the hackle stalk, and this would mean that the head would be much too bulky. The only alternative is to use the false hackle, thus involving the minimum number of turns of silk and at the same time allowing the wing to lay low over the back of the fly. The main objection that people seem to voice over the false hackle method is that the fibres tend to clump and to hang underneath the fly in an unattractive lump. I absolutely agree with them; a hackle applied like that does look absolutely awful but – and this is a very large but – if you can train your thumb to spread that false hackle round the underside of the hook-shank – to part spin the fibres in fact – you cannot tell the false hackle from the wound except that the false hackle leads to a small head and a neat wing. It is all a question of practice and of educating that thumb.

The Dressing:	*Teal and Black*
Hooks:	8 – 12, Old Numbers
Silk:	Black
Tail:	Black cock hackle
Rib:	Oval silver tinsel
Body:	Black wool, seal's fur or floss silk
Hackle:	Black cock
Wing:	Barred teal

RED-TAILED AND SILVER INVICTA

The Invicta and its variations are extremely effective wet flies when used on the reservoirs or the smaller stillwater fisheries in the United Kingdom; I have no experience of them abroad. Generally speaking the Invicta seems to work best as a top dropper on a three-fly leader; it is an excellent position which calls for 'the fly to be worked across the wave-tops', if you can do it. This is a method that I have no doubt at all is a most efficient technique for inducing a trout to take a fly. It just seems a pity that I cannot get it to work for me! Writers from before the turn of the century tell us that this is the best method of catching trout from a drifting boat. The top dropper should trip across those wave-tops and prove irresistible to the fish that has refused the two lower flies. The theory is fine, but unfortunately the practice somewhat different.

Red Tail Invicta

The problem is that either the top dropper is submerged or it is waving about in mid-air – the time it spends clipping the waves is very short indeed. True, on a couple of occasions I have had fish take the fly when it has been in this position and they have taken sufficiently firmly to stay attached but generally speaking the take comes further out, just when the flies change direction and lift in the water as the rod is starting to rise. I am certain, however, that the reason the fish takes then is the change in direction and *not* the fact that the fly is tripping the surface. It is most noticeable that when you put a change of direction into the retrieve of the fly, that is the point where the takes most often come.

If you are being rowed out on to a lake and you cast sideways from the boat and allow the flies to swing round into the whorls made by the oar strokes, it is usually when the line is just straightening and the flies are swinging round that the following fish is seduced into striking at them. On those lakes which allow trolling (or trailing, which is the correct term for towing a line over the stern of a boat) it is noticeable that certain boats take more fish than others. If you watch closely you will see that what they are doing that is different is change direction frequently. The boat that doggedly rows up the lake and then down again towing his flies behind will take fish certainly, but most of them will come at each end of the towing session when the boat turns and when the flies make an abrupt change of direction. This then should be our aim, to bring our flies to life, to make them look as a trout would expect a living creature to look and behave. No living animal, with the possible exception of man, moves in a straight line at an unvarying pace. Your aim should be to make your flies appear as live things, not mere bundles of fur and feather.

You will gather from all this that I am not a believer in the normally recommended method of fishing out a wet-fly cast from a drifting boat; I am all for spotting a fish at thirty or thirty five yards, casting six or eight feet in front of him and then pulling my fly across his nose. That, believe me, will catch you many more fish than trying to get him to take close to the boat. The other main objection I have to roll-casting the line from the boat – short-lining as it is known – is that when the fish does decide to take, the right arm is nearly always at full extension and there is no way that you can set the hook; all that results is a pricked and frightened fish. Far better to have tried for that fish when he was farther out. If he misses you can often cast at him again and he will have another go if the boat has not scared him.

The final objection I have is that to get sufficient speed of line to allow you to roll-cast again the flies are moving much too quickly. Only the last time I was out in a boat, Tuesday last it was, I was sharing it with a fellow who almost – but not quite! – condemned me for working a lure across the top while he was fishing a wet-fly team in the traditional way. True, I was retrieving that small lure quickly; that was how the trout wanted it and I am a great believer in giving them what they want. It may sound like bragging (in fact I am sure it does, but when did that ever stop an angler saying something?) but I took six fish to my companion's one. He would not accept a fly of mine to try but insisted on keeping on with his team. My little Matuka was about a quarter as long again as his biggest traditional pattern; he was fishing three flies to my one; and although he would probably have denied it hotly he was fishing them a lot faster than I was. The big difference as far as he was concerned was that he was 'fishing traditionally' and that was all he was interested in. Fair enough, but in my book he should not have condemned me, albeit under his breath, for using wicked lures and casting at, and catching, fish at thirty five yards plus when he was scaring many more by trying to catch them close to the boat. Every man to his own, I say; so long as he enjoys his fishing and it is within the rules then it is fair enough.

The Invicta – as I believe I said some time ago – is a very good fly, and so are these two variations. The Silver Invicta is a fine fly on the point of the leader as opposed to being the bob fly on the top dropper. The red-tailed version is a first class pattern fished on its own. I first saw it in use when I was fishing at Draycote with Dick Walker and his charming wife Pat. She took a lovely brownie of 3lb plus on this pattern and I cannot now tie it on to my leader without thinking of that occasion – that brownie really ripped through the water. I have often thought that trout, like nearly all fish, have a top fighting weight. It is pretty much the same as a boxer; once he puts on too much weight he becomes slow and his fight becomes sluggish. The bulk of the really good scraps I have had with trout have been from fish of 1½lb up to about 3½lb; above that they do seem to slow down. When speaking to Dick just the other day he remarked that although he agreed with me generally he did make the exception of that first year at Grafham Water when trout ran big, fast and extremely powerfully. This was very unusual and was because those rainbows were very young fish. As we all know the fight from a youngster is generally better than it is from an older fish which has perhaps started to go over the hill.

I have found that quite often the trout will refuse an ordinary Invicta and be inclined to have a go at the red-tailed version and the reverse. It seems to be a rare day when they will not show a marked preference for one or the other.

Method of tying

Begin winding the tying silk slightly behind the eye and carry it down the shank to a point just before the bend, where you tie in the tail. Take two slips from a scarlet dyed duck feather (called ibis substitute) and tie these in as you would an inverted wing. The two slips have an inbuilt curve to them so when they are tied in together, concave sides facing each other, these two curves work against each other and, with any luck, you end up with a dead straight tail.

Now fix a length of oval gold tinsel for the rib, as close to where the tail is tied as you can, and dub on yellow seal's fur or wool. I prefer wool; it is as lot simpler and quicker to dub, and with the shiny body hackle and the gold ribbing you get quite enough sparkle on the body. Run the dubbing up the shank to make a carrot-shaped body for three-quarters of its length and then tie in a ginger cock hackle by its butt-end after having stripped off the fluffy fibres from the base of the feather. If you have trouble with hackles pulling out as soon as you try to wind them, just trim off those fluffy fibres with your scissors rather than tearing them off. The scissor cut leaves tiny stubs sticking out which grip the silk and make certain that the hackle stalk does not slip as you are winding it. Grip the tip of the hackle in your hackle pliers and wind it in evenly spaced turns back to the tail; then secure the hackle by winding the ribbing tinsel forward through the hackle to the eye, where it is secured and the end trimmed off. Trim off the tip of the hackle at the tail end.

Turn the fly over in the vice to receive the false hackle of jay's blue wing feather. Tear off a section of this rather intractable feather, measure it up against the hook and then trim it off so that it measures slightly longer than the distance between the eye and the point of the hook. Lay the fibres over to the nearside of the hook and catch it in with a single turn of tying silk. Now pull the silk gently but firmly downwards and at the same moment try to spread the hackle round the bottom of the hook with your left thumb. With any luck it should spin slightly round the bottom of the hook shank and you end up with a nicely spread out hackle rather than one that hangs in a clump. Whatever else you do, do *not* try and split the hackle stalk and then wind the hackle – that way lies insanity. The only successful method with this feather that I have ever found is the technique described above.

The wing can be tricky on all the Invictas because the angle of the hen pheasant centre tail feather is very shallow indeed, and it is very difficult to get any bulk into the wing. I have found over the years that if the winging feathers are moistened, laid between two sheets of blotting paper and left overnight with a heavy weight on them they are then a lot easier to tie in. The same applies to the blue mallard wing feather used for Butcher wings. Finish the wings and then make a neat head using at least a four-of five-turn whip finish and finally run on a couple of coats of clear varnish with the point of your dubbing needle.

The Silver Invicta is rather different because it has the normal tail of golden pheasant crest. The best way of setting the tail square on the top of the shank is to moisten it between your lips before tying it in; this sticks the fibres together and you can see which way the stalk wants to bend and then allow for it when you tie it in. If you do not do this you will find that the fibres tend to flare in all directions as the silk tightens. To release the fibres from the 'glue' of your saliva you just rub them between your finger and thumb once they have dried. It may not seem the most hygienic of practices but I have been doing it for a long time now and I am still around!

The other main difference between the other two flies and this pattern is the fact that normally the Silver Invicta does not have a

Silver Invicta

palmered body hackle. I did see one tied the other day, though, where the dresser had incorporated a body hackle and I must say it did look a likely pattern; I am going to try it, and I am also going to try it with the red ibis substitute tail.

The Dressings

Red-tailed Invicta

Hooks:	6 – 14, Old Numbers
Silk:	Olive or lemon yellow
Tail:	Scarlet ibis substitute
Rib:	Oval gold tinsel
Body:	Yellow wool or seal's fur
Body Hackle:	Ginger cock
Hackle:	Blue jay wing
Wing:	Hen pheasant centre tail

Silver Invicta

Hooks:	6 – 14, Old Numbers
Silk:	Olive or brown (Sherry Spinner)
Tail:	Golden pheasant crest
Rib:	Oval silver tinsel
Body:	Flat silver tinsel or Lurex
Body Hackle:	Optional, ginger cock
Hackle:	Blue jay
Wing:	Hen pheasant centre tail

LURES

CHAPTER EIGHT

HAIRWING LURES

BASS BLOND

This is a fly which was designed by my good friend and, until recently, editor, Brian Harris. The fly is based on the late Joe Brook's 'Blond' series of flies. I should say here and now that I have not tried it myself but if Brian and his friends say it is good, then that is what it is. Brian says that it will also take pike and not just the bass it was named after, but I still incline towards black as the top pike colour. After fishing Grafham a few years ago when it was making its claim towards being the very best pike-fly water in Britain, I consider myself an expert on taking twelve inch jacks on Black Lures, Sweeney Todds and the Ace of Spades. Without doubt pike like black. I always thought it was rather a shame that disease and the Grafham staff have so effectively reduced the pike numbers: I was quite looking forward to a 30lb stock-fish-fed pike on fly gear.

This fly can be used in the surf when it is calm, or from a boat. Visible shoaling bass are a necessity. Use a shooting head which sinks fairly slowly. Fast-sinking lines can be useful from the boat. Retrieve in steady pulls through the shoals of brit; with any luck at all you will feel a hard take as the bass smashes up from below. Fly-fishing for sea-fish is something that deserves to be more popular than it is at present. It is a very interesting and effective way of taking fish. My favourite 'thing' is to fish for mackerel and gars right on the top; both species knock hell out of trout for fight and spectacular jumps.

Method of tying
Tie in your silk at the eye of a ring-eyed, nickel-plated O'Shaugnessy hook, about 1/0, and run this down to the bend, where you tie in a strip of wide silver Lurex or tinsel for the rib.

(Remember that in salt-water tarnishing occurs even faster than it does under normal circumstances, so I really think that the Lurex will be best.) Bring the silk back up the shank for half its length and tie in a strand of white Orlon. Wind the wool down the hook to where the rib was tied in and then come back up the shank making a carrot-shape by slightly overlapping each turn and, as you come farther up the hook, lapping the turns closer and closer. Rib the body with about four turns of tinsel. Take a small quantity of pale blue bucktail and tie in about half-way along the shank as a wing. Lock these fibres in place either by using locking turns of silk just round the roots of the hair or by applying a small spot of one of the super-glues. Over the butt of the hair wind a fat collar of the body material, tie in and trim off the surplus. The main wing consists of three more layers of hair; yellow, red and then, over the top of these and much longer in the fibre, white.

The head is a big, bulky affair, not just because of the hairwing which always tends to bulk up heads but also because Brian has found it to be more effective this way. The whole of the head and hook eye are varnished white and when this is dry a black eye is painted on either side of the head. What I would do

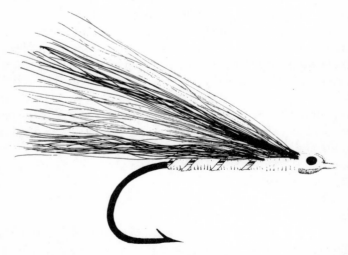

Bass Blonde

then is to allow the whole thing to dry thoroughly and then run a coat of clear varnish over the whole head, but Brian does not bother, no doubt working on the principle that those common old sea-fish are not as particular as the more 'refeened' trout!

The Dressing:	*Bass Blond*
Hooks:	1 – 2/0, nickel-plated O'Shaugnessy
Silk:	White
Rib:	Flat, wide silver tinsel or Lurex
Body:	White Orlon baby 'wool'
Underwing:	Pale blue bucktail
Wing:	Yellow, red and white bucktail
Head:	White varnish with black eyes

EDSON DARK TIGER AND EDSON LIGHT TIGER

We have here two American bucktail patterns that are good, and I mean *really* good fish-takers. I have had a lot of trout on them from our stillwater fisheries, particularly the reservoirs, although they have not done quite so well on the smaller waters. They both however suffer from one little problem – jungle cock really is necessary for both of them. They are far less effective without it. I am still in the fortunate position of having some highly treasured jungle cock capes left from the time before the ban on the import of the feathers came into force. As I remarked to my evening class some time ago, '£20 wouldn't buy one of these top quality capes these days'. This is perfectly true (if ridiculous); they are literally worth their weight in gold, and to think that these grade A capes were selling for just £1.50 wholesale! It is amazing what scarcity can do to prices. It seems only a short time ago that I used to burn the big split jungle cock feathers when the good ones were picked out of the cape – not any more! Nowadays the big feathers are split (purposely) then trimmed to shape with either wing burner tweezers or scissors to make a pair of smaller feathers; this method works very well incidentally. For those fly-dressers amongst you who are not fortunate enough to have any of the real thing left, there is now an excellent substitute available from the material suppliers, and I do not mean those terrible plastic things – I get the shudders just remembering the trouble I had with those. No, now there is a really satisfactory substitute for a natural feather. These come in three sizes and even if they do seem a little expensive at first glance, you will find the investment worthwhile, this certainly being the case with the Edson Tigers. Go on, spoil yourself!

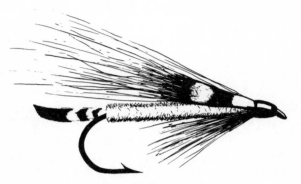

Edson Dark Tiger

The thing that annoys me more than anything about the import ban on this particular bird's feathers is that they are still being killed at exactly the same rate as before. I have several friends who live in or visit India and the surrounding countries, where the jungle fowl live, and they tell me that not only was there no real threat to the species but that they are used as a basic source of protein and are still being killed for their meat. Because the fly-dressers are no longer allowed to import their feathers, however, these are now just left to rot. These birds were never killed for their feathers; in fact there is no species of which I am aware that is killed purely for fly-dressing purposes, and no species has ever been put in danger because of flydressing (*with one possible exception – the New Zealand matuka*). If I thought that any animal or bird was being even slightly endangered and brought near to extinction through fly-tying I would give it up tomorrow, and I expect to be tying for some years yet.

I can remember several occasions when one or the other of these flies has saved the day for me. It seems that if one of them works well the other one does not on any particular day; I suppose the light conditions are the controlling factor, the same thing probably applying to many different patterns, particularly the lures and wet flies.

I recall one day fishing the Pipe Bay at Blagdon when the Dark Tiger (that is the one with the light coloured body – so, what did you expect?) was being hit really hard by the trout coming in and slashing at the shoals of sticklebacks. I picked up several fish very quickly by fishing this fly, stop–start, on a slow sinking line. If you watch a stickleback you will notice that these pugnacious little characters are the hard-cases of the mini-fish world – they are not scared of anything. They will dart along for a foot or so and then stop and have a look around, and that, it seems, is when the trout hit them; nearly every take I had came on the pause.

While I am on the subject of sticklebacks I reckon it is a shame that they do not grow to two or three feet long; then we would know what a *real* fighting fish was all about! Perhaps on second thoughts, it is not quite such a shame. They are so fearless that they could well be prepared to have a go at *us* if they did grow to that size. 'There I was being attacked by this man-eating shoal of sticklebacks. . . .'

Method of tying
We will start with the dark version. Fix your tying silk and wind it down the shank to the bend. Tie in a tail of either barred mandarin duck feather or guinea fowl. (It is a lot cheaper to use the guinea fowl and just as effective, but if you do use the guinea fowl use the wing feather for this tail, not the breast feathers.) Match up two slips to make sure the tail lies straight. Immediately after the tail is tied down fix in a length of chenille, strip off a quarter of an inch of the fluff from the end and just tie in the central cotton core, winding the chenille up the body towards the eye. Stop about three-quarters of the way up the hook because you are going to need a fair amount of room to tie in the wings and hackle. Reverse the fly in the vice and tie in a false hackle in the usual way – well, it is usual for me – using scarlet cock. Turn the fly the right way up again to take the wing.

The wing is ordinary brown bucktail; if you are not very careful you will take too much, and make the head too big because these fibres are rather thick. I would rather go the other way and use too little; you can always add more but once you have applied Super Glue to the base of the fibres there is no way you are going to get them off again without cutting them. When the wing is tied in and you are satisfied that there are no straggly bits of hair (I cannot abide sticky-outy-bits on wings, bodies or hackles – I like things neat and tidy, unless the fly is designed to be scruffy, like the Hare's Ear nymphs for instance) tie in the jungle cock or substitute on either side of the wing.

Edson Light Tiger

Decide what length you want the cheeks to be and then trim up the stalk of the feather with scissors for the right length. You are then left with the stalk and a slightly serrated surface on the stalk which, when it is tied in, will grip the silk really firmly and not allow the feather to pull out. Another way of achieving a similar effect is to strip the fibres off with your fingers and, when the stalk is tied in, bend it back alongside the hook and bind it in again with the silk. This locks it in really tightly and it will never slip; at the prices these days of jungle cock or its substitutes you cannot afford to have them come adrift after being incorporated into a fly. Make a neat head to the fly and finish with a good whip. There is no substitute for that whip-finish; it matters not whether you cheat and use one of the fancy tools now available

156

or the implements provided by Him on high for the purpose
(why else do you suppose he gave you fingers?). No, the
important thing is that without that whip-finish your fly will
surely disintegrate, no matter how much varnish you coat the
head with – half-hitches are useless.

Start the Light Tiger in the normal way, although this time
there is a tag to tie in first. The tag is of flat gold tinsel or Lurex
and you will need to use the narrow tinsel, with a width of about
one sixty-fourth of an inch. After the tag has been wound and
the end trimmed off you have to tie in a tail which is of mandarin
duck feather, the one with the attractive barring across the end of
it. These feathers are very expensive because there are so few of
them on each bird, but they are beautiful and it is worth
investing in some of them. The dressings for lots of the older
patterns of salmon flies used to specify that barred summer or
wood duck feathers should be used, but these are no longer
available to us; mandarin duck, however, is an excellent
substitute.

The body is made of twisted strands of peacock herl, which is
unribbed, so I always wind this over a coating of wet varnish;
the body then becomes virtually indestructible. The gill feathers
are the tips of two scarlet cock hackles. These are set slightly
under and to each side of the fly. The wing is really supposed to
be honey coloured bucktail but this is very difficult to obtain and
yellow is now generally used – the trout do not seem to mind.
The jungle cock eyes are again tied in as cheeks, the head finished
off in the normal way and several coats of varnish are applied to it
to give it a lovely glossy finish.

The Dressings

Edson Dark Tiger

Hooks:	6 – 10 long shank, Old Numbers
Silk:	Black
Tail:	Barred guinea fowl or mandarin duck ·
Body:	Yellow chenille
Hackle:	Scarlet cock
Wings:	Brown bucktail
Cheeks:	Jungle cock or substitute

Edson Light Tiger

Hooks:	6 – 10 long shank, Old Numbers
Silk:	Yellow
Tag:	Narrow gold tinsel or Lurex
Tail:	Barred mandarin duck
Body:	Bronze peacock herl
Gills:	Two scarlet cock hackle points
Wings:	Yellow or honey bucktail
Cheeks:	Jungle cock or substitute

CHAPTER NINE

STREAMER FLIES

SILVER GREY STREAMER

This fly is not to be confused with the salmon fly of the same name to be found in chapter 17; this is an American pattern which is very good at the back end of the season. It should be fished two or three feet down and retrieved as smoothly as possible – try not to get any pause into the pulls. This is possible by manipulating the rod as well as drawing the line with your hand. At the end of the pull the rod-top is raised to continue the movement of the fly through the water and when the line that had been gathered in the left hand is dropped it is taken smartly back to the stripping ring to make the next pull, the rod-top being lowered at the same moment. This sounds a little difficult when you are reading it but with practice it is fairly easy to keep the flies coming smoothly and steadily back to you, although it is difficult to do it for long periods.

It always strikes me as rather strange that a trout should sometimes prefer a fly to be fished in this way rather than the usual stop–start method, though I suppose I should not really be surprised – how often have I caught trout when reeling the fly back in to move elsewhere or to pack up. This can sometimes prove embarrassing, especially if you are fishing a reservoir which will not sell you a second ticket (as was the case with the Southern Water Authority reservoirs in 1978 and 1979) – Oh dear, all of a sudden you find that you are attached to your seventh trout. They do not like the fish being shaken off and you are only allowed six – a conundrum. Nowadays I always take the flies off before I make that last cast to get the line properly back on to the reel; it saves on explanations and apologies.

One would assume that the stop–start movement would be the more normal behaviour of any underwater creature; perhaps it is this very *abnormality* which is the attraction. We know that pike will often prefer a bait-fish which is different to the normal diet available to them – herring, sprat or perhaps a juicy goldfish! They will very often take one of these in preference to dace, roach or a gudgeon, their normal fare. The abnormal is more quickly spotted by the predator and like anything which is injured and behaving peculiarly it is a possible meal.

The same thing can happen with trout. You can flog away at a fish with a perfectly adequate imitation of (say) a mayfly, a pattern on which you have taken many fish previously, and it is treated with disdain. Then along comes another angler with what you consider to be an absolute monstrosity (and I have seen this happen with a mayfly which was dressed incorporating a hot-orange hackle) and the trout takes it with complete confidence. Again I think it is the built-in reflex to destroy the abnormal. This extends right through the animal kingdom; for example, albinos rarely live a normal lifespan simply because they stand out from the crowd and are therefore a more obvious target. So it is, I am sure, with the steady retrieve in fishing a trout lure; it is unusual, therefore obvious, and it gets 'destroyed'.

The Silver Grey is also very good when trout – or perch for that matter – are after the fry in the margins. Here I employ my 'sticklebacking' tactic of letting the fly lie on the bottom and just twitching it for a few seconds and then slowly increasing the speed of retrieve, the aim being to simulate the recovery of a fry which has been stunned by the attack of a fast-turning trout. This technique is often spectacularly successful.

Method of tying
To dress this fly you start by winding the tying silk from the eye – or just a shade back from it – to a point just before the bend on a long-shank hook. There you tie in a pair of slips taken from a barred mandarin duck feather, the pair being preferable to the single slip because the two curves work against each other and keep the tail perfectly straight. The Americans use wood-duck feathers but these are not available in the United Kingdom. Carry the silk almost to the eye and catch in a strip of silver tinsel or Lurex; this material is then wound down the shank to the

bend, brought up the hook again over the first layer, tied down and the end trimmed off where it was first tied in. Make certain the turns are close butted and not overlapping otherwise you will never achieve a smooth body.

The wing consists of four hackle feathers, two dyed hot orange and outside of these two barred Plymouth Rock cock hackles. When these hackles are nicely adjusted for length so that the tips match exactly, strip off all the fluff at the base of the

Silver Grey Streamer

feathers and tie them in so that they lie low along the body of the fly. Outside the wing tie in cheeks of jungle cock feathers, if you still have some, or some kind of substitute. One way or the other you are going to need the flash of the 'eyes' on this fly. One method is to varnish the head black and paint a white spot with a black centre as an eye; that works very well on almost any fly that was once tied with jungle cock, but I am afraid it is somewhat time consuming.

Finally, fix in two Plymouth Rock hackles at the eye and, clipping the tips in your hackle pliers, wind these as a collar down to the wings. Turns of silk are taken over the roots of the fibres so that they incline slightly backwards; this is to give the fly good entry. If you do not do this you will find you have got a lovely example of a dry fly streamer! It is most disconcerting when the darned thing won't sink.

The Dressing:	*Silver Grey Streamer*
Hooks:	6 – 10 long shank, Old Numbers
Silk:	Black
Tail:	Barred mandarin duck
Body:	Flat silver tinsel or Lurex
Wing:	Two orange hackles with two Plymouth Rock hackles outside
Cheeks:	Jungle cock or substitute
Hackle:	Two Plymouth Rock hackles wound as collar

APPETISER

On 12th of December 1973 I received a letter from Bob Church. It contained a fly, an Appetiser. (I reckoned that Bob must drink a fair drop of a certain fizzy beverage to give it a name like that!) I had been getting the odd enquiry from clients for this lure and I had written to Bob a few days earlier to make certain that I gave them the correct dressing. He said in his letter that it had proved deadly at Grafham and Hanningfield. I promptly tied them up and put a couple of extras in my lure-box for the start of the season. The orders were duly dispatched and I settled back to enjoy the Christmas festivities.

The first chance I had of trying the new fly was on the opening day at Weirwood. I had gone up the North bank to

Appetiser

escape the crowds round the fishing lodge and after walking about half-a-mile up the reservoir I found a spot that had relatively few people around – well no more than a dozen within a couple of hundred yards! I wondered whether I had made a mistake and ended up on the North Bank of the Nene on match day. After metaphorically shouldering my way to the water's edge I made a cast and almost on the first pull of the first cast of the season the line tightened and a trout was on, an eight inch rainbow.

I saw dozens of these small trout being killed, and I have been told that this state of affairs continued right through the season. The reason, I was informed, was that a cage holding 10,000 of these young rainbows was smashed by ice during the winter and they all escaped. There were also a lot of bigger trout killed at Weirwood that season but it was certainly a shame about those little fish.

That first fish of mine sort of . . . er . . . fell off before I could land it. So did the next six or seven that followed it in rapid succession. I quickly got fed up with this and decided to wend my way back towards the dam. The crowd had thinned slightly because a lot of people had got their limits of these little chaps and gone home. I managed to get into one of my favourite spots and found that those little fish had now deserted the place or had perhaps been killed off by the earlier inhabitants. I fished steadily on through the day and took one more small fish that I had to kill because (it would have been strictly against the rules not to of course) it was cut across the tongue and bleeding from the gills. Just as dusk fell I had a really savage take and after a fierce fight lasting three or four minutes I landed a lovely rainbow of well over 2lb. That fish took the Appetiser I had tied on at the last minute. That season the Appetiser took more trout for me than any other lure in my box.

It is also the favourite lure of a friend of mine, John Ward who runs our local gun shop. He took me along one day to a private trout pool on which he had a season ticket, and I will swear that he knew those fish by their first names! Every time I looked up his rod was bent into another one. 'How was I doing', you ask? I would sooner not answer that. However, I suppose I had better tell you – nothing . . . well, maybe that is not strictly true. At one point John took pity on me and asked me to have a try in his spot; I did and I duly hooked a trout, all twelve inches of it. It then dived into the weed-beds that you had to draw the fish past to land them, and threw the hook. John did not laugh once, he just came back into his pitch and promptly caught a five pounder . . . sometimes it is difficult to raise a smile in adversity. I have since forgiven him. All his fish came to a size 10 Appetiser fished by giving two quick jerks to the line and then pausing for a few seconds; a foot up the leader a BB shot was squeezed on to the nylon. The pause allowed the fly to be drawn down by the shot and this was when most fish came to the fly. I had no excuse; I saw what he was doing, how he induced the takes, the fly, everything. I just could not make it work for me. I am glad to say that days like that do not inflict themselves on me too often – once or twice is enough!

Method of tying
Fix a long-shank hook in your vice and after testing it for temper, run tying silk from just behind the eye to the bend. Now you have to mix a bunch of hackle fibres for the tail. The best way I know of doing that is to *cut* off about fifteen or twenty fibres from each hackle (in this case green and orange), lay them on a smooth surface well spread out, but with the tips absolutely level – the butts do not matter. You now lay the second layer on top of the first then carefully gather them up so the tips stay level. Twirl the fibres between your finger and thumb, going in one direction only (much as you would for dubbing wool or seal's fur on to silk) and you should find the colours blend and mix together nicely. Tie your mixed bunch of fibres in as a tail.

Pull the fluff off about a quarter of an inch of the end of a length of white chenille and tie in the exposed central cotton core. Wind the chenille evenly up the shank almost to the eye. Reverse the fly in the vice and tie in a false hackle using the same colours that you did for the tail and mix them in the same way. A variation of this that worked very well for me during the 1974 season was to leave the hackling at this stage and after the wings

Traditional Missionary

Shrive's Missionary

Cahill

Hairwing Montreal

Golden Olive

Fiery Brown

Teal, Blue & Silver

Teal & Black

Red-tailed Invicta

Silver Invicta ·

Bass Blond

Edson Dark Tiger

Edson Light Tiger

Silver Grey Streamer

Appetiser

White Marabou

Geronimo

Yellow Fellow

Haymaker

Vulture Matuka

were tied in to wind a green and orange hackle together, just behind the head, as a collar. If anything I think this version caught more fish for me than the original. Turn the fly the right way up in the vice to receive the wing.

Take a large bunch of marabou fibres and tie these in so that they are about half as long again as the hook; directly on top of these tie in a small bunch of grey squirrel fibres. Put a small dab of Super Glue on the roots of the fibres to secure them firmly, make as neat a head as possible and then run on several coats of varnish to make the head all shiny and pretty. The marabou wing needs to be in a fairly large quantity because when it is wetted it seems to reduce considerably in volume. The squirrel tail helps to keep the soft marabou from getting completely out of control and wrapping itself under the hook when casting.

The Dressing:	Appetiser
Hooks:	6 – 10 long shank, Old Numbers
Silk:	Black
Tail:	Green and orange cock hackle fibres mixed
Body:	White chenille
Hackle:	As for tail
Wings:	White marabou with grey squirrel tail over

WHITE MARABOU

The White Marabou is an American pattern that is also excellent on our lakes and reservoirs. It uses as its wing that most versatile and effective material, marabou feather. This feather is no longer obtained from the marabou stork but is now a substitute feather taken from the turkey. It is a strange thing but quite often we find that when a material becomes scarce or the animal or bird is placed on the protected list and a substitute has to be found, that substitute can often be better than the original material. So it is with this feather; the turkey is definitely better to use and to fish with than the original was. Of course I cannot speak about eagle feathers which were also at one time used for this purpose. It makes you wonder why fly-dressers did not use the substitute in the first place. This soft feather makes a first class winging material for stillwaters because it is so easily moved by the smallest movement of the lure through the water. All the lures using this material seem to be effective. It should be retrieved with a short, sharp pull and then a second or two's pause, to allow the fibres to open and flutter in the water. I am certain it is this fluttering which is this material's great attraction to the trout.

This pattern is also called the Marabou (White) in the book by Ray Bergman entitled *Trout*. It is a fly that the trout will sometimes take very hard indeed: use strong leaders with this one! It is not often that I get smash takes with lures; with this fly though, it can happen. I never use a leader of 7lb breaking strain or less for this fly, and certainly not in waters where the trout can reach a decent weight.

White Marabou

Method of tying

Start the silk behind the eye and go down to the bend. There catch in a length of round silver tinsel – I generally use oval myself as I do not reckon the trout can tell the difference – for a rib. Come back up the shank again almost to the eye and catch in a length of flat silver tinsel or Lurex. If you are using the non-tarnishing Lurex or Mylar, by the way, the width that is best for fly bodies is one thirty-second of an inch; the very narrow one sixty-fourth of an inch is hopeless – it is perfectly all right for ribbing but useless for winding a smooth, flat body. Wind the tinsel down the shank to where the rib was tied in, come back up the body over the first layer to just behind the eye, tie in and trim off the surplus. Rib the body with nice evenly spaced turns then tie in and trim off the end of the ribbing tinsel.

Turn the fly over and tie in a beard or false hackle of scarlet cock hackle fibres. Turn the fly the right way up again and tie in a slighly less bulky wing than that used on the Appetiser; the fibres should also be slightly longer. You will find that the marabou fibres are much easier to tie in if you slightly moisten the butts, just the part which is to be tied in – not the whole fibres or you will end up with an awful mess. It is a peculiar thing but human saliva does not, as far as I can tell, appear to rust hooks. If they are wetted by fishing and then put back into your fly-box without drying you will find that when you go to your box next you have a superb collection of rusty hooks. However, a fly which has been moistened in the mouth and then put back in the box for some reason does not rust – funny that.

Over the top of the marabou wing tie in five strands taken from the sword feather of a peacock. As I have said many times these are one of the most difficult feathers to use which you will come across in your fly-dressing; you just have to keep trying to get these fibres to lay flat over the underwing. A tip here might help a little; *tear* the fibres off the stalk rather than cutting them. This way a small amount of stalk normally clings to the butts of the feather and this holds them together and, more importantly, at the correct angle. Try the old trick for tying in jungle cock feathers; three tight turns of silk over the feather which is tied in rather long and then you squeeze the fibres into the wing with your left hand and pull the butts through with your right until the fibres are the correct length. This sometimes – but by no means always – helps; it depends rather a lot on the particular feather you are using. One can go in perfectly and another can be a real so-and-so! Along the sides of this fly tie in two jungle cock 'eye' feathers if you have them; if not a substitute will have to do. Make a neat head and then apply first a coating of black cellulose varnish and then two or three coats of clear. That way you will end up with a lovely smooth, shiny head. I know it probably does not catch any more fish with a shiny head, but it does look good. And I find that if a fly is aesthetically pleasing I fish it with more confidence – and I think I catch more fish not because of the fly's appearance to the fish but because of the way it looks to *me*.

The Dressing:	*White Marabou*
Hooks:	6 – 10 long shank, Old Numbers
Silk:	Black
Rib:	Oval or round tinsel
Body:	Flat silver tinsel or Lurex
Hackle:	Scarlet cock
Wing:	White marabou with five strands of peacock sword feather over
Cheeks:	Jungle cock or substitute (short)

GERONIMO

When I first wrote about this fly in my column in *Angling* magazine, I said that I wanted to try it matuka style. I did so and it proved to be a very good fly. The thing to remember when converting a streamer tying into a matuka (and they are virtually all capable of conversion) is that not only must the fibres be stripped off the underside of the winging feathers but the tail must be made a lot shorter than it is on the streamers. If you do not shorten the wing and its end – which of course becomes a sort of tail – you will find that you defeat the main purpose of the conversion because the tail will still twist round under the hook point during casting and in consequence spoil the fishing action of the fly.

The thing to remember when you are tying up streamer patterns is that they were never originally intended for casting; the idea was that they should be trailed behind a canoe or small boat on big Western USA rivers for the sea-run rainbows, the steelhead. The casting was kept to a minimum and in consequence the wing-tying-itself-in-knots-round-the-hook-point problem rarely arose. We have taken these patterns and are now trying to use them in a situation for which they were never intended and in consequence we find that their performance is more than a little lacking. The Matuka style of dressing on the other hand was developed in New Zealand and was used by anglers exactly as we do in the UK; therefore they are ideal and we can convert the otherwise excellent dressings of the streamers and end up with the best of both worlds.

The Geronimo was another fly from the Harris stable. Brian has been responsible for the design of several flies and almost without exception they are good patterns. What I want to know is how come a chap who has designed so many good lures professes only to be interested in nymph fishing on stillwaters? Still, for a nymph fishing purist he is not a bad fellow.

Geronimo

Method of tying

Start the silk as usual and tie in a tail of cock hackle fibres, a fairly big bunch. These are in two colours, brown (light natural red) and yellow. Mix them as described for the tail on the Appetiser. Wind the silk back towards the eye, binding down the ends of the tail as you go. This will ensure that not only has the body a nice even bed to lie on but will fix in the tail fibres really firmly.

Just behind the eye fix in a strip of gold tinsel or Lurex and wind this down the shank to the bend making sure that all the tying silk turns at the tail-end are covered by the tinsel; a fly always looks tatty if you can see tying silk at the tail. Come back up the shank to the eye with a second layer of tinsel, tie in and trim off the surplus.

The wings are made up of four slim 'cree' marked cock hackles paired and tied in back to back. An alternative which both Brian and I like, is to use four furnace or Greenwell hackles. For the collar hackles first wind on an orange hackle that is fairly long in the fibre and when this is firmly secured wind a turn or two of silk over the base of the fibres so that they lay back at the correct angle. It should lay back nicely along the wings and hug them fairly closely. The second hackle, which is bright yellow, is wound in on the dry fly angle – almost. The silk should just, but only just, take it slightly out of the vertical. If that front hackle is wrong then one of two things will happen: the fly will not work properly, or at least not as well as it was designed to work – that is what happens if it is laid back too far. If on the other hand it is too 'dry-flyey' it will behave like one and float – not a pretty sight!

The Dressing:	Geronimo
Hooks:	8 – 12 long shank, Old Numbers
Silk:	Yellow
Tail:	Mixed, brown and yellow cock hackle
Body:	Wide gold tinsel or Lurex
Wing:	Well marked cree hackles (four)
Hackles:	Rear, long fibred orange cock; front, bright yellow cock

YELLOW FELLOW

The 'Yeller Feller' is a really bright fly, somewhat similar to the Haymaker. I have a particular liking for whipping a bright fly through just under the surface on a hot, still day and watching the bow-wave close in as a big, old rainbow comes after it. The two best flies I have found for this are the Parmachene Belle and another American fly (only this time a streamer, not a wet fly like the Parma' Belle) the Chief Needabeh. To get the adrenalin flowing there is nothing like this fly-following wake and the gentle take that finally almost always comes if you manage to control yourself and not pull the fly out of his mouth.

The advice I commonly give to anyone who is trying this type of fishing – or pulling a sedge across the top during a hatch –

for the first time is 'as soon as you see a trout following *close your eyes*'; you will miss a lot of excitement but the odds are that you will catch the trout, because the first indication you will get is when the line goes taut and you feel the pull. Later on you can learn to control your impatience; it can seem a long, long time that the fish is following the fly when in reality it is only a few seconds. I can never understand it when people tell me that they get smash takes when using lures. I think I could count the number of times this has happened to me on one hand, the reason being I believe, that the trout is following along more or less directly behind the fly and his momentum softens what would perhaps otherwise have been a violent take. You can quite easily get smashed if you cast across a trout's path and pull a fly past his nose; then the takes really are savage.

Our yellow friend is also a very useful fly when the water is very coloured; Woodford bank at Chew Valley lake after a strong, persistent wind has been blowing from a southerly quarter for a few days springs to mind – it can be just like brown Windsor soup! I think in these soupy conditions there are three possible answers: you can go and fish the opposite bank with the wind at your back and very few fish in front of you; or

Yellow Fellow

you can put on a very dark pattern such as my Ace of Spades or a Black Lure which shows up really well in thick conditions; or you can go to the other extreme and select a really bright pattern, and from my skin-diving days, I seem to remember that no colour shows up better in murky water than yellow.

Method of tying
Use precisely the same technique to dress this fly that you used for the Geronimo; the only thing that changes is the colour of the materials. There is one point that has emerged since I first wrote about this fly; several people who have used it tell me that it works even better if black tying-silk is used and eyes are painted on the sides of the head using a dab of white varnish with a black or red centre. The last one sounds as if it might resemble the eyes of that character that stares back out of the shaving mirror at me after a hard night with the lads discussing the latest fly-fishing techniques over the odd Scotch or three.

The Dressing:	*Yellow Fellow*
Hooks:	10 long shank, Old Numbers
Silk:	Yellow
Tail:	White baby wool
Body:	Silver Lurex or tinsel
Wing:	Four slim, bright yellow cock hackles
Hackles:	Rear, well marked badger cock; front, short fibred yellow cock

HAYMAKER

John Young and I were sitting in a boat at Bough Beech reservoir on a hot morning; the sky was blue after weeks of rain, the water was a flat calm and no fish were inclined to feed. I was John's guest and it was the first time I had fished this water with him. We were over the deep water by the dam and I had put on a bright yellow fly that I was trying out; it was a new design and one that I thought might prove useful in the algae-thick water – you needed something bright, something that would attract a trout's attention from more than just a few inches away. The lazily-retrieved fly appeared through the murky haze and there

174

following it was a long dark shape, his nose glued to the lure. He was following literally half-an-inch behind it but he would not take. I tried speeding up the retrieve – nothing. I tried a quick pull with a slight pause – nothing. He just sat on the end of that yellow fly and looked at it; there was no way that he was going to eat it. Finally, I ran out of water and arm and the fish sheered off as the fly came really close to the boat – even the long, smooth end-of-retrieve slide through the water would not induce a take. John was watching all this as fascinated as I was but at the same time he was watching the weather. John is a farmer and he was thinking about the hay that would be drying off nicely in the sunshine. Finally he decided; he had to go. I thought it was pretty disgusting that a chap should put work before fishing but I have found over the years that these farming types get obsessive about the weather. Haymaking weather is haymaking weather and that was it.

John left me and I went back to have another try for my big brownie, but he was not going to have any of it. I feel that he thought nearly making a fool of himself once was enough for one day. I ended up drifting over the deep water and I still kept on with the yellow lure – it accounted for a limit of fish without any real effort, one being a very nice brown of well over 3lb, although I reckon he was less than half the weight of the fellow

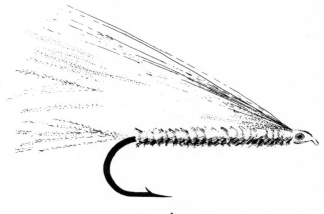

Haymaker

that had followed the fly up from the depths. Still, it was a very interesting and enjoyable day that was only marred by the fact that my host had been forced to leave early.

There really was no other name I could give this fly – the Haymaker it had to be. I have used it quite often since, when the water is dirty or algae blooms cut down visibility, and it does seem to be very effective.

Method of tying

Commence in the usual way and once the silk is down to the bend tie in a bunch of bright yellow marabou fibres for a tail. Also catch in a length of bright yellow chenille. Do not forget that this material has to have the fluffy outer portion stripped off a quarter of an inch of the central core, and it is just this core that you tie in. Wind the silk back to the eye and follow this with the chenille covering the butt-ends of the marabou as you go. Tie in and trim, leaving enough room for the wing – say an eighth of an inch or so.

There is no hackle on this pattern so tie in a fairly large bunch of yellow marabou as an underwing and over the top of this a small bunch of yellow dyed bucktail. Although I specify bucktail it does not really matter what hair it is – it is only there to stop the wayward marabou feather from going all over the place.

Run a coat of yellow varnish over the head, which should be fairly pronounced, and when this has dried paint on an eye on each side using a dubbing needle; first a coat of scarlet varnish and then a dot of black in the centre. It makes quite an attractive, if somewhat gaudy, fly.

The Dressing:	Haymaker
Hooks:	6 – 10 long shank, Old Numbers
Silk:	Black or yellow
Tail:	Bright yellow marabou
Body:	Yellow chenille
Underwing:	Yellow marabou
Overwing:	Yellow bucktail etc.
Head:	Yellow varnish
Eye:	Red varnish with black centre

CHAPTER TEN

MATUKAS

Of all the many types of lure that I have used over the years,
without doubt the Matukas have been the most consistently
successful. I should perhaps explain here that when I use the term
Matukas I am really referring to the *style* of dressing, with the
wings tied down, rather than any particular fly. Once, when I
omitted to say that I got half-a-dozen letters from irate readers in
New Zealand where this style of dressing originated. The name
Matuka comes from the bird of that name from which the
original winging feather was obtained. It is a member of the
bittern family and due to the popularity of these flies they were
put in real danger of extinction. This is perhaps the only single
species which I can think of where this has happened. Happily,
this decline has been halted for they are now completely
protected by law.

The normal substitute now used is the round-tipped flank
feathers from a hen pheasant. Many different feathers are used to
dress this type of fly, with hackles (hen or cock) coming a close
second to hen pheasant in popularity. Incidentally, hen pheasant
seems to me to make a better looking and more effective fly than
the original, which has got to be good news for this branch of
the bittern family! I have used partridge tail feathers, silver
pheasant, vulturine guinea fowl hackles and grouse as well as
several others. I am in the process of experimenting with wood
pigeon at the moment. It has always annoyed me that this bird,
the shotgunners' delight, does not supply feathers for one single
pattern of fly, unless, that is, you include the use of 'woodie's'
feathers as a rather bad substitute for heron. I *will* find an
effective pattern if it kills me.

When an ordinary lure or streamer pattern is cast there is a
great tendency for the wing to twist round and catch under the

hook-point; the fly then swims in a lopsided manner and I feel no confidence at all in its ability to catch fish in that condition. The Matukas overcome this problem to a very large extent; it is not one hundred per cent (would you believe ninety-five?), but it certainly helps when the wing is secured along the top of the body by the ribbing tinsel. The optimum length of the tail (or the end of the wing) to help stop this problem seems to be about one-third of the body length, and if the tail is kept to this length or shorter you should experience very little difficulty with this problem. The only exception which I do make to this is the Vulture, where I feel it needs a much longer tail. I have tried this fly with a shorter tail and it has proved to be nowhere near as useful. The tail should be about the same length as the body on this pattern.

On most of the New Zealand patterns it is rare to see a hackle used; in fact most of the samples of 'down-under' Matuka-type flies that I have seen tended to be fairly crude. Not that I think that the lack of a hackle makes a fly crude, but the coarseness of the hooks used and the general lumpiness of the dressings does nothing for me aesthetically. I will now sit back and wait to be deluged by dozens of beautifully dressed Antipodean Matukas. The hooks that I have seen used are what the United Kingdom angler would think of as eel hooks; these are normally the very strong, thick-wired Limerick type of hook and nearly always short-shanked. A long-shank hook makes a much more attractive fly (at least to my eyes, and I think the trout tend to agree with me, having been provided with several opportunities to try both types) and gives a much more pleasing shape to the pattern. The addition of a hackle can, on many Matukas, be a great advantage because it gives another flash of colour and therefore allows more scope for experimentation by the fly-dresser.

Since using the Matuka style of dressing my lure results have improved enormously; I am certain that if you try them you will agree with me. They appear to be difficult to dress when you have to wind the ribbing material through the wing fibres but with a little practice this becomes quite simple, and very worthwhile.

VULTURE MATUKA

This is a lure which I have used fairly extensively and with excellent results; it is another pattern invented by Brian Harris – or more correctly, he invented a streamer version and I promptly converted it to my favourite lure style, the Matuka.

I have found that generally speaking a nice steady, medium-paced retrieve seems to bring the best results. I try to smooth out the pauses in between pulls as much as possible so that the fly comes through the water at an even pace; this, incidentally, is one reason that trolling works well. I realise it is not fly-fishing as such, and is highly illegal on some waters, but this does not alter the fact that this technique does catch trout! I have tried various methods of retrieve to get this result but they all seem to have their limitations. I should be grateful to hear from anyone who has found a *really* successful method of keeping the fly coming in steadily without pauses and without winding in on the reel. I am sure we have all caught fish when winding the line back in. Sometimes the trout want a steady retrieve and you can have been fishing normally all day without a fish showing the slightest interest in your flies; you pack up at the end of the day, wind the line back and it all goes tight on you . . . 'Why didn't I try that before?' Too late, the day is done. 'Next time I'll remember to try it' and of course next time it does not work.

The main problem you are going to have with this fly is in obtaining the winging feathers, Vulturine guinea fowl hackles (the name, you see, has nothing whatever to do with those nice little dicky-birds that follow folks hopefully about in desert country). They tend not only to be rather rare but also a shade on

Vulture Matuka

the expensive side; still, once you have got a cape you have got it and it will last a fair time.

Brian invented this pattern for Grafham primarily, and his idea was to give a vague imitation of a roach fly. I have found that it works very well on several other reservoirs but just what the trout take it for I really could not say. It certainly does not look much like a young roach to me, but then I am not a trout!

The winging feathers strip and tie in nicely to make this Matuka and I certainly do not think that by dressing this streamer (or any other streamer for that matter) in my preferred Matuka-style you lose any of the effectiveness of the pattern; in fact the reverse seems to be the case. The attractiveness of more lightly dressed flies is well known and by the removal of the bottom halves of the wing fibres you lighten the effect of the wing considerably. You also dress a fly which is much less worrysome to cast.

I had a lovely day at Weirwood with this fly some years ago. The wind was really howling down the reservoir, the boat was drifting fast, but straight, right down the length of the water, there was a slight overcast and a really high wave; the trout were hitting the fly as it came through the wave-crests. I was having a clear view of all the action, and those slashing takes right up at the surface were really something to see.

Method of tying
Start the tying silk at the eye and carry it down to the bend. Tie in a fair-sized bunch of hot-orange cock hackle fibres for a tail; they should be about half the length of the hook shank. At the same point fix in the ribbing tinsel. Brian seems fond of the fine grade of Lurex for his ribs, and certainly this material is a great favourite of mine, but I find that this fine Lurex breaks all too easily – even the one thirty-second of an inch Lurex is none too strong. It does however make splendid bodies on flies such as the Butcher series. I feel that on lures the rib is perhaps better made from the much stronger oval tinsels. In these days of soaring prices I may perhaps be out of line when I say that I think that, with certain flies (like the Butchers), it is perhaps better to risk a body which will perhaps be cut by a trout's teeth rather than not

having the fish take the fly in the first place. I think that an angler has had good value from a fly if he has caught a fish on it. Every fish on that fly after the first is therefore – in my book at any rate – a bonus.

With most lures, though, I do not feel that fairly minor points, such as the type of ribbing material, are not of paramount importance and in this case where an angler is paying perhaps two or three times as much for his lure as he would for his wet fly he would feel somewhat cheated to catch only one fish on it.

The body material is chenille and you can use my standard method of tying this in – strip off a quarter of an inch from the central core and just tie the cotton in. This way you avoid giving the fly a lumpy behind. Wind the chenille up the shank being careful to keep each turn tight up to its predecessor but not overlapping. Fix the chenille about a quarter of an inch back from the eye.

Strip off the fibres from nearly all the bottom sections of two Vulturine hackles, leaving just the tips intact. Tie in the hackle feathers by the stalk. Start ribbing at the tail and carefully separate the fibres and then bind the stalk down on top of the body with the tinsel. Work your way along the wing until you get to the point where you tied in the stalks, fix and trim off the rib.

Turn the fly over in the vice and tie in the usual false hackle of the same material as the tail. Make a neat head and then run on a coat of scarlet varnish; allow this to dry thoroughly and then apply a couple of coats of clear. This is a fly that the trout normally take confidently; I think that the red head makes a striking point for the fish and therefore usually the fly is well into the fish's mouth, so you do not often get little tweaks and plucks with this pattern.

The Dressing:	*Vulture Matuka*
Hooks:	4 – 8 long shank, Old Numbers
Silk:	Black or red
Tail:	Hot-orange cock hackle
Rib:	Fine silver Lurex or oval silver tinsel
Body:	White chenille

Hackle:	As for tail
Wing:	Two vulturine guinea fowl hackles
Head:	Red varnish

BROWN BOMBER

During April 1977 my brother Don came back to England after some twenty-three years in Rhodesia – now Zimbabwe. Luckily, I managed to show him some really good trout fishing, otherwise my name – and that of British fly-fishing in general – would have been mud! He would, I am sure, have gone back to fishing his 'dams' (these are in fact reservoirs into many of which you could drop Rutland Water many times over) with such disgusting contraptions as bubble-floats. Apparently a bait-casting rod and reel are used to heave out a plastic bubble-float, half filled with water, and behind this is towed a fly. When I tried to tell him, via the cassettes with which we correspond, that this approach was perhaps not the most subtle, he seemed somewhat surprised.

When he arrived here I naturally wanted to initiate him into the pleasures of 'proper' trout fishing with the real gear, so we went to Weirwood reservoir. Don had come from tropical climes about three days earlier and the weather forecast for our first trip was not perhaps the most propitious. We stood all day, thigh-deep in ice-cold water and not a single trout showed the slightest interest in our flies. The gale howled down the reservoir. Weirwood, when it is cold and bleak, can be *very* bleak indeed! My brother's line-holding finger kept going numb from the cold, and he found that the only cure for this was to dunk it in a flask of hot soup for a few seconds; that seemed to thaw it out for an hour or so, not that it did much for the soup. It was so cold and the fish so unresponsive that by 4 pm we decided that we had suffered enough and departed. From all the anglers on the North bank that we asked only one had taken one small trout. There was silence all the way home! Next time, I decided, would just *have* to be different.

And luckily it was – press day at the new Bewl Bridge reservoir in Kent, in late April. The weather looked good, the boats were well equipped and, most important of all, the fish

182

Brown Bomber

White & Orange Matuka

Hanningfield Lure

Black Muddler Minnow

Silver Muddler Minnow

Texas Rose Muddler Minnow

Red Setter

Fuzzy-Wuzzy

Baby Doll

Jersey Herd

Stoat's Tail   Hairy Mary   Jock Scott (tube)

Avon Eagle (tube)   Usk Grub

Silver Doctor   Black Doctor

Silver Grey (salmon)   Black Goldfinch

Spring Blue   Green Highlander

were in a feeding mood. When we came in to an excellent buffet lunch we had both taken some nice fish; a bottle of wine and a good meal later we went out again, and this time we both filled our limits with no problems.

The fly that did the damage was my Ace of Spades. This is a Matuka-style dressing, and without doubt it has been my most consistently successful lure. I have used it all over the country and it has nearly always come up trumps – pun intended! We found that a long cast was needed, so we used shooting-heads backed with what is without doubt the finest shooting line available – braided monofilament. This material just does not seem to tangle at all; if the occasional small knot forms, you merely pull one end and it falls out. I find that I suffer far more, and worse, tangles when using weight-forward full fly-lines than I ever do using heads backed with braided mono'.

The style of retrieve that the fish wanted at Bewl Bridge seemed to be a long, slow pull, so that the fly was coming back a foot or so sub-surface. We got pluck, pluck, pluck – then wallop. This was why the long casts were needed; the fish were following a long way and just pulling at the fly before really taking hold. The secret was to totally ignore the plucks and just keep the fly coming at a steady pace; if you speeded up the retrieve, slowed it down, or worst of all, struck, that was it – all over, fish gone.

I think I have now found a combination of tackle, technique and I suppose a certain amount of expertise that allows me to throw a fly far farther than I ever could previously. Now I use a gunwale-high seat which is very comfortable, so that I can sit in the boat all day without suffering, a couple of Diamondback rods fitted with single-leg Fuji rings, and a number 6 or 7 AFTM shooting-head backed with Shakespeare 5000 – or its current equivalent – braided mono'. My leader length for lure fishing is normally four or five yards. I have measured a pull from the stripping ring to my full arm extension and it is a shade over a yard. In the middle of a day's casting I have counted the number of pulls needed to bring the fly-line to hand, and they seem to vary between twenty three and twenty eight. An average, say, of twenty five, plus thirteen yards of head and four yards of leader.

Brown Bomber

No matter how you work it out, that is well over forty yards virtually every cast, with very little effort indeed required. Certainly far less than would be needed to extend twenty five yards of double-taper line. I use at most two false casts and then out it sails. Just on the final shoot my left hand gives a hard downward pull to speed up the line and that is it. I find I do not need to double-haul as such; that single final pull is enough to get the line really travelling.

After a six-week holiday, Don and his wife Jean went back to Rhodesia and as he remarked to me, to 'some decent warm weather' – that was a particularly rotten English spring he chose to come visiting. A tape arrived a month or so later and he suggested that the Ace of Spades might do better in Africa if it was tied in brown. I gave it a bit of thought and came up with a very similar design to the original but using brown materials. I was dubious because, as we all know, black is not only beautiful but it catches an awful lot of fish on the English reservoirs, whereas brown has nothing like the same reputation.

I went again to Bewl to test out the new fly. Bank fishing in the early morning I had two fish to a Gold Ribbed Hares Ear nymph, both nice brownies. Once I got out in the boat I found I had to work relatively hard to catch one rainbow on the Ace of Spades and I then missed a couple that 'fell off', so I decided to try Don's brown job. It was a case of virtually every throw a coconut, and really nice fish too, three of them all over 1¾lb and they all fought very hard.

Brown is now beautiful, too!

Method of tying

Start the fly in the normal way by carrying the tying silk from eye to bend. There you catch in a length of heavy copper wire and a piece of brown chenille. Wind the chenille up the shank to make a smooth body with no gaps between turns. Bear in mind that chenille has a 'grain', so make certain that the point of the grain faces towards the fly when you tie it in; it looks slightly like an arrowhead if you hold it up to the light. Trim off the surplus at the eye.

Take two brown hen hackles, place them back to back (that is concave side to concave side) and strip off most of the fibres on the underside. Leave enough to make a reasonable tail, say a third of the body length. I used to believe that about half of the length of the body was about right but in the light of experience I have now changed my mind and I think a quarter to a third are plenty for the tail. Tie the hackles in at the eye, making sure that the wing sits vertically along the body in the style of a crest. Part the fibres, working from the tail end, and use the wire to bind down the stalks to the body, keeping the wing upright all the time and spacing the turns of rib evenly. Tie off the rib and trim at the eye.

The hackles consist of two fairly heavy bunches of cock pheasant centre tail fibre tips tied in so that they lay along each side of the body, not underneath. These hackles, applied in this way, seem to give the fly very good stability and it seems to swim steadier than with the normal false hackle. It is the same system I use on my nymph pattern the Water Tiger. (see *Fly-dressing*).

Take a wide strip of bronze mallard flank feather, trim off any of the stalk that may be left clinging to the base of the slip and then straighten out the tips of the fibres so that they are as level as possible without splitting the strip up. Then, carefully fold the slip over the top of the hackle wings so that it reaches almost the length of the body and tie it in as you would with a normal wet fly wing.

Wind a smooth head and apply several coats of clear varnish until the head comes up neat and shiny.

The Dressing:	Brown Bomber
Hooks:	4 – 10 long shank, Old Numbers
Silk:	Brown (Sherry Spinner)
Rib:	Heavy copper wire
Body:	Brown chenille
Wing:	Brown hen hackle
Hackles:	Two bunches of cock pheasant centre tail fibres on sides
Overwing:	Bronze mallard

WHITE AND ORANGE MATUKA

I have always avoided like the plague buying a season ticket on a reservoir. This is because I have felt that if you speculate quite a large sum of money on a season ticket the natural reaction is to make as much use of it as possible to get full value. This is fine if you do not have writing committments as I do. However, if you were in my position you would find that your readers would get very annoyed if you only wrote about one or two waters; you have to spread yourself around a bit.

The one exception I have made to this rule was during this current season (1980) at Ardingly reservoir in Sussex. Now that Weirwood has been taken away from the trout angler this lovely lake is the only water of any size that I have within easy driving distance of home, so I can make the ticket pay for itself by going along for an hour or two in the evenings and on a Sunday morning. This is the only reason I took the season permit for this year and it has more than paid for itself, not just in fish but in the extra enjoyment and the convenience I have had in being able to slip along for just a few hours. Notwithstanding the convenience of these tickets, they still tend to make you concentrate on the one fishery, and for a writer that just is not good enough. I doubt that I shall do it again.

Towards the back-end of the 1979 season – the first for Ardingly – the fishing got to be pretty tough; even the regulars were struggling. The same old crowd got down there each Sunday morning but where earlier in the year we had been arriving at 6 am and departing at 8 am with a limit of nice fish, now we were having to make do with the odd brace of fish and working all morning for them. Times were hard – except that is for one chap. (Have you ever noticed that there is always *one* fellow who can manage to extract fish when all around him is nothing but failure and despondency – the secret is to get to be that man.) This time though it was even more aggravating for the successful angler was not any grizzled old-timer who had learnt it all over many years' hard slog – no, this was a young 'un who was whipping us, all fourteen years of him. He was pulling into trout as if he knew their first names. It turned out that not only was he an extremely competent angler, a good caster and he got up early enough to ensure that he always occupied a prime spot, but he had a secret weapon; a fly – not all that much of a fly at first glance but nonetheless very effective for all that. It was a white lure, a very small white lure, about a size 10 long shank. This he was retrieving just sub-surface using a floating line and with a small split-shot pinched on above the first leader knot to get the line-wake away from the fly and to slightly sink it. The trout were loving it.

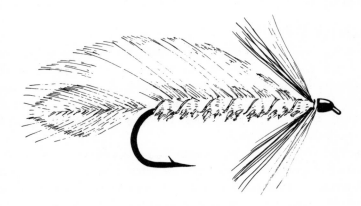

White and Orange Matuka

As is usual with any free-winged streamer-type lure the wings are the bother and they do their usual wing-wrapping-around-the-hook-point act. I did my normal conversion job and turned out a Matuka version that during the latter part of the 1979 and

189

the whole of the 1980 season has proved to be a real killer. I prefer to fish the big reservoirs from a boat; I like the fact that I can drift and so cover fresh trout all the time, and it also enables me to cart along the mountains of gear that I seem to need. I enjoy catching trout from the banks, certainly this is the case on the smaller stillwater fisheries – but generally speaking I find a boat better on the big waters. This fly cast across wind from a drifting boat has really been moving the fish for me. It is even more effective if you can spot fish just under the surface, cast to them and then pull this little lure across their noses; they cannot resist that.

Strangely, this pattern has not done a thing for me when I have tried it down deep; maybe I have just chosen the wrong times to try it but it only seems to work in the surface water – mind you, I am not complaining. I would much prefer to see all the action, anyway – I do not find it very inspiring to just have the line go tight on me as a fish hangs on down deep. That is not to say that I will not go deep to catch trout – I often do, sometimes using the dreaded lead-core line – but I, like many others, prefer to catch my fish off the top. It is where the fun is at.

Method of tying
Run your silk from the eye to the bend after pulling the first four or five inches through a ball of wax to stop it slipping on the hook-shank. At the bend catch in a length of oval silver tinsel and a piece of white chenille. Wind a neat chenille body leaving a fair amount of space at the eye so that you have room to wind on a couple of hackles later on.

Strip two-thirds of the bottom sections of fibres from a pair of white hen hackles and then tie the butts in at the eye. Separate the fibres at the tail-end by easing them forward, then wind one turn of ribbing tinsel through them and pull the fibres back over the tail so that they now lay correctly, at the same time keeping a firm hold of the rib. Come forward and separate off a small section of the hackle fibres and again take a turn of the rib, binding the hackle-stalk firmly down on to the top of the body. Work your way along the length of the hook and then tie off and trim the surplus where the body ends. The main things to make certain are that the turns of rib are really firm, that they are evenly spaced and that they lay at the same angle, one to the other. If you have got all that right you should end up with a good fly. If you have not got it right then you had better try it again until you *do* get it correct. There is no substitute for practice; nobody gets to be a good fly-dresser without putting the hours in.

The hackling is easy; you simply wind on two hackles together, a hot-orange one at the back and a white one at the front. I normally use cock hackles rather than hen; this is because hen hackles are rather more difficult to get hold off so I would rather save those for the winging. The blending of the orange and white gives a pleasing, muted, pale orange shade. Finish the fly as normal.

I have only tried this pattern for one-and-a-bit seasons so I do not know if it is going to be a permanent winner, but I have every reason to believe it will be. So often a fly comes along which produces big catches all one season and then dies the death the following year; I cannot explain it but it certainly happens with many new fly patterns. I do not think it will with this one however.

The Dressing:	*White and Orange Matuka*
Hooks:	8 – 10 long shank, Old Numbers
Silk:	Black
Rib:	Oval silver tinsel
Body:	White chenille
Wings:	White hen's hackles
Hackles:	Orange and white cock hackle wound together

CHAPTER ELEVEN

MULTI-HOOK LURES

HANNINGFIELD LURE

My feelings about multi-hook lures are fairly strong – I *do not* like them generally speaking. For a start, professional fly-dressers have to charge too much for them because the mounts are so time-consuming to make up and once the thing is dressed the wings have that unhappy tendency to wrap themselves round the hook-points during casting, thus making them swim lop-sided. My final objection is that ever present weak link where the two hooks are joined, and it is even worse with three hooks. I think however that with the advent of braided monofilament and the availability of Super Glue and the other cyanoacrylates this last problem has pretty well been solved. For all my junctions on multi-hook mounts I now use braided mono' and I have yet to have one slip, so my confidence is now starting to build up in this method – but this still leaves the other two objections.

If a census was taken of all the trout caught in the United Kingdom each season I am convinced that at least eighty per cent of them come out on lures and of that percentage perhaps half are taken on multi-hook lures. Gradually we (that is most of the angling writers) are getting the angling public to switch to the long-shank hooks as used for Hairwings, Matukas, etc. There have been a lot of red herrings flung about, with people saying that the fish can apply leverage to a long-shank hook that he cannot apply to a normal length hook, but to that I would only say one thing – rubbish. To apply leverage you must first have something firm to apply pressure to, and you must also have a fulcrum. The only way I can remember losing trout on long-shank hooks (aside from trout that just 'fall off') is when they spin and the hook catches in the net. I have lost the occasional fish like that, but I think that the same thing could happen with any hook, long-shank or short. Generally speaking then I am for long-shanked lures and agin' multis'.

One problem arises with long-shanked lures, however, and this is when you come up against a lure which appears to be effective only when it is dressed in the multi-hook version and does not work when a conversion job is done; such a fly is the Hanningfield Lure. I have tried a single hook version and the trout promptly ignored it; as soon as I returned to the two hook lure I started catching again.

This fly was invented by Dick Walker as an imitation of the colours on a small perch. Aside from trout this is also a very good pattern on which to catch perch, as I have proved at Ardingly – very often.

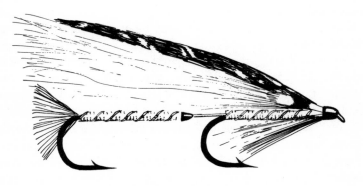

Hanningfield Lure

I think I should be perfectly happy to restrict my choice of multi-hook lures to just three: the Black Lure, the White Lure and this beastie. Compared with the other two this one looks very complicated to dress but really it is relatively simple.

Method of tying
The fist thing you have to do is to make up the mount and this, from the professional's point of view, is where the time is spent and is the reason that multi-hook lures – at least lures that are really made properly – have to cost quite a lot of money. You get nothing for nothing in this life.

Dick says that the best junction is made by plaiting three strands of 12lb test monofil' together. This works well but I think he would now agree with me that the braided monofilament is a lot better and quicker. All I do is to bind silk down the shank and up again on a long-shank hook that has had the eye snipped off with the cutting-edge of a pair of pliers. I then feed this shank up the centre of a short length – say two or three inches – of braided monofilament; it is quite easy to do as braided monofil' is hollow. I then apply a coat of Super Glue to the outside of the braid and this soaks straight through because the braid is open weave. It locks everything up tight and even if left at that the junction will not slip – at least the ones I have tried have held firm. However, to make doubly sure I now whip tying silk in two layers up and down the hook while the adhesive is still wet, and that *really* fixes it.

The front hook again is whipped in open turns and then the braided mono' is carefully laid along the top of the shank and whipped down tightly. Glue is applied and then the end of the braid is laid back over itself and whipped down again, effectively locking it into position. When I have tried to pull a junction apart with just the straight whipped joint and without doubling it over I have never managed to shift it, but with clients' flies I like to make completely sure so I double it. The braid is fairly rough so the silk finds plenty of sufaces to grip but I am pretty certain that just the glueing would probably hold all right. However, better safe than sorry – eh?

After the mount is completed the next job is the tail. Dick's idea for this is very neat and easy and, as with so many of his ideas, original. You carry the silk down to the bend of the rear hook where you tie in an orange hackle, wind several turns inside the bend, tie in and trim off the surplus. Draw your forefinger and thumb back along the hook and pull all the fibres back behind the hook and then, taking one cut with sharp scissors, trim the fibres off square so that they reach slightly past the bend of the hook. A nice neat tail results which is not at all the normal type of tail. In future if I design any more lures, I am going to keep this method in mind – it really is most effective.

After completing the tail, tie in the ribbing tinsel and carry the silk up the shank to the joint. Catch in a strand of Daylight Fluorescent white wool and wind this down the hook to the tail and then come back up again over the first layer and tie in and trim off where it was first fixed. Rib the body with nice even turns of the oval tinsel. Make a neat whip finish, varnish the whip, and hang the half fly up so that the varnish gets a chance to dry off thoroughly. You can always be doing another while this is happening.

When the varnish is really hard on the rear hook set the front hook in the vice and again wind the silk down to the bend; in fact you now repeat exactly what you did on the rear hook, except that you do not varnish the head yet and of course you omit the tail. When the body and ribbing are completed the fly is turned over in the vice to receive the false hackle, which is in two sections. The first to be applied is the longer hackle of hot orange cock and in front of this you tie in a slightly shorter fibred beard of bright blue cock hackle. Turn the fly the right way up again.

The wing is of white goat hair tied in to reach almost to the tail and over this a roof wing of a single strip of speckled turkey feather is laid. This wants to be rather dark; I use the lower part of the feather that provides the white tipped turkey for the salmon-fly underwings – waste not want not, I reckon.

Either side of the wing tie in a jungle cock eye feather or a substitute. I did try painting on eyes either side of the head but it did not seem as effective. Keep the jungle cock feathers fairly short. Whip-finish the head and apply varnish until it is nice and smooth and shiny.

The Dressing:	*Hanningfield Lure*
Hooks:	8 long shank, Old Numbers; Dick specifies silvered but I prefer bronze
Silk:	Black
Tail:	Hot orange cock, wound and clipped
Rib:	Silver thread (oval silver tinsel)
Bodies:	White fluorescent wool or nylon
Hackles:	Orange and blue cock
Wing:	White goat hair with speckled turkey over
Sides:	Jungle cock or substitute

CHAPTER TWELVE

MUDDLER MINNOWS

BLACK MUDDLER

In my first book, *Fly-dressing*, I discussed the standard, gold-bodied version of the Muddler Minnow, and in writing of that pattern I said that I preferred a ball-shaped head. Tom Saville took me to task in my original article in *Angling* magazine and said that the head, to be at its best, should be cylindrical. In the intervening period I have changed my views considerably, not to Tom's viewpoint but to Dick Walker's. Dick said that he found the best shaped Muddler head to be cone-shaped, and now I am pretty sure he was right – as usual. I have done considerable experimentation with all three shapes and the cone came out on top by quite a wide margin; in an election the others would have lost their deposits!

The Black Muddler is a Richard Walker pattern and I know it has proved to be a very effective fly for many anglers; I have tried it a few times but it has not produced any very special results for me as yet. This is the problem of course when an angler is in the position that I am, writing about fishing and fly-dressing; there are only so many flies that you can use and like everyone else I have my favourites. I test what patterns I can personally but quite often I have to rely on customers and friends telling me how they get on with particular flies, and so it has been with the Black Muddler.

Method of tying

This fly is started in the normal Muddler fashion by tying in the silk about a third of the way down the shank – that allows you to spin the deer body hair freely on the bare hook-shank – and taken down to the bend where the ribbing tinsel is caught in. The silk is then taken back up the shank and a piece of black floss

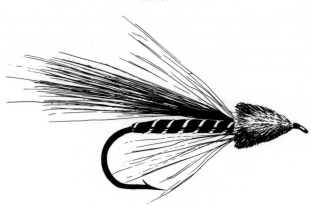

Black Muddler

silk is tied in; this is then wound down the hook and then taken back up again to the point where it was first tied in, making a smooth double layer of silk. There it is tied in and trimmed. I prefer to make my bodies a slight carrot shape, but Dick seems to use mostly level bodies; I doubt if it makes much difference but I think my shape looks better.

Once the body is applied satisfactorily you rib it with the tinsel and tie in and trim off the surplus at the right-hand end. A fairly hefty bunch of black dyed squirrel tail fibres are now tied in and a couple of locking turns can be applied round the roots of just the hair. If you decide to use locking turns you will find them quite satisfactory but nowadays I just trim off the ends of the fibres neatly and put a smear of Super Glue over the butts and this locks them in even more securely. If you use the glueing method you must put the fly away for a few minutes before applying the deer hair otherwise the glue will stick to the deer hair and it will not spin – I know!

The deer hair is now applied by taking two loose turns of tying silk over a pretty hefty bunch of the stuff and then tightening the silk with a downward pull, with the result that the hair flares round the shank. Remember, though, that the hair will not flare properly unless you do this on a bare shank – it will not do it over silk. When you trim up the head on this fly there is no ruff of hairs left at the rear of the head as there is on

197

the normal patterns. Dick prefers to have the heads on his Muddlers rather longer than the normal ones, which was why I suggested that a space of a third of the shank should be left silk-free rather than the more usual quarter.

The Dressing:	*Black Muddler*
Hooks:	8 long shank, Old Numbers
Silk:	Black
Rib:	Fine oval silver tinsel
Body:	Black floss silk
Wing:	Dyed black squirrel tail
Head:	Deer body hair

SILVER MUDDLER

This pattern, as far as I know, was my idea; at least I have not seen anybody else write about it to date. This fly has sometimes been very effective indeed – not always, but then what fly is? – but certainly often enough for it to warrant you dressing some. There was a day when I had several fish follow a standard pattern almost up to the boat but they just would not take it. I was using a floating line with the lure fishing just sub-surface and you could see a dorsal fin break water behind the fly – it was difficult not to get very excited indeed! The trout would follow about three or four inches behind the fly and when the speed of the retrieve was altered the fish just kept the gap the same. However excitement changed to annoyance with my inability to induce a take. It was dead frustrating I can tell you!

I got pretty fed up with this after it had happened half a dozen times and I decided to switch flies – but, what to, that was my problem. I looked through my lure box and because they obviously wanted a biggish fly I tied on a Sweeney Todd, with no result whatever; it was completely ignored. It was then that I remembered all the fiddling about with Muddlers during the close season; maybe one of those would turn the trick: I tied on the silver bodied version without any expectation of success; perhaps the blighters were just having a let's-drive-Collyer-out-of-his-mind kind of a day. I have noticed they do this every once in a while just to cut me down to size, and very effective it is too

– knocks the old ego about no end. Anyway, on went the new fly and I cast it to the same spot where the fish had been showing previously. Wallop, and number one was on after just one pull of the line. From then on it was nice consistent sport; not one of those days when it is a fish every cast, but very pleasant and consistent, a fish every quarter of an hour or so – just the way I like my fish spaced in fact. I packed in about lunch-time with an eight-fish limit bag which, according to my quite fallible memory, weighed about fourteen or fifteen pounds – very nice.

Silver Muddler

Method of tying
Leave the normal Muddler gap at the front of the hook and then wind the waxed end of the silk down the shank to a point just before where the bend starts to curve. Tie in a tail of two slips taken from opposing feathers from an oak turkey wing. After that tie in a length of oval silver tinsel and run the silk back up the shank to where it was first tied in. Catch in a length of flat silver tinsel or Lurex and wind this down the shank to where the tail was fixed. Make certain that the tinsel covers all turns of silk at the tail-end, otherwise it looks decidedly scruffy. Rib the flat tinsel body with the ribbing tinsel, tie in and trim off the surplus.
  A wing of brown squirrel tail fibres is now tied in and locked into place with either locking turns of silk or with a cyano-

acrylate adhesive. Tie in a wing of oak turkey over the hair-wing. Now spin on a head and ruff of deer hair, making certain that the first bunch of deer hair you tie in faces towards the tail of the fly because you want to leave as many of the tapered tips of the fibres pointing towards the back as you possibly can. Fill the entire clear space at the front of the hook with hair and then trim it to shape with sharp scissors, being very careful to leave a ruff of the pointed fibres all round the rear portion of the head.

The Dressing:	*Silver Muddler*
Hooks:	4 – 12 long shank, Old Numbers
Silk:	Brown (Sherry Spinner)
Tail:	Oak turkey wing
Rib:	Oval silver tinsel
Body:	Flat silver tinsel or Lurex
Underwing:	Brown squirrel tail
Wing:	As for tail
Ruff and Head:	Deer body hair

TEXAS ROSE MUDDLER

This fly is another of our Dick's patterns; at least it is one that he popularised in the United Kingdom, although I do not believe he designed it. This fly does very well if it is fished really fast just sub-surface on a floating line. The best method is to use a shooting head and to squeeze on a split-shot a foot or two up the

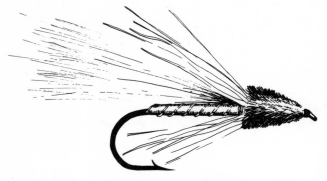

Texas Rose Muddler

leader; this just sinks the fly and reduces the wake so that it does not scare the fish. Sometimes it is better to leave out the split-shot if you are fishing from a drifting boat and the wind is really blowing; then the fly wants to create as much wake as possible as it skims the wave-crests. This really is fascinating fishing if you can see the fish as they come for the fly.

The method of dressing this pattern is precisely the same as for the Black version so I shall not repeat it here. Merely change the materials.

The Dressing:	*Texas Rose Muddler*
Hooks:	8 long shank, Old Numbers
Silk:	Orange
Rib:	Fine oval silver tinsel
Body:	Orange floss silk
Wing:	Yellow bucktail
Head:	Deer body hair

201

CHAPTER THIRTEEN

UNCLASSIFIABLE PATTERNS

RED SETTER

One day a few years ago I was fishing at that home of monster rainbows, Avington fishery in Hampshire, when I met a New Zealand angler over here on holiday. We got talking about fish and fishing and he introduced me to a fly that I had heard of but not seen, and certainly not tried, the Red Setter. This fly has been the centre of a controversy in America because some people feel that it is tied up to represent two salmon eggs and that this is what the fish take it for. Well, I know that if I wanted to dress up an imitation of a couple of fish eggs I am certain I could do a better job of it than this pattern does. I think the truth of the matter is that the fish takes it for precisely the same reason it takes any other lure – whatever that is.

My New Zealand friend gave me one of his stock of Red Setters and I thought that I would try it. I fished it deep-sunk in the hole at the top of the second pool, and on the second or third retrieve everything went tight and I was into my first trout of the day. I then caught another couple of fish and decided that I ought to ease up because otherwise I was going to get my two brace limit within about twenty minutes. I went off on a grand tour of the lakes to see how the other anglers were doing and to take some photographs – I should have known better. I have had this happen to me too often in the past; you save a fish or two and ease off during the prime feeding time and what happens? I will tell you what happens – you do not catch another fish, that is what happens; or, perhaps more accurately, does not happen. The stillwater trout angler has to be an opportunist, he has to take his chances while he may. If the fish are feeding for a while, then hit them hard; it may well be your last or only opportunity of the day.

202

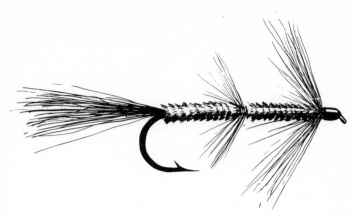

Red Setter

The retrieve I used on that day was a slow figure-of-eight that, coupled with a small split-shot pinched on to the leader about three feet from the fly to get it to sink fairly deeply, brought the fly back to me just off the bottom. I must say it was not particularly inspiring fishing, the line went tight and the rainbows swam around under the rod-top until I slipped the net under them. These were three and four pound fish and certainly the rainbows at Ardingly reservoir fight far harder than this at about one-third of the weight. Perhaps it was because they were relatively newly introduced stock-fish or perhaps it was because the lakes are relatively shallow. I have often observed that fish – almost any fish – fight harder and longer over deep water, and if that water is also gin clear then the fight tends to be even more spectacular. This business of deep, clear water is perhaps best illustrated by mentioning pike. I had never been very impressed with the way pike fight until I began to catch them at the gravel pits at South Cerney in Gloucestershire; there they really gave me a workout. They could have been an entirely different species from the sluggish wet-sacks that I was used to catching in the muddy, shallow Sussex lakes.

Method of tying
After winding the silk from eye to bend as usual catch in a large

bunch of long, brown squirrel tail fibres. At the same point tie in the central core of a length of chenille; the colour of this should be a fairly deep (not hot) orange. Wind the chenille up the shank for half of its length, tie in and trim off the surplus. Now wind a medium-large hackle in front of the rear portion of the body; pale ginger is the colour you want. Slope the fibres over the body by turns of silk, then catch in the chenille again and wind the front portion of the body. Once again you wind a hackle in front of the chenille but this time make the hackle slightly longer in the fibre than the rear one. Finish the head neatly and varnish.

The Dressing:	Red Setter
Hooks:	10 – 14 long shank, Old Numbers
Silk:	Brown (Sherry Spinner)
Tail:	Unbarred brown squirrel tail fibres
Body:	Orange chenille in two halves
Hackles:	Two pale ginger cock hackles

FUZZY WUZZY

This pattern positively screams 'TROUT' – it really seems rather a shame that I cannot catch anything on it! It looks something like a Wormfly, which we know is a good killer, and it has that tasty, crunchy look to it. I have yet to have a trout cast a second glance at it. Of course this is almost certainly just the way, the place, the speed or the depth at which I have fished it because, since I first wrote about it, I have had several people tell me just how good a fly it is and that they have caught monster bags and monster fish on it – makes you sick.

Like its close relative the Red Setter it seems that the retrieve has to be very slow and very deep to be at its best. It fishes well along dam walls I am told and if the hackles are tied to stand out at the dry-fly angle it tends to bounce over snags, boulders and such. The consensus seems to be that red is the best colour overall, with yellow coming in close second.

I think I may try this fly using a system which is very effective indeed when drifting. On the drift over deep water on our reservoirs it is almost impossible to fish the flies at any depth because the boat moves over the line as it sinks and you cannot keep in contact with the fly. The only answer seemed to be to anchor or to use the side-casting techniques that the Northampton lads employ. But by anchoring you only cover a relatively small area of water and the tendency is to be constantly casting over the same fish. If you have shelled out for a boat you might just as well get the best from it; this means that you want to be constantly fishing to different fish and not hammering the same few as you would fishing from the bank.

Fuzzy Wuzzy

I have never seen anyone using this particular technique on any of our reservoirs but I do not by any means claim to have been its originator. It is really very simple; what we want to achieve is for the sinking line, lead-core or whatever, to get to a predetermined depth and to be covering fresh fish all the time. First of all you have to turn round in the boat and face backwards. Now cast back into the wind; it does not matter how far so long as the head on your line is out through the top ring. *Shake* out the following line, monofilament, braided mono' or whatever the backing is, until you have all you want laying on the water behind the boat. You now hold the rod and watch the line slowly begin to straighten until eventually it tightens up. The sinking portion has now reached its maximum depth; if you want it to go deeper you have to shake out more line. The length of line you have to retrieve each time is determined by the depth of the water you are fishing over. If you are fishing shallow water you need only a small amount of line out. Correspondingly if the water is very deep you will need much more to allow the weighted line to sink. There is of course another factor which affects it and that is the speed of drift, but this is relatively minor because with any real ripple on the water you drift quite a long way in a surprisingly short time.

When the line begins to tighten you start the normal retrieve. On many waters it is not a legal technique to allow the line to just trail inertly over the back of the boat; it is also a bore and on top of that it is not a particularly productive method of fishing. By employing the usual retrieve and imparting stops and starts, pauses and darts to the fly, you are far more likely to attract the attention of a trout.

The real advantage of this method is that it allows you to cover many fish that would not normally see a fly because they habitually live in the deeper water that is seldom reached by the usual methods. Almost any fly pattern can be used when Deep-Drifting, which is the name I have given this technique, but it seems to be most useful when using a lure of some kind; an Ace of Spades does very well, as does the Hanningfield Lure, but I have also used it to fish a team of nymphs or buzzer pupae – the latter can really get a whizz on when rising through the water. It is also quite effective with wet flies. I have no doubt that some reservoir manager is reading this and wondering how he can get it banned – it always happens when a newish or unusual method is thought up. I feel though that it is merely another tactic to add to the stillwater angler's armoury. From the fishery manager's point of view it could prove to be very useful because it could well catch some of those fish that are least likely to be caught by any other method, the fish that are seldom seen, the blighters that sit down deep and are not in the least interested in coming up in the world!

After that slight diversion I suppose I had better get back to talking about the Fuzzy Wuzzy. As I said earlier, I think I will try this fly using the Deep-Drift method; I think it may work very well indeed.

Method of tying

Wind your tying silk from the eye to the bend and tie in a small bunch of black squirrel tail fibres as a tail. Immediately in front of this catch in a length of whatever colour chenille you fancy. Wind the silk up the shank for about a third of its length and then follow this with the chenille. Tie in and trim off the surplus chenille. In front of this tie in a black cock hackle and wind it on in the normal spider fashion. Catch in the chenille again and wind it up the remainder of the shank, leaving just enough room at the eye to take another wound hackle – make the front hackle slightly longer in the fibre than the rear one. Tie off with a good tight whip-finish and varnish the head. The colours and types of materials you could use to dress this type of fly must be almost infinite, so you may find it interesting to experiment. Whatever else you do though, when you have tied some up, try them Deep-Drifted next time you are out in a boat; I think you may be in for a very pleasant surprise.

The Dressing:	*Fuzzy Wuzzy*
Hooks:	6 – 10 long shank, Old Numbers
Silk:	Black
Tail:	Black squirrel tail
Body:	Chenille, almost any colour
Hackles:	Black cock

BABY DOLL

This is a fly – if you can call it that – which I have no particular love for, although there is no denying that it does catch fish. It catches a lot of fish – in fact it catches far more than its fair share of fish. Aesthetically pleasing it is not, but there is no denying that trout like it and who are we to argue?

It was invented not by Bob Church as is commonly thought but by Brian Kench, but Bob has written so often about it that it has become closely linked with his name.

I tried another version which, would you believe, was even more repulsive than the original – a brilliant, fluorescent green Baby Doll that actually caught quite a decent fish for me at Ardingly when there was a very heavy algae bloom and the water was like pea soup. I saw him move on the top, plonked the 'fly' down ahead of him, pulled it through and he whacked it. I have never raised the courage to try it on again. Maybe one day when I am desperate. . . .

Method of tying
It really could not be much simpler. All you do is wind the tying silk from eye to bend and catch in a double strand of white baby wool. Fold this back out of the way and come up the shank to the eye and tie in a single strand of wool. Wind this down the shank to where the two strands were tied in and then carefully take a turn of wool over the tying silk to hide it. Wind the wool back up the body over the first layer, tie in and trim off at the eye. Bring the ends of the two strands over the body and pull them tautly so that a back is formed; tie down and trim off at the eye again. Wind a neat head and whip finish and then apply several coats of varnish. Trim off the tail to about half the body length and then bush it out by picking out the fibres with the point of your dubbing needle until it is as fluffy as possible. This fluffing out seems to be critical; I am told it does not work anywhere near as well unless this is done.

Baby Doll

When I dress this fly I normally try to get the body to a slight fish shape by starting to wind the body wool in the middle of the shank rather than at the end. I also slightly overlap some of the turns to get this shape. My clients seem to prefer it this way rather than the more usual – and I am sure the original – method of tying with a flat body.

The Dressing:	*Baby Doll*
Hooks:	Normally 8 – 10 long shank but sometimes better on 10 – 12 normal length, Old Numbers
Silk:	Black
Tail:	White baby wool well fluffed out
Back:	As for tail
Body:	As for tail
Head:	Black tying silk

JERSEY HERD

Of all the flies I have written about over the last fifteen years the Jersey Herd is perhaps the fly that has been most messed about by the professional fly-dressers. When Tom Ivens designed this pattern it was supposed to imitate a small fish and was tied with a bulked-up underbody to give it the right shape. The normal pro tying is a body which is flat. The tinsel normally used is gold rather than the copper which Tom tied with. Variations of hackle colour are common, with yellow being the most usual, rather than the correct colour which is rich orange. Usually the hackle is a mile too long in the fibre as well.

Some time ago I sent Tom a sample of a material called Goldfingering which is available from most draper's shops. This product is available in many colours, one of which is copper. It is virtually impossible to get copper-coloured flat tinsel unless you buy either the very fine grade or the same material in sheet form. I dressed some Herds with the copper-coloured Goldfingering and they looked quite attractive; the bodies tended to be a bit lumpy but this is merely the limitation of the material. They do catch fish, but I much prefer the flat copper Lurex; I take my material from the sheet because the thin strands are too narrow to wind a decent body. Another point which is usually omitted on this pattern is the pronounced head of a wound peacock herl.

In fact what the poor old public ends up with is almost anything but the fly that Tom designed, and what must make it even more annoying from his point of view is that if you now send a client a Jersey Herd dressed correctly he promptly sends it back because 'it's the wrong fly' – the professionals' alterations have now become accepted as the correct pattern. Another snag is that these gold bodied, yellow hackled, headless wonders do catch fish – that makes it even more aggravating!

I assure you that if you dress up the correct tying you will find that no matter how useful you have found the horrid messes you have been using in the past, this dressing is better. (You have stuck your neck out there Collyer!)

Method of tying
Run the tying silk down the shank to the bend and there catch in several strands of bronze peacock herl, leaving the tips sticking out past the bend of the hook to form a tail. Carry the silk back up the shank towards the eye and fix in a length of floss silk – any colour will do. Leave a gap of at least a quarter of an inch at the eye. Wind the floss silk to make a fairly bulky underbody in the shape of a fish. If you decide to try the Goldfingering, tie that in in the centre of the hook and wind towards the head then come right back down the shank to the tail, taking close-butting turns. Finally take it back up the shank again towards the eye and tie off; this should result in a reasonably fishy shape.

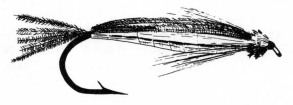

Jersey Herd

For Tom's original dressing, carefully cut off a strip from the copper sheet about a sixteenth of an inch wide, tie this in at the forward end of the floss-silk underbody and wind it down the hook to the tail, making it as smooth as you can. I find it is very helpful at this stage to run on a thin layer of cellulose varnish along the top of the first tinsel layer and then wind the tinsel back up the body over the varnish while it is still wet; you have to be a little careful because it can tend to slip. The varnish will spread round the body to a certain extent and when it dries it will make the body much stronger and certainly more impervious to trout's teeth. Tie in and trim off the surplus tinsel.

In front of the body wind an orange cock hackle to make a collar (four or five turns of a short-fibred hackle should be sufficient). Slope the fibres back along the body with a turn or two of silk. The back and head are the peacock herl, which is carried forward over the top of the fly and tied in at the eye. The head is then wound after twisting the herl into a rope and applying a drop of varnish to the hook. The herl is tied down, the ends are then trimmed off and a neat whip-finish is made at the eye. And that, with any luck at all, should look something like the Jersey Herd as Tom Ivens designed it.

The Dressing:	*Jersey Herd*
Hooks:	6 – 8 long shank, Old Numbers
Silk:	Black
Tail:	Peacock herl
Underbody:	Floss silk
Body:	Flat copper tinsel or Lurex
Back:	As for tail
Hackle:	Short-fibred, deep orange cock hackle
Head:	As for tail

As a supplement to this section on lures I feel it would be appropriate to explain how I go about splicing fly-lines and making up shooting-heads. I now use these for perhaps eighty per cent of my fly-fishing, even for dry flies and nymphing.

Now that we have the advantages of braided monofilament and the ideal method of splicing lines into it by using the new, fast adhesives we really are getting the best of both worlds – the distance that has always been the big attraction of shooting-heads plus the lack of tangling that the braided mono' gives. The almighty birds-nest was always the big drawback with using shooting-heads backed off with plain or flatted monofil' in the past. Now I find that I get far less tangling with shooting-heads than I do with full fly-lines; one tug on the braided mono' and it nearly always just falls out and the tangle disappears.

At one time I used rather fiddly methods of splicing fly-lines to

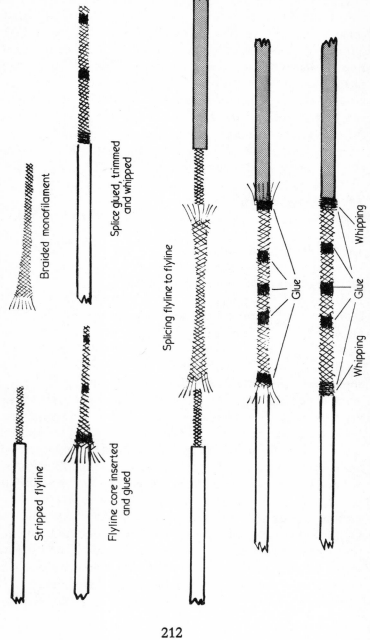

SPLICING FLYLINE TO BRAIDED MONOFILAMENT

Braided monofilament

Splice glued, trimmed
and whipped

Stripped flyline

Flyline core inserted
and glued

Splicing flyline to flyline

Glue

Whipping

Glue

Whipping

212

make up sink-tips, float-tips and so on. I now have a much simpler and quicker technique which seems to be virtually foolproof. Say you want to join a sink-tip shooting-head together. This is how you go about it.

For a start off we will splice the back of the head to the braided monofil'. Using an electric-wire stripper pull off about an inch or so of the dressing (the plastic outer skin) on the end of the fly-line. Get a large darning needle and thread the core of the fly-line into the centre of the braided mono'. Make certain that the core is inserted for at least its own length up the braid because the braid is very inclined to fray. Put three small dabs of Super Glue 3 or whatever other fast curing adhesive it is that you are using on to the outside of the braid and rub it quickly between a layer of old cloth to make certain it penetrates – you have to be quick because otherwise the line will stick to the cloth. Give it a minute or so and then give the junction a hard pull to make certain that it has really taken. Trim off any of the frayed end of the braid and make certain that it butts up cleanly to the fly-line.

Now get your bobbin holder and pull off about a foot or so of silk. Take the splice between the fingers and thumbs of both hands, hold the end of the silk at the splice and then swing the bobbin holder round and round. If you keep the fly-line taut you will find that you can get quite a neat whipping by this method. When you have sufficient turns and it looks neat and tidy insert a loop of thread under a turn of the silk and then whip over this again by spinning the bobbin holder. Cut the end of the silk, push it through the loop, pull the loop through the turns of silk and there is your completed whip. Run a little cellulose varnish or adhesive over the whip and that is it. You should have a really attractive, tapered and very professional looking splice.

For the junction of the sinking portion of the sink-tip to the floating part remember that you will have to use a sinking portion which is about two sizes heavier than the floating line. This is because the sinker is always a lot thinner for the same weight and you do not want a fast step-down along the line when you are casting. Assuming you would normally want a number 8 line to work your rod properly, what I would do is to splice a length of number 9 sinker to a length of number 7 floater. This should then result in roughly – very roughly – a number 8 line. It is not all that critical because it would be unusual to splice in more than about three or four yards of sinking line on to about seven yards of floater, thus making up your sink-tip head to the proportions that most people can handle.

To make the splice all I do is to strip off about an inch of the plastic outer layer of both pieces of line, and then thread them into the centre of a short length of braided monofilament using a large-eyed needle. When they are fully inserted apply a dab of cyanoacrylate in about three different spots; make certain that the glue goes all the way round – and through – the braid and then repeat the same thing on the other side. I cut the fraying ends back so that there is no overlap and do a whip using my bobbin holder. The whip is just to stop the ends of the braid fraying. A drop of cellulose varnish over the whip finishes the job.

Another way of doing it, which is not quite so sure but which looks a whole lot prettier, is to insert into a hole in either end of the fly-line a short piece of roughened and tapered monofil' and to push the ends tight together. This worked very well for a couple of seasons but I was always a little nervous of it. Using the braided mono' I have complete confidence in the junction.

To fix your leader to the tip of the fly-line all you do is again use the braid, splice that to the fly-line and then pull the end of the leader into the other end of, say, three inches of braid and glue, and whip as before. The beauty of this method of joining your leader into your fly-line is that the junction is near enough smooth and there is no knot to jam in the top-ring when you are playing a fish. It enables you to use a really long leader if necessary and if the fish wants to run, even though the leader is well into the rings, he can do so with no risk of the leader breaking. It is far superior to any other method that I have tried. Fly-lines have never been so versatile since these two products, cyanoacrylate adhesive and braided monofilament, have become available.

SECTION FIVE
SALMON FLIES

CHAPTER FOURTEEN

HAIRWING FLIES

STOAT'S TAIL

Hairwing salmon flies are becoming increasingly popular as the years go by. Do you know why? I shall tell you (you knew I would, didn't you?) — it is because they are easier and much quicker to dress than the traditional patterns and therefore they generally cost quite a bit less to buy. The truth is they also catch just as many fish as the older, more involved and much more colourful flies, which I think is sad. You would think that if you were to put in that much extra work and effort on dressing a perfect fully dressed salmon fly the least you could expect would be a couple of extra fish for your pains, but I am afraid it just is not so. Those fish really do not care how long you slaved over a hot fly-dressing bench.

We do not know why a salmon takes a fly or bait on its non-feeding-spawning-run up river, but the fact that, on occasion, this does happen is enough for most anglers. I must admit that I know the feeling. You have been flogging away all week on an entirely unresponsive series of so-called salmon pools; anything — and I do mean *anything* — that will induce a take and remain legal is welcome. I honestly feel that of all the frustrating fishing that the United Kingdom offers the angler, salmon fishing takes the biscuit. If you have ever seen me without my hat you may have noticed that the youthful hairline is receding — that is what salmon fishing does for you. The trouble is that it is the one form of fishing to which the application of logic is totally useless. Thus it is that those thoroughly frustrating, beautiful fish will as happily eat a Stoat's Tail or a Hairy Mary as they will a Jock Scott — or even, let it be whispered, a Collyer's Blue! No soul, dammit!

There are very few hairwing salmon flies that can be regarded as even vaguely complicated to dress. Perhaps the most involved is the Garry or Yellow Dog. This one though is the proverbial piece of cake, and if you can make a reasonable job of a Sweeney Todd you will find this one even easier.

Stoat's Tail

Method of tying

Start winding the tying silk slightly back from the eye of the hook or iron, as the hook is usually called when used in salmon fishing (don't ask me why – just to be quaint and to confuse newcomers to the sport I expect). Tie in a fair length of silk, say four inches or so. You hold that very taut in your left hand at an angle of about forty-five degrees away from the iron and towards you. If you then wind the silk in fairly close turns you should – always assuming you managed to decipher that little lot about angles and all – get the turns of silk sliding down the taut end on to the shank in very close-butted turns. Keep doing this until you are well over the spur of metal that makes up the loop eye of the iron. This, if it is done properly, should mean that the layer of silk comes off the spur smoothly rather than dropping abruptly. You will find it well worth doing this because it results in a better finish on the body.

218

Once you are clear of the spur it is all right to carry the silk down to the bend in open turns; this saves quite a lot of time and makes not the slightest difference to the finished fly. At the bend the ribbing tinsel is tied in and it is worthwhile tying this in with a long tag-end so that it reaches almost the full length of the shank — to the start of the spur anyway. If you carefully wind the silk over the tag-end of tinsel so that it lays along the near side of the shank it again helps to make the shank smooth by evening out that drop-off.

Tie in a length of stout, black floss silk behind the spur, wind this down to where the rib was tied in, then come back up the body past the spur, tie in and trim off the surplus silk. The body should be slightly tapered and to get this effect all you have to do is, when winding the second layer, make the turns closer and closer together as you move towards the eye. The turns should be very slightly overlapping at the bend but be almost completely overlapping as you approach the eye. Rib the body with evenly spaced turns of tinsel and tie off at the eye.

The fly is now taken out of the vice and reversed, making sure that the weight of the bobbin holder holds everything taut, otherwise it will all disintegrate before your very eyes. This means that the fly is now sitting in the vice belly-up at an angle of about thirty degrees out of vertical. (This is getting worse than my children's geometry lessons!) The false hackle is now applied to the underside of the hook. If the initial turn of silk is placed on the feather fibres lightly and then pulled downwards fairly sharply, with the fingers removed from the hackle, you should find that the fibres flare slightly. The effect is exactly the same as with the deer-hair ruff and head on a Muddler Minnow, but because the feather fibre is much softer and is not being spun on a bare hook-shank the effect is less drastic and much more controllable. The idea is that the hackle should encircle the bottom half of the hook-shank, giving a very similar effect to the traditionally wound and separated hackle without having the unfortunate tendency to cock the wings up into the air that the thick hackle stalk gives. It really is much better; you just try it and see if you do not agree with me.

The fly is now taken out of the vice and put back the right

way up again. The wing is supposed to be made of stoat's tail (the black tip fibres) but there are so few of these on a stoat's tail that everybody uses natural or even dyed black squirrel tail fibres instead; I have yet to meet the salmon who could tell the difference, or the angler for that matter! When you wind the silk over the hair tie them in securely in the centre of what will be the head of the fly, not along the entire length of the head. This is because the head can then be tapered by holding the scissors at an angle (here we go on with the geometry lessons again) making just one smooth cut through the hair. You cannot do this if you have carried the silk right up to the eye. The other reason for the centrally wound silk is so that there is a space left to allow you to wind two locking turns, just round the hair itself, and then to wind turns of silk over the locking turns and the ends of the wing and blend everything into a neatly shaped head, as smooth as possible. These days I rarely use locking turns though. I just apply a dab of Super Glue to the ends of the hair and that secures everything very tightly; I have yet to have any hair slip after using this method.

Once the head is finished apply a coat of thick black cellulose varnish and then one coat of Vycoat or a couple of layers of clear cellulose varnish. After this treatment you should end up with a beautifully glossy smooth head that will not make the slightest bit of difference to the fly's fish-taking ability but will please me no end if ever I get to peer into your fly-box.

The Dressing:	Stoat's Tail
Irons:	1/0 – 10 ordinary forged or low water irons
Silk:	Black
Rib:	Oval silver tinsel
Body:	Black floss silk
Hackle:	Black cock
Wing:	Black, stoat's tail fibres or squirrel's tail

HAIRY MARY

I have never taken a salmon on this fly but I know from the many reports I hear about it that it can be a very good pattern indeed. It can sometimes prove effective when it is dressed in the very small sizes on low-water irons, say 6 through to 12, and then fished greased line style. This technique involves fishing the fly so that it barely skims under the surface of the stream during low-water conditions, when the salmon are notoriously difficult to tempt. Using this method they can sometimes be induced to come up and have a go at a small fly but as with anything to do with these lovely, perverse fish nothing – and I do mean nothing – is certain. Remember when dressing this or any other fly for low-water fishing that the irons are made very long so that the dressing can be condensed on the front of the hook rather than spread right along the shank as is normal. The theory is that the fish will strike at the dressed part of the fly and

Hairy Mary

therefore cannot avoid being hooked because the bite and bend of the hook are taken before the dressing can be reached. That is the theory, but I have yet to be convinced of it in practice. I have taken a fair few salmon and grilse on ordinary trout flies in these low-water conditions and the rate of hookings as opposed to nudges, plucks and pulls that came to nothing seemed very similar to that experienced when using normal low-water dressed flies.

221

The method of tying the Hairy Mary is precisely the same as that used for the Stoat's Tail so I will not go through the same thing again; just substitute the appropriate, different materials and follow the instructions for the other fly.

The Dressing:	*Hairy Mary*
Irons:	1/0 – 10 ordinary forged or low-water irons
Silk:	Black
Rib:	Oval gold tinsel
Body:	Black stout floss silk
Hackle:	Black or blue cock
Wing:	Brown bucktail or squirrel tail

CHAPTER FIFTEEN

TUBE FLIES

JOCK SCOTT (TUBE)

I do not like tube flies. I think they are rotten to dress, difficult to cast (especially the big brass ones) and they have virtually no aesthetic appeal. Having said all that I must now add that the darned things *do* catch salmon. 'And what', you may ask, 'has that to do with it?' I agree. Salmon flies are supposed to look pretty, not so much for the fish's benefit but for ours; these great, lumpy, ungainly tube flies could never be called attractive, so why do salmon show so little aesthetic taste by trying to eat the things? (I have heard it rumoured that on occasion salmon will even sink so low that they will have a go at such things as spinners, small fish, prawns, or even worms. I suppose if they are that far down in iniquity a tube fly must appear quite sporting.) I am pretty sure that the reason they take a tube fly is all that hair waggling around in the water and the thick, meaty looking outline of the body. There is of course another possibility – sheer cussedness!

It is often said that tube flies are easier to dress than conventional patterns. Believe it not! Any idiot can tie a few strands of hair on to a tube and call it dressed, but it is my opinion that you have to take exactly the same amount of care and use the same expertise to dress these flies that you do with the fully dressed patterns. That still does not mean that I have to like the darned things. Remember that when you are dressing tubes, the materials should be applied as sparsely as possible, otherwise you will end up with something vaguely reminiscent of a scruffy feather duster.

I think it is about time I started to try and say something in the favour of the tube flies – it is not easy. They do offer one advantage over normal salmon flies; they are armed with a treble

223

hook which, through being able to stick into a fish from three directions at once, will perhaps offer a better hooking potential. Generally though they are fairly fine in the wire and this can lead to a bigger fish 'falling off' – remember a salmon is a very powerful adversary. Another advantage is that if a hook is damaged it can be replaced. The treble does have this rather evil tendency to swing round and catch the nylon leader during casting, and though various methods have been tried to prevent this occurring, nothing has yet proved to be the complete answer. Perhaps the best bet is to whip a short length of plastic tube (the stuff used to make coarse-fishing float caps is ideal) on to the back end of the tube and then pull the shank of the treble up into this; it is an improvement but it is still not one hundred per cent.

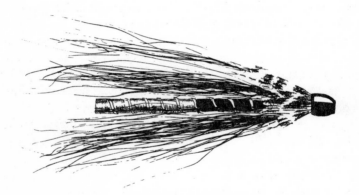

Jock Scott (Tube)

In their smaller sizes tubes do offer the angler variety inasmuch as he can add short lengths of tube, complete with dressing, to get a number of effects. For instance you can tie up a dozen or so short pieces of tube with different coloured hair and body materials, then slip five or six of these on to the leader to achieve different effects; it also makes for a very flexible fly which works rather better in the water than does the normal solid hook. I have used this idea several times for stillwater trout and it does seem to work very well. The only problem I have come up against is that during casting the pieces of tube do have a tendency to slip up the leader. I stopped this by pinching on a tiny split-shot and sliding this down to the top of the fly. I have not as yet tried this system for salmon but I see no reason at all why it should not be a winner.

Any of the standard, fully dressed salmon flies may be converted to make a tube pattern by simply substituting hair for feather and by simplifying the dressing. The basic advantage of dressing on tubes is that the 360 degrees of hair gives great mobility in the water. You can of course still use feathers in the tyings but the whole point of it is to get that mobility of the hair working for you.

A little experimentation in the use of different materials will not hurt. If the standard dressing calls for jungle cock feathers (and you have still got some) there is no reason at all why these should not be incorporated into the dressing. You will find that it is better to use three or four rather than the two used on the conventional flies.

Method of tying

To start dressing a tube fly, then, the first thing to do is to mount the tube in the vice. The best way I know of doing this is to clip the eye off a salmon iron that will fit tightly into the tube; It is as well to keep a selection of different size irons to fit the various sized tubes that you will use. There is also, just available, a series of special tube inserts that are made specifically for this job; I have not as yet tried them but they seem like a good idea. I always thought the clipped-off salmon iron was a little crude.

Set the hook in the vice and slide the tube firmly on to the shank. You will see that most tubes have slightly belled ends to stop the dressing slipping off; this seems like a good idea on the face of it but I have often tied tube flies on straight tubes and no clients have yet sent them back because the dresing had slipped. The heavy brass tubes normally have a plastic or nylon insert so that the leader material will not be cut by the metal.

The silk needs to be very well waxed and is started at the right hand end as it would be for any normal fly. This is then wound down to the back of the tube, there the rib is tied in. I should perhaps say at this point that some fly-dressers use no body materials at all and just dress the head end with the wings. In my opinion it looks awful, but sad to say the fish do not seem to mind very much. As I said earlier, salmon show very little taste in these matters. Carry the silk back up the tube to about half way along, catch in a length of golden-yellow floss silk, wind this down to the rib and back up again, tie in and trim. Carry the tying silk forward to within about an eighth of an inch from the end of the tube and catch in a length of black floss silk. Wind this down to butt up tightly to the golden-yellow floss, then again wind back up to the point where it was first tied in, fix and trim. Now run the ribbing tinsel right up the body and make certain that all turns are as evenly spaced and as tight as possible.

It is necessary to leave out some of the normal dressing operations used on the fully dressed flies; for instance it would look ungainly to put on the veiling and central butt on the Jock Scott. However try to achieve the basic elements of the fly; in this case the yellow and black floss and the silver rib have to suffice. It certainly does not look as pretty, but I suppose there are folk who would argue that it is a lot quicker and just as effective. No soul, some people.

The wings are what makes a tube fly what it is — whatever that is — and it must be born in mind during the time when you are applying the wings that you should use a lot less than you think you are going to need. Be very, very sparing with the hair and any other winging materials — if you are at all heavy handed you will end up with a walloping great head. The other thing to remember is that the silk and hair is applied in very small bunches, working from left to right. Try not to make two turns of silk in the same position but make each securing turn to the right of its neighbour. Each succeeding clump of hair is tied in front of the preceeding one, while the tube is rotated on the hook. The whole winging operation, even on the biggest flies, has to be condensed into no more than a quarter of an inch, and half of that would perhaps be better.

One of the major problems with tube flies is how to dry the heads once they are dressed. You see, you will need the salmon hook mount for the next fly you are going to dress and it can be expensive if you destroy lots of salmon irons. What I have done is to drive some ordinary panel pins right through a piece of timber and I then stand the tubes upright on these to dry. I usually slide a small length of tube over the panel pin first, just enough to hold the dressing away from the board, so that the wing on the dressed tube does not become distorted while it is drying. They do need to be stood vertically; if you try to dry them horizontally you will find after the first layer or two the varnish tends to droop.

The Dressing:	Jock Scott (Tube)
Hooks:	According to tube size, trebles
Silk:	Black
Rib:	Oval silver tinsel
Body:	Rear half golden yellow floss silk; front half black floss silk
Wings:	Red, yellow, blue and black bucktail or any suitable hair with guinea fowl hackle outside
Cheeks:	Optional, jungle cock or substitute
Head:	Black varnish

AVON EAGLE (TUBE)

The Avon Eagle is, for a tube fly, very attractive; it is all light, bright and airy. I must confess that I have never caught a salmon on it but plenty of my friends and clients have so I know it is a fly well worth the tying. It is relatively unusual in the tube fly world in as much as it has not got hair wings. They are made from feather fibres, marabou plumes and golden pheasant rump in fact. Yes I think even *I* could almost work up a little enthusiasm over this tube pattern!

This dressing is the normal one that I supply when asked for this fly and nobody has yet complained; it is merely a simplified version of the fully dressed pattern.

Method of tying

Take your tying silk from right to left down the tube and at the end catch in *three ribbing tinsels* – twist (though generally oval silver tinsel is used these days), broad flat silver tinsel, and then

227

again twist or oval. Dub on for a quarter of the tube's length some lemon coloured seal's fur, followed in equal sections by bright orange, scarlet and fiery brown. Wind one section of twist ribbing in nice even turns up the body and tie off just short of the end of the tube, leaving enough room for the wing to be tied in. Follow the first rib by the flat silver tinsel and make absolutely certain that it butts up really tight all the way round the tube to the first rib. Tie in and trim. Finally bring up the other rib on the rear edge of the flat tinsel, once again butting it close up. Tie in and trim off the surplus of that one too. You should find that you have a most pleasing effect with the three ribs over the attractive body colours.

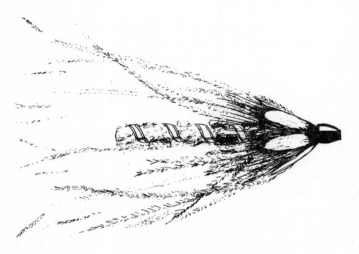

Avon Eagle (Tube)

Now tie in bunches of yellow dyed marabou fibres working your way round the circumference of the tube. This feather is somewhat fractious so I tie in three or four golden pheasant gold coloured rump feathers so that they tend to control the very soft marabou substitute feather. I generally take three or four tightish turns of silk over the stalk end of the rump feathers and then ease them through the silk so that I get a good even spread of fibres round the tube. You can now add some widgeon fibres around the outside of the wings but I think that this can tend to make the fly appear rather heavy, so I normally leave it out. Jungle cock or its substitute is absolutely essential though; this adds the final touch and the resulting fly is really – for a tube! – very attractive indeed.

The Dressing:	*Avon Eagle (Tube)*
Hooks:	According to tube size, trebles
Silk:	Black
Ribs:	Twist or oval silver tinsel, broad flat silver tinsel, and then silver twist or oval
Body:	Lemon, orange, scarlet and fiery brown seal's fur in equal sections
Wings:	Yellow dyed marabou substitute, golden pheasant gold coloured rump feather
Cheeks:	Jungle cock or substitute
Head:	Black varnish

CHAPTER SIXTEEN

GRUBS

USK GRUB

This pattern is one that I am told is a very handy one to have by you. It is not a fly I have used very much (damn it Collyer, be honest, it is not a fly you have used at all!) but nonetheless it does, from all the reports I hear, seem to catch a fair number of salmon. But that, I am afraid, is 'only hearsay evidence' as they say in all those court-room soap operas on television. Still, I am sure that if you tie a few up and tuck them away in the corner of your box there will come a day. . . .

Method of tying
Apparently, just to help to confuse everybody, there are at least three different dressing of the Usk Grub. This one, I am assured, though is the most popular and effective of the trio.

Tie in the silk in the normal way and carry it down to the bend. Wind the normal tag but do not bother about winding the layers of silk in front of it to make a bed. There is no tail as such on this fly. Secure a golden pheasant red breast feather by the centre fibres, not by the stalk – that way you will not have a great lumpy stalk wound round the end of the hook. Wind this to form a hackle in the bend of the hook; carry the tying silk slightly over the turns of feather to hold it at the correct angle, sloping back over the bend of the iron. Tie in a rib of oval silver tinsel. Wind the tying silk back up the shank for about half its length and tie in a piece of floss silk. Wind this down to the breast feather and then come back over the first layer to get a really smooth finish. Rib with the tinsel. An alternative is to wind a body of seal's fur dubbing; I think that makes a better fly than the one using floss silk. Lay on two scarlet cock hackle tips as veiling, one over and one under the hook, and in front of these

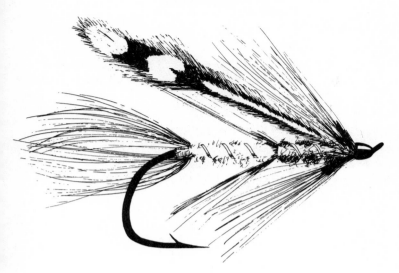

Usk Grub

wind on a light furnace (Greenwell) hackle.

The front half of the body is again either seal's fur or floss silk ribbed with oval silver tinsel. The wing, if such you can call it, is simply two largish jungle cock feathers set back to back and tied in to reach the full length of the body. The front hackle is again furnace cock, light in colour but a fair bit longer in the fibre than the central one. Varnish the head and make certain it is as smooth and neat as possible.

The Usk Grub is generally tied on double hooks. These are a bit of a so-and-so to dress flies on because the loose hook always tries to cut the silk as you wind it. Most disconcerting! I have yet to be convinced that double hooks offer any advantage over singles, except perhaps that they would tend to make the fly swim in a more stable plane, but even then I think any advantage would be marginal. Anyway, if you fancy dressing it on doubles, the best of luck to you!

The Dressing:	*Usk Grub*
Irons:	1/0 – 10 ordinary forged, singles or doubles
Silk:	Black

231

Tag:	Round silver tinsel
Tail Hackle:	Wound golden pheasant red breast feather
Rib:	Oval silver tinsel
Body:	In two halves: back half yellow or orange seal's fur or floss silk; front half black seal's fur or floss silk
Veiling:	Tips of two scarlet cock hackles, over and under the rear half of the body
Centre Hackle:	Light furnace cock
Wing:	Jungle cock or substitute
Front Hackle:	As for centre hackle but longer in the fibre
Head:	Black varnish

CHAPTER SEVENTEEN

FULLY DRESSED FLIES

SILVER AND BLACK DOCTOR

The Doctor series of salmon flies is an excellent basis for a day's salmon fishing; they have, in their elegant combinations of colour and shade, killed many fish. There are two items, the main points of recognition, which remain virtually fixed throughout the series; they have scarlet heads and butts, and there is usually a fair amount of silver in the dressings. Apart from this the different tyings take into account shades that will prove effective under most weather conditions: for instance, I would use the Black Doctor with far more confidence in coloured water than I would the silver or blue version. The reverse applies in bright conditions, of course, although there have been occasions . . . but let us not cloud the issue.

Method of tying

I will tell you stage by stage how to dress the Silver Doctor and you can substitute the appropriate materials for the black version if you want to dress that. The full dressing for both will be given at the end. So, fix your salmon iron in your vice and wind close-butted turns of silk over the spur as you did for the Stoat's Tail to smooth out the drop-off. Carry your silk to a point just before the bend and catch in a length of round or oval silver tinsel. I usually use oval because it lays better and makes a neater job; round is specified in the original dressing, but the salmon do not seem to mind. Then wind four or five turns down the shank to the left, come back up over those turns with another layer, fix in and trim off the surplus. Make sure the tag is neat and the turns are tight and butted close up to each other. In front of the tinsel tag wind another one, this time of golden yellow floss silk.

For the tail select a golden pheasant crest feather; you want one with only a slight curve to it. Tie it in to lie straight along the shank, making certain it is perfectly vertical and not leaning off to one side or the other. Follow this with a 'blue chatterer' feather (which I replace with two bright blue slips taken from a kingfisher's wing) and tie them both in as you would the tail on a normal wet fly such as a Butcher. The slips are paired to face inwards (back to back) and to follow the curve of the golden pheasant crest feather.

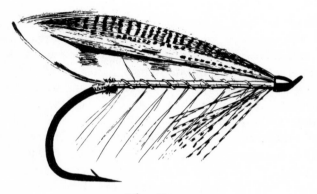

Silver Doctor

I always wind the butts on these flies by dubbing the wool on to the tying silk, never by winding the wool on in a strand – it is much neater. Now tie in the ribbing tinsel of oval silver and run the tying silk up the shank as far as the spur, binding down the ends of the tail and ribbing tinsel as you go and keeping them to the nearside of the hook – this helps to overcome the lump made by the spur. Tie in flat silver tinsel and wind down to the butt, then come back up over the first layer and tie in and trim about an eighth of an inch from the eye.

We now come to the bit that can cause apoplexy amongst the more traditional fly-dressers. *I* do not believe that there is any advantage to be gained by doubling the body hackles on salmon flies. I feel that it makes a far neater and better fly if the fibres are stripped off one side of the stalk and the hackle is then wound in the normal way. Try both methods and see which you prefer but my feeling is that the doubled hackles make the fly too heavy; the stripped hackle gives a much lighter effect. I prefer it anyway. Turn the fly over in the vice and tie in a throat hackle of a bunch of widgeon fibres. I often use the soft part of a teal's breast feather, that makes an attractive hackle.

Having turned the iron the right way up again tear off a dozen or so fibres from a large golden pheasant tippet feather, match this with a bunch taken from the opposing side of the feather and then tie them in so that they lay as low along the back of the fly as possible. This forms the supporting underwing for the main roof-wing.

Take two opposing strips from a golden pheasant tail feather and tie them in so that they form a roof over, but not completely hiding, the tippet fibres. Now marry strands of scarlet, blue and yellow swan or goose with strips of florican and speckled bustard over the top. The way you marry feather strips is quite fascinating but it is far, far easier to demonstrate than to describe – however I will try my best. The first thing to remember is that only strips from the same side of each feather will marry up with each other properly; it is no use at all trying to marry opposing sections taken from different feathers (there is one exception to this – naturally!). Take small sections of perhaps three fibres from each of the feathers you wish to marry, the scarlet being on the bottom. Hold that strip in your left hand between your finger and thumb and lay a strip of blue swan alongside it so that the two edges *touch but do not overlap*. Take hold of the butts of the two strips with the forefinger and thumb of your right hand and with your left finger and thumb stroke the two strips towards their tips. If you do it correctly they should have fused into one strip. All you do now is add the next section of fibres and build up your wing until that side is complete. You then do the same thing for the other side. Hold them together gently by the top of the wing and you should find that the bottom flares open slightly so that you can lower the completed roof over the underwing and then just tie it in in the normal way. You should still be able to see some of that underwing.

Very narrow strips of barred summer duck feather or its substitute, mandarin duck, are now married to equally narrow strips of teal. Here and now I warn you that you will have trouble with this part of the dressing; compared with mandarin duck and barred teal the main wing will seem a piece of cake! Once you manage to get these feathers married they are tied in on either side of the wing. A drop of lick helps no end to stop them trying to spring out from the side of the wing. If you have ever bought any of my flies you will now realise that they have probably been well annointed with Collyer-type saliva – that is why the fish like them of course! A good drop of stuff, that.

Over the whole of the top of the wing goes a *narrow* strip of bronze mallard feather; I fold a double width strip as I do when making wet fly wings of this material. Finally add a topping of golden pheasant crest. Make certain that this lies close over the top of the wing just meeting and touching the crest feather in the tail; this forms the lovely halo that completes the fully dressed salmon fly. There is, however, on these patterns one final thing to be done and that is to complete the head. It should be short and neat. The original dressing specifies that scarlet wool should be used, but I do not like heads made of wool; you will get a far better effect by using scarlet varnish, with at least two coats of clear over the top.

I have always used black silk to dress these flies, as I do for all my salmon patterns, but the other day my friend Tony Claydon suggested that I should be better off using either brown or scarlet silk. The dubbing on the butt would not show the colour through so much and the head would take the scarlet varnish better. I now use brown silk for these patterns; it is a definite improvement. Thanks, Tony.

The Dressings

	Silver Doctor
Irons:	5/0 – 8 ordinary forged
Silk:	Brown (Sherry Spinner)
Tag:	Round or oval silver tinsel and golden yellow floss silk
Tail:	Golden pheasant crest and blue kingfisher wing

Butt:	Scarlet wool
Rib:	Oval silver tinsel
Body:	Flat silver tinsel or Lurex
Hackle:	Pale blue cock
Throat:	Widgeon
Wing:	Tippet in strands, golden pheasant tail over; a mixed sheath of scarlet, blue and yellow swan or goose, florican bustard, speckled bustard and light mottled turkey tail; married narrow strips of barred summer duck or substitute and teal outside the sheath; bronze mallard over; golden pheasant crest over all
Head:	Scarlet wool or varnish

Black Doctor

Irons:	As for Silver Doctor
Silk:	Brown (Sherry Spinner)
Tag:	Round or oval silver tinsel and lemon floss silk
Tail:	Golden pheasant crest and Indian crow or substitute
Butt:	Scarlet wool
Rib:	Oval silver tinsel
Body:	Black stout floss silk
Hackle:	Claret cock (dark)
Throat:	Speckled guinea fowl hackle

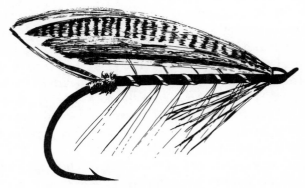

Black Doctor

Wing:	Tippet in strands with golden pheasant tail over; mixed sheath of scarlet, blue and yellow goose or swan, florican bustard, peacock wing and light mottled turkey tail; married strips of barred summer duck or mandarin duck and teal on sides; bronze mallard over; golden pheasant topping over all
Head:	Scarlet wool or varnish

SILVER GREY (SALMON)

This fly is a real sparkler, light and attractive. It seems to catch fish for me best when there is good light; not necessarily bright conditions but clear, clean light. I have never caught stale fish with this pattern, no kippers or long-term residents that have seen it all before. Perhaps it has been mere coincidence but all the salmon (well, the three or four) I have taken on the Silver Grey have been fresh-run fish. True a couple were grilse and well under the 10lb mark but they were in superb condition. I am thinking here particularly of the West Wales rivers; that is where this fly has served me best.

It has often been said to me that salmon flies must be the most difficult of patterns to dress – well this simply is not so. All a fully dressed salmon fly is is complicated, not difficult. The trickiest fly to dress really well is a small, split-winged, dry trout fly. If you can tie one of those to perfection no salmon pattern should prove to be any problem; they are all fairly easy if you follow a few basic principles.

Make sure that all the different stages in dressing the body *slightly* overlap the preceding stages. For example, we have just tied in a tail, and the butt of an ostrich herl is now to be wound on. Make certain that it overlaps both the tag-ends of the tail and any turns of tying silk and hides them. The only exception I make to this is the butt itself. I never overlap this because the fibres would be squashed out of shape; the body material does *always* lie up closely to it though, no gaps.

The next rule applies just as much to trout flies and lures as it does to salmon patterns. The ribbing *must* be evenly spaced and tight; that really does make a difference to the finish you obtain.

The wings should always be well married on the fully dressed flies; if the strands spring apart on the bench before they are tied in, the wing will never be a good one when it is completed. The golden pheasant topping in the tail and over the wing should form a halo round the wings with the tips just touching; if they are slightly apart it does not matter too much, but they must always be of exactly the same length. If the topping over the wing is pressed lightly downwards it should kiss the tail feather tip exactly. The final point is the head; this should be short and fairly compact. On the streamer and lure patterns the heads are normally fairly long and tapering but this is never the case with salmon flies. Try to compress the head into as short a space as possible, conducive to the wing and other materials being firmly and properly fixed. The head on any fly is greatly improved by the application of several coats of varnish rather than just one. To get that beautiful glossy, professional-looking head apply a coat of thick coloured varnish first, then add a couple of coats of clear varnish after the first one has dried thoroughly. It makes a big difference to the appearance of the fly.

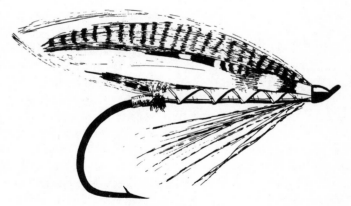

Silver Grey (Salmon)

Method of tying
Run your tying silk down the shank of the iron in the usual way making certain that the drop-off from the spur is as smooth as possible. Form two short tags, first of oval silver tinsel and then

239

golden yellow floss silk. Tie in a tail of golden pheasant crest with mandarin duck barred feather over the top. Now wind a butt of black ostrich herl. I will go into this operation in slightly more detail because we have not as yet covered the best method of applying it. If you look closely at a length of ostrich herl you will see that the fibres point away from the butt and they form a shape somewhat similar to an arrowhead. They also lean over to one side of the stalk. The stalk side must be tied pointing to the right otherwise each succeeding turn will crush the previous one and you will get a terrible mess. Tie the herl in by the butt-end as tight up to the tail and tag as you can get it and then wind from left to right until you get a fluffy flue-brush effect; make certain each turn is as tight up to its predecessor as you can get it. Wind for about the same distance as the length of the two tags. The older style salmon flies (some dressers still tie them this way today) were dressed with very long butts and tags and the wings were extended about half as far again as the length of the hook. Normally the tags were taken well round the bend of the iron. I prefer to dress mine on the straight and I like the wings to be only a shade longer than the length of the hook. I do not think my style is any better than the older arrangement, it just suits me.

After the butt is secured and the surplus trimmed off the next item to tie in is the ribbing tinsel, which is oval silver. Carry the silk back up the shank to the end of the spur and tie in a length of flat silver tinsel or Lurex, wind this down to the butt and then come back up again over the spur and tie in and trim about an eighth of an inch from the eye. Select a well-marked badger cock hackle and strip one side of the fibres off; this is the method I prefer to use but most fly-dressers use the doubling technique which I feel gives too heavy an effect. Tie in the hackle stalk by the butt-end and wind it down the shank to meet the rib; now wind the rib through the hackle going in the opposite direction. (Clockwise with, say, the hackle and anti-clockwise with the ribbing tinsel; this will then lock the stalk to the body in several points instead of just one at the tail end. If you ever enter a fly-dressing competition the fly will look much neater if the rib follows the stalk, but if I am judging it you will lose marks because the hackle will be very insecure if the fly is used for fishing instead of sitting in a frame behind glass.)

Turn the fly over in the vice ready to receive its false hackle of widgeon or teal; use the soft, open fibred feathers for this, not the dense ones that you would use for the winging on wet flies.

The winging is by the same method you used for the Silver Doctor; the only difference, aside from the colour of the swan feather strips, is that one of the nastiest feathers of all is used along the top of the wing sheath – golden pheasant centre tail. Earlier in this chapter I said that you must always lay the strips for marrying together so that only strips from the same side of each feather come together; now I am about to tell you about the exception to this rule (there usually is one you know!). For years I struggled to try and get golden pheasant centre tail strips to marry in properly, but they were always troublesome. Then one day I was fiddling around with materials and I decided to try to marry them in the wrong way round – I knew it was against all the rules, of course . . . and it worked beautifully. The strips went in just right and sat there just as I had always wanted them to. This method does not always work; some feathers it works with and some it does not – do not ask me why, I did not design the bird! There is a further difference on this wing from the Doctor series; you require either jungle cock feathers or their substitute down each side of the wing. Finish the head as normal.

The Dressing:	*Silver Grey (Salmon)*
Irons:	3/0 – 8 ordinary forged
Silk:	Black
Tag:	Oval silver tinsel and golden yellow floss silk
Tail:	Golden pheasant crest with mandarin duck over
Butt:	Black ostrich herl
Rib:	Oval silver tinsel
Body:	Flat silver tinsel or Lurex
Hackle:	Badger cock
Throat:	Widgeon or teal
Wings:	Tippet in strands; over this but not completely hiding it, married sections of white, yellow

and green swan or goose, bustard, florican
bustard and golden pheasant tail; strips of
pintail or teal married to barred summer or
mandarin duck set along the sides; brown
mallard over; topping over all

Cheeks: Jungle cock or substitute

Head: Black varnish

BLACK GOLDFINCH

This fly is an Irish pattern. The big difference between the Irish
flies, aside from their brogue of course, and the Scottish and
English patterns is that they do not include jungle cock eye
feathers in their dressings. This is a big advantage now that the
import of these feathers has been banned and we are forced to
think about using substitutes. This rather odd fact has made me
wonder over the years whether there really is any great advantage
in having jungle cock eyes on the flies from this side of the
water. Certainly the Irish flies seem to catch plenty of fish and
that, without doubt, is the final criterion.

Method of tying

Fix in your tying silk and wind it down to the bend in the
normal way. Tie in a tag of, first, silver tinsel; I generally use
oval but round is normally specified. This is followed by yellow
floss silk. Do not make the tag too long. The standard dressing is
for a tail of one golden pheasant topping, but I generally prefer
to use two to match up to the two used over the wing. With
just one I feel the fly looks somewhat unbalanced. Whatever, tie
in your tail of either one or two crests. Wind a neat butt of black
ostrich herl; this should be wound very close to the tail so that
the crests spring out from the butt with no gap showing.

Catch in your ribbing tinsel, oval gold, and run the tying silk
back up the shank almost to the eye, where you tie in a length of
black floss silk. Wind the floss smoothly down the body until it
reaches the ostrich herl and then wind it back up the shank; tie in
and trim where it was first secured. Tie in a hackle by the stalk
after either doubling it or stripping off one side of the fibres and
wind it palmer fashion down the shank to the ribbing tinsel,

which is then spiralled up the shank in the opposite direction taken by the hackle in order to secure it really firmly.

Turn the fly over in the vice and apply a false hackle to the throat. For some strange reason blue jay wings appear to be a little difficult to get hold of just recently so a perfectly good substitute is blue gallena (blue dyed guinea fowl hackle). This is certainly the case on the bigger sizes of fly where the jay fibres are just not long enough to reach the correct distance. In fly-dressing, proportion is perhaps the single most important aspect of a fly. Turn the fly the right way up again to receive its wing.

Black Goldfinch

The wing really is very easy after some of the complicated Scottish patterns. Tie in tippet fibres in strands as a base for the married feathers. Now, marry up four strips – two for each side – of deep, almost golden, yellow and red goose or swan feather. The red should be at the top of the wing and because there are only two strips a side they have to be much wider than is normal for most married wings. Tie them in to form a roof over the golden pheasant tippet fibres. Carefully tie in two golden pheasant toppings over the wings so that they form a halo with the tail feather. On the sides of the wing tie in two Indian crow substitute feathers, wind a neat, short head, whip finish and then apply varnish until the head is smooth and shiny.

The Dressing:	*Black Goldfinch*
Irons:	3/0 – 10 ordinary forged
Silk:	Black
Tag:	Round or oval silver tinsel and yellow floss silk
Tail:	One or two golden pheasant toppings
Butt:	Black ostrich herl
Rib:	Oval gold tinsel
Body:	Black floss silk
Hackle:	Claret cock
Throat:	Blue jay or blue gallena
Wings:	Golden pheasant tippet in strands; yellow and red swan or goose
Toppings:	Two golden pheasant crests
Sides:	Indian crow substitute
Head:	Black varnish

SPRING BLUE

This is another Irish salmon pattern which is very popular in its country of origin but which is seldom used elsewhere. This is a pity because it really is a rather good fly and I am certain that if it was given a fair trial in other countries it would prove very useful indeed. I have caught quite a few trout on a slightly simplified version when drift fishing and using a team of flies; it makes an excellent bob fly. All I did was leave out the tag, the Indian crow in the tail, the butt, the underwing of golden pheasant tippet fibres and the topping. You are then left with a rather attractive trout pattern that the fish seemed to like. However, folks, we are not supposed to be talking about trout flies here, this is the salmon section.

Method of tying

Wind the silk from the eye to the bend and make a tag of either round or oval silver tinsel and yellow floss silk. Tie in a golden pheasant crest with Indian crow substitute over the top; tie it in so that the Indian crow follows the curve of the topping. It is best not to tie in the stalk of the feather, which can force the crest downwards, but rather to take a section of the web from

Spring Blue

the side of the feather and use that instead. Wind a black ostrich herl butt and tie in an oval silver tinsel rib in front.

Dub on a body of blue seal's fur and when you almost reach the eye catch in a hackle which should be as close to the same shade as the seal's fur as possible. Wind this down the body palmer fashion and then secure it with the ribbing tinsel in the usual way. Tie in a false hackle of lemon-yellow cock at the throat.

The base of the wing is again golden pheasant tippet fibres in strands and over this is laid a roof of married goose or swan strips in the order, from the bottom, red, yellow and blue. Wide strips of teal feathers are now tied in to lie tight up against each side of the wing; they should reach no more than about two-thirds of the length of the wing. Over the top of this little lot tie in strips (or, as I prefer to do, a wide single folded strip) of bronze mallard and over the top goes a golden pheasant crest. The head is finished in the normal way.

A pretty sight is a well-dressed Spring Blue.

The Dressing:	Spring Blue
Irons:	5/0 – 10 ordinary forged
Silk:	Black
Tag:	Round or oval silver tinsel and yellow floss silk

Tail:	Golden pheasant topping and Indian crow substitute
Butt:	Black ostrich herl
Rib:	Oval silver tinsel
Body:	Blue seal's fur
Hackle:	Blue cock
Throat:	Lemon yellow cock hackle
Wing:	Golden pheasant tippet in strands; married strips of red, yellow and blue swan or goose; wide strips of teal down the sides; bronze mallard over, and a topping over all
Head:	Black varnish

GREEN HIGHLANDER

This fly seems to me to be at its best – and like the child, 'when it is good, it is very, very, good' – when it is used in fairly heavy water conditions and if dressed in the larger sizes. I like to see a fair amount of colour in the water when I tie on a Highlander. I have always thought of it as perhaps my first choice for a spring pattern. I had a lovely salmon of 24¼lb on a Green Highlander fishing it really deep in water that I could not see into more than about six inches. The main thing though was not what *I* could see but that the salmon could see that fly swinging across his nose and then decided that he wanted it.

All the fully dressed patterns we have talked about have been those classed as mixed-wing flies. This type of fly is perhaps more difficult to dress than the built-wing flies such as the Jock Scott. This is because the built-wing patterns have usually got a far more rigid underwing made of such materials as white-tipped black turkey tail. This type of underwing provides a great deal of support for the married wing that covers it; on the mixed-wing patterns there is either no underwing at all or it consists of golden pheasant tippet in strands, which is much softer.

Method of tying
Run tying silk down your hook to a point just short of where the bend begins. Catch in a strand of round silver tinsel (oval is what I normally use) and make a short tag. Build up the turns of

246

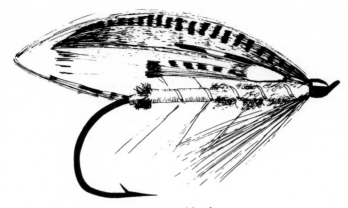

Green Highlander

tying silk behind the tag so that they form a bed which is perfectly level with the tinsel; this is to take the tail of golden pheasant topping and barred summer or mandarin duck. This is a very necessary operation on virtually any fully dressed salmon fly; if you do not make this bed the tail will be thrown high up by the tag and it will completely spoil the look of the fly – remember, no self-respecting salmon is going to *look* at a badly dressed fly, is he? After the tail is tied in, wind on a butt of black ostrich herl, making certain that the fibres point towards the rear of the iron; if you get that wrong you will also put the salmon off! Directly in front of the butt tie in your rib of oval silver tinsel; vary the width of the tinsel according to the size of the fly you are dressing.

Wind the tying silk back up the shank for about a quarter of the body length and tie in a piece of golden yellow floss silk. Take the floss down the shank to come tight up to the butt and then wind it back up the shank again over the first layer, making certain it is smooth and even. Trim off the surplus. Dub on the rest of the body of bright green seal's fur (some dressers prefer a body of wound floss silk but I think the seal's fur looks better), wind the dubbing, or floss, to a position just behind the eye of the iron making certain you have left enough room for the wing. Wind on a body hackle of Green Highlander colour cock hackle. Turn the fly over and tie in a throat hackle of yellow cock.

Put the fly back in the vice the right way up again and select a large golden pheasant tippet feather and strip off all the fluffy fibres at the base. *Tear* out a section from either side of the feather and lay these back to back, then tie them in just as you would for any other wing; if you want the fly to look a real mess then just try tying in the tippets as strands, but don't say I didn't warn you!

Marry up the winging strips in the order given in the dressing and tie these in as a roof over the tippets. If you have any, tie in jungle cock feathers either side; if you have not got any then use one of the good feather substitutes. On the outside of the jungle cock tie in the dyed feather of an Indian crow substitute. And finally, as with all my salmon flies, I like to tie in the topping. This is not an easy feather to manipulate and I find it makes life a lot easier if it is tied in last of all.

The Dressing:	Green Highlander
Irons:	3/0 – 4 ordinary forged
Silk:	Black
Tag:	Round silver tinsel
Tail:	Golden pheasant crest with barred summer duck or mandarin over
Butt:	Black ostrich herl
Rib:	Oval silver tinsel
Body:	First quarter golden floss silk, remainder green floss or seal's fur
Hackle:	Cock hackle dyed Green Highlander
Throat:	Lemon cock hackle as beard
Wings:	Tippet in strands (or strips); yellow, orange and green swan or goose, florican bustard, peacock wing, golden pheasant tail; married strips of barred summer or mandarin duck married to narrow strips of teal; bronze mallard over
Sides:	Jungle cock or substitute
Cheeks:	Indian crow or substitute
Topping:	Golden pheasant crest
Head:	Black varnish